RELIGIOUS DIVISION
AND
SOCIAL CONFLICT

Books from Social Science Press

The Enigma of the Kerala Woman: A Failed Promise of Literacy (HB)
Edited by SWAPNA MUKHOPADHYAY

Cultural History of Modern India (PB)
Edited by DILIP M. MENON

Delhi: Ancient History (PB)
Edited by UPINDER SINGH

Unbecoming Modern: Colonialism, Modernity and Colonial Modernities (HB)
Edited by SAURABH DUBE AND ISHITA BANERJEE-DUBE

After the Iraq War: The Future of the UN and International Law (HB)
Edited by BERNHARD VOGEL, RUDOLF DOLZER AND MATTHIAS HERDEGEN

Social and Economic Profile of India (HB)
(In full colour)
PEEYUSH BAJPAI, LAVEESH BHANDARI AND AALI SINHA

India and China in the Colonial World (HB)
Edited by MADHAVI THAMPI

Everyday Politics of Labour: Working Lives in India's Informal Economy (HB)
GEERT DE NEVE

Viramma: Life of a Dalit (PB)
VIRAMMA, JOSIANE RACINE AND JEAN-LUC RACINE

Lived Islam in South Asia: Adaptation, Accommodation and Conflict (HB)
Edited by IMTIAZ AHMAD AND HELMUT REIFELD

Tamil Nadu Human Development Report (Text in two colours)

Reforming India's Social Sector: Poverty, Nutrition, Health and Education (HB)
Edited by K. SEETA PRABHU AND R. SUDARSHAN

Human Security in South Asia: Energy, Gender, Migration, and Globalisation (HB)
Edited by P.R. CHARI AND SONIKA GUPTA

Middle Class Values in India and Western Europe (HB)
Edited by IMTIAZ AHMAD AND HELMUT REIFELD

Religion and Personal Law in Secular India: A Call to Judgment (HB)
Edited by GERALD JAMES LARSON

WTO Agreement and Indian Agriculture (HB)
Edited by ANWARUL HODA

Sikkim Human Development Report 2001
MAHENDRA P. LAMA

Trade, Finance and Investment in South Asia (HB)
Edited by T.N. SRINIVASAN

The Everyday State and Society in Modern India (HB)
Edited by C.J. FULLER AND VÉRONIQUE BÉNÉÏ

Children's Lifeworlds: Gender Welfare and Labour in the Developing World (HB)
OLGA NIEUWENHUYS

FORTHCOMING

Cultural History of Medieval India (PB)
Edited by MEENAKSHI KHANNA

Globalization and the Millennium Development Goals (HB)
Edited by MANMOHAN AGARWAL AND AMIT SHOVON RAY

Regulation, Institutions and the Law (HB)
Edited by JAIVIR SINGH

RELIGIOUS DIVISION AND SOCIAL CONFLICT

The Emergence of Hindu Nationalism in Rural India

by
Peggy Froerer

Social Science Press
NEW DELHI

Published by
Esha Béteille
Social Science Press
69 Jor Bagh, New Delhi 110 003

© Social Science Press 2007

Distributed by Orient Longman
3-6-752 Himayatnagar
Hyderabad 500 029
and
1/24 Asaf Ali Road
New Delhi 110 002

ISBN 978-8-18735-827-5/8-18735-827-0

Set in Plantin 10/12
Typeset by Eleven Art, Delhi 110 035
Printed by Yogesh Pracashan
at Ravindra printing Press, Delhi 110 006

In memory of my father
Robert E. Froerer

Contents

List of Figures

List of Graphs

Acknowledgements

Like every academic endeavour, this book has been a collaborative effort, and it would be impossible to credit by name all of those who in various ways have contributed to its completion. My deepest gratitude is to the people of Mohanpur, who warmly welcomed me into their lives and looked after me during my fieldwork. Amongst these people, I especially want to thank Sumitra, my 'sister' and research assistant, who helped me to settle in to the village and made it possible for me to carry on with my research. I am also indebted to my host family, Johnny Tamba (Bahadur), Johnny Tengio (Hirimani), Nana, Nani and Johnny, for allowing me to live in their house and for sharing all aspects of their lives with me. Along with Johnny Tamba and Johnny Tengio, I would particularly like to thank Prema Tamba and Prema Tengio, Carmella Tamba and Carmella Tengio, and Vero Tamba and Vero Tengio, for their patience, love and laughter.

In Mohanpur, I also wish to express special thanks to the Patel for giving me his blessings and allowing me to become a *'gaon ki beti'*. I am also deeply grateful to Bachan, who acted as teacher and confidante from the day I arrived, and to Rameswar, Santu, and Panchram, who helped me 'to understand'. Special thanks are due to Jerome and Shantilal, whose companionship and assistance with various aspects of fieldwork were invaluable. I also wish to thank Munan Khan for inviting me into his home and providing me with endless cups of tea, and Jugla for patiently enduring my stumbling questions.

I am extremely grateful to Father Thomas, without whose

suggestions and advice I would never have chosen this fieldsite. I also thank the priests and nuns in Madanpur, especially Father Shanti, Father George and Sister Laurencia, for first suggesting that I work in Mohanpur and for their exceptional generosity throughout my fieldwork. During my many trips to Korba I was always given a ready meal and treated to lively conversation from the priests at the Kosabadi Catholic Church and from the workers in the Kalyan Vanvasi Ashram. Thanks must also go to Santosh Mishra, whose ice cream shop served as a welcome retreat during my excursions to Korba. My frequent visits to Raipur during my second period of fieldwork were made tremendously comfortable by the warm hospitality of Renu, Sunil and Bittoo. For this, I will always be grateful.

In Delhi, I owe a tremendous debt of gratitude to Nagaraj Adve and Anita Roy, for providing much needed support, along with a comfortable and greatly appreciated haven away from fieldwork. To Anita, especially, I am grateful for encouraging me to 'get on with it' and complete the monograph. I also thank Veena and Sharif Rangnekar, and Dilip and Sonu Rangnekar, for their encouragement throughout the duration of my fieldwork. I am extremely indebted to Dwijen Rangnekar, for his constant support throughout my research. His presence during my first period of fieldwork made a significant difference to the way that I was accepted in the community, and his insights and suggestions provided the basis for many of the ideas that have emerged in this monograph.

The research on which this book is based was generously funded by several institutions. I am grateful to the Research Institute for the Study of Man, from whom I received a Fieldwork Grant. Research was also supported by an Overseas Research Student award from the University of London; the Alfred Gell Memorial Studentship and a Malinowski Fund Grant from the Department of Anthropology at the L.S.E.; a Radcliffe-Brown Award from the Royal Anthropological Institute; and a thesis writing grant from the Guggenheim Foundation. This monograph would have been impossible to complete without the support of these institutions. An earlier version of Chapter Five was published in *Contributions to Indian Sociology* (2005, Vol. 39 No. 1, pp. 39–73). I also thank Blackwell for granting permission to publish material from an article that appeared in the *Journal of the Royal Anthropological Institute* (2006, Vol. 12, pp. 39–59).

The development of this research really began in 1992, when I first travelled to New Delhi and enrolled as a postgraduate student at Jawaharlal Nehru University. It was there that I discovered anthropology and began the intellectual journey that would result in the completion of this monograph. While those to whom I owe a debt of gratitude are too numerous to name, I would especially like to thank Professor Rajiv Bhargava and Professor Majid Siddiqi for their role in nurturing my naïve intellectual curiosities. Throughout my field research, I continued to be affiliated to J.N.U., receiving supervision and advice from Professor Dipankar Gupta, to whom I am very grateful. For her friendship, which has endured beyond those JNU days, I would like to thank B. Kiranmayi. Others who have had a much greater impact on my intellectual development than they can possibly be aware, and to whom I will always feel deeply indebted, include S. Anitha, Mathew Joseph C., Nattu and Sukti, Sanjay A., Susan and Samira, along with Pronob, Sohini, Ria, Raja and Rocket.

In the process of carrying out research and completing this monograph, I have been extremely fortunate to work under the supervision of Professor Jonathan Parry and Professor Chris Fuller at the LSE. Both willingly endured countless drafts of my PhD thesis, on which this monograph is based, forcing me in the end to produce a significantly better book than I otherwise would have done. Their guidance, constructive criticism and dedicated encouragement throughout all stages of my doctoral and post-doctoral research have been invaluable, and I sincerely thank them for the support and inspiration that they continue to offer me.

I have also enjoyed the intellectual support and critical comments from a large number of people who have contributed in different ways to the development of this book. Special thanks go to my post-graduate peers who participated in the writing-up seminars in the Department of Anthropology at the LSE, where ideas and draft chapters were presented for the first time. I am also grateful to Massimiliano Mollona, Richard Chenhall and Albert Schrauwers for commenting on specific chapters at earlier stages of this monograph. I thank David Mosse and Jock Stirrat for being such thorough and constructive examiners. I am extremely grateful to Esha Beteille, for her persistence and patience in bringing this book into being, and to Meenakshi Chawla, for her invaluable editorial assistance. Many thanks go to Milo Wakelin for his map-drawing skills and to Fiona Bluck for proofreading the manuscript. I am also grateful to the anonymous reviewer, whose astute and useful comments made me think more deeply about the issues I wanted to address in this book. Special thanks go to Tadesse

Wolde, Todd Sanders, Deborah James and Rita Astuti who, in different ways, have been extremely encouraging throughout various stages of research. I am also grateful to Elizabeth Ewart, Catherine Allerton, Hayley Macgregor and Eva Keller for their constant encouragement and support.

I owe an immeasurable amount of gratitude to my parents, Robert E. and Marilyn B. Froerer, who have supported me in countless ways throughout the duration of this research. My father, Robert E. Froerer, died shortly after I returned from fieldwork, and it is to his memory that I dedicate this book. I am also grateful for the support and encouragement that I have always received from my aunt and uncle, John and Gayle Richards. I learned much from both 'John Uncle' and my brother Jared, whose visits during different stages of fieldwork reacquainted me with issues I had long since taken for granted. Finally, Evan Killick has provided me with unwavering intellectual and emotional support throughout the preparation of this monograph. I am grateful to him for the endless discussion and painstaking re-reading of different drafts, and especially for putting up with my frustrations and persuading me to carry on.

Note on Transliteration

In the area where I conducted my fieldwork, a mix of Hindi, Chetriboli, Chhattisgarhi and Kurukh is spoken. Standard Hindi is used in schools and by government and church officials, whereas Chetriboli, Chhattisgarhi and Kurukh are spoken in the village. Kurukh is a Dravidian-based language spoken by the Oraons, and has no relation to Hindi. Chhattisgarhi belongs to the eastern Hindi language branch, and Chetriboli is a dialect of Chhattisgarhi. Many of the features of Chetriboli and Chhattisgarhi are the same. For example, *o* is used instead of *e* for personal pronouns: *mor* and *tor* are used instead of the standard Hindi *mera* and *tera*. Many words are shortened versions of Hindi: *kaun* (meaning 'who') becomes *ko*; *kya* (meaning 'what') becomes *ka*. One distinguishing feature between Chetriboli, Chhattisgarhi and Hindi is with the suffix '*an*' and '*itch*': in Hindi, the word 'like', or 'like that', is '*aise*'; in Chattisgarhi, the word becomes '*aisan*'; in Chetriboli, the word becomes '*aisitch*'. While I carried out my fieldwork in a combination of all three languages, unless otherwise denoted, I use standard Hindi in the text. In translating Hindi words I have given priority to the way they sound. Diacritical marks are used only in the glossary, which is intended to aid the reader and includes only those words that appear several times in the text. The following vowel pronunciations apply:

à: long a (as in ah)
ã: long long ee sound (keep)
å: long u sound (boot)

Glossary of Selected Terms

adhikàri:	proprietor; keeper; patron; servant
àdivàsi:	tribal; original inhabitant
akal samay:	time of scarcity
andhviswas:	blind belief; superstition
ànganwàdi:	nursery school teacher
angrakshak:	guardian spirit
angrezi davài:	English medicine
anumati:	permission
anusàr:	as one; one and the same (according to)
arkhi:	liquor distilled from the *mahua* flower
asli:	genuine
baiga:	local healer
bara:	big
baṛa dev:	big god
badmàsh:	rascal
bahar:	outside
Baiga:	village priest
balidàn:	blood sacrifice/offering
basti:	neighbourhood; locality
bhagwàn:	god
bhàshà:	language
bhut ka bimàri:	ghost's illness
bhitar:	sacred room

bhut:	ghost; spirit
bidi:	Indian cigarette made from *tendu* leaves
bimàri:	illness
bimàri pujà:	illness/healing ritual
buti kàm:	wage labour
chapràsi:	helper; assistant
Charismas:	Catholic revival meeting
chaukidàr	
(kotwar):	guard
chhuà chut:	untouchable, polluted, dirty
chhotà àdmi:	small man (refers to low caste people)
chowk	
(chauk):	sacred space or square where *puja* takes place
chowrà	
(chaura):	shrine
chulhà:	cooking hearth
chup chàp:	secretly, quietly
churmur:	fried snacks
damru:	protective talisman
dàru:	beer
davài:	medicine
dehàti:	country person; rural dweller
dev ka	
adhikari:	keeper/servant of the deities
devatà	
(devtà):	deity
devràs:	sacred grove
dhàn:	seed rice
dhàn ginte:	seed-rice counting: a divination method
dharm	
(saran	
dharm,	
adi dharm):	traditional Oraon religion
dhup:	incense
dismil:	one one-hundredth of an acre
dukh:	misfortune
gahanà:	a piece of mortgaged land; a mortgage arrangement
gàon:	village
garam:	hot

ghar vapasi:	homecoming
ghumne:	visit; visiting
girjà:	Church (specifically Catholic mass)
git:	song
girvin:	a type of mortgage arrangement where land is exchanged for money or jewellery
Gaura:	local festival celebrating the marriage between Mahadev and Parvati
goli:	pills; medicine
gotr:	clan
gràm sabhà:	village-level government
gunia:	healer
hàjari kàm:	wage labour
Hindutva:	Hindu-ness
isài:	Christian
jagha:	space (especially for a deity)
jai jai:	a common greeting (literally long live)
jamin:	land
jangli:	rustic; uneducated; forest dweller
jhanjh:	cymbal-like musical instrument
jaributi:	herbal medicine
jàti:	caste
jhàr phukna:	sweeping/blowing action used at times of illness, to ritually sweep the disease downward out of the body of the patient
jhupna:	possessed state
kabjà jamin:	encroached land; land without legal title
kandi:	a measurement of roughly 40 kg
katta:	Kurukh term meaning non-Oraon person or non-Oraon culture
khet:	paddy field
khunt-kattidàr:	original settler or lineage holder
kohà pàni:	big feast; Oraon pre-wedding ceremony, sponsored by the groom to decide the wedding date
kurtà pyjàmà:	long shirt, loose trousers; clothing of 'city folk'
Kuṛukh:	language/culture of the Oraons
kutumb log:	inlaws; affines

lak:	tree from which the sap is harvested, sold and used to make bangles
lota pani:	brass watering vessel; also an Oraon engagement ceremony
lungi:	sarong; wrap-around, skirt-like garment warn by men
madad:	help, assistance
Mahàshiv-ràtri:	Hindu festival (especially associated with city Hindus)
Mahaseva:	most important occasion of worship
mahilà sangat:	women's organization
mahuà:	(*Bassia Latifolia*) flower from which local liquor is brewed
màlik:	owner, manager
mantra:	sacred spell
mission civilisatrice:	civilizing mission
mistri kàm:	construction work
mukhià:	headman
munshi:	foreman; supervisor of tendu collection process
nàd:	spirit (Kurukh)
nakli:	counterfeit
nimantran:	invitation
nissàn:	sacred drum
niyam:	rule
naukari:	service; respectable job
pakkà:	pure, absolute
pàgal:	mad
pakaṛnà:	to catch (euphemism for becoming possessed)
panchàyat:	village council
pandit:	Brahman priest
pine wala bhut:	drinking ghost; ghost which causes drunken behaviour
pattà dekhnà:	leaf gazing; a divination method
Patwàri:	government-appointed official who oversees local land records
parchà:	land title document
parhài-likhà log:	people who read and write; educated people
parikshà:	test; examination
Patel:	village headman

patta:	land title document
prachàrak:	follower, organizer
pràsada:	divine grace
pràthnà:	prayer
pujà:	worship
pujài:	space where rituals/*pujas* are performed
purà viswàs:	pure, complete faith
purvaj:	ancestors
ràjà:	king
rastà:	road, path
reghà:	type of mortgage arrangement where the landholder gives land to a creditor for a fixed return
riti rivàj:	custom; tradition
sàdhàran:	simple
sadhu:	wandering holy man
sahàji:	sharecropping arrangement where the landholder splits his harvest with the tenant
sahàrã (shahàrã):	city
sahàri wàlà (shahàrã wàlà):	city fellow
sakti:	power
samàchàr:	news
samàj:	community
samdhi:	inlaws; affines
Sangh Parivàr:	the family (refers to the group of Hindu Nationalist organizations and sympathizers, including the RSS, BJP, VHP)
sarài:	a tree found in central India, the sap of which is used to make incense
saril bimari:	body/physical illness
sarkàri:	government
sarpanch:	elected head of village or group of villages
seàn log:	elders
sevà karnà:	ritual service; doing service to the gods
shaitàn:	satan; evil deity
shaitàn kà kàm:	satan's work
shuddhi:	re-conversion

sida, bilko	
sada khana:	vegetarian food (literally, 'straight' food)
sikshit	
davài:	educated medicine
sikshit	
bimari:	biomedical illness (literally, 'educated' illness)
sindhur:	red vermillion powder used for anointing deities
sthàn:	sacred space belonging to deities
sui pàni:	injection
sukti:	type of jungle leaf harvested and eaten by Oraons
supà:	winnowing basket
surakshà:	protection
shuru se:	since the beginning
swàgat:	welcome
tehsil:	subdistrict
tendu patta:	jungle leaf out of which bidi (cigarette) is made
tikrà:	dry field, for the cultivation of pulses and vegetables
tonhi:	witch
uppar pàrà:	upper locality, neighbourhood
vanvasi:	adivasi (literally forest dweller)
ved:	healer (of herbal medicine)
viswàs:	faith, belief, trust, respect
zyàdà:	large amount

CHAPTER ONE

Introduction

In September 1998, a particular incident took place in a village that I will call Mohanpur, located in a forested region of Chhattisgarh, central India, which signified the moment when militant Hindu nationalism became a patently visible force in this area. It was early evening, a time when most people had retired to their homes to prepare for the evening meal. The exception was a group of about ten young men belonging to the local Hindu community. Like most evenings, they were engaging in 'time-pass', an activity that usually consisted of loitering about, ogling local girls and playing cards.

This particular evening, they had congregated along the forest road at the edge of the village to share a bottle of local liquor. As equal portions were being poured into makeshift leaf-cups, the sounds of a vehicle could be heard some distance away. This was unusual, for vehicular traffic was still rare in this part of Chhattisgarh—particularly after dusk—due to impassable roads and the potential dangers of the jungle. As they consumed the drink, the young men speculated about who could be driving through the forest at this time of the night. Soon, they recognized the jeep belonging to the two Catholic Fathers, who were returning to the mission station in the neighbouring village.

As the vehicle drew nearer, the young men spread across the road, forcing the jeep to come to a halt. One of them ordered two others to 'bring fire' and instructed the rest to surround the vehicle so that they could burn it. He then accused the Fathers of wanting to 'turn all Hindus into Christians, like elsewhere in India'. Because 'local Hindus do not want to become Christians', he argued, the Fathers had instead decided 'to bring the Hindu community down' by encouraging local Christians to make and sell liquor to the Hindus. These accusations were met with vocal concurrence from the rest of the group and fierce denials from the Fathers, who insisted that they had no such conversion agenda. To the contrary, the Fathers claimed, they were actively counselling local Christians to avoid liquor production and consumption.

Throughout this heated exchange, the Fathers remained seated nervously in their jeep. The two young men who had gone to fetch fuel for a fire had returned and now stood on either side of the vehicle, wielding cans of kerosene and large pieces of burning wood, waiting for the order to torch the jeep. Nearly an hour or so later, the Fathers were finally allowed to proceed, but only after agreeing to employ more stringent tactics against those members of the local Catholic parish who continued to produce and sell liquor, and to conduct their annual village mass not in the Christian locality on the opposite side of the village, but at the local Hindu shrine in the village square.

This incident, which was narrated to me by the Fathers and by several of the young men involved, occurred during the period of anti-Christian violence that spread across India between 1997 and 2000. It was directly connected to the Hindu nationalist movement which, since the late 1980s, has been arguably one of the most pervasive and divisive political forces that have spread across Indian society. While this movement has recently experienced electoral setbacks at the national level, it continues to influence the course of Indian politics at the state and local levels, and its ongoing and often violent penetration into everyday life will continue to have far-reaching implications for years to come.

It is the emergence of Hindu nationalism in this mixed, Hindu/Christian *adivasi* (tribal; literally, original inhabitant) village, and the impact that this has had on the lives of local people, which are the principal concerns of this book. Based on nearly two years of fieldwork that took place between October 1997 and August 1999, it provides an explicitly ethnographic approach to the wider understanding of the process by which Hindu nationalist ideology is successfully transmitted in rural *adivasi* areas. In particular, it examines the role played by 'conversion specialists' (Brass 1997: 16; 2003), or those RSS activists who serve as the primary facilitators in this process.

The concerns of this book have been shaped by the growing influence of the RSS (Rashtriya Swayamsevak Sangh; literally

Association of National Volunteers or the National Volunteer Corps), whose increasing attention in this area paralleled the period during which my fieldwork was conducted. Along with other proponents of Hindu nationalism, the RSS is part of what is sometimes referred to as the 'saffron brigade'—those political and cultural groups most visibly associated with militant Hindu nationalism—due to their appropriation and widespread use of the saffron colour, which is traditionally associated with mainstream Hindu rituals. When I first began my research in October 1997, this organization was relatively unknown in the area. The four RSS activists or organizers (*pracharaks*) who visited Mohanpur every few months to conduct meetings amongst a few interested young men held the interest of the majority of locals more for their motor bikes and fancy clothes than for their message of Hindu unity. By the time I completed my research nearly two years later, visits by these activists had increased to a weekly frequency. While Mohanpur was by no means the only village in the area in which these cadres were active, it is an examination of the particular strategies that they employed during this period to gain wider access to the *adivasis* in this particular village that is the focus of this book. Analysis is based on events that occurred between 1997–9, and specific aims are twofold: to identify the local conditions and cleavages that have contributed to the transmission of Hindu nationalism in this community, and to explore how nationalist ideology is tailored by individual activists to correspond with local concerns. The broader objective is to understand the manner by which, through the instrumental involvement of its activists in local level issues, groups like the RSS are able to gain a legitimacy on the ground, and to extrapolate from this analysis in relation to the complex link between the growth of Hindu nationalism at the grass-roots level, and broader discourses on Hindu nationalism.

Approaches to Hindu Nationalism

Mitigating the 'backwardness' of India's *adivasi* communities is one of the objectives that has recently figured in the agenda of the RSS. Along with other members of the Sangh Parivar ('the family'), that complex of Hindu nationalist organisations that includes the political branch, the Bharatiya Janata Party (BJP) and the 'cultural' wing, the Vishwa Hindu Parishad (VHP), the long-term aim of this organization is the spread of *Hindutva*, or 'Hindu-ness', and the transformation of Hindu culture into an undifferentiated, unified whole, for the purpose of achieving 'one nation, one people, one culture' (Khilnani 1997: 151). This kind of singular Hinduism assumes that India has always been 'fundamentally Hindu', a community united by geographical origin, racial connection and religious belief (see Thapar 1991). Indeed, the very notion of *Hindutva* equates religious and national identity, where an Indian is defined as a Hindu, and the Hindu faith in turn, is defined as the core of Indian nationhood (cf. Gopal 1993; Madan 1997; McKean 1996; van der Veer 1994: 1).

There is an extensive body of academic work within the social and political sciences devoted to analysing the origins and contemporary manifestations of the Hindu nationalist movement, much of which is likely to be familiar to readers of this book. One section of the literature explains the success of Hindu nationalism in terms of systematic organizational work, creative political strategies and mobilizing ideologies (Basu et al. 1993; Jaffrelot 1996; Kanungo 2002; Sharma 2003). Another section interprets Hindu nationalism in more cultural and historical terms (Bhatt 2001; Ludden 2005; Sarkar 2001; Vanaik 1997), or examines the movement in terms of 'religious nationalism' (Juergensmeyer 1993; van der Veer 1994). Others use the Ayodhya confrontation as a specific point of departure (Gopal 1993; Nandy et al. 1995), while still others link the movement to the larger disjuncture between democratic mobilization and governance (Hansen 1999; Khilnani 1997).

Alongside this research is a great deal of comparative literature that views Hindu nationalism, together with other 'nationalisms', as a product of modernizing and globalizing forces unfolding throughout much of the contemporary world (Kapferer 1988; Marty and Appleby 1993, 1994 and 1995).[1] This scholarship on Hindu nationalism, in turn, belongs to a more general discourse on nationalism that has been produced over the past two decades, largely in response to the growing prominence of nationalist movements across the globe (seminal studies include Anderson 1983; Eriksen 2002; Gellner 1983; Smith 1971, 1992). Finally, the processes outlined in this literature can be viewed within the context of more competitive religious assertions

---

[1]For comparison with ethnic-nationalist movements outside of South Asia, see Ben-Ami 1992; Glenny 1999; Joseph 2004 and Pratt 2003.

taking place across the globe (see Mahmood 2005; Saberwal and Hasan 2006).[2]

Most of this literature situates the antecedents of Hindu nationalism within historical traditions such as the late nineteenth and early twentieth-century German ideas of the nation and ethnic nationalism, nineteenth-century Hindu revival and reform movements, Christian missionising practices, scouting and the British police (Andersen and Damle 1987; Bayly 1999; Gold 1991; Jaffrelot 1996; see Thapar 1985 and 1991). Contemporary manifestations of the Hindu nationalist movement, moreover, are framed against the backdrop of a postcolonial context that has been informed by the struggle between parties, factions, personalities and ideologies for the political governance and reconstruction of India (cf. Chatterjee 1993).

As Ludden (2005: 18–19) acknowledges, this struggle, which is underpinned by the gradual disintegration since the mid-1970s of the Congress party's hold over the Indian state, is principally concerned with the legitimacy of the state and the distribution of state resources and power. Since the early 1990s, this struggle has also been shaped by economic liberalization and an increase in urban, middle-class affluence and consumerism. Furthermore, it has been informed by the upsurge in and increasing demands of lower-caste political parties and social movements, shifting loyalties and vote blocs, and the (re)interpretation of shared cultural symbols and national heritage (see Hansen 1999; Kohli 1990). These phenomena undoubtedly have given added impetus and legitimacy to wider Hindu nationalist campaigns across the country. However, it is also recognized that the continuing momentum of Hindu nationalism has become regionalized (see Hansen 1996), and it is in this context that the BJP and other proponents of the Hindu right have gradually enhanced their power and that, in the 1990s, *Hindutva* 'emerged as a solid competitor for popular loyalties' (Ludden 2005: 19).

While a detailed review of this literature would unnecessarily duplicate by now familiar arguments, that have sought to explain

---

[2]Valid comparisons can certainly be made with the ways in which religious movements are becoming increasingly assertive and even violent in their methods of propagation across the globe (see Mahmood 2005 and Saberwal and Hasan 2006). It is important to bear in mind, however, that the Hindu nationalist movement, being fundamentally political, is not equivalent to such processes.

how and why Hindu nationalism and other nationalist movements arise, the purpose of drawing attention to this extensive discourse is to highlight what has generally been ignored: namely, the grass-roots processes that examine precisely how nationalism is manifested and spread at the local level, and how ordinary persons' engagement in nationalist projects evolves.[3]

It is true that there is a great deal of attention on the spread of Hindu nationalist sentiment and violence in urban settings. Available accounts include a focus on the Hinduization of public and ritual space in urban sites of conflict (see, for example, Fuller 2001; Hansen 1996); the introduction of new rituals or 'invented traditions' created for political purposes in urban areas (cf. Anandhi 1995: 36–43; Fuller 2004); or the personal accounts of the victims of (largely urban) communal violence (e.g. Kakar 1996). Additionally, there are a number of works that cursorily mention the 'social upliftment' strategies being employed by Hindu nationalist organizations in rural, *adivasi* areas (see Hansen 1999: 103–6; van der Veer 1994: 135–6).

Detailed ethnography, however, is sparse, and there is no work to date that documents and analyses the precise manner by which Hindu nationalism is being introduced amongst *adivasi* communities in specifically rural areas. We know that, due to impediments like inaccessible roads and lack of electricity, access to and participation in 'mainstream' urban culture is often limited. This means that the methods by which Hindu nationalism is routinely transmitted in urban areas, which rely heavily on people's access to mass media and to popular forms of public participation, must of necessity be very different (cf. Farmer 1996; Varadarajan 1999).

Existing scholarship has hinted at such differences. In his revised edition of *The Camphor Flame*, for example, Fuller (2004: 262–89) notes a recent study of the Banjara (an 'ex-criminal' tribe) in rural Rajasthan, which mentions how RSS activists have spent months endearing themselves and their ideology to the local community. But this study does not analyse the process by which Hindu nationalism

[3]One recent exception outside of the literature on South Asia includes Jean-Klein's (2001) ethnographic account of 'nationalist production in everyday life' in Palestine during the Intifada. This work offers a timely criticism to studies that ignore the process by which ordinary people engage in what she calls 'self-nationalisation' (p. 84). Another critical contribution to this literature is Billig's (1995) more general work on 'banal nationalism', which examines the unnoticed, everyday habits that contribute to the ideological reproduction of nations (and nationalism).

is introduced to and accepted by this community. Moreover, while the basic theme of 'cultural unity' amongst all Hindus is fundamental to the overall project of Hindu nationalism, available discussions indicate that this theme has unique manifestations. In the tribal-dominated Jharkhand area (now a state), for example, we are told by Hocking (1996: 225) that *adivasi* Christians have been characterized by Hindu nationalist activists as being outside the bounds of the Hindu nation, creating a threat against Hindu society; and in Gujarat, leaders of the Sangh Parivar reportedly urge *adivasi*s to assert their Hindu-ness and defend their threatened religion against exploitative Muslim traders (Baviskar 2005: 5108; cf. Lobo 2002: 4844–9). Beyond the generalized descriptions of how members of the Sangh Parivar modify their message to suit the situations and histories of different communities however, the specific activities in which these activists engage at the local level remain largely undocumented and unanalysed.

There is perhaps reason for the lack of ethnographic attention to rural, *adivasi* communities, foremost being the fact that Hindu nationalism has, until recently, been concentrated 'in the heart of India's urban middle classes' (Hansen 1999: 7; Jaffrelot 1996, 1998). Support from this sector unquestionably contributed to the political success of the movement in recent years, most notably in 1997 when the BJP first came to power as the head of India's national coalition government. Since the early 2000s, however, this support has declined. A consequence of this was the defeat suffered by the BJP in the 2004 national elections.[4] At the same time, it is notable that the party came to power in states with sizeable *adivasi* populations, which included Madhya Pradesh, Jharkhand, Rajasthan and Gujarat.

In short, it is clear that this movement has successfully spread from its urban centres into more 'backward', rural areas, achieving popular and electoral support from India's dispersed *adivasi* communities. It is equally clear that, given the anti-Christian violence of the sort

[4]Reasons for this decline in support from the urban middle classes are complex, and can be attributed to a combination of economic liberalization and rapid globalization, and the disillusionment of the middle classes, who are more interested in the stable world of enduring material benefits than in the destabilizing reality of *Hindutva* and other forms of religious activism (see Corbridge and Harriss 2000 for detailed analysis). Moreover, as religious tensions are being corrected, self-interested secular opportunities are becoming more important (cf. Varma 2005). This gives new salience to the modernist idea that economic development secularizes society because religion becomes private (Fuller n.d.).

described at the beginning of this book, a detailed ethnographic analysis is necessary to facilitate greater understanding of the way in which this movement has succeeded in gaining widespread support in such communities. This book is an attempt to provide such an analysis.

The RSS, *Adivasis* and Christianity

Within Hindu nationalist discourse, cultivating a fear of the threatening 'abstract Muslim' remains the 'decisive ideological bedrock' that underpins the movement (Hansen 1999: 12). Protecting the 'Hindu nation' against conversion to Islam, in turn, has been central to the Sangh Parivar's campaigns. These campaigns culminated in the destruction of the Babri Masjid in 1992, an important mosque in Ayodhya, north India, which resulted in widespread violence against Muslims across India (see Nandy et al. 1995; Noorani 2000: 73–89).

Even as anti-Muslim sentiment remained the 'master narrative' (Varshney 2002: 34) underpinning Sangh Parivar attempts at consolidating the Hindu nation, attention of the RSS and other organizations was directed towards Christians across India in the mid-1990s, with a particular focus on Christian *adivasi* communities. The reason for this shift revolved around the view that Christians, as 'foreigners and non-Hindus', pose a threat to the national Hindu majority because they have been engaging in 'divisive and subversive' activities, particularly amongst the minority and 'backward' *adivasi* communities (cf. Hocking 1996). Part of the RSS's broader interest in tribal communities is thus related to the wider threat that the Christian and other non-Hindu communities present to the Hindu nationalist quest for political and cultural supremacy. In response to this threat, campaigns like *ghar vapasi* (homecoming) or *shuddhi* (re-conversion) were instituted in *adivasi* regions across Chhattisgarh, Jharkhand and other states to 'reclaim the souls' (Baviskar 2005: 5108; cf. Bunsha 2006) of Christian *adivasis* who, through conversion, had 'strayed' from the Hindu fold. Such campaigns were accompanied by more violent measures, and between 1997 and 1999, a period that coincided with my own research, the RSS and other members of the Sangh Parivar were implicated in a number of well-publicized atrocities against Christian communities.[5]

---

[5]Atrocities included the burning and destruction of churches (throughout *adivasi* districts of Gujarat, 1998), the rape of nuns (in an *adivasi* district in central Madhya

As I discuss in Chapter Three, the issue of conversion has been a point of contention amongst Hindu nationalists since the late nineteenth century, when a wave of mass conversion movements, to both Protestant and Catholic faiths, took place across India, largely in the tribal belts in north-eastern and central India. These movements, which continued through the mid-twentieth century, created apprehensions amongst Hindu nationalists who, at the time, alleged that such conversions were related to 'illegitimate methods' such as the provision of material inducements (see Shourie 1994). Interestingly, one of the earliest voices to raise the alarm against Christian missionary activity in central Indian tribal areas in the mid-twentieth century was Verrier Elwin, a champion of *adivasis* and author of numerous early ethnographies on tribal culture (see Elwin 1939, 1943, and 1947). Primarily concerned about the essentially western values espoused by Christianity and the effect that such values would have on the survival of traditional tribal cultures, Elwin charged missionaries with 'indulging in psychological abuse of the tribals by alienating them from their own culture' and '[asserting] their cultural superiority to effect conversions' (Thakkar 1941: 4–5, cited in Prasad 2003: 89).[6]

Concern for the impact and influence of Christianity on (especially) lower caste and tribal communities in Madhya Pradesh eventually led to a government enquiry on missionary activities, whose conclusions and recommendations were outlined in a report published in 1956 (see Niyogi 1956).[7] This report, with its charges

---

Pradesh, late 1998), and the murder of a foreign missionary and his two young sons (in an *adivasi* district of neighbouring Orissa, early 1999). See Anonymous (1998a, b and c), Anonymous (1999a, b, and c), cf. Baviskar (2005: 5108); Bhatt 2001: 196–202; Cooper (1998), Filkins (1998), Goldenberg (1999), Pati (2003: 53–7); Singh and Mahurkar (1999).

[6] For an incisive critique of Elwin's 'ecological romanticism', and of the way in which the RSS and its adjunct organizations have both echoed and appropriated Elwin's position in their contemporary efforts to facilitate inroads into tribal areas through both re-conversion and the sponsorship of social welfare programmes, see Prasad (2003: 73–105).

[7] Recommendations of what came to be known as the 'Niyogi Committee Report' included a ban on all foreign and mission agencies in tribal areas; the severing of foreign support of and connections with Indian Churches; the prohibition of the use of medicine and education as a direct means of conversion; and the prohibition of circulation of literature meant for religious propaganda (see Niyogi 1956: 155). That such recommendations could conceivably be applied to the contemporary efforts of the Sangh Parivar to (re)convert *adivasis* into 'proper' Hindus is not a position shared by

against missionaries as 'anti-national', its claims of conversion through 'material inducements', and its recommendations to ban Christian proselytization, continues to have a significant impact today (cf. Bhatt 2001: 198–202; Prasad 2003: 73–5). The charge of 'forced conversion' in particular, is regularly levelled against contemporary Christian and Muslim leaders by members of the Sangh Parivar, who fear the further dilution of the Hindu majority. After all, Hindus can only remain a 'majority' as long as such communities do not declare themselves to be outside that majority (see van der Veer 1994: 28)—by, say, converting to Christianity.[8]

While the issue of conversion is at the centre of the Sangh Parivar's shift towards Christian communities, it is interesting to note that the RSS does not recognize the possibility of 'conversion' to Hinduism, particularly with respect to *adivasi* people who, the organization has consistently claimed, are 'very much Hindus, though they have no knowledge of the [Hindu] religion' (cf. Golwalkar 1966; Kanungo 2002: 149).[9] The discourse of 're-conversion', however, is acceptable to the RSS, for it is accompanied by the unquestioning recognition of *adivasis'* original identity as 'Hindu'. The fact that they have strayed from this identity makes their 're-conversion' justifiable (see Pati 2003: 3).[10]

---

the RSS, which consistently disputes the possibility that *adivasis* have been historically anything other than Hindu (see cf. Golwalkar 1966; Kanungo 2002: 149).

[8]The historical relationship between the RSS, *adivasis* and Christianity is clearly more complex than noted here. According to Prasad (2003: xvii), for example, it was Elwin's call for a ban on all Christian missionary activity in central Indian tribal areas that initially 'facilitated the penetration of right-wing Hindu nationalists in tribal areas', thus enabling the creation of the Niyogi Committee in the first instance. While a more comprehensive examination of this relationship would be useful, this is not the objective of this book. For further detail and analysis, see Pati (2003), Prasad (2003: 73–105), and Sundar 2006.

[9]By extension, the issue of conversion to Hinduism has been studiously ignored by scholars, although it has been addressed indirectly in terms of 'the Hindu mode of tribal absorption' (Bose 1941) or 'Sanskritization' (Srinivas 1965; cf. Sundar 2006: 358; Thapar 1985: 17). See Pati (2003) for a recent exception.

[10]As Sundar (2006: 358) observes, the position of the RSS on 're-conversion' is also bolstered by the state, which treats Hinduism as the default religion for *adivasis* by classifying the latter as 'Hindu' in government census reports, and regards 'conversion' in terms of recruitment *from* Hinduism *to* Christianity or Islam (cf. Robinson and Clarke 2003: 13–18). Pati (2003: 2–3) also reminds us that until recently, the idea of 're-conversion' has also been accepted unquestioningly by many scholars (see Jordans 1977; Oddie 1977).

While the shift toward Christian communities necessarily draws on historical fears about mass movements and invokes the issue of conversions (see Sarkar 1999: 76–7), it is also impelled by what van der Veer (1994: 135) calls the 'politics of inclusion'. To date, the larger 'community' of *adivasi* people, which comprises over 8.2 per cent of India's population, has yet to be encompassed within the 'Hindu fold' and as such remains an important obstacle to the long-term political agenda and the comprehensive success of the Hindu nationalist movement. The fact that Christians number less than 2.5 per cent of India's current population suggests that the Sangh Parivar's shift in attention toward Christian *adivasi* communities is less a defence of a threatened religion in the face of conversion and more a calculated tactic aimed at breaking out of its urban and upper caste 'cocoon' (Hansen 1996: 210) and expanding the movement's political support base (cf. Panikkar 1999: xviii) which, as discussed above, has traditionally been drawn from urban, upper-caste, middle-class sectors (cf. Jaffrelot 1998). According to Sarkar (1999: 98–9), this shift could also be related to the Sangh Parivar's wider discomfort with aspects of the globalization and liberalization processes that have rapidly unfolded under a BJP government. In a cultural and political context that is rooted in nationalist, indigenous values, Christians, with their 'foreign' origin, and as representatives of western imperialism, provide a convenient 'surrogate'—in place of multi-national companies—against which Hindu nationalists can reconfirm their nationalist agenda (see Sarkar 1999: 98–9).

Regardless of the precise nature of this shift, it is clear that the attention of the Hindu right toward *adivasis* has been driven not only by the threat of conversion that has been newly fuelled by the RSS, but by the more practical concerns of electoral representation and the need to move beyond traditional bases of support (cf. Jaffrelot 1998). Historical events such as the mass conversions of tribal people have shown the Sangh Parivar that they cannot take the Hindu identity of marginal groups like *adivasi*s for granted.[11] And while it

[11]The BJP's mid-1990s policy of courting marginal groups was not without risk, as the party risked losing a substantial portion of its support amongst its upper caste bases. According to Jaffrelot (1998: 69), this was one of the reasons why, in a process called 'indirect mandalization', the BJP made alliances in the 1996 elections with regional parties with a strong base among the low and intermediate castes, rather than directly promoting such people within its own party.

would of course be naïve to hold that *adivasis* constitute a single group or 'community' of people, it is undeniable that they are seen as an important political constituency that comprises a potentially sizeable vote bank.[12]

It was partly in response to this potential that in the 1990s, the Hindu nationalist agenda for *adivasi* communities came to revolve around a twofold strategy: to bring *adivasis* into the Hindu mainstream by revealing to them their 'true' identity as 'Hindus'; and to counteract minority Christian cultures that have taken *adivasis* away from the Hindu fold (Almond et al.1995; cf. Basu et al. 1993: 67).This strategy was underpinned by the implicit assumption that *adivasis* had failed to conform to the 'civilized' standards of caste Hindus, and it was accompanied by the aim of mitigating this general 'backwardness' of *adivasi* communities (cf. Baviskar 2005: 5105; Kanungo 2002: 149–57). As I discuss in Chapter Two, the sort of 'backwardness' with which the RSS is concerned locally refers to those practices that underpin traditional *adivasi* cosmology and forms of worship, such as the propitiation of village and forest deities with alcohol and blood offerings. Such customs, described by the villagers as *dehati* (rural) or *'jangli'* (wild) Hinduism, are contrasted to the forms of worship found within 'mainstream', *sahari* (city) Hinduism, where the 'big gods' (*bara dev*, e.g. Ram, Shiva, Krishna) are worshipped with offerings of incense and flowers.

To advance their aims of reforming these 'backward' practices, the RSS has, since 1996, mounted a number of educational and cultural campaigns in rural *adivasi* villages across India. Locally, these include the setting up of nursery schools for the purpose of communicating a relevant 'cultural ethos' to young village children; the introduction of mainstream Hindu holidays and the instruction of local *adivasis* in the 'proper' way of Hindu worship; and the organization of village training meetings for 'infusing the qualities of nation-building' and spreading *Hindutva* ideology (cf. Kanungo 2002: 149–57; Nandy 1995) for a discussion on similar campaigns being propagated in tribal

---

[12]This importance was made manifest in the 2004 elections, which saw the BJP come to power in states (Madhya Pradesh, Jharkhand, Rajasthan, along with Chhattisgarh) with relatively substantial *adivasi* populations. To be sure, support for the RSS does not automatically translate into votes for the BJP, and the establishment of a direct electoral link between these two groups would require actual figures and greater statistical and ethnographic analysis. Here, I am only suggesting the possibility of such a connection (see Chapter Two).

districts in Orissa). The specific ideological message communicated during the course of these meetings revolves around the urgent necessity for the creation of Hindu nation to counter the threats of alien 'others' (Muslims and Christians) (Basu et al. 1993: 37). I discuss these issues in more detail in the following chapter.

While such campaigns are important to the wider agenda of integrating disparate minority communities into the Hindu fold, they have only been marginally successful in transmitting to local people the kind of long-term communal sentiment that is required for the broader expansion of the movement. As we shall see in Chapters Two and Three, villagers remain more concerned with their 'traditional' practices and rituals, which they perceive to be superior to, and which often have very little in common with the mainstream Hindu variety. In view of this, local RSS activists have been forced to seek out different ways by which local people can be integrated into the *Hindutva* project.

Mimesis, Civic Activism and the 'Civilizing Mission'

There are two primary strategies that have been successfully employed by RSS activists to augment local support and propagate Hindu nationalist ideology. The first is through the process of sustained engagement in civic activism. Aimed at the community as a whole, this strategy includes the sponsorship of a local biomedical treatment alternative (discussed in Chapter Four) and the promotion of citizens' rights and assistance with countering local corruption (outlined in Chapter Five). In line with the broader *Hindutva* agenda, this strategy has its roots in the nineteenth century Hindu reform movements noted earlier that attempted to defend, redefine and create 'Hinduism' on the model of the Christian religion (Thapar 1985: 18). Viewed as an 'alternative welfare system' (Kanungo 2002: 150–2), it is patterned after the kinds of civic activism or social 'upliftment' programmes in which the Christian missionaries have traditionally engaged, and which have historically revolved around the educational and health concerns of 'backward' *adivasi* communities (cf. Niyogi 1956; see Chapter Three).

One of the objectives of this book is to demonstrate how the particular strategies being employed by RSS activists are underpinned by the broader mimetic relationship that the organization has with the Church.[13] Throughout India, the more visible forms of mimesis include the re-conversion programme mentioned above. Equally, the Vanvasi Kalyan Ashram (Tribal Development Centre) and the Vidya Bharti (literally, India's knowledge), affiliates of the RSS that are concerned with the physical welfare and education of tribal communities, are patterned after the Church's long-term engagement in the social upliftment of more vulnerable communities (cf. Baviskar 2005; Prasad 2003: 73–105; Sundar 2004).

While engagement in such programmes provides an obvious point of entry into *adivasi* areas by members of the Sangh Parivar, the latter's success is achievable only if Christianity and its associated 'good works' are discredited and its efforts replaced by those of the RSS and its affiliated organizations (cf. Panikkar 1999: xviii-xix). This is obviously made difficult by the Church's strong presence in *adivasi* areas. Nowadays, for example, Christian-sponsored schools and hospitals are sprinkled throughout much of India's tribal regions and receive considerable support from local *adivasi* communities, both Hindu and Christian alike. In view of this, it could be said that the primary obstacle to the recruitment of *adivasis* into the Sangh Parivar is the Church itself. As we shall see in Chapter Five, the RSS activists' ability to successfully endear themselves to the community as a whole is made easier by the failure of the state to guarantee entitlements to local *adivasis* and to prevent their economic rights from being infringed (cf. Robinson 2003: 372). It is by responding to this failure and participating in the kind of civic activism that benefits both Christian and Hindu members of the community that RSS proponents have achieved an important degree of local legitimacy within the village.

One of the issues I hope to bring out in this discussion is how the RSS's engagement in civic activism can be construed as a kind of 'civilizing mission'. Taken from the French *mission civilisatrice* and based on concepts of the Enlightenment and the French revolution (Mann 2004: 4), this idea was used as a powerful tool to legitimize nineteenth century colonial rule. It was underpinned by the dual assumptions that French culture was superior and that colonial subjects were too backward to govern themselves and thus required 'upliftment' (see Conklin 1997: 1).

In tandem with ideas that underlined this French concept, notions of 'improvement', betterment', and 'moral and material progress' of

[13] Throughout this book, 'the Church' refers broadly to 'Christianity', and more specifically to the local Catholic Church institution. The context in which these usages alternate should be clear.

colonial subjects who were regarded as 'inferior' characterized the civilizing mission that became the 'sole ideology of British colonialism in India' (Mann 2004: 24). Indeed, Britain's civilizing mission was accompanied not only by the idea that the British were entitled to educate or 'improve' their Indian subjects, but that they had a duty to do so (ibid.).[14]

As I discuss in Chapter Three, there are clear historical connections between this kind of civilizing mission and Christianity in India. The transformation of early British civilizing attitudes into a more coherent form began as early as the late eighteenth century, with the growth of England's Christian movement (see Mann 2004: 6). The diffusion of Christianity throughout India was regarded as the most effective means to civilize India's peoples, amongst whom *adivasi*s were considered to be the most backward and '*jangli*' (wild) (ibid. 7; cf. Bryce 1810: 112–14).[15] Colonial medicine in particular was considered to be a useful tool for civilizing the bodies of people (cf. Arnold 1993; Mann 2004: 14), and modern biomedicine continues to be viewed by both the Church and the RSS as a useful civilizing method (see Chapter Four).

Similar to the way the colonial civilizing mission enabled officials to bring *adivasi*s closer to British notions of efficiency and conformity, the current 'civilizing mission' allows the RSS (and the Church) to actively pursue the same. Skaria (1999: 200), who has outlined how the British conceived of the 'civilizing mission' with respect to the *adivasi*s of western India, notes how the colonial civilizing mission was underpinned by two strategies: to protect tribes from the outside world, and to protect them from themselves. Where the former included liquor merchants, traders and other people from the plains, the latter included 'high-spirited boisterousness' and a propensity for plundering, along with alcoholism and human sacrifice (ibid.; cf. Padel 1995). Indian state officials took over the original civilizing mission after Independence and extended the same ideology: tribal groups were construed as the 'younger brothers' of more civilized, plains Indians, and therefore had to be helped out of their primitiveness (cf. Skaria 1999: 278).

---

[14]The idea of the 'civilizing mission' is obviously more complex, historically and conceptually, than this discussion lets on. In the first instance, the British civilizing mission was not only restricted to its colonial subjects; it was, at once, based on and extended to society at home (see Mann 2004: 30). For extended analyses, see the volume edited by Fischer-Tine and Mann (2004) and Conklin (1997).

[15]For an eloquent and engaging discussion on the discourse of 'wildness', its associations with notions of 'primitivism' and (in India) '*jangli*-ness', and its historical relationship with and opposition to 'civilization', see Skaria (1999).

The contemporary civilizing mission in which the RSS is engaged is underpinned by comparable strategies. As I discuss in Chapters Six and Seven, present-day threats from the outside world include the possibility that material wealth will enable local Christians and the Church to acquire land that belongs to local Hindus. Strategies employed by the RSS to combat these threats are accompanied by efforts to protect *adivasi*s from the harms of their own traditions. The latter can be seen both in the context of the RSS activists' active discouragement of 'backward' beliefs and encouragement of 'proper' 'civilized' ways of worship and acting (see Chapter Two), and with respect to their strategic intervention in local health treatment practices (discussed in Chapter Four).

In short, in the same way that British colonial officials regarded Indian peoples as uncivilized, the ethos and values that propel the RSS's own civilizing mission is underpinned by the idea that contemporary *adivasi* cultures require 'civilizing' the saffron way: that is, they need to be introduced to the 'correct' notions of Hindu practice and groomed to defend the Hindu nation against threatening religious minorities (cf. Skaria 1999: xii). Similar strategies are, of course, being effected by the Church. As intimated in the above discussion, previous accounts of Hindu nationalism have not fully appreciated the role of the Church, or the broader way in which such strategies are patterned after historical Church practices. Indeed, even as the RSS continues to be the active agent in this process, the particular manner in which Hindu nationalism has been introduced locally represents a response to the historical practices and contemporary presence of the Church. Bearing this in mind, Chapter Three focuses on how the local Church, through the spiritual and material 'diabolization' of 'backward' Oraon beliefs and practices, is advancing its own 'civilizing mission'.

Local Disputes and the 'Threatening Other'

The active engagement in 'civilizing' strategies, manifested in the form of medicines and other material assistance, has enabled RSS activists to successfully legitimize their presence locally and to endear themselves to both Christians and Hindus. This seemingly constructive outcome is the product of one of the more insidious means through which *Hindutva* is propagated in this area and elsewhere; for, under the auspices of 'good works', it conceals the more aggressive communal agenda that underpins the Hindu nationalist movement as a whole.

The second strategy through which *Hindutva* has been propagated locally is more directly related to this wider agenda, and that is the communalization of local grievances and the promotion of the 'threatening other'. Specifically, it is by involving themselves in the local land and liquor disputes, and attaching these to the 'one-nation, one-culture' agenda that the RSS activists have successfully facilitated the spread of Hindu nationalism.

This strategy is strikingly parallel to the processes discussed by Tambiah (1996) in his study of ethnonationalist conflicts in twentieth century in South Asia. Focusing his analysis on Sri Lanka, Pakistan and India, Tambiah seeks to understand the trajectory of communal riots and collective violence that is commonly manifested within different sites of ethnic conflict. He draws particular attention to the process whereby local incidents and minor disputes between individuals regularly evolve into wider conflicts and communal riots between larger numbers of people who are only peripherally involved in the original dispute.

Tambiah characterizes this particular process with the terms 'focalization', whereby the original incident or dispute is 'progressively denuded of its contextual particulars', and 'transvaluation', where the incident is then 'distorted and aggregated into larger collective issues of national or ethnic interest' (Tambiah 1996: 81). While these are decidedly cumbersome terms, they are nonetheless very useful, for the processes to which they refer are similar to the kinds of strategies that are being employed in Mohanpur. It is in Chapters Six and Seven that we shall see how local-level disputes are distorted and stripped of their particular context and then attached to broader Hindu nationalist concerns.

These processes are compounded by the influence and involvement of what Brass (1997: 16) calls 'conversion specialists', another useful category that refers to those 'propagandists' or activists who appeal to wider, more enduring (and therefore less context-bound) loyalties such as race, religion, and place of origin (cf. Tambiah 1996: 192). Like Tambiah, Brass is referring specifically to the instigators behind collective violence. He seeks to explain how collective violence often evolves out of circumstances that are not necessarily communal in nature (Brass 1997: 6), and is critical of existing accounts that attribute to the emergence of communal riots as 'spontaneous acts'.[16] He holds

---

[16]Brass also provides a very convincing argument about how the elevation of such incidents into communal confrontations or riots is related to how they are interpreted and articulated by the press, and by politicians and other authorities. He demonstrates that the persistence of so-called 'riots' is indeed largely related to their functional utility for dominant political ideologies (cf. Brass 1997: 6–7).

that there are invariably specific, identifiable individuals who work intentionally to produce such riots (ibid. 8). The role of such individuals is twofold: that of the 'fire-tender' (ibid. 16), who 'fuels' or maintains local tensions and communal animosities, and that of the 'conversion specialist', who transforms or 'converts' a particular incident into a potentially violent, riotous event (cf. Brass 2003: 32–3).

While I do not claim that the kind of conflict that I discuss in later chapters is akin to the violent riots to which both Tambiah and Brass refer in their separate studies, I do contend that there are important parallels with respect to the role of the individuals who serve as the primary instigators in converting local conflict into communal tensions. As Brass suggests, these individuals, or 'conversion specialists', tend to occupy formal and informal roles in organizations that actively seek to represent members of another group as an enemy or threat to their own community (ibid. 16). Locally, the individuals who serve in this role are the RSS *pracharaks* who visit the village on regular occasions. As I demonstrate in Chapters Six and Seven, it is the transformation of local Christians into the 'threatening other' that is the primary objective behind their involvement in local tensions.

As suggested above, the successful implementation of this particular strategy, both in tribal Chhattisgarh and throughout India as a whole, is predicated on the perception of the 'threatening other', or those whose origins and therefore allegiances apparently lie outside of this community (Jaffrelot 1996: 2; Hansen 1999). Many scholars have addressed the importance of propagating the perception of the 'other' for the purpose of conveying legitimacy to a community and its aims (see Das 1995; Frietag 1989). The incident narrated at the beginning of this book is an illustration of the potentially violent manner in which this kind of perception can be manifested.

In order to grasp the importance of this perception, it will be helpful to briefly consider its theoretical antecedents. For this, we must turn to the concept of ethnicity, a notion idea that underpins the idea of the 'other'. The term 'ethnicity' was first mentioned as a point of social analysis by Max Weber (1968 [1922]: 385–96; cf. Smith and Hutchinson 1996). Ethnicity and the definition of social and cultural boundaries emerged as a critical problem in anthropology when Leach (1954) put forth his argument that social units are produced by subjective processes of categorical ascription, processes which are not necessarily related to the observers' perceptions. Leach's ideas had a major influence on Barth (1969), who is largely hailed as setting the framework in which the study of ethnicity was to proceed. Following Leach's general perspective, Barth placed emphasis on the cultural practices that produce and mark boundaries between ethnic groups. He advocated an interactional approach to the study of ethnicity, and focused on how the ethnic group was subjectively defined and understood through its relationship with others. The first fact of ethnic group identity, then, became the application of systematic distinctions between two groups: 'us' and 'them', or the 'other' (see Moerman 1965; Nash 1989).

General discussions of ethnic identity since Barth's work have been dominated by a set of oppositions: primordialism, which assumes that there is something fixed, natural or innate ('primordial') about human identity and social groups; and instrumentalism, which holds that social identities are products of external ('instrumental') political or social processes. The former generally includes ties based on origin, blood, language, or religion (cf. de Vos 1983; Epstein 1978; Geertz 1963; Isaacs 1975; Nash 1989), whereas the latter claims that ethnic identities are created by social and political factors and consciously manipulated by powerful individuals (see Brass 1974, 1979; Cohen 1974; Cohn 1987; Glazer and Moynihan et al. 1975; Robinson 1977).

More comprehensive discussions of ethnic group identity attempt to synthesize these positions and view ethnicity as a collective identity that naturalizes cultural attributes such as language, descent, religion or territorial occupation, and attaches these to groups as their innate possession and historical legacy (Bentley 1987; Brass 1991; Eriksen 2002; Smith 1992; Tambiah 1989; Tonkin 1989). Any one or more of these components are in turn subjectively claimed or socially accorded, depending upon the context and calculation of advantages.

Like other nationalist movements that revolve around the promotion of ethnic politics (see Kapferer 1988; Marty and Appleby 1993; Smith 1992), Hindu nationalist objectives tend toward the instrumentalist kind, with its proponents using a strategy of ethno-religious mobilization to propel primordialist claims that assert the idea that a 'Hindu Indian nationhood' should attract everyone who is conceivably classified as a Hindu by blood or descent (Jaffrelot 1996:6).[17] According to most

[17]A useful framework in which to conceptualize Hindu nationalism is Anthony Smith's notion of 'ethnic nationalism' (1971, 1992). This model starts from 'a recognizable cultural unit' whose primary concern is to 'ensure the survival of the group's cultural identity' (see also Jaffrelot 1996: 13). Here, Smith argues that European modernity caused a sense of backwardness and decline among colonized peoples, from

analysts, the larger political strategy built around the Hindu nationalist quest for power can only succeed in a context where 'they' are perceived as posing a threat—real or imagined—to the majority community of Hindus (Hansen 1999: 208). And indeed, the perception of the 'threatening other'—those whose origins and therefore allegiances apparently lie outside of this community—has been called the 'cornerstone of the Hindu nationalist movement' (Jaffrelot 1993: 522).

Locally, Christians and the Church are the most obvious 'other', both with respect to the way they epitomize the RSS's primary object of mimesis, and the way they represent a palpable 'threat' to the RSS's saffron agenda. In an effort to cultivate the specific notion of the Christian 'threatening other', RSS activists have actively persisted with a strategy of transforming local grievances into wider communal issues through the dual processes of 'focalization' and 'transvaluation' discussed above. The discourse surrounding the creation of the 'threatening Christian other' is, of course, compounded by the Church's parallel agenda of transforming backward Oraon *adivasi*s into 'proper' Christians. It is in Chapter Three that I undertake a detailed examination of the relationship that local Oraons have with the Church, along with the present-day contributions that the Church has made to the emergence of Hindu nationalism. Chapters Six and Seven are devoted to a fuller analysis of the manner by which such grievances, which are seemingly embedded in caste-based economic interests that revolve around the acquisition of land and the sale of drink, are activated and linked to nationalist issues.

In this analysis, we shall see how the general concern that the Hindu community has for the Christians' increasing wealth, land and overall economic advantages is inextricably related to the issue of the infringement of prior rights and to local power relations and structures of domination. This can be partly explained in terms of what Horowitz (1985: 186) calls the 'politics of entitlement', or the issue of rights and legitimacy that one group claims over another. While it is not my intention to engage substantively with the wider arguments that Horowitz examines in his influential study of the dimensions of ethnic group conflict, I find his ideas about the role that group entitlement

---

which a certain elite section then set about reforming their traditions by endowing them with a 'Golden Age', similar to what Hindu nationalists have done. See also van der Veer (1994), whose discourses on 'religious nationalism' also rely on a particular conceptualization of historical developments in Europe.

plays in such conflicts to be very useful in trying to understand the trajectory that local grievances have taken.

According to Horowitz (1985: 201), group legitimacy and group rights are related to 'ownership': to be legitimate is to have both a right to the territory as well as a right to exclude others from it. Some of the foundations of group legitimacy include prior occupation, or 'indigenousness'; possession of a 'special mission' (usually religious in character) to occupy a particular territory; and 'traditional rule', or the invocation of an 'earlier glory' or a golden age that informs contemporary claims to a territory (ibid. 202–5).

It is the notion of indigenousness that constitutes the most widespread and powerful claim to group legitimacy and entitlement: the closer the identification of the group with the soil, the more powerful the claim (ibid. 207–8). This idea resonates with Weiner's (1978) notion of 'sons of the soil', which also evokes historical claims of 'belonging' and collective aspirations to own and rule the land (p. 13–14). Like Horowitz, Weiner was interested in the wider issues and origins of ethnic conflict. His specific focus was on the conflict and resentment that arise when migrants from one or more ethnic communities are economically more successful than the local 'sons of the soil'.

According to Weiner (1978: 10), one of the more critical dimensions of ethnic conflict is the extent to which local and migrant groups battle over access to or control over economic resources, such as land. In tandem with these observations, the primary grievances around which group conflict and tensions have revolved in Mohanpur are specifically underpinned by the claims that the 'sons of the soil', the Ratiya Kanwar Hindus, have over land. What they see as their rightful entitlement has recently come under threat by the Oraon Christians, a community of industrious outsiders who have recently migrated to the village.

As we shall see later in the book, the economic or material basis that frames such grievances makes it possible to interpret the disputes and tensions as an ordinary caste conflict, whereby the Ratiya Kanwar high caste 'sons of the soil' and other members of the Hindu community attempted to 'level' (Tambiah 1996) or diminish the margin of advantage enjoyed by the upwardly mobile, low-caste community. The central concern here is the way that increasing tensions between the Hindus and Christians have been framed by both the (re)allocation of scarce resources (land) traditionally belonging to and controlled by the higher-caste Ratiya Kanwar Hindus, and the increasing economic wealth, helped by liquor profits, of the low-caste, newcomer Oraon Christians (see Brass 1974: 34).[18]

While the basis of these tensions is related to group entitlement, the 'time of arrival' issue is also pertinent here and serves, as Horowitz (1985: 202–4) has observed, to invoke a sense of proprietorship and superiority. As we shall see in Chapters Six and Seven, it is not a question of who actually came first that governs the strength of claims to local land. Indeed, according to Horowitz (ibid.), the issue of who arrived first is not always important. Instead, it is the way in which such claims and the pre-existing tensions have been appropriated and used by the RSS to represent what could have been classified as an ordinary caste conflict in terms of *Hindutva*.

Locally it is these pre-existing tensions that have provided the RSS with a convenient platform from which to strategically extend its ideological agenda. As Weiner (1978: 7) has pointed out, when competing groups belong to different ethnic or caste communities, and when the issue revolves around competition over or access to economic wealth, then ordinary caste conflicts can and do become exacerbated into larger ethno-nationalist issues—particularly if one or both groups are organized and guided by a group of elites (cf. Brass 1974: 45). In other words, what could have been interpreted as the tensions distinctive of an ordinary caste conflict have rapidly become communalized by the instrumental involvement of members of the RSS, who strategically shifted attention from caste to religious affiliation, thereby emphasizing the idea of the Oraons as the 'threatening other' to the local Hindus.

Instrumentalism and the Spread of Hindu Nationalism

It will be clear to those familiar with the literature on Hindu nationalism that the two principal strategies described above—we shall call them 'civilizing' and 'aggressive'—are underpinned by what Jaffrelot (1996) identifies as 'emulation' and 'stigmatization'. Jaffrelot uses these terms to describe the more general endeavour of the Hindu right which,

---

[18]The scenario described here has interesting parallels with the situation observed so long ago by Bailey (1958), with respect to the aspiring low-caste community, the Boad Distillers, whose economic success through engagement in liquor sales and land acquisition had important political repercussions for the community as a whole.

from the late nineteenth century onward, sought to both emulate and stigmatize those aspects of (initially) western society that were at once useful and threatening to Hindu society (1996: 11). According to Jaffrelot (ibid.), this endeavour was originally manifested in terms of the tension between cultural preservation and modernization, which was resolved through the invention of a 'Vedic Golden Age' that was both indigenous and in accordance with modern values.[19]

Following on from Jaffrelot's analysis, I argue that the use of these strategies and the successful spread of Hindu nationalism to specifically *adivasi* areas is predicated on the 'instrumentalist' involvement of self-interested, powerful outsiders, such as proponents of the RSS, who employ their positions to engage in forms of civic activism and to communalize social identities and relations by actively promoting the idea of the 'threatening Christian other'. This process is a part of the broader identity-building strategies of the contemporary Hindu nationalist movement, which attempt to assimilate or appropriate the cultural traits, ideas and organizational principles that give those 'others' their superiority and prestige (cf. Jaffrelot 1996: 16).

Here, I find Paul Brass's (1974: 37–45; 1979) analysis of ethnic group politics to be constructive, particularly with respect to the importance he gives to the involvement of political organizations in the promotion of ethnic group loyalties to a nationalist agenda. Indeed, Tambiah's (1996) arguments highlighted above, about the instrumental role that elites (or propagandists like the RSS) play in engendering highly selective and often distorted local accounts of disputes, were in many ways anticipated by Brass, whose 1979 study of elite groups noted how leaders of ethnic movements invariably select certain symbols from traditional cultures, attach new value and meaning to them and use them to mobilize the group, defend its interests and compete with other groups (1979: 51).

It is true that Brass probably overemphasizes the extent of the power and influence of political organizations led by elites when he writes that 'they shape group consciousness by manipulating symbols of group identity to achieve power for their group' (1974: 45).[20] It would also be an over-simplification to argue that these strategies

---

[19]Jaffrelot (1993b) also employs the notion 'strategic syncretism' to describe the same process.

[20]For further criticisms, see Brubaker, Rogers and Laitlin (1998), Jaffrelot (1993a: 80), Robinson (1977), van der Veer (1994: 30) and Varshney (2002).

were employed *solely* on the basis of elite self-interest or the involvement of an outside political organization. My point in highlighting this issue, however, is to emphasize the directed and instrumental way that *Hindutva* ideology is made relevant to local contexts. As we shall see in the analysis that follows, elites, who are represented by the local RSS activists, are 'disproportionately important' (Horowitz 1985: 104) in the local context, and it is their agenda that has facilitated the emergence of Hindu nationalism. It is for this reason that Brass's analysis provides a useful framework for this book.

Situating the Study: Mohanpur, Chhattisgarh

This book draws on research that was carried out between 1997–9 in Mohanpur, a village located in one of the more densely forested subdivisions (*tehsil*) of Korba district in Chhattisgarh, central India (see Map 1).

At the time of fieldwork, Mohanpur, along with other villages in the area, was relatively cut off from the urban 'mainstream' due to thick jungle and inaccessible roads. The 40-kilometre distance to Korba, the nearest city and district headquarters, took an average of four hours to reach by cycle or bus, and local people thought this distance to be quite far. Indeed, most villagers, who earn their livelihoods through a combination of rice-cultivation and the collection and sale of non-timber forest products, had never made the journey into the city. Instead, people regularly travelled to villages that were located within what was considered to be within a comfortable walking or cycling distance (10 to 12 km) of Mohanpur. These excursions mostly took place for the purpose of calling on kinfolk or attending festivals and other ritual events, or with the objective of looking for work or purchasing or selling local produce or other goods (see Chapters Six and Seven).

At the time of fieldwork, Mohanpur had a population of 886 that was spread across 163 households and eight *jatis* (castes or social groups).[21] The largest village in the *tehsil*, Botli, was located around 12 km from Mohanpur and had over 500 households and a population of over 2200. This was unusual, however, as most villages

---

[21]Throughout this book, I use these terms interchangeably. See below for a discussion on the complexities of the terms 'caste', 'tribe' and '*adivasi*'.

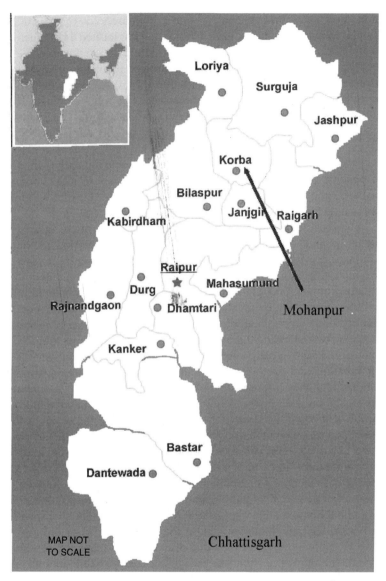

Figure 1.1: Depicting India/Chhattisgarh/Mohanpur

in the area averaged between 145 and 200 households (600–1200 people). While the nearest village, Chuidorha, was located 4 km north of Mohanpur, the village with the most dominant presence in the area was Manpur, which was situated around 6 km to the east of Mohanpur. With a population of around 1650 spread over 315 households, Manpur was also considered to be a large village. It housed both the Catholic Church, which served all Oraon Christians within a 20 km range, and the government middle school, which catered to pupils from villages within a 10 km radius. Manpur was also known for its three large shops that local people regularly visited to purchase their government-subsidized supplies of rice, flour, kerosene and other goods that were not available in one of the four shops in the village.

A second village to which people from the surrounding area regularly flocked was Parsakhola. Situated just over 6 km to the southeast of Mohanpur, Parsakhola hosted the only weekly market (*bazaar*) within a 12 km range. Every Thursday afternoon, itinerant traders from around the district would descend on Parsakhola to sell their wares, which included clothing and blankets, water pots and cooking vessels, fresh produce, fish, and any number of useful items. Notwithstanding this abundance of goods, the primary reason that most local people dressed up and travelled to the market was for meeting and greeting friends and family from neighbouring villages. This was illustrated by the fact that regular visitors who spent the afternoon at the *bazaar* rarely returned with anything but a small packet of *churmur* (fried snack) for their children or younger siblings.

In addition to its relative geographical distance from the urban mainstream, there was little regular access to 'popular' Indian or Hindu culture via television and other media at the time of fieldwork due to the lack of electricity in Mohanpur and other villages in the area. Most local people, for example, had never seen the popular Indian epic, the Ramayana, that was serialized on the government-sponsored television channel, Doordarshan, in the late 1980s;[22] nor did they have access to newspapers and other print media. While I do not wish to give the impression that the village and surrounding area were unusually isolated, it is important to bear in mind that this relative

---

[22]This is significant, particularly since such programmes are widely perceived to have possessed communal undertones that were later appropriated by the leaders of the Sangh Parivar (see Farmer 1996: 102–8).

geographical and cultural distance from the Hindu and Indian 'mainstream' contributed to the 'backward' or *jangli* label that outsiders and urban-dwellers—including RSS *pracharaks* and Catholic priests—had given this and other villages in the surrounding area.

Like all other villages in the area, the majority (93 per cent) of Mohanpur's inhabitants are *adivasi*. The Hindu community, which is dominated by the Ratiya Kanwar *jati*, comprises three-quarters of the population (646 people, 122 households); the Catholic Christians, all Oraon, make up one-quarter (241 people spread over 42 households). This comparatively large number of Christians is unusual in this area. For example, over half of the 22 villages that are located within the 20 km area that is served by the Church in Manpur have no Christian presence; the remaining villages have an average of around ten to fifteen Christian households, all of which are Oraon. Reasons for the uncommonly large number of Christians in Mohanpur are related to the Oraons' migration history and will be addressed in Chapter Three.

One of the objectives of this book is to show that it is partly due to the relatively large Christian presence that the RSS has been able to successfully employ its instrumentalist strategies in the manner that it has done in Mohanpur.[23] This is not to say that the process by which Hindu nationalism is introduced and the impact that it has on local relations in this area is in any way unique to this village. Indeed, the kinds of activities in which RSS *pracharaks* engaged locally and that are discussed in the following chapters—namely, the establishment of nursery schools, the introduction of mainstream Hindu festivals, and the inculcation of *Hindutva* in the course of 'training meetings' conducted with young men—have been replicated in all neighbouring villages. What I hope to demonstrate is that the kind of process by which the RSS has succeeded in Mohanpur can be found in other areas across India where there is a strong presence of potential 'threatening others'. Locally, this 'threatening other' happens to be the Christian Oraon community.

---

[23]The situation would likely be very different in neighbouring districts, such as Surguja or Jashpur, where both Christian and non-Christian Oraons are more dominant, and in neighbouring states, such as Jharkhand, where there is an ongoing movement to have the traditional Oraon religion recognized as '*sarna dharm*' or '*adi dharm*' and classified alongside Christianity and Hinduism in the census (see Roy 1985; Sundar 2006). At this time, however, I have no data on the situation in such areas.

It is in Chapter Two that I will consider more fully the local caste rankings and inter-caste relations. Here, however, it is important to note that I am most concerned with the relationship between the Ratiya Kanwars, who are the local 'high caste', and the Oraons, who are the lowest caste in the village. A more considered examination of not only the perspectives of each individual *jati*, but also of the wider, intra-Hindu caste relations would of course provide a more nuanced understanding of the processes by which Hindu nationalism is manifested locally. However, as we shall see in the pages that follow, it is the relationship between the Ratiya Kanwars—the most numerically and politically dominant Hindu caste in the village—and the Oraons—the sole Christian caste—which constitutes and therefore represents the broader communal relationship between the local Hindus and Christians as a whole. By extension, it is this relationship that has been most affected and transformed by the presence and involvement of both the RSS and the Church.

Notwithstanding the dominance of the Ratiya Kanwar perspective, throughout the course of this book I tend to use the term 'Hindu' when discussing the local Hindu community as a whole. While the Ratiya Kanwar and other local groups have traditionally referred to themselves by their caste or clan name (see Chapter Two), my usage of this term reflects the fact that 'Hindu' is being increasingly employed by both Ratiya Kanwars and other *adivasis* and non-*adivasi* Hindus to juxtapose themselves to local Christians. As I shall argue in Chapters Six and Seven, reasons for this are related to the growing influence of the RSS. I also tend to use the terms 'Oraon' and 'Christian' interchangeably, as both of these terms represent a single group. Further discussion about the complexities and local usage of these social categories will take place in the following two chapters.

At the time of my fieldwork, Chhattisgarh made up the eastern and south-eastern region of Madhya Pradesh. It became a separate state in November 2000, and currently boasts of a population of nearly 21 million, three-quarters of which dwells in rural areas. The region is rich in natural resources, and includes large deposits of minerals such as aluminium, iron ore and coal (Chaudhuri 2001: 84). 44 per cent of the state's total land area is covered by forest, and timber accounts for around 40 per cent of the state's total forest revenue. Additionally, more than 70 per cent of India's total production of *tendu* leaves, which are used to make the *bidi* cigarettes, comes from the Chhattisgarh forests (ibid: 86–8). Both the timber and the *tendu* industries, along with the collection and sale of minor forest produce, serve to supplement the agricultural-based incomes of the majority of the state's 6.5 million *adivasi* people who, like the residents in Mohanpur, are concentrated throughout the forested areas.

Chhattisgarh's early history reveals a distinctive pattern of minor kingdoms whose leaders were typically from junior branches of major ruling families to the north (cf. Flueckiger 1996: 5). According to one popular account, Chhattisgarh was formerly known as Kosala, or 'land of treasure'. It comprised one of three kingdoms belonging to the Gond tribals, who lost this kingdom to a Rajput dynasty in the second century A.D. (Prakasam 1998: 18–24). After this, it was divided into 18, and then 36 forts (see Danda 1977). The name Chhattisgarh refers to these 36 forts, a concept that is documented in folk histories and that continues to have contemporary significance to tribal and non-tribal Chhattisgarhis (Flueckiger 1996: 5). This region officially came under British rule in 1854 (Babb 1975: 122–3), and was divided into two districts, Raipur and Bilaspur in 1861. There have been numerous bifurcations since then, and today, Chhattisgarh state is comprised of sixteen districts.

Chhattisgarh is considered to be the most important rice-growing region of this part of India (Danda 1977: 97). Even now, its plains are known as India's 'rice bowl', and around 85 per cent of the population is dependent on agriculture (Chaudhuri 2001: 86). This is a figure that encompasses the majority of tribal people in the region, and in the specific area where I conducted my fieldwork, most households are largely, if not entirely, dependent on wet-rice cultivation.

According to Babb (1975: 9), the main 'ethnographic break' in this region is between the central plain, which is mostly populated by 'caste Hindus', and the outlying, forested hill region inhabited predominantly by tribal people. The geographic barrier of Chhattisgarh's hill regions, combined with its distance from major urban centres and the Hindi heartland of the Gangetic plains, is one reason why the plains region has received relatively less attention by early ethnographers (cf. Flueckiger 1996). Babb's (1975) notable work on popular Hinduism in the plains region was the first extensive ethnographic study after Elwin's (1946) collection of Chhattisgarhi folklore. Greater attention has been devoted to the area in more recent times, with Flueckiger's (1996) contemporary study of Chhattisgarhi folklore and gender, Dube's (1992, 1998) work on the Satnami community in Raipur, and Sundar's (1997) anthropological history of Bastar. Most recently, Parry has undertaken research on industrial labour and caste relations amongst steel plant workers in Bhilai (1999a, 1999b, 2000, 2001).

One thing that much of this literature has in common is its recognition of a strong sense of 'Chhattisgarhi identity' and the Chhattisgarhi 'way if doing things' (Babb 1975: 11). Cultural characteristics that are thought to be uniquely 'Chhattisgarhi' include dress and jewellery, along with ritualized friendships and local festivals, as well as language (Flueckiger 1996: 6–8).

'Tribes' and 'Adivasis'

A major factor contributing to this 'Chhattisgarhi identity' is said to be the strong impact of tribal people in the region. There are at least forty-two communities in Chhattisgarh officially classified as 'Scheduled Tribe' (ST) (Chaudhuri 2001: 84). In comparison with the caste Hindus who largely populate the plains region, these communities have been the focus of much earlier anthropological work.[24] This literature notes how these communities have tended to become submerged in the surrounding caste Hindu culture, due to the Sanskritizing processes which come from fairly intimate contact with the Hindus (see Babb 1975). In spite of their relative assimilation, however, there is a fair amount of anthropological literature that focuses on the retention of specifically 'tribal' aspects of Hindu culture (see Gell 1982, 1987; Jay 1968; Orans 1965). As we shall see in Chapter Two, the majority of local groups in Mohanpur reflected this sort of 'tribal Hinduism': on the one hand, they were culturally and officially classified as 'Scheduled Tribes'; on the other, they belonged to 'caste' groups, wherein purity was an index of hierarchical rank and difference was a marker of separation (Fuller 1996: 12; Padel 1995: 17).

Groups categorized as 'Scheduled Tribes' in India today are generally those formerly called 'tribes' by the British (see Bates 1995; Cohn 1987; Skaria 1997). The identification of 'tribes' involved a

---

[24]See Dube (1951), Forsyth (1889), Fuchs (1973), Ghurye (1959), Grigson (1949), and Russell and Hiralal (1916). Additional information on tribals in Chhattisgarh can be found in very generalized collections on tribal people in India (Ghurye 1959; Mamoria 1952; Majumdar 1958; Roy 1912, 1915, 1972, 1985; Roy and Roy 1937; von Fürer-Haimendorf 1982). More contemporary work focuses largely on the Gonds, the largest tribal group in India whose population spreads across various districts in Chhattisgarh (Gell 1992; Gell 1987 and 1997; Mehta 1984).

relationship between the British concept of the more 'civilized' Hindu society, defined by their understanding of the caste system, and the 'primitive', wild periphery that dotted the edges of its social and geographical domain.[25] Groups that could not be classified into major caste or religious categories were labelled instead on the basis of general impressions about their physical and socio-cultural isolation from mainstream, caste-bound Indian society (Béteille 1977).[26] Early studies by British colonial administrators like Dalton (1872) and Risley (1891, 1908), as well as the works of Roy (1912, 1915), Elwin (1943, 1950) and other scholars reflect the difficulty experienced by colonial officials in deciding where a caste ended and a tribe began.[27] This difficulty was augmented by the classification and description of several communities as 'tribe' and 'caste' that changed from one census to the next (cf. Béteille 1998; Kulkani 1991; Sengupta 1988).

The term 'tribe' evolved into legal and common contemporary usage with its official categorization in the Constitution of India. In 1950, the President of India drew up lists or 'Schedules' of castes and tribes in order to demarcate underprivileged sections of society to receive government funds and benefits (Galanter 1984, Unnithan 1994: 113).[28] In 1952, the Report of the Scheduled Caste and Scheduled Tribe Commission published what was considered to be the 'common features' of tribal groups. These included holding animistic beliefs, living naked or semi-naked, hunting and gathering, consuming meat, and having a propensity for drink and dance (Mathur 1972: 460). These features, which carried overtones of 'jangliness' and invited comparisons with more 'civilized' societies, have been compounded by exaggerated claims about *adivasi*s being geographically 'isolated' or culturally different from mainstream caste-

---

[25]Skaria (1997: 728) reminds us that the 'wild man' had been an abiding concern of European popular and elite culture, going back at least to medieval times (see also Bartra 1994). The figure of the 'primitive' was also wild in the sense that it was separated from civilization by time: the conceptual opposite of primitive being modern (cf. Kuper 1988; Skaria 1999: 193–6).

[26]Even before terms such as 'wild' (*jangli*) and 'wild tribes' (*janglijati*) were ascribed to such groups by the British, such communities often described themselves and were referred to by surrounding communities as '*jangli*' or *janglijati* (see Skaria 1999: v).

[27]See Ghurye (1943); Bailey (1960a, 1960b); Desai (1977); Dumont (1961); Sinha (1965).

[28]These Schedules directed that 'the State shall promote with special care the educational and economic interests of the weaker sections of the people and in particular of the Castes and Tribes and shall protect them from social injustice and all forms of exploitation' (Mandelbaum 1970: 574).

Hindu society (see Dube 1977). As we shall see throughout the course of this book, such ideas which are encapsulated within the term '*jangli*' continue to predominate among local *adivasis* themselves. While employed occasionally in tongue-in-cheek fashion when juxtaposing themselves with 'city people' (*sahari log*), the term '*jangli*' is used more seriously by local people to signify a more fundamental opposition between their traditional *adivasi* practices and the customs and values they associate with urban caste Hindus.[29] This term is also used by RSS *pracharaks* and Catholic Fathers to underpin and validate the contemporary civilizing missions of the RSS and the Church.

Unpopular as these criteria have been among those scholars who dismissed such a classification as a 'typical case of fiction creation by Government officers' (Mathur 1972: 460; see Hardiman 1987 and Baviskar 1995 for further criticisms of this term), they remain prevalent today within popular Indian society, as well as amongst those scholars for whom 'a tribe is a "tribe" that is included in the list of Scheduled Tribes' (Pathy et al. 1976: 401–6).

It is partly because of the problematic nature of the notion 'tribe' that the term *adivasi* (original inhabitant) has become increasingly preferable for researchers and activists. This term itself is not without criticism, however, and scholars continue to contest its sociological validity and dispute its precise meanings (Baviskar 2005: 5106; cf. Skaria 1999; Sundar 1997). Hardiman (1987: 12), for example, notes that the idea that *adivasis* are 'autochthonous' or 'original' is challenged by the fact that many *adivasis* groups are known to have actually migrated into areas in which they now reside, having displaced existing inhabitants in the process (see Prasad 2003: 1–33). Such criticisms notwithstanding, the term *adivasi* has acquired increasing legitimacy not only because it is employed in administrative and political contexts, but because it is used by *adivasis* themselves to differentiate their communities and cultural practices from non-*adivasis*, and to claim political material resources from the state (see Baviskar 2005: 5106).[30] It is for these reasons that I prefer the term *adivasi*.

It is pertinent to note that this term has fallen out of favour with the RSS and other members of the Sangh Parivar, which has adopted

---

[29]While the term '*dehati*' (rural) is also used to denote a similar opposition, '*jangli*' is more comon.

[30]*Adivasis* are eligible for special government benefits, a type of 'affirmative action' that includes reservations in employment and elite educational institutions, scholarships, and so on (Desai 1975; Kulkani 1991; Singh 1972).

the term *vanvasi* (forest dweller) to denote 'tribal'. Reasons for this preference relate to the wider *Hindutva* project that, as noted earlier, assumes that India is 'fundamentally Hindu' (see Thapar 1991). The term *adivasi*, which implies that tribal people are the 'original inhabitants' of India, threatens the dual RSS claims that the Aryans, with their ancient Vedic civilization and Hindu culture, were the original inhabitants of India, and that Indian culture is, therefore, synonymous with Hindu culture (cf. Kanungo 2002: 96–8; Sundar 2006: 375; Thapar 1985: 17).[31] The term *vanvasi*, in contrast, allows the RSS to propagate the view that the Aryans, not *adivasis*, were indigenous to India and that, far from being 'outside the Hindu fold', the 'forest dwellers' have traditionally had an honoured place within Hindu society (cf. Kanungo 2002: 149–50; Prasad 2003: 1–2).

It is precisely because of its strong *Hindutva* connotations that I do not use the term *vanvasi*. My alternating usage of *adivasi* with tribe and caste throughout this book, however, reflects both the impossibility of a clear distinction between these terms, as well as the ambiguities generated by early academics and administrators, and the ongoing attempts by contemporary scholars to understand and theorize the differences between these categories and communities. Finally, and not withstanding the broader connotations that continue to be associated with the term '*jangli*', my usage of this term reflects the fact that it remains an important ethnographic category, utilized by both local people to distinguish themselves from city dwellers and customs, and by RSS *pracharaks* and Catholic Fathers to justify their respective 'civilizing' agendas.

Entering the Field

Although I did not know it at the time, the relationships that I would foster with both the villagers and local RSS activists were indelibly marked by my method of arrival and introduction into the village. Before beginning my fieldwork, my intention had been to study the ethnic relationship between Christian and Hindu *adivasi*s in a part of Chhattisgarh where the Church had a relatively long presence. At the advice of one of my Ph.D. supervisors in London, I got in touch

---

[31]See also the report produced by Sabrang Communications entitled 'Adivasi vs. Vanvasi: The Hinduization of Tribals in India Foreign Exchange of Hate' at www.outlookindia.com/specialfeaturem.asp?fodname=20021120&fname=irdf&sid=11.

with a Catholic priest who had worked in this part of Chhattisgarh some 20 years ago. I arranged to meet this priest in Korba, from where we travelled for three hours by jeep to a Catholic mission station lying at the edge of a small village called Manpur. The two priests and four sisters residing at the mission had been warned of my imminent arrival, and I was welcomed with a round of 'Jesu'. I spent the next two days talking with the priests and sisters about my research interests. After expressing concern for my ability to endure the hardships of an area with no electricity or running water, they suggested that Mohanpur, located 6 km from the mission station, might be the most suitable place to carry out my study. This village was considered to be attractive not only because it was ethnically diverse but also because it was home to a young Oraon woman named Sumitra, who spoke English and Hindi, as well as Kurukh and Chetriboli.[32] Sumitra had learned English and Hindi when she was sent, like many local Oraon girls, at the age of fourteen or fifteen to work as a domestic servant for an English-speaking Christian family in Mumbai.

My first introduction to Mohanpur took place when I accompanied the priests and sisters by jeep to an evening mass at the home of one of the Oraons. To reach the *uppar para*, or upper neighbourhood where most of the Oraon Christians reside, it is necessary to travel along the dirt track through the main *basti* (neighbourhood, locality) where the majority of the Hindu community lives (see Map 2).

As we saw in the anecdote narrated at the beginning of this book, the presence of any vehicle in the village is always an unusual event. On this particular occasion, the presence of a white foreigner inside the mission jeep not only created additional curiosity, but also served to mark my connections with the Church.

Upon making my introductions and explaining my research intentions, it was decided that I would live in the attached room of the home of a young Oraon Christian couple, Bahadur and Hiramani, along with their two-year-old son, Johnny, and Bahadur's elderly parents. Bahadur was considered to be something of a leader of the Oraon Christians and, with a large home and extra room, he had the

---

[32]In the area where I conducted my fieldwork, standard Hindi is used in schools and by government and church officials, whereas Chetriboli (a dialect of Chhattisgarhi) is spoken by all villagers and Kurukh (a Dravidian-based language) is spoken by the Oraons (see note on transliteration). I carried out my research in a combination of all the three languages.

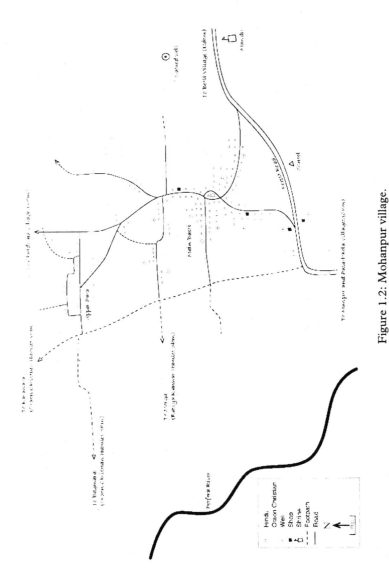

Figure 1.2: Mohanpur village.

The distance between the Oraon *basti* (*uppar para*) and the Hindu *basti* is half a kilometre.

space that my presence required. It was here that I would stay for the next twenty two months with Sumitra, who would serve as my research assistant.

I was told months later that, due to the nature of my arrival, the Christians had assumed that I was as pious as the priests. This explained their devout behaviour in the early weeks of my research, which was exhibited by an uncharacteristically high level of church attendance and weekly prayer meetings. The Hindus, on their part, assumed that I was a missionary and, though polite, mostly regarded me with curious caution. It didn't help that I lived with the Oraon Christians and wandered around the village during the first few weeks with Sumitra, one of the most devout of all the local Oraons.

In the early stages of fieldwork, I made it a point to visit and introduce myself to members of each household and, with Sumitra's help, to explain as simply as possible the nature of my research. I realized fairly quickly, however, that Sumitra's presence was not only hampering my progression with linguistic proficiency, but was also hindering my access to local Hindus, who had little to say to me when she was around. My daily forays into the Hindu *basti* with an Oraon Christian guide must have seemed very odd indeed. Sumitra's own discomfort also served to highlight the limited and often strained nature of the interactions between these two local communities.

My decision, six weeks into fieldwork, to leave Sumitra behind when I visited the Hindu *basti* marked a turning point with my relationship to the members of the Hindu community as a whole. Although I knew that my association with Christianity would always remain, I tried to minimize this as much as possible by spending the majority of my days in the Hindu *basti*. I began by 'hanging out' in one of the local shops owned by a member of the Hindu community. My perch on the shop stool allowed me a privileged place from which to observe the constant flow of both Hindu and Oraon Christian customers, and to familiarize myself with names and make friends with people who would later become my closest informants. I also began to collect basic genealogical and demographic information. This process provided me with a valuable 'social map' of the village that was to prove integral to later attempts to unravel local ethnic and social relations. As my presence became routine and my linguistic skills improved, I was accepted as a 'daughter of the village' and invited into people's homes and lives, where I spent time observing and participating alongside them in their daily activities. I was taught how to weave mats and tie brooms, and I was shown how to make liquor and to tell the difference between a useless weed and a valuable medicinal plant. I was also invited to participate in healing and possession rituals, and to observe local *panchayat* (village council) and women's council meetings. This research was accompanied by monthly excursions to the mission station in Madanpur, where I would chat with the sisters and priests after mass, and to Korba, where I would pick up copies of old newspapers and the post.

It was during these early months that I became aware of the presence of, and was introduced to, the four RSS activists who came regularly to the village to conduct training meetings with young Hindu men. One of these activists, Raj, figures prominently in this book as the principal 'propagandist' or 'conversion specialist' (Brass 1997: 16) in the transmission of Hindu nationalist ideology to the local community (see Chapter Two). After much convincing that I was neither a Christian nor a missionary, he and his RSS friends were finally satisfied with the academic nature of my presence, and I was invited to visit them at the RSS ashram on my monthly visits to Korba.

Nine months or so after I began my fieldwork, I felt that my presence in the village as a researcher who was 'writing a book about the people of Mohanpur' had become accepted by both the locals and members of the RSS alike. My attendance at both Christian and Hindu festivals and healing rites, marriages and meetings, had become routine and expected, and if I was absent, then someone would invariably be sent to fetch me. Fifteen months into fieldwork, I was once again reminded of my Christian 'links' when I was suddenly summoned by the chief of police in Korba. This was in early January 1999, just after the murders of an Australian missionary and his two young sons. This family had lived for years in the neighbouring state of Orissa, and had been burnt to death in their jeep by alleged members of the Bajrang Dal, a militant group that was part of the Sangh Parivar. Because I was a white woman working alone in a mixed Christian/ Hindu *adivasi* village in an area that borders Orissa, the police chief became concerned for my safety. It took a great deal of time to convince him that I felt quite safe in the village, and that the attention given to me by his deputies following this incident was in fact more disturbing— both to local people and to my research—than any perceivable threat from militant members of the RSS, who by then considered me to be their friend.

This incident was followed by an upsurge of anti-Christian violence and sentiment across other parts of India. In light of this kind of violence which, at the time of writing, continues in *adivasi* areas where there is a strong Christian presence, and in view of the recent political success of the BJP in states like Chhattisgarh, the need for a distinctly ethnographic analysis of the manner by which Hindu nationalism is being inculcated in such areas and the role that the RSS and its activists play in this process, is urgent. And while I do not presume to be able to explain the particular form that such sentiment takes outside of its specific manifestation in Mohanpur, the issues with which this book engages are ongoing and present wherever the RSS and other members of the Sangh Parivar operate. For this reason, it is intended that this book should have wider applicability beyond the particular analysis provided in the ethnography that follows.

This book can be seen as having three parts. The first part examines some of the 'backward' practices that set local *adivasi* traditions apart from more 'proper', mainstream Hindu and Christian traditions. Principally descriptive, this part sets the stage for later sections that focus on how the relationship between local Hindus and Christians has been appropriated and transformed by the RSS and the Church. Chapter Two focuses on the dominant local caste, the Ratiya Kanwar 'sons of the soil', who have historically controlled and continue to dictate most ritual and political affairs that concern the wider Hindu community. This chapter also discusses some of the more general ways in which members of the RSS have gained access to the village. Chapter Three gives a brief account of the missionization processes in which the Church has historically engaged and discusses how such processes provide the basis for the strategies in which the RSS is involved. The greater part of this chapter is devoted to an examination of the relationship that local Oraons have with the Church, along with the present-day contributions that the Church has made to the emergence of Hindu nationalism in this area.

The second part examines the 'civilizing strategies' in which the RSS has engaged to legitimize its presence and represent its agenda to the local *adivasi* community. Focusing primarily on local peoples' responses to this agenda, detailed ethnographic consideration is given to two specific strategies. The first, which is the subject of Chapter Four, is related to local conceptions of illness and healing, and revolves around the sponsorship and installation by the RSS of a biomedical 'doctor'. A second strategy through which the RSS has gained local support, which is the focus of Chapter Five, is by lending its legitimacy to those who wish to contest the domination of the local headman. The objectives behind the RSS's involvement in this issue are impelled by the 'politics of inclusion', the result of which is the promotion of citizens' rights and democratic representation. It is argued that these methods together are part of a more implicit strategy to 'emulate' the successful methods that the Church has historically employed in its proselytizing efforts in *adivasi* areas, with a view to gaining further local legitimacy.

The third part examines the more aggressive strategies that the RSS has employed to propagate its agenda. Specific focus is on the role of local RSS proponents in the promotion of the 'threatening (Christian) other' and the transformation of local tensions into wider issues of communal and nationalist concern. Particular attention is on the local economic interests that underpin growing tensions between the Christian and Hindu communities, and on how the 'politics of entitlement', or the contest for worth and place, helps to explain the emergence of communal sentiment. Chapter Six is specifically concerned with land relations and the growth in land tensions between the 'original settler' Ratiya Kanwar Hindus and the 'first clearer' Oraon Christians. The objective is to provide a detailed outline of the origin of such tensions, in order to demonstrate their appeal to the RSS as an effective 'conflict symbol'. Chapter Seven examines the link between land tensions and liquor disputes, along with the relationship that both communities have to land, labour and access to cash. Specific attention is on how these tensions have been appropriated by RSS activists who then strip such tensions of their local particulars and attach them to one of the most powerful discourses of the Hindu nationalist movement: the 'threatening other'.

With respect to the broader concerns of this book, I try to show how RSS emphasis on the 'Hindu-ness' of local *adivasi* Hindus, in opposition to the 'threatening Christian', is an attempt to include the former in a sort of 'imagined community' of Hindus (Anderson 1983). This is a process whereby Hindu nationalist proponents, through engaging in forms of civic activism and communalizing local disputes, are persuading Hindu *adivasis* that they share traditions and aspirations—and therefore allegiances—with the wider mainstream Hindu community (cf. Tambiah 1996: 21).

CHAPTER TWO

Adivasi Hindus and the RSS

O ne of the principal arguments of this book is that the successful spread of Hindu nationalism into rural *adivasi* areas can be attributed to the manner by which RSS activists tailor their strategies to the particular situation that exists at the local level. In order to understand the motivation behind the kind of strategies being employed by RSS activists in Mohanpur, and to appreciate the impact that these have had on the lives of local people, it is necessary to centre the ethnographic examination on the primary local groups at whom such strategies have been targeted, and on the cultural practices and beliefs around which such strategies have been moulded.

The primary strategies employed in this village are underpinned by the broader cleavage between the Hindu and Christian communities, and the specific focus of this chapter is on the former. While intra-Hindu caste hierarchies and roles are briefly considered, a more extended discussion is devoted to the dominant local caste, the *adivasi* Ratiya Kanwars. As we shall see below, it is this caste as the local 'sons of the soil', that has historically controlled and dictated most ritual and political affairs that concern the wider Hindu community. A more detailed focus on the perspectives of each individual caste would of course, provide a more substantive account. It is true, for instance, that the non-*adivasi* castes—the Panika, Chauhan and Yadav—have a different historical relationship to mainstream Hindu society than their *adivasi* neighbours. However, such castes comprise only 9 per cent (15 out of 164 households) of the otherwise *adivasi*-dominated village population. Moreover, as noted earlier, such a discussion would take away from the wider issues with which this book is concerned: namely, the social relationship between the 'high-caste' Ratiya Kanwar and 'low-caste' Oraon communities, and the way that this relationship has been appropriated and transformed by the RSS and the Church.

A second objective of this chapter is to consider what both local *adivasis* and RSS activists categorize as '*jangli* Hinduism', and to examine how this is distinguished from what is considered to be more 'proper', mainstream Hinduism. As we shall see throughout the course of this book, the cultural practices and beliefs that underpin the former both constitute the kind of 'backward' *adivasi* traditions that the RSS seeks to 'civilize' and represent the primary obstacle in their local efforts to do so.

A final aim of this chapter is to consider the interest that the RSS organization has in *adivasi* communities more generally, and that local RSS activists have in the Mohanpur *adivasi* community in particular. Focus will be on the way in which RSS activists have gained access to the village, with specific attention on Raj, who serves as the principal propagandist or 'conversion specialist' (Brass 1997: 16) in the transmission of *Hindutva* locally. This discussion will set the stage for later chapters, where it will become clear that the emergence of Hindu nationalism in this area is largely due to the instrumentalist involvement of RSS proponents in local affairs.

Hindu Community, the Ratiya Kanwar Caste and the Gandhel Clan

The Hindu community (*samaj*) comprises three-quarters of the village population and is divided into seven *jatis*. These include Ratiya Kanwar, Majhuar, and Dudh Kanwar, which are all categorized as Scheduled Tribe (ST), or *adivasi*; Yadav, which is categorized as 'Other Backward Caste' (OBC); and Panika, Chauhan and Chowk/Lohar, which are classified as 'Scheduled Caste'.[1] As mentioned earlier, the Christian (Catholic) community is made up solely of Oraon *adivasis* (ST).

---

[1]Other Backward Caste, or OBC, is the official classification that designates traditionally lower (but not untouchable) castes; Scheduled Caste, or SC, is the category that designates so-called 'untouchable' castes, or Dalits.

The Ratiya Kanwars, who have resided in this area 'for nine or ten generations', comprise nearly half of the village population.[2] Their local dominance is largely due to a combination of high-caste rank, 'first settler' status and landownership. According to local accounts, the Majhuars and Dudh Kanwars immigrated to the village from elsewhere in Chhattisgarh two generations after the Ratiya Kanwar settled in the area. With the exception of the Panika, who moved to the village just two generations ago to serve as the village watchman (*kotwar*), the other four castes that make up the rest of the Hindu population have lived in the area for three to four generations. They were invited to reside in the village by the Ratiya Kanwars in order to perform economic and ritual services for the local high caste groups. The Oraon Christians migrated to the area from a neighbouring district just one generation ago and are presently the second largest caste in the village. They, like their predecessors, came in search of land and were given permission by the Ratiya Kanwars to reside in the village.

The caste ranking of local groups does not follow the mainstream caste hierarchies found in other parts of India (cf. Singh 1993a and 1994), and many scholars might find this surprising. For example, the Yadav (OBC), Panika (SC), Lohar (SC) and Chauhan (SC) are normally considered to be higher in the caste hierarchy than *adivasis*, or those classified as ST. Locally, however, the OBC and SC castes are classified *below* the dominant Hindu *adivasi* castes, but above the Christian Oraons, who fall lowest in the hierarchy (see Table 2.1).[3] This ranking, like Mayer's (1996: 34–5) classic study of caste hierarchy in another central Indian village, represents the broad consensus of not only the inhabitants of Mohanpur, but of those of other villages in this part of Chhattisgarh. It is based on local norms of pollution and untouchability and, as demonstrated below, is most visible in terms of occupation and commensality.

Locally, each *jati* is divided into a number of clans (*gotr*) and is strictly governed by rules of endogamy. Within the Ratiya Kanwar

[2] According to Singh (1994: 484–91), the Ratiya Kanwar (or Rathia Kawar) are one of twelve endogamous divisions of Kanwar hailing from Raigarh and Surguja districts of Chhattisgarh. They trace their origin to the Kauravas of the Mahabharata (cf. Russell and Hiralal (1923 [1916]: 389–403).

[3] While Oraons acknowledge and abide by this local hierarchy, they also insist that such rankings are completely different in areas such as Pathalgaon (in the neighbouring district of Jashpur) or Jharkhand where, they claim, they are considered to be the dominant 'high caste'. I currently have no ethnographic data to substantiate such claims, which are comparatively, very interesting.

Table 2.1: Caste Hierarchy of Local Groups

Caste	Status	Households	Population
1. Ratiya Kanwar	ST	75	418
2. Majhuar	ST	27	130
3. Dudh Kanwar	ST	4	30
4. Yadav	OBC	8	27
5. Panika	SC	3	21
6. Lohar	SC	2	11
7. Chauhan	SC	2	8
8. Oraon	ST	43	242
Total		164	887

jati, and indeed within the village as a whole, the Gandhel clan is the most powerful. Members of this clan were the first to arrive in the area and, 'since the beginning' (*shuru se*), have led the village in political and ritual affairs. The most influential members of the local *panchayat* also come from this clan, along with most of the government-appointed and salaried positions in the village, including two of the three *anganwadis* (nursery teachers), the *sarpanch* (an elected village representative), and the *munshi* (*tendu* collection 'foreman'). The power of this clan, moreover, is economically strengthened by the fact that its members own or have rights to the most productive agricultural and forestland (see Chapters Six and Seven).

Within the Gandhel clan, there is one particular lineage that has always held the reins of ritual and political power amongst the Ratiya Kanwars. These are the descendants of Moharsai (the current headman's great-grandfather), whose great-great-great grandfather was one of the founding members and 'original settlers' (*khuntkattidars*) of the village. The village headman (Patel) and priest (Baiga), hereditary roles that are typically passed on to the eldest son, traditionally and currently come from this lineage (cf. Pathak 1994: 78). Such features of local dominance run parallel to those outlined in an earlier study by Srinivas (1959) and include numerical strength, economic and political power, and ritual status (cf. Dube 1968).

Like other local caste groups, all Ratiya Kanwar clans were 'invited' by the Gandhel clan to live in the village between two and four generations ago. The latter were in need of '*kutumb log*' (literally, affines or relatives) to perform various ritual services related to marriage and death, and to act as potential marriage partners. Today, these six

Table 2.2: Ratiya Kanwar Clans in Mohanpur

Ratiya Kanwar caste	No. of households	Population
Gandhel	58	297
Libri	8	52
Deheria	3	30
Jiourda	2	11
Khunta	2	10
Pantha	1	12
Porga	1	6
Total	75	418

clans comprise only one-third of the Ratiya Kanwar population, the rest of which is made up of members of the Gandhel clan (see Table 2.2).

The dominance of this clan is largely connected to the tradition and status that comes from being the 'sons of the soil' (Weiner 1978). As we shall see below, this dominance is also augmented by the ritual authority that comes from being the '*dev ka adhikari*' (deities' proprietors), a responsibility that accompanies the role of 'first settler'. More recently, this dominance has been reinforced by the growing influence of members of its younger, more educated generation. Raj, the RSS activist whom we will meet later on, and his two brothers—Santu, a local shopkeeper, and Panchram, the local 'doctor', whom we will meet in Chapter Four—act as the unofficial leaders of the younger generation of Ratiya Kanwars. The occupational interests of these men regularly take them to the city, and the tales of their excursions are looked upon as exciting, if not exotic, by the majority of local people, whose own forays outside of the village do not usually extend beyond the 15 or 20 km range within which most of their affines reside. It is in Chapter Five that we will see more clearly why the growing influence of the younger Gandhels, by virtue of their association with Raj and other RSS activists, has gone uncontested by other members of the Hindu community.

While the Ratiya Kanwar caste dominates local political affairs, there is a great deal of ritual and economic interdependence between the Hindu castes. It is here that caste hierarchies and roles become most apparent. All local castes derive their primary income from agriculture. Beyond this, however, and in traditional occupational fashion, members of the Yadav caste take care of cattle-herding, the Chauhan families are responsible for goat herding, and the Lohar caste sees to the blacksmith needs of the village (see Singh 1993a). This labour is compensated daily by individual families in the form of a portion of uncooked rice. Moreover, members of the Ratiya Kanwar high-caste (*bara jati*) are responsible for officiating at all ritual events, whereas lower castes like the Chauhan are in charge of the polluting jobs of playing the leather drums at all village rituals, and members of the Panika caste are responsible for cleaning up after such rituals. Once again, such caste-specific occupations include other pollution-related jobs, such as assisting in the birth of a child, washing the soiled linen associated with birth or death, or disposing of cattle carcasses, are performed by the Chamars, an untouchable caste whose members are scattered in neighbouring villages. All Hindu castes, moreover, employ and assist members of their community during the most labour-intensive period of the agricultural season, such as weeding and harvesting times. People are ordinarily compensated with seed-rice for this sort of labour, and only on rare occasions, such as when there are an inadequate number of workers from within the Hindu community, will members of the Oraon Christian community be called. Reasons for the latter are to do partly with convenience: Hindus, I am told, do not like to make the trek to the *uppar para* to call Oraon Christians for work when plentiful labour is available in their own *basti*. Increasingly, however, Hindus do not like to see members of the Christian community benefit at the expense of a Hindu labourer. I will discuss this issue more fully in Chapters Six and Seven.

Caste hierarchies within the Hindu community are also visible in terms of rules of commensality, which become particularly obvious during the feasts that accompany marriage and death ceremonies, as well as during times of communal labour (*madad*; see Chapter Seven), when individuals who assist others with *bara kam* (big work, such as weeding, transplanting, or harvesting a crop) are typically paid with a meal. The four high castes (Ratiya Kanwar, Majhuar, Dudh Kanwar, Yadav), for example, are considered to be ritually 'equal' (*barabar*), and on such occasions will indulge in the 'symmetrical exchange' of food and drink (cf. Mayer 1960; Parry 1979: 97). None of these castes takes food or drink prepared by or from the hands of any village 'low castes' (Panika, Chauhan, Lohar) who on such occasions will present their higher caste guests with a portion of uncooked rice, lentils and raw vegetables, which will then be prepared and consumed at the home of the recipient. Whereas lower castes will take food from higher castes, no Hindu castes will take food from the Christian Oraons who, since their immigration to the village, have been considered to be '*chhua chut*' (untouchable) by the entire Hindu community (cf. Chapter Three). With respect to the public expression of relations between both high and low caste groups, and between the Hindu and Christian communities as a whole, such prescriptions are 'founded on an ideology of pollution' (Parry 1979: 101) and are strictly enforced and respected by all local castes today. As we will see in Chapter Three, this ideology has most recently been employed by the village headman for the purpose of restricting Hindus' access to the Christian-owned machine to which all villagers regularly take their par-boiled rice for threshing. Amongst individuals, however, such prescriptions are regularly but quietly broken, particularly when the form of commensality involves the consumption of liquor (see Chapter Seven).

In contrast to the situation within the Hindu community, there is a striking absence of ritual and economic interdependence between the Hindus and the Oraon Christians. The latter as a whole serve no specific ritual or economic role for the former, although individual exceptions include the sole Oraon woman who is occasionally called by Ratiya Kanwar households to assist in the birth of a child, and those members of the Oraon community who sell alcohol and act as moneylenders to the Hindus (see Chapters Six and Seven). This lack of interdependence is related in part to the Oraons Christians' 'outsider' status: they are a migrant community that has 'come from outside' (*bahar se aye*); they speak a language that is not from this area; they are largely economically dependent on the world beyond the village; and, most importantly, their deities are from outside the dominant ritual and territorial realm. I discuss this status, along with the wider relationship between the Hindus and the Christians and some of the ways that it has contributed to the strategies employed by the RSS, in the following chapter.

For now, I turn to the kinds of beliefs and practices that constitute what both the local people and outsiders identify as '*jangli* Hinduism' and examine the dominant role that the Gandhel clan and Ratiya Kanwar castes play in the maintenance of '*jangli*' Hindu beliefs.

Adivasi Hinduism

It has often been noted in the literature on popular Hinduism that great gods (or 'big gods')—Ram, Shiva, Krishna—are thought to be less involved than local deities in the affairs of ordinary villagers. Consequently, their powers are limited and they are often ignored (cf. Fuller 1992: 29–56; see also Babb 1975; Mayer 1960). This phenomenon is very pronounced amongst the Hindu *adivasis* in this area, who rarely invoke the 'big gods' at ordinary rituals because they are 'too far away'. The kind of divine beings with which local Hindus primarily do interact include ancestor spirits, along with the myriad clan, village and jungle deities. The latter are territorial beings that belong first to the land and subsist on whichever human community happens to live in their vicinity.

All local deities, including the ancestors (*purvaj*) who have died a good death, require their own ritual spaces (variously called *sthan, jagha,* or *pujai*). These are located within the household and village boundaries, as well as within the jungle—usually inside a sacred grove (*devras*), tree, stream or rock that the deity itself is said to have chosen. It is thought that the latter are the deities' real (*asli*) homes, where public worship takes place and where offerings on behalf of the village as a whole are made. Deities are said to own and therefore control the area surrounding their sacred space, which can include forest and agricultural land, bodies of water, agricultural yields and forest produce. If humans trespass on these areas without permission, or if they disturb the resident deity outside of designated 'safe' times of mornings and afternoons, then they risk the deity's revenge. This can result in crop failure, serious illness, or even death. These spaces are largely under the care and management of the Ratiya Kanwar caste. As the owners of most of the land on which ritual spaces lie, it is the responsibility of this caste to look after the regular propitiation of these deities and the maintenance of their sacred grounds.

Importantly, local deities are neither housed nor worshipped in the small village temple, which is located nearly half a kilometre away from the village centre. This temple is reserved for the propitiation of 'big gods'. It is in a constant state of disrepair, much to the chagrin of the pandit who visits the village from the city three or four times throughout the year to conduct a 'proper' Hindu *puja* during one of the mainstream festivals (Divali, Rath Yatra, and Dashahara) that are marked locally. While this priest is treated with respect during his visit and offered a meal and a place to sleep in the home of the village headman, very few people attend these 'proper' *pujas* or indeed take any notice of the purpose behind his visits. Instead, villagers can be found at the local version of these celebrations, where dancing, drumming and drinking routinely accompany possession rituals that honour and invoke the blessings of local deities. In addition to being 'invited' to and worshipped at these mainstream festivals, local deities also have their own festivals at which they are specially honoured. These festivals are seasonal and normally run parallel to the agricultural calendar.

As elsewhere in Chhattisgarh where 'religion is a done thing' (Babb 1975: 31–2), people in this area worship their deities by 'doing *puja*'. *Pujas* carried out on behalf of the whole village are normally performed by the village priest, the Baiga; *pujas* devoted to specific clan and ancestor deities are carried out by the household patriarch. All *pujas* and the offerings made therein carry with them the same purpose: keeping the deities happy and ensuring the well-being and protection (*suraksha*) of the community, crops, family or individual (cf. Babb 1975 and Fuller 1992 for extended discussions on popular Hindu worship). These and other deities have the power to cause illness, the death of humans or cattle, or crop failure, if not regularly propitiated through *puja*. Local offerings made during *puja* invariably correspond to everyday practices. For example, the smoky substance created when *dhup* (incense) is sprinkled onto hot coals is described as being 'like the *bidi*', the local cigarette that is smoked by village men and passed around to guests at every social gathering as a sort of welcome (*swagat*): as humans like to smoke *bidi*, so deities like to inhale *dhup*. Likewise, a few drops of local liquor made from the *mahua* flower are first offered to a number of deities because, I was told, 'like us, they also enjoy the drink', and on more than one occasion a particular illness has been attributed to the neglect of this seemingly insignificant practice. Depending on the context, *pakka* or 'mainstream Hindu' offerings such as rice, coconut and milk are also included. Unsurprisingly, more elaborate rituals, such as those that revolve around marriage, death or an annual festival, require more expensive offerings. These invariably include *balidan*, a blood offering of a chicken or goat or, on rare occasions, a buffalo or even a pig. Such offerings are considered by local people, the RSS and the Church alike to be particularly representative of '*jangli rivaj*' (backward customs).

It is important for the overall protection of the household that the Hindu household patriarch worships the numerous village and ancestor deities within his own home and 'by his own hand'. Such worship takes place in specially constructed spaces that are cordoned off from the rest of the house. Once ritually installed, strict rules come into effect to protect the sanctity of these spaces. These mainly revolve around the ban of undesirables from the premises: low caste individuals, menstruating women, drunk men. In addition to the performance of regular household worship, all public *pujas* must be replicated in each home by the household patriarch. If such rules are observed, then it is believed that the household should receive regular protection and blessings.

While the primary forum through which humans worship and interact with deities is *puja*, deities also communicate with local people through dreams, where they make demands or give orders or warnings. The most direct means of communication, however, is possession (*jhupna*) (cf. Eschmann: 1978: 81). Whether in the form of illness, a sudden, trance-like state of dissociation, or a formally staged performance brought on through the mediation of the village Baiga and the sound of drums, possession by deities of their human subjects is one of the most potent and visible signs of divine presence. As we shall see in Chapters Four and Five, possession is another cultural practice that is perceived by the local people to be particularly '*jangli*': while city people could conceivably become possessed by a '*jangli*' *devata* (forest deity) when they visit the village, it is believed that such people never become possessed in the city by 'big gods'.

Local Deities and Gandhel Patronage

All local deities are believed to have once been human themselves. This is not uncommon. As Fuller (1992: 50) notes, 'the absence of any absolute distinction between divine and human beings' is widespread in rural practices, particularly those that revolve around local or 'little' deities (see also Russell and Hiralal 1923 [1916]: 400). In this area, most deities are believed to be the original Gandhel settlers, including Thakur Dev, a deity that is common to all villages in this part of India and that serves as one of the village guards (*chaukidar*). Like other local deities, Thakur Dev is ritually looked after by members of the Gandhel clan: his *devras* is located in the vicinity of the Patel's fields, and his village shrine (*chowra*) is located in the Baiga's courtyard. A second '*gaon devata*' (village deity) is Diharan Devi, the most powerful local female goddess who has equal strength and is regarded with as much fear and respect as Thakur Dev (cf. Fuller 1992: 40–8). A tutelary deity of the Gandhel clan, her *devras* lies at the edge of the village very near to the Patel's family compound. She takes centre stage during the marriage season, when grooms from all village Hindu castes must offer her a female goat (*bakri*). This is to request her protection and ensure fertility of the bride, as well as to fend off any jealousy that Diharan Devi deity might feel towards the newcomer. Without such propitiation, her punishment is fierce: the bride could die.

Perhaps the most important village deity is Mahadev, the 'god's god, the biggest god' (*devata ka devata, sabse bara devata*). An incarnation of Shankar (Shiva), Mahadev is said to have been 'brought from the city long ago', for he is not an original *dehati* ('*jangli*') *devata*.[4] He resides in the village *chowra*, the most important shrine within the village boundaries, located just outside the ruling Gandhel family compound where it was built by the first settlers. The regular and public propitiation of this deity is the responsibility of the village Baiga, who ensures that two coconuts hang all the year round at the *chowra* in a constant propitiatory state. On one occasion, I accompanied the Baiga to observe the *puja* that was performed during the ritual exchange of old coconuts with new, a process that occurs two or three times annually. As he firmly attached the fresh coconuts to the top of the *chowra* and completed the *puja*, the Baiga smiled and said, 'we *jangli* people use coconuts for our deities. We cannot afford flags'. While flags are commonly used by *adivasis* at festivals and *yatras*, he was specifically referring to the saffron flag that RSS *pracharaks* often carried with them on their visits to the village.[5]

The most important event at which Mahadev is honoured is Gaura, the local festival that celebrates the 'marriage' between Mahadev

[4]The fact that the most important and powerful village deity, Mahadev, is the local incarnation of Shankar (Shiva), represents the way in which *adivasis* in this village and in the surrounding area have been subjected to more mainstream Hindu ideas and beliefs. In spite of certain parallels with mainstream Hindu practices, however, I hesitate to call this particular example a form of sanskritization (Srinivas 1952: 213). For instance, there is no acknowledgement by local *adivasis* themselves that they have been 'actively' seeking to raise their status by 'sanskritizing' or adopting mainstream Hindu deities or other beliefs and practices. Equally, the adoption of Mahadev as a local deity has not been accompanied by other customs and practices identified with sanskritization, namely vegetarianism and teetotalism. The presence of Mahadev could be called 'sanskritization' only insofar as it represents an extension or spread of what Srinivas calls 'Sanskritic deities' to 'outlying groups' (p. 215).

[5]As noted earlier, the saffron flag (and, more generally, the saffron colour) is traditionally associated with mainstream Hindu religious rituals and processions. Today, it has been appropriated as an important symbol of the Hindu nationalist movement. In this village, this flag serves as a visible presence of the RSS and a marker of Hindu superiority (cf. Hansen 1999: 108). I return to this issue later in this chapter.

(Shiva) and Gaura Rani (Parvati).[6] Figures that symbolize these gods are carefully constructed out of sacred clay. In the local celebrations, Mahadev is always represented by the Gandhel lineage, while Parvati is alternately represented by one of the Gandhel clan's affines or *kutumb* (Deheria, Libri, Porga, etc.). The Gaura festival, along with other festivals in which various deities are honoured, includes specific dances that are performed by men and women alike, to the beat of traditional drums and *jhanjh* (brass cymbals), and often under the influence of copious amounts of liquor. The local deities in whose honour such festivities are held are said to be pleased when they see that people are enjoying themselves.

This festival is also said to be a major *seva karna* (service) on behalf of all local deities, who are invited to the celebrations and who make their presence known during the nightlong possession ritual. Mayer (1981), referring to Western India, notes that '*seva*' is distinguished from '*puja*' by virtue of the former being 'without thought of benefit or return', and the latter being 'a transaction', made with the expectation of something in return (1981:167; see also Fuller 1992: 70). However, in the case of the local Gaura celebration, there is very much an expectation of return. This can be seen in the requests for protection and prosperity made by the local people in exchange for public propitiation throughout the year.

I highlight this specific ritual not only to illustrate how mainstream Hindu gods are incarnated as village deities, but also to demonstrate the ritual dominance of the Gandhel clan and Ratiya Kanwar caste. Because Mahadev is always represented by the Gandhel clan and Parvati by other Ratiya Kanwar clans (or Gandhel affines), the protection of the village is in many ways completely in the hands of the Ratiya Kanwar caste. More critically, Gaura celebrations serve to re-establish the connection and relationship between the most powerful individual in the village, the Patel, and the most powerful and feared jungle deity, Kaleshar. The dominance of the Gandhel clan in general, and the authority of the Patel in particular, are contingent upon remaining in the favour of this deity. I discuss this issue at length in Chapter Five.

Because of their ritual dominance, the Gandhel elders, and

[6]Locally, this festival is always celebrated in early January, although the *Sociological Survey of Bhilai* (1968: 74) mentions that 'Goura-Gouri' is celebrated in September. See also Babb (1975: 157–60) for an example of how Gaura is celebrated by the Gonds in another part of Chhattisgarh.

particularly those from the Patel's family, refer to themselves as the 'deities' proprietors' (*dev ka adhikari*). This notion is not unlike that noted in Sundar's (1997: 25–30; 2002) anthropological history of Bastar, where members of the founding (and most dominant) lineage also 'owned' and looked after the local gods (cf. Sontheimer 1989). Locally, the status of *adhikari* goes back to 'the beginning' when the first Gandhel settlers were directed through possession to a particular spot in the jungle and ordered by Kaleshar to reserve it as his *devras*. Other jungle deities were 'discovered' when members of the Gandhel family became ill after unknowingly trespassing on a particular part of the forest or agricultural land. The 'discoverer' of the deity or the person on whose lands the sacred space lies is believed to have been singled out: 'chosen', as it were, to be the *adhikari*, the keeper of that particular deity and its sacred space.

Carrying out the ritual and physical obligations that accompany the title of *adhikari* is a mixed blessing. At one level, it is said to be a great service, in return for which increased protection from misfortune is granted. Likewise, the social prestige that the Gandhel family gains from the honour of being 'chosen' by local deities contributes to their position of power in the village. The involvement of at least one Gandhel elder in all but the most private family or household ritual is mandatory because of their *adhikari* status, a rule that gives the Gandhel clan a great deal of control in the timing and organization of most ritual events in the village.

While their ritual and social status is high, however, the potential danger that accompanies this status is also great. If the *adhikari* fails to perform a mandatory village ritual, the costs for which he alone must bear, then his family is held responsible and will be inflicted with the wrath of the resident deity. The financial and temporal costs of physically maintaining the ritual site can also be exorbitant. During my fieldwork, the sacred village well was made '*pakka*' (complete) and lined with concrete at the behest of the well's resident deity. The entire expense for this, which included the cost of the concrete along with several goats that were sacrificed at the completion of the task, amounted to thousands of rupees and was met exclusively by the owner of the land on which the well was located.

In short, disregard for the duties that accompany the prestigious position of *adhikari* runs the risk of a vengeful deity. As we shall see in Chapters Four and Five, it is precisely these kinds of beliefs and practices that not only represent the '*jangli*' traditions that the RSS wishes to 'civilize', but also serve as the chief obstacles to their attempts to do so. Other kinds of customs that are considered to be particularly 'backward' include the traditional authority that is vested in the local headman. It is to this subject that I now turn.

Traditional Authority and Local Politics

The kind of dominance wielded by the Gandhel clan and Ratiya Kanwar caste is unusual compared to other villages in this area, where the power of a village headman is typically dispersed and shared between the 'big men' of several lineages or castes who sit on the village council (*panchayat*) (see Dube 1955: 46–7; Sharma 1978: 108–30). Traditionally, the main function and responsibilities of this council were to mediate and rule on local disputes and other matters of local concern. Anyone with a particularly important issue that required public addressal was allowed to call a meeting.

In recent decades, the village council was replaced with a state-administered system of self-government, called the *gram sabha*. This new body, which locally comprises Mohanpur and two neighbouring villages, including Botli and Kudwari, is governed by a single elected representative, the *sarpanch*. Traditionally, the local ruling elite was in the most favourable position to be elected to such a post, and the office of *sarpanch* often became another mechanism by which the local Patel could extend his traditional power and be represented within the modern state system (see Pathak 1994: 82). At the time of fieldwork, however, the *sarpanch* who represented Mohanpur was a man who hailed from Botli.

In the eyes of the state, this elected official has greater power than any individual village headman (cf. Mayer 1960, Srinivas (1969 [1955]). As the first point of contact for state officials, such power and responsibility traditionally include the signing of documents verifying people's eligibility for loans, distributing monies to local labourers involved in state-sponsored public works projects, and verifying the identity of individuals who should be included on the list of beneficiaries for ration cards and other poverty alleviation programmes (cf. Pathak 1994: 81–3). In Mohanpur, however, the powers of this official are not recognized by the village headman who, in spite of being invited, not only boycotts all *gram sabha* meetings, but also retains his local position of authority with respect to state officials. It is in Chapter Five that reasons for this will become clear.

The Patel also continues in his position to lead the village *panchayat* that, instead of a group of elders from different castes or lineages, is dominated by men from the Ratiya Kanwar caste.[7] This means that the direct permission, involvement and support of both the Patel and the senior members of this caste are necessary before any political or economic decisions that affect the village as a whole, can take place. Whether the issue revolves around the ritual and practical maintenance of rules of untouchability or the mediation of a land dispute or customary grazing rights, the decisions of the Ratiya Kanwar elders serve to dominate the wider Hindu community. As we have seen, reasons for this are related to the relationship that the Gandhel 'original settlers', who are the most powerful Ratiya Kanwar clan, have with divine beings. In view of this situation, it is unsurprising that the authority of the Gandhel clan and, more broadly, the Ratiya Kanwar caste, remains uncontested by other members of the Hindu community. Significantly, and as we shall see in later chapters, it is this dominance that defines the wider relationship between the Hindu and Christian communities.

While the Ratiya Kanwars dominate local affairs, members of subordinate castes—including the Oraon Christians—continue to feel indebted toward them. It is this clan, after all, that originally gave permission to later immigrants to settle in the area, and that designated land on which they could build their houses and make their fields. It is for this reason that the Oraons and others often talk about the generosity that the 'sons of the soil' have shown their ancestors before them. This indebtedness is regularly expressed in terms of the political support that the Oraons and other local castes feel they must offer the current headman with respect to local *panchayat* issues.

In spite of the general sense of duty that all local groups demonstrate toward the Ratiya Kanwars, relations between this caste and other groups are not without conflict. Dissatisfaction during the period in which my fieldwork took place was specifically directed at the Patel, who rules over village affairs in an unusually autocratic manner (see Chapter Five). As we shall see throughout the course of this book,

---

[7]Women are not allowed to sit on this council, although they are permitted to attend the meetings.

this dissatisfaction has evolved into wider tensions between different castes in the village and acquired broader political implications.

For now, it is necessary only to mention that the Patel, along with other members of the Ratiya Kanwar caste in general, has traditionally been a supporter of the Congress Party, the BJP's main political opponent at the national level, and the political party that ruled the state of Madhya Pradesh at the time of my fieldwork. During this time, Mohanpur was part of the Rampur constituency located in Korba District, Madhya Pradesh. The local member of the legislative assembly (MLA) who represented Rampur was also a member of the Congress Party. In 1998, halfway through my fieldwork, the Madhya Pradesh State Assembly elections took place. While the Congress party returned to state power with a simple majority, the incumbent Congress Party candidate for Rampur lost to the BJP candidate, Nankiram Kanwar, by over 30,000 votes. His victory was helped by the votes that were unexpectedly cast in his favour by people from Mohanpur, a village that, until the 1998 election, had been a traditional Congress stronghold.[8]

I later discovered that, apart from the Patel's own family, the only other group that voted as a bloc for the Congress Party candidate during the 1998 election was the Oraon Christians. The majority of all other castes, including most of the Gandhels and the other Ratiya Kanwar clans had, for the first time, shifted their votes to the BJP, making the village evenly split between the BJP and Congress. The reason for this shift was, I was told, related to the wider dissatisfaction that people in this part of the state, then Madhya Pradesh, had with incumbent Congress Party representatives and their alleged neglect of *adivasi* concerns. This interpretation was consistent with a trend in the neighbouring constituencies of Sakti and Champa, both of which saw Congress party incumbents ousted by BJP candidates. As we shall see in Chapter Five, however, it is clearly possible that local discontent with the Patel contributed to this shift in support away from what is known locally as 'the Patel's party'.

In tandem with this shift has been an increasing involvement in local affairs by RSS activists who, while not directly active in electoral politics, have been tremendously influential in the successful promotion of the *Hindutva* ideology. In order to understand the wider impact

---

[8]For more extensive commentary on India's electoral politics, see Jaffrelot (1996), Kumar (2003), and Roy (2000).

that the RSS has had locally, it is useful to outline the history of the organization and examine how its relationship with local villagers has evolved.

The RSS: Some Historical Notes

The RSS, or 'national volunteer force', is largely considered to be the leading organization of the Hindu nationalist movement, responsible for implementing *Hindutva* ideology at the national level.[9] It was started in 1925 by K.B. Hedgewar, a medical doctor and nationalist, in response to the rise in Hindu-Muslim riots that spread across India in the early 1920s. Amongst Hedgewar's early mentors are counted B.S. Moonje, a leader of the Hindu Mahasabha (Hindu Association), the 'proto-Hindu' nationalist organization that first advanced the idea of the 'Hindu nation' against the threatening Muslim 'other' in the early twentieth century (cf. Andersen and Damle 1987: 26–70; Jaffrelot 1993: 18–21). Hedgewar was also inspired by the writings of V.D. Savarkar, an early Hindu nationalist ideologue who first proposed the notion of '*Hindutva*', articulated in his 1923 work, *Hindutva: Who is a Hindu?* This work lay out the ideological framework—that to be an Indian citizen is to be a Hindu—around which the Hindu nationalist movement revolves today (see cf. Bhatt 2001: 77–111; Jaffrelot 1993: 25–33). This militant discourse was further strengthened under the leadership of M.S. Golwalkar, a prominent ideologue who succeeded Hedgewar in 1940 as leader of the RSS. It is Golwalkar's book, *We or our Nationhood Defined*, which is regarded as the RSS 'bible' today (Noorani 2000: 18; cf. Kanungo 2002: 35–67).

While not expressly a 'reproduction of European fascism' (Jaffrelot 1993: 51), this organization and its founding fathers were strongly influenced by late nineteenth and early twentieth-century Italian and German ideas of the nation and ethnic nationalism (Hansen 1999: 41, 80–4; see also see Benei 2000: 209–10; Jaffrelot 1996). Golwalkar's book in particular was influenced by German ethnic nationalism, specifically in regard to the most important criteria that underpinned the concept of a Hindu nation: geographical unity, a shared race,

---

[9]The history and contemporary activities of the RSS have been the subject of a large body of research and scholarly writing (see Andersen and Damle 1987, Basu et al. 1993; Hansen 1999; Jaffrelot 1996; Noorani 2000).

religion, culture and language (Jaffrelot 1996: 54–5).[10] As mentioned earlier, the organization has also been strongly influenced by the historical relationship that it has with Christianity.[11] Indeed, as this book will argue, the strategies in which the RSS has engaged both nationally and locally are constituted by this relationship.

Since its inception, the primary mission of the RSS has been to unite and organize Hindus on nationalistic lines against colonial British rule and against the proselytizing influence of Muslims and Christians. The latter, viewed as 'foreign races' and enemies of India, were called upon to adopt the Hindu culture and language and merge with the 'Hindu race'. Following the alleged involvement of the RSS in the death of Mohandas K. Gandhi in 1948, a ban was placed on the organization. This was later lifted in 1949, after which the RSS began to expand its interests in education and social welfare.

From the mid-1960s onward, this organization has been accorded an increasing degree of public respectability. It has played a seminal role in the establishment of other principal members of the Sangh Parivar such as the BJP, formed in 1980 (cf. Louis 2000: 30–80), and the VHP (Vishva Hindu Parishad), founded in 1964. The aims of the latter include strengthening links among Hindus living outside of India, and checking Christian proselytization within India and welcoming back those among the tribal populace who had 'gone out of the Hindu fold' (Bhatt 2001: 179–207; Hansen 1999: 101–7; cf. Katju 2003). This latter activity is carried out by the Vanvasi Kalyan Ashram (VKA, or 'Tribal Development Centre'), an affiliate of the VHP that was set up in the 1940s in Chhattisgarh (cf. Sundar 2006; 2004). The original remit of the VKA was to establish schools, *ashrams* and boarding facilities for tribal children. Reflecting the wider mimetic relationship that the Hindu right has with Christianity, these were not only patterned after existing Christian facilities but also served as a way of combating the dominant Christian presence and mission education in *adivasi* areas.

[10]As Jaffrelot (1993a: 77) and others (Alter 1994: 567–8; Gold 1991: 577; Nandy 1983) point out, there is a certain irony in the fact that the identity of *Hindutva* was crystallized through the application of political and value concepts from the West.

[11]Interestingly, most of those individuals who are considered to be the 'founding fathers' of *Hindutva*, along with many of the *pracharaks* (activists) who serve on behalf of the contemporary Hindu nationalist movement (including the local liaison between the RSS and Mohanpur village), were educated in Catholic institutions (see Andersen and Damle 1987; Hansen 1999).

In line with broader *Hindutva* goals, the VKA's more expansive objective was to 'produce nationalistic leadership' among tribal people and bring them more into the mainstream of national life' (see Andersen and Damle 1987: 133–7; Hansen 1999: 103). It has more recently branched into medical care and vocational training, and currently runs a large number of hospitals and vocational training centres across Chhattisgarh and other parts of India (see Hansen 1999: 103–7; Jaffrelot 1993: 322–3). It has been particularly active in targeting Christian tribal communities in western India (Maharashtra and Gujarat) (cf. Baviskar 2005: 5108).

Another affiliate of the RSS is the Vidya Bharati an umbrella body that manages primary schools (Saraswati Shishu Mandir) across India. Part of the RSS interest in education, which officially began in 1952 with the launch of its first primary school, stems from the view that the 'denationalizing heritage left behind by the British' had corrupted the educational mainstream (cf. Andersen and Damle 1987; Sarkar 1996: 240). The RSS aimed to counter this problem by inculcating 'true national education that teaches the student to be proud of his/her Hindu heritage' (ibid: 243). Today, the single school that marked the RSS's initial incursion into education has grown into a network of over 17,000 schools across India, ranging from single-teacher, one-room structures in remote villages to large, multi-class complexes catering to thousands of pupils in urban areas. These schools cater predominantly to lower-middle class students (cf. Basu et al. 1993: 45–50; www.vidyabharati.org).

To augment its support base, finally, the RSS has regularly targeted boys and young men from around the age of twelve to their early twenties. These youths are recruited because they are of an 'impressionable' age and because they demonstrate a strong 'capacity for loyalty and obedience' (Basu et al. 1993: 17; 35–7). They are invited to attend regular meetings at a local RSS branch or unit (*shakha)* wherein various training programmes geared toward bodily comportment, physical discipline and exercise regularly take place. This physical training is combined with the inculcation of the *Hindutva* ideology and is nowadays carried out in all of the 25,000 *shakhas* that the RSS claims, exist across India. The aim is to build up a powerful body of disciplined and organized volunteers who are capable and prepared to unite the Hindu community and defend the Hindu nation against 'threatening others' (cf. Hansen 1999: 93; Andersen and Damle 1987).

The RSS in Mohanpur

The RSS is an extremely hierarchical organization (cf. Andersen and Damle 1987: 84–9). From the basic branch or unit of organization—the *shakha*—wherein rituals and physical training are carried out, to the state and national assemblies, there are numerous committees and departments that comprise the RSS's 'pyramid of authority' (ibid: 86). In this area, the organization's regional 'headquarters' are based in Raipur, the capital of what is now the state of Chhattisgarh. Senior leaders in Raipur liase with local *pracharaks* in provincial towns like Korba, although the latter are occasionally called to attend meetings and 'training camps' in Raipur (cf. Kanungo 2006 for detail on the crucial role played by *pracharaks* in the broader Hindu nationalist movement). It is at such meetings that leaders give orders and pass on information about issues related to the broader goals and practical implementation of *Hindutva*. However, it is important to bear in mind that, in this area at least, there is no systematic campaign or directive that is regularly communicated 'from above' to local *pracharaks* about the specific strategies by which Hindu nationalism should be communicated amongst the area's *adivasi* people, beyond the general strategy of bringing tribal people into the Hindu fold and counteracting Christian influence (Andersen and Damle 1987; Basu et al. 1993). Decisions about specific strategies to employ are left to the discretion of the local *pracharaks*.

The headquarters of the RSS in Korba are located in the local branch of the VKA, which doubles as a boarding school for young tribal boys. Local people—Christians and Hindus alike—also know that they can avail of the VKA's hospitality (including a hot meal and a place to sleep) if they find themselves stranded in the city overnight. While many VKA branches across India have been the site of political tensions between Hindu nationalists, left-wing activists and Christians (cf. Hansen 1999: 106; Sundar 2006), the VKA in Korba has seen no such tension to date.

It is here that local RSS activists live and coordinate the activities that they carry out within the district. Amongst these is Raj, a young man in his late-twenties who hails from Mohanpur village itself and who is a member of one of the more prominent local Ratiya Kanwar families. Like many RSS *pracharaks*, Raj had benefited from a Catholic school education and had harboured dreams of going to the university and 'becoming a big man' (*bara admi*). He left home after finishing Class XII (some twelve years earlier) in search of a better life in the city. Having no possessions or money at the time, he frequented the VKA branch, which doubled as an RSS *ashram*, in Korba. From there he received meals and a place to sleep in exchange for the odd bit of work. Like other ambitious young men who had worked hard to escape their rural, *adivasi* roots, Raj's dreams of making something of himself in the city were inevitably hindered by fact that he lacked the requisite connections and patronage that would help him to pay the exorbitant 'fees' (bribes) and ensure him a place in the local college, or at least to acquire a respectable job (*naukari*).

Feeling increasingly disappointed about his unfulfilled expectations, he began to devote his full attention to the *ashram*. He attended daily *shakhas* and participated in 'training meetings' (*baudhik*), where more senior cadres would communicate the core doctrine of *Hindutva*. This message can be summed up as follows:

... Hindus alone constitute the Indian nation, since they are the original inhabitants and sole creators of its society and culture. Hinduism is uniquely tolerant, and hence superior to any other faith, but its tolerance has often been mistaken for weakness. The Hindu nation has been repeatedly conquered by aliens, particularly Muslims and then the Christian British, and must acquire strength through RSS *sangathan* to counter all present and future threats. The subsequent entry and takeover by foreigners created the illusion that India was a land of many different and equal cultures. In truth, however, all cultural traditions survived by Hinduizing themselves— otherwise they remained alien, distanced, oppressive. (Basu et al. 1993: 37)

According to Basu et al. (ibid: 36–8), the appeal of this message is its basic simplicity: it is devoid of complexities and debates, and requires no mastering of difficult texts. Potential disciples like Raj learn that it is only through this message—that Christians and Muslims are a threat to the Hindu nation and therefore must be contained— that the discourse of Hindu harmony could be achieved.

Convinced by this rhetoric, Raj became increasingly committed to the RSS. He abandoned his plans to go to the university and formally joined the organization as a full-time *pracharak* in the mid-1990s. His knowledge and familiarity with the villages that are scattered throughout the surrounding jungle made him a valuable member of the organization, and he quickly became the primary liaison between the local branch of the RSS and the area's *adivasi* people. Since joining, he has dedicated himself to communicating the *Hindutva* ideology to as many people as possible, making regular visits with other activists to Mohanpur and other villages in the area in order to conduct 'training meetings' and engage in other activities, outlined below, that are geared toward this objective. Like other *pracharaks*, he receives no remuneration for this work, although his living and travel expenses are all provided by the RSS. His position is, he proudly tells me, 'just like *naukari*'.

In short, Raj is a local 'son of the soil' who, after failing in his efforts to go to the university and become a 'big man', committed himself to the RSS and became steeped in the *Hindutva* ideology. As we shall see throughout the course of this book, Raj is the principal 'propagandist' in the transmission of Hindu nationalist ideology and communal sentiment not only in Mohanpur, but in neighbouring villages as well. He is what Brass (1997: 16) calls a 'conversion specialist', or a person who occupies a formal role (like *pracharak*) in the RSS, who is devoted to the advancement of one particular community (Hindus), and who is instrumental in propagating the idea that a particular community (like Christians) is the primary threat to this advancement (see Chapter One).

While Raj does have a central role in the emergence of Hindu nationalism locally, it is important to point out that it is not the intention of this book to examine the history of his involvement in the RSS; nor is it the objective to consider more fully the nature of his personal commitment to the spread of *Hindutva*. An examination of this sort has been carried out elsewhere;[12] what is more, this would detract from the primary purpose of this book, which is to take the analysis to the next stage: namely, the manner by which Hindu nationalism is successfully transmitted by committed activists like Raj to *adivasi* villages like Mohanpur.

In Mohanpur itself, Raj is something of an icon. His unusually high level of education compared with the local norm was the result of relative family wealth and birth order: as the third of five brothers, Raj's father could afford to spare him from the usual participation in agricultural labour and to invest in his education at the more superior Catholic-run primary and secondary schools in the area (see Chapter

---

[12]For a detailed account of the factors that motivate a young man to become an RSS *pracharak*, the process of recruitment, and the commitment and loyalty that they have, see Kanungo (2006). See also Andersen and Damle (1987); Basu et al. (1993).

Three for further discussion on why the latter are considered to be more superior).[13] Raj's access to the outside world through his affiliation with the RSS has also conferred upon him a type of social status which, when combined with his position as a member of the most dominant local caste, makes him very respected and influential amongst younger members of the Hindu community. Raj draws attention to this status by making a point of calling on the Patel, in the same manner as other important outsiders, whenever he visits the village.

Raj's influence extends particularly strongly over a group of around ten young men from local Hindu castes, including those involved in the jeep incident mentioned at the beginning of this book. Early on in his visits to the village, Raj issued an invitation to all young men in the village—Hindus and Christians alike—to participate in his 'training meetings' and learn more about the *Hindutva* ideology. The first meeting, which was conducted in the courtyard of Raj's parents' home, attracted around 24 young men. Both married and unmarried, most of these men were educated to Class V and ranged in age from late-teens to their thirties. Having limited prospects beyond the village and a future replete with hard agricultural labour, they were curious about what kind of opportunities the RSS could offer. As elsewhere in India, it is this category of person—young, male, limited education—that is most commonly targeted by RSS activists.

After this, however, numbers diminished to a core group of around ten. These consisted of two Majhuars, one Lohar and seven high caste Ratiya Kanwars (including Raj's two younger brothers). The most common excuse given by those who did not return to follow-up meetings was that they had no time, or were burdened by work. While I do not intend to explore the personal agendas and internal motivation of those young men who did carry on attending these meetings, their reasons invariably included the pursuit of opportunities in the city. In the early days of Raj's visits, most of these ten young men expressed

[13]Class VIII is considered to be an extremely high level of education locally. In spite of assertive government initiatives that target rural *adivasi* children, such as free school meals, subsidized books and fees, education in this area is still perceived to be quite 'useless'. This is why children are typically removed from school after Class V, when they are at an age when their labour can be better utilized in the fields. While parents want their children to be able to read, they do not see any need for continuing their education beyond this point. In spite of a few 'success' stories such as that of Raj, the majority of those who have gone beyond Class V have received no tangible benefit from their efforts.

the hope that affiliation with Raj and his powerful organization might offer them some useful returns in the future. One of these young men named Gulap, was even taken to the VKA ashram in Korba for several months to assist with maintenance of the building. He told me how excited he had been at first. 'I thought that joining Raj and going to work at the ashram would lead to some proper *naukari*. This is why I spent so much time there'. He returned from the ashram after three months, disillusioned with the fact that he had been made to do most of the cooking and cleaning at the ashram, and with the fact that neither Raj nor the other RSS *pracharaks* followed through with their promises of getting him 'proper' (paid) work.

In addition to Gulap, these other young men were occasionally taken to the ashram in the city in order to participate in events organized by the local *shakha*. When Raj's visits to the village increased, all were issued with *khaki* shorts and white shirts, the standard uniform worn by young RSS *pracharaks* across India. Considered to be much fancier than the *lungis* (wrap-around cloth) ordinarily donned by village men, this uniform is worn with pride by these young men. According to Baviskar (2005: 5105), this is symbolic of the advances that militant Hindu nationalism has made in this and other *adivasi* areas.

These young men have proved to be very useful to Raj and the two or three other RSS *pracharaks* who regularly accompany him to promote various 'cultural' activities in the village, such as the introduction to local people of 'proper' Hindu ways of worship during a mainstream Hindu holiday. Most often, however, these young men are summoned to participate in an evening 'training meeting' to learn more about the *Hindutva* ideology, or to simply 'hang out' in the company of Raj and his RSS friends when they visit the village for the day. The extent to which they are willing to support Raj's more aggressive efforts in inculcating communal ideas locally will become evident later on in the book.

In addition to the meetings, Raj and the *pracharaks* who regularly accompanied him solicited the involvement of these young men in setting up a local nursery school, modelled after the primary schools run by Vidya Bharti. While the village did have a functioning *anganwadi* (nursery) programme,[14] around halfway through my

---

[14]The *anganwadi* (literally courtyard play) is a government-sponsored nursery programme located in most villages and towns across India. Government-appointed nursery workers are usually women who live in the locality and are trained in various aspects of health, nutrition and child development. They are responsible for soliciting

fieldwork, Raj decided that the village needed a 'proper' nursery school. Its aim was to give three- to five-year old children a 'head start' on reading and literacy, and to communicate a relevant 'cultural ethos' through the teaching of nationalist songs and the narration of stories valorising *Hindutva* principles. It was arranged that one of the ten young men mentioned above would undertake the teaching for a small stipend of Rs 300 per month.

Word spread throughout the village that a 'new school' for very young children would be opening soon. The mild interest that was initially expressed quickly waned, however, as people realized that the children who attended this school would not receive a free meal, unlike those who attended the existing *anganwadi* programme. In the end, only five children (three of whom belonged to Raj's brothers) signed up for the school, which met every morning in a room within Raj's family's household. Raj was confident that the numbers would increase as people realized the value of this school, particularly in view of the poor alternatives: the Church boarding school (to which most Oraon Christians sent their children), and the state-sponsored *anganwadi* programme which, according to Raj, 'did nothing but offer children a bit of food'.

The RSS and *'sahari/jangli'* Distinctions

As discussed earlier, one of the most important obstacles to the RSS efforts of inculcating *Hindutva* ideology amongst *adivasi* communities and expanding its electoral support in this area and elsewhere in India is the Church. Reasons for this will be further explored in the following chapter. A different kind of hurdle that the RSS faces includes the 'backward', *'jangli'* practices and beliefs that are popularly associated with *adivasi* cultures and that are presumed to be so different from caste Hindu culture. Locally, such practices revolve largely around that relationship that people have with their deities, and to which the majority of people remain strongly devoted.

It is specifically through proselytization measures like the introduction of mainstream Hindu festivals and 'proper' ways of

---

the participation and supervising the play and pre-school education of all local children aged 2–5. Locally, the *anganwadi* programme meets thrice-weekly for two hours, at the end of which participating children are provided with a free meal of wheat porridge.

worship that the RSS *pracharaks* are actively attempting to dissuade local *adivasis* from engagement in such practices. To illustrate, several months into my fieldwork, Raj and the other *pracharaks* pulled up on their motorcycles at a shop in the centre of the village. The appearance of outsiders on motorcycles (or any vehicle) was so infrequent, that such an occasion generally merited a small crowd of curious villagers. On this particular morning, however, most of the men and women had long since departed for work in their fields. This left only children to gather around as Santu, the shopkeeper, came out to greet the men, whose visits to the village were becoming gradually more frequent. '*sahari-wallah*' (city folk), whispered one child, as the four climbed off their bikes and took off their sunglasses.

Draped around Raj's neck and matching his saffron shirt was a saffron scarf that had the words *Shri Ram* inscribed across it.[15] Two of the other *pracharaks* sported similar scarves that they wore along with white *kurta-pyjama* (long shirts and trousers). The last was in jacket and 'full-pant', formal wear in contrast to the *lungi*-clad, barefoot Santu and the other villagers. Additionally, all four men wore shoes, which they made a great show of dusting off when they climbed off their bikes and all four sported a '*choti*', a small clump of hair on the back of the head that extends three to four inches longer than the rest of the hair. According to villagers, this is the style favoured by *sahari* or '*pakka* Hindus' (city Hindus, or pure, 'real' Hindus), the wandering *sadhu* (holy man) or the *pandit* (Brahman priest) who visits the village thrice yearly.

After greetings of 'Jai Shri Ram' (long live Lord Ram)[16] were exchanged, the customary tea and bath were offered to the dusty foursome, who had just completed a two-hour journey from the city through thick jungle and snaking, unpaved roads. Declaring that they had no time for such pleasantries, the men demanded cool water instead. Mohanpur was their first destination in a planned four-village visit, and they had to begin immediately if they wanted

[15]RSS discourse on 'Hindu culture' emphasizes the foundational significance of Ram, one of the most important gods in the Hindu pantheon, to the Hindu nation. The significance of Ram as a symbol or metaphor for the 'Hinduness' of Indian culture took on new prominence in the late 1980s, with the broadcasting of the Hindu epic, the Ramayana on national television, and again in the early 1990s with the Ramjanmabhoomi agitation (see Hansen 1999: 174–5; Nandy 1995).

[16]This greeting is especially favoured by 'city' or 'proper' Hindus, and its usage in the village, in contrast to the local preference of '*Johar*', '*Jai Ram*', or simply '*namaste*', suggests an immediate connection to the RSS.

to complete their project that day. After a quick drink of water, Raj instructed Santu to gather all the village women together. He then went off to inform the village headman of his plans and issue the obligatory invitation.

The group reassembled fifteen minutes later with mixed success. Santu was able to gather only five women together: one was his aged mother and one was his wife; two had several small children in tow, as they suckled even smaller ones; and one was Dhankumer, the most outspoken woman in the Hindu community. Their complaints about being pulled away from important work were offset by the excited chatter of five teenaged girls who had also been summoned by the *sahari wallas* and who thought it quite fine that they were given a temporary reprieve from their daily routine. Raj returned shortly after. Having had no success in locating the village headman, he had instead brought along Durga, the 12-year-old grandson of the village headman.

As the group assembled in front of Santu's house, Raj informed them of the purpose behind this visit. 'Today is a very important day', he announced in Hindi. 'It is Mahashivratri, a sacred festival that has been celebrated by Hindus in the city and all over India. On this day, all good Hindu women should fast and go to the temple to honour their husbands and pay respect to Lord Shiva'.[17] This was the first time that most villagers had heard about this festival, and the more outspoken Dhankumer lamented in a mix of crude Hindi and the more familiar Chetriboli that 'we did not know about this city people's holiday. We have never celebrated it here in this village. What to do? We have already eaten our morning rice'. Raj assured her that it was okay that she and the others knew nothing about this sacred day; that this was in fact, the reason why he and his city friends had come to the village today, in order to teach them about the festival and to show them how it must be observed.

He then instructed Durga to fetch a long branch, to which he attached his saffron Ram scarf, making a crude flag. A small drum and a set of cymbals were retrieved from the village school and two girls were ordered to begin playing and singing. Though their repertoire was quite vast, most of the songs they knew were specific to their local tribal culture. Raj informed them that these were unsuitable for the

---

[17]According to popular Hindu tradition, on this day Lord Shiva created his idol in the form of a *linga*. The day is marked by Hindus across India by fasting and visits to the temple. In the village, the holiday was directed toward women only, who were specifically told that they should pray for their husbands' well-being.

occasion, and instructed them to sing the National Anthem instead. The group then began marching. Durga, in the lead with the flag, was followed by a small crowd of children and teenaged boys, the singing girls and then the women. Santu's elderly mother carried a basket on her head containing the standard items needed for a *puja*, and the four *sahari-wallahs* brought up the rear.

The procession made its way slowly northward through the Hindu *basti* and then bypassed a curious group of onlookers from the *uppar para*, the Oraon Christian locality. The Oraons had not been invited to this event, and as the group passed they wondered aloud in Kurukh 'what these *katta* people [Hindus] were up to'. The local temple, a half-kilometre east of the village, was also avoided, since it was locked and in a state of disrepair. Although there was a caretaker who lived on the grounds of the temple, it remained unused for most of the year. Once the group had left the outskirts of the village and entered the jungle, the flag was allowed to droop, the singing and drumming stopped and enthusiastic chatter ensued. The four *sahari-wallahs* found it difficult, in their shoes and full-pants, to keep pace with the women and girls, who strode swiftly and comfortably barefoot, their saris pulled up above their knees.

After some 3 km, the group stopped at the base of a small hill. As the women sat on their haunches, waiting for the *sahari-wallahs* to catch up, Durga and some of the older boys mounted the flag onto the top of a tree close to the path. Quite a ruckus ensued as the women and girls resumed their playing and singing, reverting back to more familiar local songs. Their enthusiasm was more pronounced this time, in part to scare away bears that were known to frequent the jungle.

The group then made its way to the top of the hill, where the boys searched around until they found a small, little-used shrine consisting of two football-sized stones that lay at the base of a tree and a larger, crudely carved figure of Lord Shiva, which rested on top of the stones.[18] All of this had been concealed by thick, overgrown foliage, which was quickly chopped away with the axes carried by the boys. Raj instructed the group to sit down around the tree and ordered the women and girls to introduce themselves to the men. The girls giggled as they stated their names and their father's names; the women put

---

[18]While this relic potentially represents a historical connection to mainstream Hinduism, no one could tell me how long it had been there.

their heads down and refused. Uttering their own names aloud is something that women in this area are prohibited to do after marriage, and these women were not prepared to indulge such a request at this time.[19] Raj's mother scolded her son for even considering such a request, and the other men laughed, saying something about *dehati 'jangli' rivaj* (rural backward custom). Eventually, the outspoken Dhankumer introduced herself and the other four women by their natal village and husband's name, the acceptable local custom.

One of the *kurta-pyjama* clad men then stood up and, again in Hindi, explained to the women how privileged he felt to introduce the Mahashivratri festival to them. It had been celebrated for centuries, he informed them, and it was important that they, like all good Hindus across India, should celebrate this festival from this day forth, every year on this day, with a special flag ceremony and *puja*. He then narrated the origins of the festival in a speech that took nearly thirty minutes. For all but Dhankumer, much of the Hindi was probably too sophisticated to follow. The rapt attention initially displayed by the group was soon replaced with quiet gossip as the women fussed over the nursing children and the girls, long since bored, threw small sticks at the boys. The group was admonished by Raj several times to be quiet and listen to this man, who had come all this way to introduce this important festival to them.

At the end of the speech, Raj requested Dhankumer to state how she and the other women felt about Mahashivratri. She protested that she could not speak well and did not know what to say. Raj encouraged her, saying that she only needed to thank these good men for coming so far, and to promise that she and the rest of these women would celebrate this festival every year on this day, from this day forward. Dhankumer then stood up and, with hands pressed together in *namaste* form, shyly repeated exactly what he had told her. She first apologized for the collective ignorance of the women that such a festival even existed, and blamed this on the fact that 'we are just '*jangli*' women, we don't know anything'. She then said how grateful the women were to these kind men for teaching them about this important day, and promised that they would trek to this spot every year on this day to celebrate this festival.

[19]After marriage, women are known by the names of their natal villages. See Sundar (1997: 42–3), who makes a similar observation about women in Bastar district, Chhattisgarh.

After her speech, a small *puja* was performed at the base of the tree by the men and teenaged boys. One boy applied red powder (*sindhur*) to each stone; another spread five small piles of rice (representing the local deities) near the base of the tree and sprinkled powdered incense (*dhup*) onto some smouldering coals. Mimicking the actions of their elders, the boys then invoked the names of local deities ('*jangli*' *devatas*), informing them of this sacred day and thanking them for their presence and understanding. Raj interrupted them, telling the boys that that they must also invoke Shiva and the other 'big gods' (mainstream Hindu deities such as Ram, Krishna, and Brahma). A coconut was then broken and offered to the deities, and the group dispersed. The women went off to attend to their neglected work, and the *sahari-wallahs* sped off to introduce Mahashivratri to the next village. Later that evening, I met the two women who had been suckling small children during the introduction of Mahashivratri. I asked them what they made of this incident. One of them said 'who knows, I did not understand'; the other grumbled that 'we have enough festivals to celebrate here in the village. Why do we have to also celebrate *sahari* people's festivals?'

I have narrated this particular piece of ethnography at length in order to illustrate one of the more common strategies used by the RSS to inculcate 'proper' Hinduism amongst 'backward' *adivasi*s: the introduction of mainstream Hindu festivals and ways of worship. Through the ignorance and reaction of the women and boys, we are offered a glimpse of the kind of people at whom this particular strategy is aimed: *dehati* (rural) tribals, with their inferior dress and comportment, language and beliefs. Mainstream Hinduism, represented in the story by 'big gods', Ram scarves and Hindi, is nothing new to this community of *adivasis*, whose engagement with '*sahari* Hindu' culture has a long and rich history.[20] What is new is

---

[20]For extended discussion on the complex interactions between *adivasi* and mainstream Hindu cultural and religious practices, see Baviskar (1995: 85–105). The long history of *adivasi* engagement with Hinduism is also well documented within tribal oral and ritual traditions. Locally, for example, the manner in which the Ratiya Kanwars' trace their origin to the Kauravas of the Mahabharata is illustrative of the scope of engagement with Hindu traditions (cf. Russell and Hiralal (1923 [1916]: 389–403). Singh's (1993b and 1993c) edited collections also document the influence of the classic Hindu epics, the Ramayana and the Mahabharata, on oral tribal traditions and folk rituals (see also Mishra 1993a and 1993b). Likewise, Eschmann (1978a, 1978b and 1978c) examines the relationship between tribal culture and Brahmanic Hindu traditions, focusing specifically on the tribal origin of the

the proselytizing way in which the present bearers of this kind of Hinduism—the RSS—are enlightening 'backward' *adivasis* on how to become good Hindus.

Unlike the group of ten young men over whom Raj and the other *pracharaks* extend considerable influence, the majority of local people was at this stage (early 1998), comparatively ignorant about what constitutes 'mainstream Hindu' practice, and even less concerned about the precise *Hindutva* agenda of the RSS. This ignorance, which was highlighted in the above anecdote, was related to the fact that this area is cut off from the geographical and cultural mainstream due to the lack of roads and electricity. While less than half of all adult men in the village have actually been to Korba, the majority of the women have not ventured beyond the roughly 25 km range within which their natal villages lay.

It is generally acknowledged by all villagers that there is a great deal of difference between themselves and their 'backward' village customs, and the only other kind of Hinduism about which most people have some level of knowledge: '*sahari*' or city Hinduism, represented by the itinerant Brahman priest who visits the village two or three times per year. This kind of Hinduism is also characterized by the slick-dressing RSS *pracharaks* who arrive on motorcycles and sport abrupt mannerisms, big gods and saffron towels. Having little else to judge by, nor indeed little interest or need to do so, local people place the RSS *pracharaks* and their brand of Hinduism into the same category as other outsiders of like manner and appearance: '*sahari* Hindus', who bring *sahari*-Hindu festivals and ways of worship to *dehati* or '*jangli*' *log* (rural or backward folk).

Hinduized Jagannatha cult in Orissa (see also Eschmann, Kulke and Tripathi 1978). Commenting on this long engagement, Bose (1941) demonstrates how traditional tribal customs are often modified in the process of interaction between tribal communities and more dominant Hindu groups. Indeed, it is common to assume that such interaction has always resulted in a one-way direction of influence, whereby, through processes of 'sanskritization', or the 'imitation' of high caste customs and rituals by lower castes, high castes influence and transform the customs and beliefs of 'lowly groups'. Srinivas (1952: 226–7) reminds us that this is incorrect by pointing to the way in which Brahmins have been historically influenced not only by tribal deities but also by modes of worship. Brahmins in South India have commonly made votive offerings of an animal to village-deities during smallpox or cholera epidemics (cf. Pati's 2002: 4–6 recent reminder of the consequences of viewing 'sanskritization' or Hinduization as a 'one-way process').

In addition to the general distinctions between '*sahari log*' (city people) and *dehati* '*jangli*' *log*, local people recognize that there are other visible indicators, along with numerous social practices, that differentiate local groups from their city counterparts. Language is one such distinction by which Hindus and Christians alike collectively differentiate themselves from their city counterparts. '*jangli bhasha*' (local languages like Chetriboli and Kurukh) are spoken by local people, whereas Hindi is a city language (*sahari bhasha*) spoken by *sahari wallahs*, by people who can read and write (*parhai/likai log*), and by 'big men' (*bara admi*): the local Fathers during mass, visiting RSS *pracharaks*, and the police and visiting government officials.

Hindi is not only a city language; it also represents a culture that is different from local practice. This differentiation is starkly emphasized when *sahari wallahs* arrive to introduce a new festival like Mahashivratri to villagers using a language in which the latter are not particularly comfortable. The intentional use of Hindi on this occasion is in part linked to the political agenda of the RSS, which advocates Hindi as the 'language of Hindus'.[21] Although the majority of local people are not familiar with this agenda, they are aware that this language represents a culture different from their own.

This is underscored by the strong connection that local people make between their own '*jangli*' language and their '*jangli*' customs, such as the rituals in which local people engage in possession. Here, the communication between the possessing deity and its human agent within contexts such as, for example, the Gaura celebration, takes place only in Chetriboli. This was illustrated to me on one occasion when a young man from the village suddenly became possessed upon the return of a wedding party. In his state, he raved about a particular offence committed by the groom prior to the wedding, for which the new bride would be punished. This was an unusual event for two reasons. First, this young man had never before been 'visited by a deity', and people were startled by his sudden possession. Secondly, the 'deity' was communicating in Hindi, and everyone present knew that possessing spirits only communicate in one of the *jangli* languages; they do not speak Hindi. The Hindi-speaking 'spirit' was accused of

---

[21]This association is historically linked to earlier Hindu revival movements beginning in the nineteenth century when the Hindi language and Hindu beliefs were 'warmly intertwined' and placed in opposition to Urdu and Islam (cf. Kumar 1991a, 1991b).

being a fake by the veteran medium who was present, and the young man was thrown out of the celebration.

Other distinctions between '*jangli*' and city customs (*rivaj*) or practices concern ritual leaders. In *sahari* Hinduism, the leader is the Pandit (the Brahmin priest) who is known to officiate at all ritual occasions (weddings, funerals, festivals, etc.), and indeed, without whom the occasion cannot proceed. As mentioned earlier, Pandits do make the occasional appearance in the village to officiate at more mainstream holidays such as Rath Yatra. However, the village has its own priest and spiritual leader, the Baiga, in whom all ritual knowledge is supposed to be vested, and who officiates at all local ritual events and mediates between local deities and the community at large during spirit possession.

Healing and medicine is another arena wherein '*jangli*' and *sahari* cultures are differentiated. In the city, people are afflicted by *sikshit bimari* ('educated' illnesses) and cured by *sikshit davai* (literally 'educated' medicine or biomedicine) and doctors. Villagers, on the other hand, are afflicted by angry deities and use '*jangli davai*' and consult a healer. Also, city people are not plagued by the same illnesses as *adivasi* people, because the cause (deities' wrath) and conditions (the jungle) do not exist in the city (see Chapter Four).

In addition to these distinctions, the 'big gods' (*bara devatas*) that city people worship are represented only indirectly, through iconographic images: namely, 'photos' (bright, gaudy posters) or carved figures. Interaction with these gods is indirect, and either takes place through the mediation of a Brahmin priest or through worship of the photographic representations. According to villagers, city people only have to look at the photo of the god, wave a stick of incense around, and recite a prayer in order to placate the deity. While the walls of many local Hindu households feature similar posters of Hindu gods, these are not 'worshipped' in the same way but hung for decorative purposes. Whereas 'big gods' are represented by posters, local deities are represented by certain stones. Unlike 'big gods', moreover, interaction with local deities is invariably direct. It is commonly manifested through a human agent and takes the form of possession, trance or illness.[22]

[22]For additional analysis of the distinctions between 'mainstream' Hinduism and 'tribal religion', see Eschmann (1978a: 81–2). Further discussion of illness and possession takes place in Chapters Four and Five, respectively.

Hindu man from neighbouring village worshipping sahari *Hindu style. Photographs of Shiva, Ganesh and other 'big gods' are seen adorning the wall.*

City gods also demand impossible things of people, especially with regard to food, drink and sex. Villagers find *sahari* Hindu food restrictions to be very restrictive, and the prospect of abiding by them elicits serious apprehension. *Adivasi* people simply cannot worship *sahari* gods, I was told, because the latter demand 'straight, absolutely vegetarian food' (*sida, bilko sada khana*), and definitely no alcohol. In contrast, '*jangli*' gods, like *adivasi* people, are non-vegetarian and require offerings of meat (blood) and alcohol. Sex, it is believed, is also not approved of by the big gods. A 'husband/wife meeting' (*pati/patni milne*), one of the local euphemisms for sexual intercourse, ceases in the city because the big gods do not approve. This is demonstrated by the well-known 'fact' that city folk have very small families: 'one, maximum two children'. But 'how can *jangli* folk abide by this?' I was asked rhetorically. 'We need a lot of children to work our land and fields. And '*jangli*' *devata*s understand this!' This is why the rule regarding sex for *adivasi* people is 'however many times you can'. If you want to worship the big gods, I was warned later on, it is better that you do so after you have children.

Perhaps the most important issue differentiating '*sahari*' and *'jangli'* Hinduism concerns land and forest. Local customs are largely governed by the relationship that people have with their local deities, and this relationship is inextricably linked to land. Very simply, local people are obliged to worship and propitiate their forest deities because the latter own the land from which people derive their livelihoods. In the city, in contrast, there is no forest in which *'jangli' devatas* could exist and from which they could rule over their human subjects. It is for this reason that city people worship 'big gods' who are not jungle or land dependent.

Conclusion

Clearly, the kinds of practices described by local people as *'jangli'* Hinduism are not dissimilar to the kind of Hinduism practised by more mainstream caste Hindus (cf. Fuller 2004). However, it is by highlighting the distinctions and emphasising the *'jangli*-ness' of such practices that the RSS can justify their broader 'civilizing mission' in this particular area and elsewhere. The RSS is of course not alone in its attempts to civilize 'backward', *'jangli'* practices and transform *adivasis* into proper Hindus. Other members of the Sangh Parivar, namely the VHP, are also actively involved in campaigns against those practices that it finds 'un-Hindu' and 'uncivilized'. Like the RSS, the focus of the VHP is largely on those traditions that underpin *adivasi* cosmology and forms of worship.[23]

The purpose of presenting a detailed ethnographic overview of the specific features of *'jangli'* Hinduism here was to understand the wider motivation behind the specific strategies being employed by RSS activists in Mohanpur, and to appreciate the impact that these have had on the lives of local people. It is important to reiterate that when I began my fieldwork, members of the RSS were visiting the village on an average, once every other month or so. Within a year, these visits had increased to a weekly frequency, often coinciding

---

[23]Highlighting ethnography from Orissa, Kanungo (2002: 150–1) notes, for example, how the VHP successfully campaigned against the practice of *dhangda dhangdi*, or the practice whereby young tribal girls and boys congregate at the *Thakurani ghara* (the abode of the goddess) in order to choose their respective premarital partners. According to Kanungo (ibid. 172, ff. 52), the VHP disapproved of 'staying together' outside the institutionalized bonds of marriage and proudly demolished numerous *Thakurani gharas* in an effort to abolish this objectionable practice.

with mainstream Hindu festivals such as Divali or Holi. On such occasions, RSS representatives would arrive in the manner described in the Mahashivratri vignette for the purpose of showing local *adivasi* people how to observe the festival in the appropriate, mainstream Hindu fashion.

Like the strategies that will be examined in later chapters, the introduction of Mahashivratri and the insertion of mainstream Hindu 'big gods' into local forms of propitiation represent another way in which RSS activities are modelling their efforts and activities after successful Christian practices. The form of mimesis in this particular case is related to the process of inculturation, or the 'insertion' of Christian tenets into non-Christian cultural ideas and practices (see Mosse 1994b; Stewart and Shaw 1994; Stirrat 1992: 45). As I discuss more fully in the following chapter, this is a common missionisation strategy that has been aggressively pursued by Church officials since the Vatican II Councils in 1962–5. It is hailed by local priests to have been instrumental in the increasing piety of the local Oraon Christians.

Another objective of this chapter has been to show, ethnographically, how the RSS, through Raj gained access to the local community. As a local 'son of the soil', Raj used his connections in his efforts to establish a strong *Hindutva* presence in Mohanpur, as well as in other villages that he visited regularly with the other RSS *pracharaks*.

In spite of the efforts of Raj and the other 'conversion specialists' to inculcate mainstream Hindu ideas into local cultural practices, and notwithstanding the participation of the ten young men in RSS-related activities, these kinds of campaigns have not been especially successful in propagating the message of Hindu unity. The introduction of Mahashivratri and 'proper' Hindu ways of worship, for example, held little long-term interest for the majority of the Hindu community, who remained more concerned with their 'traditional' *adivasi* practices and rituals than with mainstream Hindu forms of worship. Additionally, the nursery school that was started so enthusiastically by Raj and the other *pracharaks* was closed down after less than two months due to lack of local participation and support: its five pupils lost interest, and the appointed nursery teacher, who had not been paid his promised stipend, left the project in disgust. Finally, few of the young men over whom Raj wielded such influence seemed particularly well versed or terribly interested in the *Hindutva*-based subject matter some 12 months into the meetings. By the time

I completed my fieldwork in 1999, this group included only four semi-regular participants.

While the campaigns mentioned above have been marginally effective in bringing awareness of the Hindu nationalist agenda to certain members of the local community, in other words, none have been particularly effective in transmitting to the local people the kind of long-term communal sentiment that is required for the broader expansion of the movement. As we shall see in Chapters Four and Five, the failure of these kinds of campaigns can in part be explained by the dominance that the Ratiya Kanwars continue to maintain over political and ritual affairs, and the respect and loyalty that this caste continues to command.

Other strategies, however, have been more than marginally successful in the spread of Hindu nationalism, and it is an examination of these to which the remainder of the book is devoted. Such strategies revolve around the engagement by the RSS in more legitimizing tactics such as the social upliftment of the community as a whole, and around the RSS's propagation and cultivation of anti-Christian sentiment.

It will become clear throughout the course of this book that the impact of the RSS in this area is largely a function of its relationship with the Church. This is both implicit, where the Church's historical and present day practices have served as a model for the RSS's mimetic activities, and more explicit, where the Church and local Christian community have specifically been stigmatized as the 'threatening other'. The contribution that the Church itself has made to this process is the subject of the following chapter.

CHAPTER THREE

Adivasi Christians and the Church

I n the previous chapter, we were introduced to the Hindu
community and to some of the campaigns that local RSS
pracharaks have instituted to propagate the *Hindutva* agenda
amongst local *adivasis*. These included the active promotion of 'proper'
Hindu practices through the introduction of mainstream Hindu
festivals. The ignorance and reaction of local people to the RSS activists
and their delivery of Mahashivratri provided a glimpse of the kind
of 'backward' Hinduism practised in the village as well as the
perceptions that local people have of the RSS and their particular
brand of 'city Hinduism'.

By replacing Ram towels with crucifixes and Mahashivratri with
Mary's birthday, a similar account of how 'proper' Catholic conduct
is being inculcated in the local *adivasi* Christian community could
easily be narrated. Owing to the vast literature that exists on nineteenth
and twentieth-century missionization processes in India, this kind of
account is by now, reasonably familiar.[1] However, it useful to return
briefly to this literature, in part, to recall how the activities of early
missionaries contributed to the conversion of large numbers of *adivasis*
to Christianity. More importantly, it is useful to re-examine these
processes because they provide both the basis for the mimetic practices
in which current proponents of Hindu nationalism engage and the
present-day rationale behind the Sangh Parivar's apprehensions about

---

[1] See Bowen (1936), Forrester (1977), Neill (1985), Oddie (1975) and (1977),
Pickett (1933), Sahay (1976) and (1992) and Webster (1976).

Christian conversion. And while the recent emergence of Hindu nationalism and the trajectory of communal tensions are due principally to the increasing involvement of the RSS in local affairs, I intend to demonstrate in this chapter that the particular manner in which Hindu nationalism has been introduced locally is a response to the historical practices and contemporary presence of the Church.

I begin by briefly considering the history of Christian missionary activities and the Church's general civilizing mission. I then turn to the local Oraon Christians, whose 'outsider' status and relationship with the local Hindu community is further explored. Like the ethnography presented in the previous chapter, this will provide the basis for a more comprehensive understanding of the processes by which the Christian community has been transformed into the local 'threatening other'. The greater part of this chapter is devoted to an examination of the relationship that local Oraons have with the local Church. Specific attention is on how the Oraons' 'Christianness' has been cultivated by the Church, and on the present-day contributions that the Church has made to the emergence of Hindu nationalism. Drawing on the perspectives of both the Oraon Christians and the local priests, I demonstrate that it is through the spiritual and material 'diabolization' (Meyer 1999) of traditional Oraon beliefs and practices that the Church has made its own contributions to the creation of the Christian 'other' and, by extension, the emergence of Hindu nationalism. My alternating usage of the terms 'Oraon' and 'Christian' reflect the fact that all local Oraons are Christian, and all Christians in Mohanpur are Oraon.

Christian Missionization and *Adivasis*

The existing ethnographic and historical literature on Christianity and missionization processes in India is largely divided between south India and central India. The former concentrates on low-caste or untouchable experiences that date back to at least the sixth century AD (cf. Caplan 1987; Kawashima 1998; Mosse 1994); the latter focuses on the mass conversion movements that spread throughout tribal areas from the mid-eighteenth century onward (Bayly 1994; Dube 1977; cf. Prasad 2003: 75–84; Sahay 1976 and 1977). This chapter is concerned primarily with the latter.

The earliest recorded missionary presence in central India was the Free Church of Scotland, a Protestant mission established in

1840 in Nagpur, Maharashtra. This was considered to be an area 'ideally suited to become the centre of pioneer work from the point of view of Christian missionaries' (Neill 1985: 317). A second Protestant Mission, the Gossner Lutherans from Germany, arrived in Chhotanagpur (a region located in what is now the state of Jharkhand) in 1845 (Mahto 1971; Sahay 1968). After actively proselytizing for five years amongst 'higher classes of natives' with no results, missionaries turned their attention to the more marginal and 'dispossessed' groups, notably the untouchables and *adivasis*. It was speculated that these groups might be more susceptible to the gospel (Sahay 1976: 27). Indeed, this shift resulted in the first four Oraon converts to the Lutheran Church.

By November 1858, the number of Oraon Lutheran villages in Chhotanagpur had grown to 205, and missionary efforts spread into Chhattisgarh (Roy 1912: 236; cf. Dube 1995). The missionaries had also begun to actively assist and advise tribal people in court cases regarding traditional *adivasi* land rights. The impression rapidly gained ground that 'to become a Christian was the best means of shaking off the oppression of the landlords' (Tete 1990: 55), and by 1868 there were 10,000 converts to the Lutheran Church (Mahto 1971; cf. Niyogi 1956; Roy 1912 and 1915). Lutheran missionaries became increasingly wary of such large numbers of people who ostensibly wished to become Christians 'of their own accord'. They attempted to shift their proselytizing efforts back to the 'spiritual' as opposed to the 'secular' or material aspects of Christianity (de Sa 1975: 88).

It was perhaps due to the decreasing material support that *adivasis* received from the Lutheran missionaries following this shift that many converts left the Lutheran church and joined the Catholic church, which was established in Chhotanagpur in 1869. In the early period of the Catholic mission, the Jesuits' proselytizing practices consisted of strict evangelism with a focus on 'inner conversion': they did not advocate on behalf of tribal people. Consequently, the Catholic church had no converts until 1873, and very few by 1880. Conversion on a mass scale to Catholicism began in 1885 under the direction of Father Constant Lievens. Called the 'greatest missionary since St. Francis Xavier' on account of his 'sensational apostolate in Chhotanagpur' (cf. Bowen 1936; Sahay 1968: 925), Lievens familiarized himself with the agrarian troubles and tenant laws, advised tribal people on legal matters and urged them to refuse illegal demands from the landlords or to pay rent without receipts. Once the mission began to be perceived as a source of assistance against the landlords, *adivasis* began to come to the missionaries as whole families and villages. In time, as a condition for his help, Lievens began to demand baptism.

The Catholic mission also joined other missions in participating in other kinds of 'non-evangelical' activities, such as education, medical services, famine relief, and cooperative banking societies. Such activities together led to phenomenal results: by 1889, Lievens had succeeded in converting around 75,000 tribal people (Mahto 1971; cf. Niyogi 1956). This success reflected a general shift in Catholic missionizing practices across the world, which favoured group conversion and seldom emphasized the individual's 'inner experience' (cf. Green 1995; Sahay 1976: 15–31).

As demonstrated by this brief account, conversions during the late nineteenth and early twentieth century amongst tribal communities in central India took place predominantly in the form of a 'mass movement'.[2] The implication here, is that the adoption of the new religion becomes a collective, as opposed to a personal act (Caplan 1987: 217). Indeed, one issue that troubled both administrators and missionaries of the time revolved around whether *adivasis* converted out of genuine spiritual belief, or whether they were induced to convert via material means and association with a powerful group of missionaries (Tete 1990, de Sa 1975, Sahay 1976). Implicit in this issue is the question over the capacity for 'primitive' tribal groups to possess such 'genuine' motives. This question also relates to the process in which the social category of 'tribe' was historically constructed in opposition to more 'civilized' Hindu society (see Bates 1995; Skaria 1999). Sceptical administrators did not feel that 'primitive' tribals were capable of experiencing such a sophisticated cognitive transformation (cf. Hardiman 1987: 154).

Whether 'genuine' or 'materially motivated', recognition of the real or perceived power of Christian missionaries was clearly a major factor in conversion (Hardiman 1987: 163). The association of Christianity with discourses of power, along with its specific link to the colonial project, has been systematically acknowledged by scholars on missionization processes within and outside of India.[3] Within central

---

[2]Scholars estimate that approximately half of the Catholic community and around 80 per cent of the Protestants in India are descendants of mass movement converts (Pickett 1933: 5–21; Sahay 1976: 29).

[3]See Hardiman (1987); for comparative examples outside of India, see Comaroff and Comaroff (1991), Rafael (1988) and Stirrat (1992).

India, Christianity not only offered *adivasis* the means by which they could combat exploitative landlords and moneylenders; it also provided them with a 'replacement community' (Devalle 1992: 163), which was accompanied by a new system of schooling and education, along with new moral and legal codes that would enable *adivasis* to achieve a certain level of social mobility.

As mentioned earlier, there are clear historical connections between the kinds of social upliftment activities in which the Church historically engaged to diffuse Christianity throughout central India, and the civilizing mission that was characteristic of the British colonial project (cf. Bryce 1810; Fischer-Tiné and Mann 2004). Although the colonial state as a matter of policy attempted to distance itself from missionary activities, colonial officials who were based in *adivasi* areas were often supportive of missionaries who, it was felt, could serve as agents in the broader civilizing mission (cf. Dube 1995; cf. Hardiman n.d.). With their explicit emphasis on the 'moral and material progress' of 'inferior' and 'dispossessed' tribal communities, such activities continue to underpin the 'civilizing mission' in which the Church is engaging within *adivasi* communities in the present day. As we shall see in Chapter Four, the biomedicine available at the local Church dispensary is linked closely with the healing power of Christ and is considered by local Church officials, to be a particularly useful proselytizing tool (cf. Arnold 1993).

For some critics of these early missionization processes and dubious conversion tactics, it is this 'replacement community' that has threatened traditional cultures and practices and taken *adivasis* away from the 'Hindu fold' (Niyogi 1956; Shourie 1994). Nineteenth-century Christian missionaries who championed tribals in land disputes against Hindu landowners were accused by local Hindus of being anti-national and therefore anti-Hindu (see Weiner 1978: 190). Christian converts, by extension, were accused of feeling 'closer' to non-tribal Indians and European Christians, than to non-Christian tribals who were still part of the 'Hindu fold'. This was evidenced by the identification of some Christian tribals first and foremost with their religion, and only later with their ethnic origin (Singh and Jabbi 1995).[4] This sense of connection to a foreign 'community' purportedly persists to the present day. It is ostensibly more prominent among

[4]The issue of social identification was likely more complex than this. Pati (2003: 21), for example, notes the opposite trend, whereby Oraon Christian converts in Orissa, when asked about their identity, suppressed their Christian connection in favour of their tribal links.

Catholic Christians, whose loyalty with respect to socio-religious and even political matters is allegedly dictated by pronouncements from Rome, and whose allegiance to the Indian nation is therefore questioned (cf. Bhatt 2001: 198–202; Sahay 1976:157 for further discussion on the RSS and VHP's narrative of a 'global Christian conspiracy').

As noted earlier, it is this latter issue in particular, that continues to be invoked by the RSS to justify increased attention and militant action within Christian communities across India. As we shall see in the course of this present chapter, however, while local Oraons retain a strong sense of superiority with respect to their material and educational advantages over their Hindu neighbours, they identify themselves first as *adivasi*, using the terms 'Oraon' or 'Kurukh' people, and only secondly by their religious identity (Christian or *isai*). It will also be demonstrated in this chapter, and more broadly in the book as a whole, that it is through the concerted and sometimes aggressive tactics exercised by both the Church and the RSS that these identities and relations are becoming communalized.

Oraon History and Migration

There is much speculation about the origin of the Oraon people, who are today scattered throughout north, northeast and central India (Grignard 1909; Kujur: 1989: 80–1; Roy 1915). The fact that their language, Kurukh, is Dravidian-based suggests a south Indian origin (Roy 1915). It is popularly believed that they migrated from south to north India, where they fought in the 18-day battle described in the Mahabharat on the side of the Kauravas. From the north, they eventually migrated south again to west Bihar, where they were ruled by their own king for several centuries, enjoying what Kujur calls their 'golden age' (1989: 30). Sometime between the twelfth and sixteenth century, they migrated to Chhotanagpur (located in present-day Jharkhand), where the majority of Oraon *adivasis* reside today. A combination of land alienation and the search for employment was behind the mass migration of *adivasi* people (including Oraons) out of Chhotanagpur into the neighbouring region of Chhattisgarh in the late nineteenth and early twentieth century (see Weiner 1978).

Most of the Oraons in this area are descendants of converts who joined the Catholic Church during one of the mass conversion movements that took place in Chhattisgarh in the 1930s. The Oraons immigrated to Mohanpur in 1970 from Pathalgaon, a town in the neighbouring district of Jashpur around which most of their villages were scattered, and where most still have extended family.

The first three Oraon settlers, Dewar Tirkey, Pachki Kirketta, and Garibsai Kujur, came to this area 'in search of land'. Having heard of the abundant jungle located some four days' walk from Pathalgaon, they sought permission from Mohanpur's village headman to bring their families and settle alongside the small Hindu community that, then, consisted of 40 households. The headman agreed, on two conditions: that the Oraons build their homes a half-kilometre away from the main village, and that they refrain from using the village well. The Oraons were considered to be untouchable (*chhua chut*) by local Hindus, who did not wish to maintain anything beyond minimal contact with the newcomers. These conditions were in common with other prescriptions of untouchability elsewhere in India that included reduced social contact and residential segregation (Deliege 1992; cf. Mayer 1960).

Interactions between the Oraons and local Hindus during the initial years in the village continued to revolve around strict rules of untouchability, mostly concerning the consumption of food and access to communal water sources. One factor that contributed to the general ostracism of the Oraons during these early years was their reputation for making a yearly human sacrifice to their ancestor spirits. This practice allegedly occurred immediately following the autumn harvest, when the head of each Oraon household was obliged to sprinkle the blood of a (preferably male) stranger over the household's fields to ensure the following season's fruitful harvest. Historical and ethnographic records intimate that this practice was also performed by other *adivasi* groups in central India (Mitra 1935; cf. von Furer-Haimendorf 1944). Contemporary scholars such as Padel (1995) and Sundar (1995), however, have questioned this record, and I have never come across any reference in the literature regarding this practice amongst the Oraons.[5] Rumours about the Oraons' involvement in human sacrifice accompanied them to Mohanpur, and today local

[5]On the inconclusive proof of the existence or non-existence of human sacrifice amongst *adivasis* in Bastar, central India, Sundar (1995: 371) reminds us of the importance of considering what this belief means to different people: 'to the British, human sacrifice was an organized evil that had to be suppressed, while to the people of Bastar, sacrifice was (and is) a central metaphor of existence grounded in the agricultural ritual' ... 'The belief in the existence of the practice is a belief about the extraordinary power of their gods who can make such demands, as well as the power of humans who are capable of performing the act'.

Hindus admit that they used to be very frightened of these newcomers, taking particular care to avoid them around the time when the sacrifices were said to take place. Nowadays, local Oraons insist that they have never participated in this custom. They do admit, however, that it was a practice in which their ancestors indulged, 'before they found 'Jesu'. At least two Oraon families have stories about how their grandfathers narrowly escaped being the victims of such a sacrifice, and most insist that this sort of practice still occurs today, amongst more '*jangli*', non-Christian Oraons in other parts of Chhattisgarh and Jharkhand.

A year after the three original Oraon settlers moved their families to Mohanpur, four more families followed, along with a trickle of others in later years. All migrated for the same reason: the search for cultivable land. At the time of their arrival, only one member of the original party of settlers had the cash with which to legally purchase land in this area. The other immigrants were given permission by the Ratiya Kanwar elders to clear and cultivate the section of forestland that fell alongside the Petfora, the local river. This was very fertile land that had been left uncultivated by members of the local Hindu community due to the danger of offending the deities and spirits that were believed to live alongside the river. Warned of this danger, the Oraons chose to proceed with the cultivation of the land. As the elderly Pachki, the only surviving original settler, told me, 'It was very good land, and we were so poor. We were not afraid of those deities who lived there; they did not belong to us.' It is this land that would become the subject of ethnic and communal tensions in later years, as outlined in Chapter Six.

When the Oraons first migrated to the area, there were insufficient numbers from their community to provide adequate assistance in clearing and making this land into cultivable fields, and no one had any livestock with which to drive the ploughs. Moreover, the less destitute members of the Hindu community refused to assist the Oraons, or even to loan them the use of their livestock. As such, it was three to four years before the Oraon immigrants began to reap any sort of harvest from their efforts. Their narratives of these initial years in Mohanpur are infused with tales of hardship, poverty and hunger— tales with which local Hindus concur. According to the current village headman, who was a young man at the time, the Oraons were 'very dirty and very poor when they arrived, with no land, no cattle, no homes—nothing like what they have today. They sometimes begged us for a bit of rice, and sometimes we gave it. But we Hindus also had very little, barely enough to feed our own families. What could be done?'

Indeed, the early 1970s were a difficult period for everyone in the village. Local Hindus had faced two consecutive monsoon failures before the Oraons' arrival. This not only affected their agricultural harvest, but also reduced the supply of jungle produce—roots, mushrooms, greens, *mahua*—on which they had traditionally depended to supplement their primary food supply of rice. Nowadays, the whole community refers to this period as the most serious 'time of scarcity' (*akal samay*) in living memory.

While Hindus made do with what little agricultural and forest produce they managed to harvest, most of the adult Oraon Christian men went off to Korba, the growing industrial township 40 km from the village, to seek work. It was at this time that the coal, aluminium and electricity plants that today comprise Korba's main economy, were being constructed or expanded, and Oraons were able to obtain work as casual labourers on these sites. They would travel to the town in groups of two or three, returning to the village every two weeks or so with bags of rice for their families. It was considered to be a difficult journey that had to be made by foot through dense jungle. It was at this time that the Oraons' local reputation for 'hard work' and for earning their livelihoods from 'outside' the village was firmly established amongst the Hindu community, who even today, do not engage in outside wage labour to the same extent as the Oraons (see Chapters Six and Seven). That they were forced to seek work outside of the village to see them through this period was nothing new to the Oraons, who will 'do anything' to earn a living. Pachki, who worked as a labourer in Korba during this time, often reminisced about how Oraon people have always gone 'here and there', searching for work wherever they can. 'Where there is a possibility of getting work and earning money', I was told, 'you will find Oraon people.'

Today, the Oraons are the second largest group in the village, numbering 43 households and 242 people, and making up just over a quarter of the local population. The Oraons used to be led in spiritual and political affairs by two of the three original migrants, Dewar Tirkey and Garibsai Kujur. These men were powerful healers who commanded a great deal of respect amongst members of both the Oraon and Hindu communities. They were also the primary mediators 'in those days' between the Oraons and their deities and ancestor spirits. According to the descendants of these men, their presence and authority had been the primary obstacle to the Oraon's budding Christian faith. Similarly, it is the opinion of the local priests that the deaths of these elders in the mid-1990s marked a turning point for the Oraons' relationship to the Church. This is a subject that I explore in relation to the influence of the Church later in this chapter.

Nowadays, there is one person who serves as the Oraon's unofficial leader and spokesperson. This is Bahadur, my adoptive 'brother' and host who, in spite of only being in his early thirties, enjoys an unusual level of respect amongst members of both the Hindu and Oraon communities. He goes unfailingly to all village *panchayat* meetings and acts as advisor and confidant to the Oraon community as a whole. His authority, however, is by no means comparable to that of the village headman, particularly with regard to contentious issues such as the curbing of liquor sales (see Chapter Seven).

Oraon Christians' Wealth and 'Outsider' Status

In contrast to their impoverished beginnings, nowadays, the Oraon community as a whole enjoys a relative material dominance that surpasses even the landholding Ratiya Kanwars. This is largely related to their wage-based labour activities that take place outside of the village, about which I go into detail in Chapters Six and Seven. There are varying degrees of prosperity among individual Oraon households: some are considered to be wealthier than even the village headman, while others are extremely poor. None, however, are as destitute as some of the poorer Hindu households, and indeed, the Oraons as a whole, are considered to be 'rich' by local standards. As we shall see throughout the course of this book, it is the alleged origin of the Oraons' relative wealth that has served to fuel the wider tensions between the Christian and Hindu communities.

The Oraons' wealth is represented in the first instance, by their houses, which are generally larger, more spacious, single-family dwellings, as opposed to the often crowded, joint family 'compounds' in which most Hindus live. Moreover, most Oraon families own one (and sometimes two) of the most important local prestige goods, a bicycle, compared to perhaps only half of all Hindu families. The first motorcycle in the village was also purchased by an Oraon shopkeeper, as were the first two of the three televisions that the village boasts of. While the latter are relatively useless consumer durables due to the fact that there is no regular electricity supply, the prestige attached to the ownership of such goods serves as an important indicator of wealth (cf. Stirrat 1989: 94–115). The first diesel-powered threshing machine was also purchased by an Oraon shopkeeper, and the only two hand-held pesticide pumps are owned and rented out by Oraons.

The Oraons for their part, attribute their relatively superior material status to a combination of hard work and 'Jesu's' approval'. As Bahadur, once remarked, 'when we arrived we had nothing: no land, no homes, no food. What were we to do? We had to work. We had to get food from somewhere. And now see all this. Through our hard work, we have large homes, land, bicycles; our children are being educated. 'Jesu' has blessed us.' The issue of how the Church has influenced present-day Oraon practices and beliefs and ostensibly enabled them to assume a relative material advantage over their Hindu neighbours is discussed later in this chapter. For now, it is important to say that the Oraons' relative prosperity has not gone unnoticed by local Hindus. My friend, Pratap, a well-off member of the dominant Gandhel clan, once compared the Oraons, 'who came with nothing when they arrived in this area twenty years ago, and who have now become very rich', with his own 'people', the Ratiya Kanwars, who have been here 'for over 500 years', but who still have not 'gone up' in material and social status.

In spite of their material prosperity, Oraons are considered by all Hindus to be the most inferior caste in the village. The Oraons' untouchable status is used to reinforce the high caste status of dominant local groups. One incident that illustrates this concerns the diesel-powered threshing machine, owned by Jugla, an Oraon shopkeeper. For most of my fieldwork, all villagers, Hindu and Christian alike, took their par-boiled seed rice (*dhan*) to Jugla for threshing, paying a nominal fee for the service. Several months before I concluded my fieldwork, a similar, second-hand machine was purchased by the village headman. He soon discovered that the majority of Hindus continued to go to Jugla because of the superior quality of rice that the latter's machine produced. In response, the headman called a *panchayat* meeting and ordered all high-caste Hindus to stop taking their seed rice to Jugla's shop, on the basis that it was being defiled by the low-caste Oraon customers' rice. This case likely had more to do with the headman's attempt to augment his position of power and to recover his investment in purchasing his own threshing machine than with his concern for the purity of the local Hindus (see Chapter Five). However, this incident does illustrate how caste hierarchies and local rules of untouchability can be regularly invoked.

Prosperous Oraons, heading off to their mortgaged landholding.

In spite of their untouchable status, the Oraons continue to feel indebted to the Ratiya Kanwar caste in general and the Gandhel clan in particular for the generosity that the then-headman demonstrated by permitting them to reside in the village. This indebtedness is regularly expressed in terms of the political support that the Oraon community feel they must offer the current headman with respect to local *panchayat* issues. I return to this issue later in the book.

As mentioned in the previous chapter, because of their untouchable status, and because the Oraon Christians do not serve any specific ritual or economic role for the Hindus, there is little daily or informal interaction between individual members of the Oraon Christian and Hindu communities. People *within* the two communities interact on a daily basis, assisting each other with a piece of work in the home or fields, or visiting each other informally at home to share advice or gossip. But it is very unusual for this kind of interaction to take place *between* individuals from the two different communities. Exceptions to this include the local Yadav cow-herders and Chauhan goat-herders, who interact with both the Hindus and Christians on a twice-daily basis when they collect and later deposit their owner's livestock. Likewise, local shopkeepers (two Hindus and two Christians) have regular interactions with customers from both communities. Apart from this, the only time that ordinary people might come into contact with each other is at a chance meeting en route to the fields or in the context of alcohol consumption. This is particularly true for women, who do not enjoy as much freedom for 'visiting' (*ghumne*) local households and making journeys outside of the village as men.[6] For the most part, however, people from different communities do not meet or engage with each other on a day-to-day basis.

People do interact in more formal contexts, such as the mortgage negotiations that take place between the (invariably) Hindu landowner and the Oraon Christian creditor, or the sale of an item such as a sleeping mat (made and sold by Oraon women) or some sort of local produce (usually grown and sold by Hindus). Both communities occasionally participate in communal labour activities sponsored by the other, and representatives from all castes attend each other's festivals. Moreover, people from different communities meet at local *panchayat* or women's

[6]Research suggests that tribal women do in fact, enjoy a relatively greater degree of freedom of movement compared to non-tribal women across India. For further discussion on these issues, see Srinivas (1977), Mehta (1984) and Srivastava (1990).

meetings. But even here, direct interaction is kept at a minimum, as people tend to sit in segregated community clusters.

The lack of integration between the two communities is reinforced by the fact that the Oraon Christians are spatially located in the *uppar para*, a half-kilometre outside of the main village *basti*. It takes 10–15 minutes to walk between these two sections, which are connected by a well-trodden dirt path (*rasta*). Additionally, there are four outlying hamlets, three of which are comprised entirely of Oraon households. These are scattered within a roughly 3 km radius of the main *basti*.[7] Lack of engagement is thus related to the practicalities of the spatial distance between the Hindu and Oraon *bastis*: it is simply too far for people from different communities to make anything but work-related visits to the others' localities or homes. Indeed, my own daily forays between the *bastis* meant that I quickly became a major source of news and gossip, and my arrival at anyone's household was invariably greeted with queries about news from the other *basti*.

The Oraons' 'outsider' status is also underlined by linguistic differences. Locally, Oraons speak Kurukh, a Dravidan-based language that has no relation to Chetriboli, the dialect of Chhattisgarhi spoken by local Hindus. Although Oraons understand and speak this dialect with their Hindu neighbours, they speak Kurukh amongst themselves, often in front of and about local Hindus, who do not understand Kurukh.

The Oraons take great delight in the fact that they can communicate in a language that the local Hindus cannot understand. The Hindus are aware that they are at a disadvantage, saying about the Oraons that 'they can understand our language, but we cannot understand theirs.' Oraons, in turn, sometimes bemoan the fact that their Hindu neighbours have made no effort to learn their language, in spite of having lived amongst them in this area for thirty years. Apart from the handful of children who have been educated at the mission school, there are only a few young Hindu men who can understand basic Kurukh.

In addition to being the name of the principal language in which Oraons communicate, Kurukh is a term used by Oraons when referring to themselves and their customs. I was often reminded that the Oraons

---

[7]This distance is only an approximation. Locally, the notion of distance is generally conceived of and measured in terms of walking time. For example, the distance between the main village and one of its hamlets, Bagmara, is '*adha ghante*' (half an hour's walk through the jungle), while that between the village and the city, Korba, is '*che-saat ghante*' (six, seven hours' walk).

were 'Kurukh people' who have 'Kurukh traditions'. The Oraons in turn refer to all Hindus of the village collectively as '*katta* people' who do '*katta* things'. *Katta* is a rather ambiguous Kurukh word that has both ethnic and linguistic connotations. While it could roughly be translated into 'non-Oraon' or 'non-Kurukh', the meaning is more complex than this. It not only distinguishes a local resident Hindu from a local Oraon, but it also distinguishes local people from both non-resident and city Hindus: only a Hindu person from Mohanpur is called *katta*, while a Hindu person from, say, the neighbouring village of Basin is referred to as *Basin-hin* or *Basin-wallah* (person from Basin), and a person from the city is simply a *sahari wallah*.

The question 'is he Kurukh or *katta*?' is commonly asked of strangers approaching the Oraon *basti*, establishing both the ethnic identity and the language to be spoken. The local Hindus to whom it refers are not meant to know that *katta* refers to them, although visiting Oraons from neighbouring villages and districts are familiar with the usage of this term, the rules of which apply in their own village as well. For the Oraons, caste distinctions within the Hindu community are of little significance, and the usage of *katta* for their neighbours instead of the specific caste or clan name shows how the Hindu community as a whole is viewed more like a block caste category.[8] Indeed, my questions to my Oraon informants regarding the caste membership of a particular Hindu villager were often met with exasperation and the inevitable response of 'who knows, he's just *katta*.'

It is clear that there are numerous factors that contribute to the Oraons' 'outsider' status and, by extension, serve to shape the relationship that this community has with local Hindus. It will also become clear that the Oraons' 'outsider' status, combined with the lack of physical interaction and spatial integration between the Christians and the Hindus, plays a role in the way in which the RSS has so successfully involved itself in local issues. The significant point for our purposes at this time, however, is that the categories 'Christian' (*isai*) and 'Hindu' are not the primary ethnic distinctions that local people use to identify themselves or to refer to the other. For all local people, in other words, religious categories are downplayed in favour of (block) caste ('Oraon', '*katta*' or 'Ratiya') and clan ('Deheria',

---

[8]Parry (1999b: 136–7) makes a similar observation with respect to Satnamis living in Bhilai, for whom the category 'Hindu' is a 'block-caste' category, defined in opposition to the 'Satnami' community. See also Dube (1998) on how the construction of this Hindu 'otherness' for the Satnamis occurred in the late nineteenth century.

'Gandhel') terms. One of the objectives of this chapter is to demonstrate how the Oraons' 'Christian-ness' is being stressed by the Church, and to show how this has contributed to the transformation of local Christians into the local 'threatening other'.

Christianity and the Church in Mohanpur

While the Oraons converted to Christianity two generations ago, most of the community admit that they did not become practicing Christians until long after their migration to Mohanpur. In the same year (1970) that the first Oraons arrived in Mohanpur, a Catholic mission belonging to the St. Vincent Pallottine religious order was established in the neighbouring village of Manpur, 6 km away, to serve the growing Oraon Catholic population that lived within roughly a 20 km range. This religious order was founded in 1835 by a German called Vincent Pallotti. Its headquarters are in Rome and its regional base is in the neighbouring district of Raipur. The particular calling or 'charism' of this Order revolves around 'service' to the poor. Priests who are posted to this area see themselves as 'agents of progress' in the form of education, medical care and other charitable works conducted amongst local tribal communities.

The first two priests who were stationed at the Mission in the early 1970s frequently donated rice and wheat flour to the most impoverished Oraon families, and helped them to build their own well. One of the striking details about the Oraons' narratives of when they first arrived in the village, in addition to their enduring memories of hunger and hardship discussed earlier, is the kindness and generosity of the priests. The two priests who were attached to this particular mission during my fieldwork—one from Kerala (South India), the other, an Oraon *adivasi* from Jashpur district, Chhattisgarh—describe the local Oraons as 'rice Christians' (see Forrester 1977; Webster 1975), due to their willingness to accept mission donations in the past. Contrary to those who criticise such actions (Niyogi Report (1998 [1956]; Shourie 1994), which in the past led to large numbers of converts, local priests see nothing wrong with such assistance. One of the priests even admitted to me that it was necessary, sometimes, to feed the belly before concentrating on the soul.[9]

---

[9]It is interesting how the local priests' position on the Oraons' conversion and early commitment to Christianity contrasts with that attributed to the Christian

*Fathers stationed at Manpur during period of fieldwork conducting
a wedding service at the Catholic Church.*

The original mission station, or the '*bangla*', as it came to be
called locally, consisted of two small mud and thatch structures that
served as the church house and the priests' residence. In the late
1970s, a dispensary and health clinic were also constructed, and
two Catholic Sisters-cum-nurses joined the Fathers at the compound.
These Sisters belonged to the St. Francis Assisi congregation, a
Catholic Order that is also dedicated to service to the poor and that
is often 'paired' with Pallottine priests. A school and hostel were

---

missionaries in context of the Niyogi Report (Niyogi 1956). In the latter, the missionaries
reportedly denied that the mass conversions that took place in the 1930s in central
India were 'rice conversions' (conversion out of material inducement), and insisted
that such conversions were 'genuine' ('inner' or 'personal'). Implicit within the comments
made by the local priests is not only the issue of whether such conversions are 'genuine'

added in the early 1980s, along with two additional Sisters who were trained teachers. Two of the Sisters who were in residence at the time of my fieldwork were Oraon (one each from Chhattisgarh and Jharkhand), and two were South Indian (from Kerala). As observed by Hardiman (n.d.) and others (see Comaroff and Comaroff 1986; 1991), it was believed by Church authorities that a grand church structure and compound raised the local status of missionaries. It was also an effective means to reinforce the 'civilizing' agenda and the authority of the Church (cf. Dube 1995: 180). To this end, the final addition to the mission station was the conversion of the mud and thatch church building into a large concrete structure. By the late 1980s, the wooden fences that surrounded the property had been replaced with iron, and the compound was completed.

Sisters in residence at Manpur during period of fieldwork. The two Sisters on the right serve as nurses in the Catholic-run dispensary; the two on the left serve as teachers to the Oraon Christian boarders.

---

or 'spurious', but also whether temporal 'inducements' are actually incompatible with the spiritual aspect of conversion. As noted in the introduction to this book, such issues remain politically sensitive throughout India today. While comprehensive consideration of the meaning and process of conversion is clearly beyond the scope of this book, for further discussion, see Hefner's (1993) edited volume on the historical and anthropological considerations of conversion. See also the useful volume edited by Robinson and Clarke (2003), which focuses mainly on the social, political and historical aspects of the conversion process within India; cf. Oddie (1977) and Pickett (1933).

While the whitewashed Church with its stained-glass windows is the most visibly imposing feature of the compound, the dispensary and clinic are the primary vehicles through which the Church engages in social service and interacts with both Oraon and Hindu *adivasis*. As mentioned earlier, this is in line with broader Christian practices that historically have used medical institutions, as well as schools, to establish and legitimize their presence and spread Christianity amongst *adivasi* people. Hospitals in particular were thought to provide the 'best point of contact' between missionaries and potential *adivasi* converts (Carstairs 1928: 239), where superstition could be countered and where patients and their families could be 'taught Christianity' (cf. Kawashima 1998: 139). Surgery especially was believed to 'open many a closed door to missionary influence' as well as to provide the most dramatic proof of the superiority of western medical technique (Hardiman n.d.).[10] Nowadays, local priests insist

Catholic Church, the most visibly prominent feature of the Catholic compound, Manpur.

[10]Medical missionaries, or 'clinical Christianity' (Fitzgerald 2001) as it was sometimes known, was not recognized as an effective method of proselytization until the latter half of the nineteenth century (see Cavalier 1899; Dennis 1899; Williams 1982). This was attributed to the long-held conviction that medical work would distract from the purpose of conversion, and to the fact that the medical profession had not, before the mid-nineteenth century, gained respectability (Williams 1982: 272).

that conversion of Hindu *adivasis* to Christianity has never been part of their broader agenda. They do admit, however, that the prevention of the Oraons' 'backsliding' into what they identify as superstitious customs and beliefs is an ongoing task.[11]

Locally, regular utilization of the dispensary by Oraon Christians did not come about immediately. The Oraons' initial distrust of the dispensary revolved around a combination of unfamiliarity with biomedical techniques and practitioners, and devotion to their own healers, who believed that angry deities and ancestor spirits were the main source of illness (see Chapter Four). When the clinic first opened, moreover, there was a strong association between the medicine of the dispensary and Jesus. The medicines and 'potions' that were distributed by the Church through the dispensary were said to be sanctioned by Jesus. As such, these not only provided competition to traditional healing methods, but also threatened the power of Oraon healers and healing practices (cf. Dube 1998: 74). This was a time 'before we were proper Christians', I was told by the nephew of one of the healers. 'It was a time when we had *andhviswas* (superstition; literally, 'blind faith'; see Parry 1994: 227–8) and believed that our illnesses were caused by *bhut* (ghost, spirit). Instead, we went to our own healers who would perform *puja* and give us *bhut ka davai*' (literally, ghost's medicine). Although no records were kept at the dispensary until the early 1980s, the current nurses claim that the dispensary saw only a few hundred patients in the first few years of its existence. According to those old enough to remember, it was not until the last of the Oraon healers died in the mid-1990s that the Oraons started using the dispensary regularly.

It has taken longer for local Hindus to make systematic use of the clinic, for reasons that will become evident in the following chapter. Nowadays, most Hindu families do visit the clinic, and many

---

Mission establishments reportedly gave little consideration to the idea that medical assistance might provide evangelism with added legitimacy (cf. Fitzgerald 2001: 105). By the early twentieth century, however, medicine had a significant place in most Christian missions.

[11]Cf. Kawashima (1998: 138–9), who documents how the prevention of re-conversion to Hinduism was a stated priority for Church Medical Missions in late nineteenth and early twentieth-century Kerala. The problem of re-conversion was also noted by Fitzgerald (2001:115–16), who reports on missionary complaints of the difficulty of keeping new converts from 'straying outside the Christian fold' and returning to traditional forms of healing, particularly when faced with the 'crucial test of disease'.

acknowledge and seem grateful for the role that it has played in treating them at times of serious illness. Currently, nurses see up to a thousand patients per month, around three-quarters of whom are Hindu. This is in part, due to the fact that the clinic has been the only primary healthcare centre in the area, catering to the basic medical needs of *adivasis* living within a 20 km range. It is also a reflection of the demographics of this area, which is comprised of a roughly three-to-one, Hindu/Christian ratio. But this is still a worrying figure for RSS advocates. As I shall argue in the next chapter, the monopoly that the Catholic dispensary has had on healthcare in this area is in part, the motivation behind the RSS's sponsorship of a local Hindu man to undertake a training course in primary health care and establish himself as the village 'doctor'.

As elsewhere in India, education is the other vehicle through which the Church engages in 'service to the poor'. Very few Oraons who were children at the time of the school's construction in the early 1980s were actual boarders at the school. But this had to do with cost, not with scepticism about the priests' motives. The school has always charged a nominal annual fee to its boarders, which goes toward the children's board and is supplemented by the Church. The Rs 150 that was charged when the school first opened was an impossible amount for most Oraon households to afford in those days. Nowadays, the school charges around Rs 800 per year, a substantial sum that most Oraon households struggle to pay. It serves 180 children between first and eighth standards, and is divided equally between boys and girls aged five to sixteen. The boarders hail from six neighbouring villages and mostly consist of the grandchildren of the original Oraon settlers to this area. Additionally, there have generally been between two and six Hindu boarders every year since the school was first opened. Amongst these is Raj, the primary link between the village and the RSS, as well as his two younger brothers. In the two years that I lived in the area, around eighteen boarders came from Mohanpur, including Raj's two teenaged nieces.

All of the children who board at the mission school adhere to a daily regime that is geared towards their spiritual and secular education. The one-hour morning mass is followed by two hours of classes and tuition conducted by the two Sisters and two trained teachers who also reside at the mission compound. The children then go off to attend classes at the government school located a half-kilometre away in Manpur village. In the evening, they are given two additional hours of tuition. Any spare time that the children have is mostly spent doing odd work for the compound, such as weeding the vegetable gardens or sweeping the dirt drive.

Most students and many parents complain of the strictness of the regime, along with the increasingly high fees and the fact that the children are made to work in their spare time. However, most parents are also grateful for the educational benefits their children are receiving, particularly when compared with the effectiveness of the local government schools. The latter are considered to be 'useless' by most students and their parents, and it is generally agreed that the kind of tuition offered at the mission school gives students an advantage over others who only attend ordinary government classes. This is the primary reason that Raj and his brothers use to justify their own participation in Catholic school education.

Religious Identification: Oraon 'Christian-ness' and Piety

The steadily increasing legitimacy and patronage of the Church's medical facilities by local Hindus have prompted the RSS to install its own 'doctor'. The mission school and hostel, in contrast, have not been of great concern for local RSS proponents. This is perhaps because the latter caters mostly to Oraon Christians and does not attempt to expand its student body by actively soliciting the enrolment of local Hindus. This could also be related to the fact that the majority of RSS *pracharaks*, along with those who occupy leadership positions within the organization, have themselves benefited from some degree of Christian school education. It is true that this kind of schooling has traditionally been the best educational alternative in rural *adivasi* areas is of general concern for the RSS as a whole. This is partly the impetus behind the attention and involvement of groups like the VKA and other Sangh Parivar organizations in setting up increasingly reputable non-Christian school alternatives in such areas (cf. Sundar 2004).

Although it has been illegal for Christians to actively proselytize in Madhya Pradesh and Chhattisgarh since 1991, the RSS and its sympathisers argue that the mere existence of the school and dispensary is a form of missionization (Shourie 1994). More generally, and as we shall see throughout the course of this book, it is the presence of the Church itself, combined with its history of mass conversion movements, that represents the possibility of proselytization and thus underscores the increasing attention of the RSS in this area.

These possibilities notwithstanding, the local priests maintain that there has been no active missionization of non-Christians since the mission station was first built. They also maintain that their commitment to the healthcare and educational needs of local people is actually secondary to their fundamental objective of strengthening the Oraons' Christian faith. This objective has been met with gradual success, if such success can be measured in terms of improved attendance at Sunday mass, the decrease in indulgence in what the Church considers to be 'superstitious' practices and the increasingly visible indicators of the Oraons' Christianity.

Such indicators revolve primarily around what Dube (1998: 74) describes as the 'moral discourse about Christian decency'. Since the mission station was established in Madanpur, the Oraon women's 'social skin' (Turner 1980) has been gradually adorned with less jewellery than their Hindu neighbours. The former tend to restrict their bodily ornaments to simple bangles and a rosary or necklace with a charm of Mary, Jesus or the Pope attached, for 'remembrance and protection'. In contrast, members of the Hindu community wear chains with pictures of Hindu gods attached, along with protective amulets or '*damru*' filled with medicinal herbs and numerous bangles on both arms. Oraon women have also stopped wearing the traditional nose rings worn by other *adivasi* women in this area because, I was told, Jesus did not wear such jewellery.

The practice of tattooing the arms, ankles and chest, once mandatory for all *adivasi* women from the age of puberty onward and still sported by Hindu girls and women today, has also stopped amongst Christian women at the behest of the local priests, who actively discourage the practice because 'it goes against Jesus to defile one's body like this'. Nowadays, such tattoos can only be found amongst middle-aged or older women. This 'moral discourse' has also been extended to clothing and the idea of bodily shame (cf. Dube 1995: 180–1). Oraon women, who traditionally wore only a sari draped around their shoulders, are nowadays regularly advised that they should cover their breasts with blouses. This distinctive sign of Church-imposed physical modesty further sets Oraon women apart from their Hindu neighbours.

Religious identity, finally, is revealed upon entering the house. In contrast to the pictures of Hindu gods or national leaders that decorate the walls of Hindus' houses, Oraon's have pictures of Jesus and Mary tacked up on their inside walls and crosses painted or etched on the outside walls.

While these visible indicators serve to differentiate the individual along the lines of religion, it is important to reiterate that the Oraons' 'Christian-ness' as a social distinction is rarely acknowledged. Instead, it is their low caste status that has been given greater importance and that is often used to reinforce the high caste status of the dominant local group. This was illustrated in the incident regarding Jugla's threshing machine discussed earlier. Indeed, until very recently, Hindus in the village rarely referred to the Oraons' 'Christian-ness' or identified them as Christian (*isai*) except in the context of specifically Christian holidays (*isai tyauhar*) that are marked by the Oraons.

As mentioned earlier, this could have something to do with the fact that in this village, all Christians are Oraons. As such, it is not necessary to distinguish non-Christian Oraons from Christian Oraons, or the Oraon caste as a whole by their Christian identity. But this could also be attributed to the fact that it has only been in the past few years that the Oraons have started to become 'proper Christians'. The priests attribute this growing piety to the deaths of the two influential healers mentioned above, which occurred between two and three years before I began my fieldwork. These healers were considered by both the priests and the Oraons to have been the primary link between the Oraons and 'Satan's work', and by extension, the primary obstacle against the development of the Oraons' inner faith in Jesus and demonstration of proper Christian practice. To the priests' obvious delight, the deaths of these healers have been accompanied by the steadily decreasing observation of traditional Kurukh practices and indulgence in traditional medicines.

The Oraons' growing piety is also due to the fact that in the past decade, most of the grandchildren of the original settlers reached school-age and were sent to be educated at the mission boarding school. Except for Christmas and Easter holidays, children are not permitted to leave the compound and return home, and the only time that parents are encouraged to visit their children is at Sunday mass. This rule has had a remarkable effect on the increasing Church attendance of local Christians, most of whom have at least one child or grandchild who attends the school. It is also telling that Church attendance typically plummets by about three-quarters during the summer holiday.

It is during the annual Christmas mass that the Church witnesses nearly complete attendance. There is a festive atmosphere at this late-night service that Oraons are loath to miss. Local Oraons will also attend the special mass that is conducted in each village during the summer and monsoon months, when regular Church attendance is at its lowest. Apart from the Christmas mass, the one event in which at least one member from every Oraon household will participate is the Way of the Cross procession at Easter. This procession begins at the Church and is led by the priests, who are followed by the schoolchildren and a crowd of around one hundred Oraon Christians from surrounding villages. Village men take turns to carry the cross as the procession slowly winds its way to the top of a small hill located some two kilometres away. This is the only time of year when a large group of Christians gathers outside of the compound, and the occasion is met with curious glances from Hindu onlookers. Once the group reaches the hill, the previous year's cross is taken down, a mass is conducted and the new cross is mounted in its place.

The Way of the Cross ceremony has been described at length in various ethnographies on local Catholic culture (see for example Cannell 1999; Stirrat 1992: 68–72). The significant point here is that, apart from the mission compound itself, the small cement platform on which the cross is mounted is the only other sacred space or 'social territory' (Tambiah 1996: 53; 234) claimed by Christians in this area. This is in contrast to the numerous sacred shrines, groves and other territories devoted to Hindu deities dotted around the forest. Unlike many such territories, no effort is made to protect the cross, which is 'planted' into a two-foot hole inserted into the platform. Likewise, the hill itself is not deemed to be particularly special, and indeed, many local Hindus and Oraons regularly graze their livestock around the place where the cross is mounted. It is this space, however, that would come under threat from Raj and the other local RSS activists halfway through my fieldwork, a significant issue to which I return in Chapter Seven.

The Oraons' growing faithfulness can, finally, be attributed to the proactive measures taken by local priests in recent years, including the introduction of 'Charismas', the four-day 'revival' meetings that were launched in 1996. These are held annually at the Church and, with the combination of sermons, songs, meditation and spontaneous speeches by members of the congregation, appear to mimic the 'revivalist' charismatic meetings of contemporary fundamentalist

Christian churches (see Caplan 1987). Local Oraons are encouraged to attend these meetings with the promise of daily meals and spiritual blessings. Today many Oraons claim that they have become 'closer to God' only after attending one or two of these 'Charismas' programmes.

A more general strategy hailed to have been instrumental in the increasing piousness of the Oraons, is the process of 'inculturation', or the 'insertion' of Christian tenets into non-Christian cultural ideas and practices (see Mosse 1994b; Stewart and Shaw 1994; Stirrat 1992: 45). Since the Vatican II councils in 1962–5, which reassessed the role of the Church particularly with respect to non-western Catholics, the Church has advocated the integration of local practices into Christian liturgy in order to 'spread the Christian message' in a more culturally contextual and appropriate manner.[12] It was thought that communities would 'apprehend the message of the Gospel better if they do so in their own terms' (Stewart and Shaw 1994: 11).[13] Locally, inculturation has been manifested by the transformation of numerous myths, rituals and festivals that Oraons traditionally celebrate, most of which revolve around the worship and propitiation of their deities and ancestor spirits. These have been infused with Christian themes largely emphasizing Christ's goodness and protection.[14] In addition to the reinterpretation of the traditional meaning, the Oraons are encouraged to donate the offerings that they would have otherwise made to their deities and ancestor spirits to the Church. These offerings are then used to help feed the schoolchildren.

[12]Prior to Vatican II, the Church's position was dominated by policies that revolved around its claim 'to have a monopoly of the truth and its commitment to the idea of a universal Church' (Stirrat 1992: 43). By the 1950s, it was clear to many within the hierarchy of the Church that the position and teachings of the church were anachronistic to the twentieth century world (Mosse 1994b: 85; Stirrat 1992: 43–4). The Vatican II reforms also did away with Latin liturgy and looked at the role of women in the church and at the religious orders and their relevance to modern life. See Sahay (1992: 85–8) and Tirkey (1980) on the impact of the Vatican II transformation on Oraon Catholic culture.

[13]As Stewart and Shaw (1994) further assert, anthropologists would probably label many instances of inculturation as 'syncretism', in so far as they involve the combination of diverse traditions in the area of religion (1994: 11). These authors go on to say that representatives of the Catholic Church would dispute this usage, reserving 'syncretism as a distortion or loss of the Truth of the Christian message' (*ibid.*). Cf. van der Veer (1994) for a discussion on the meaning and application of the notion of 'syncretism' in anthropology and history.

[14]See Roy (1985 [1928]), Sahay (1976, 1992) and Tirkey (1980), for further details on how other Oraon rituals and festivals have been reinterpreted and adapted by the Church. For a discussion of inculturation in the wider Indian context, see Mattam (1991).

'Jesu', *Shaitan* and *Viswas*

As mentioned in the previous chapter, the RSS is engaging in similar kinds of 'inculturation' strategies with the introduction of Mahashivratri and the insertion of mainstream Hindu 'big gods' into local forms of propitiation. Such strategies have not been as successful as the Christian variety, which have resulted in the increased visibility of Christian-ness and improved public attendance at the weekly mass. In spite of such improvement, however, the Oraon community is still considered by the local priests, along with the Oraons themselves, to be 'weak' in faith. In the words of one of the priests,

the Oraon people may have accepted a Christian version of their myths, but this does not mean that they take the message of Christ into their hearts. Even now, with all of our efforts, Oraons perform their own rituals, they narrate their traditional tales alongside the Christian one, and they are involved in Satan's work (*shaitan ka kam*). It will take many generations before Oraons really come to Jesus.

According to the priests, the primary obstacle to the Oraons' transformation into proper Christians is their *andhviswas*, or superstition, which is underpinned by the continuing veneration of Kurukh deities and ancestor spirits.[15] Traditionally, these included countless 'superior and inferior' gods and spirits, the highest being *Dharmes*, the 'creator and controller of gods' (Roy 1915: 22). Beneath *Dharmes* sat the spirits of ancestors (*pāchbāl, purkha*), as well as the myriad village deities and spirits (*devatās*) and the malevolent beings (*nad*). As part of the missionization process in central India, the Kurukh term '*nad*' was translated into the term 'Satan' (*shaitan*) (see Kujur 1989: 169; Roy 1915: 107).[16] Today, the term '*nad*' is used by local priests to classify not only malevolent beings, but to encompass the numerous deities and ancestor spirits that are incompatible with Christian belief and that still figure in Oraon people's lives. In tandem

---

[15]See Belmont (1982) for an extended discussion on how the notion of 'superstition' has been constructed in opposition to the Christian religion and the appropriate worship of the Christian god. See also Stirrat (1992: 93).

[16]The selection of specific deities as 'God' and the identification of other beings as agents of the 'Devil' were historically a common practice amongst Christian missionizing traditions across the world (Horton 1971; cf. Meyer 1999). Sundar (2006: 359) has also noted how contemporary Christian propagandists point to similarities between Oraon religious traditions and Christianity, in that both are founded on a belief in *Dharmes*, or one 'supreme god'.

with Church rhetoric, even the Oraon elders admit that these beings are just different names for Satan (*shaitan ka nam alag alag*).

Regular propitiation of these beings has diminished with the increasing influence of Christianity, and nowadays these beings are kept in good humour with a single blood sacrifice offered annually by three local Oraon elders. As part of the continuing effort to discourage worship of what they clearly categorize as 'Satan', and to create what Stirrat (1992: 178–9) has identified as the necessary 'opposition of two absolute states', the local priests repeatedly tell the Oraons in Sunday sermons that they must choose between Jesus and Satan (good and evil), and that each choice has a consequence.[17] Following Satan or indulging in 'Satan's work' (*shaitan ka kam*) by invoking the deities or ritually worshipping the ancestors results in suffering and misfortune (see Kujur 1989: 239). The only way to ensure protection is by abandoning these practices and choosing and maintaining a steady faith (*viswas*) in Jesus.[18]

Instead of discarding their deities and traditional 'Kurukh practices', in 'syncretic' fashion (Stewart and Shaw 1994), Oraons have incorporated Jesus into the existing hierarchy that encompasses the whole range of supernatural beings with whom they have traditionally engaged. In a sort of 'gradation of relative benevolence and malevolence' (Stirrat: 1992: 85), at the top of this hierarchy and reigning as 'king of the gods' (*devata ka raja*) sits Jesus, who Oraons assert, is the most powerful and good of all beings. Beneath Jesus sit the myriad deities and the ancestor spirits who, if not propitiated regularly, do not protect the Oraons from illness and misfortune.

While Oraons have not entirely discarded their worship of traditional Kurukh beings, they do seem to have accepted the Church's view that Jesus is the most powerful deity and that their relationship with Jesus is consequently the most beneficial and protective. One of the most visible forms of protection is the 'Christian talisman' (*isai damru*): the rosary, which is worn both 'to remember Jesus' and to ensure protection against evil. One example of the rosary's power

[17]See Stirrat (1992: 88–9), who also talks about how the 'mythic structure of Catholicism' at a local Catholic shrine in Sri Lanka is based on a series of paired oppositions: God and Satan, good and evil, and so forth. There are a number of other writers who discuss how things 'of the Church' are brought into a 'relation of opposition to tradition'. See for example Green (1995) and Meyer (1996: 210).

[18]*Viswas* is a complex notion variously glossed as faith, respect, belief (see Stirrat 1992: 179). As with all indigenous notions, the problem of translation is implicit here (cf. Jolly 1996 and Rafael 1988).

concerns Raju, a smart young Oraon man from the village. While cycling off to the bazaar one day, he suddenly came across a beautiful girl with long flowing hair, standing alone on the road. She came towards Raju and asked if she could accompany him. Frightened, he refused, and told her to wait for the next person, for he was in a rush. He admitted that while drawn to her beauty, his heart was 'big with fear'. To calm himself, he made the sign of the cross and 'thought of Jesus'. When he pulled out his rosary, the girl vanished.

Later on, there was much discussion about this incident. The girl's immediate disappearance at the sight of a rosary suggested to Raju that this had been Satan in disguise. Raju's uncles agreed and decided that if this incident had happened to a '*katta* boy', or to someone like Sanjeev (a non-church going Oraon Christian about the same age as Raju), then he surely would have succumbed to the girl's advances and taken ill, or perhaps been killed, for he would not have had the protection of Jesus.

While Jesus' protection can be called upon through the sort of demonstrative faith illustrated here, he won't always settle for such public displays. Oraons have learnt that receiving Jesus' protection is contingent upon the person having 'complete faith' (*pura viswas*). As my friend Vero Tengio, a mother of seven, explained,

'Jesu' is able to see you from afar. And when he sees that you are doing *shaitan ka kam* (Satan's work), he cries because he feels very badly. Even if you wear a rosary, he'll remember that you also perform *shaitan ka puja* and he'll look away when you need him. How can he come to your aid if you don't respect him?

Vero Tengio is partly parroting the local priests, who regularly preach that the only way to expect Jesus' assistance is to believe, from the heart, that God is more powerful than Satan. However, the experiences that she and other Oraons have had, support this axiom. Take, for example, the encounter narrated by Manglu, a respected Oraon elder and healer.

I was spending the night in my field hut, protecting the groundnuts from wild pigs and foxes. I was sitting on my haunches, stirring a small fire with my axe. Suddenly, there stood a very large, human-like animal in front of me, with the body of a bear and the face of a man. I knew it was *shaitan*, because his eyes were large and blinking red, like a torch going on and off, and he was standing five feet off the ground. He kept staring at me, with his red eyes, and squatted down near to me, on the other side of the fire. At first I became stiff with fright; I couldn't move. But *shaitan* just squatted there, in front of the fire, looking at me; he did not touch me. After some time, I built the fire bigger and became less frightened. After one hour, maybe two, *shaitan* moved toward the village. He went so quickly, his feet did not touch the ground. I left the field hut and ran home. I don't know, maybe he would come back for me. The next morning, I heard the death wails of some Hindu women. I knew what it meant. The same *shaitan* who visited me in the night went to the *katta basti* (Hindu locality) and strangled my friend around the neck, in his sleep. Killed him. *Shaitan* didn't harm me because I am Christian; I have faith (*viswas*) in 'Jesu'. *Shaitan* only troubles *katta* people (Hindus), because they believe in him.

While I do not wish to enter into a discussion about the nature of Manglu's 'belief', it is important to note that Manglu and other Oraons insist that his faith and recognition of Jesus's power over Satan saved him from certain death. Had his *viswas* been weak, or had he been a Hindu, then it is assumed that he would have met the same fate as his Hindu neighbour. While Manglu was not denying the existence of *shaitan*, he was, by virtue of his *viswas*, denying him the power to cause harm (see Obeyesekere 1968: 22).

In addition to protection from the clutches of *shaitan*, the existence of 'complete faith' can also be rewarded with blessings. The wife of my adoptive brother, Bahadur, had been childless for nearly a decade. During this time, they had consulted a number of different healers and tried numerous ritual cures, all to no avail. Throughout this period, Bahadur was known to be a bit of a *badmash*: a man of bad character, who drank a lot and stayed away from home for nights on end, carrying on with other women. Moreover, he did not go to church in those days. As he put it, 'although I said 'Jesu' and wore a rosary, I did not have Jesus in my heart.' Ten years into the marriage, when Bahadur's desperation for a child nearly drove him to take a second wife, a new priest was transferred to the local parish. This priest told Bahadur that if he would start to pray and believe in Jesus 'from the heart', then he would be blessed with a child. Within a year, his son Johnny was born. Needless to say, Bahadur attributes Johnny's arrival to the power of Jesus, brought on by his own 'change of heart': *viswas* exchanged for child.

It is examples like these that confirm to the Oraons that Jesus is the most powerful god, and that there is a being called *shaitan* that can bring only harm and that exists in opposition to Jesus. The latter, moreover, is capable of taking on many forms, one of which was encountered by Manglu. The Oraons accept these two propositions, perhaps because their own traditional gradation of benevolent and malevolent beings is somewhat analogous to the Christian concepts of 'good' and 'evil'.

But what they cannot accept is that the ancestor spirits and deities, who have protected them in the past, are merely guises of Satan, or that the rituals they indulge in to honour these beings are, as the Church teaches, *shaitan ka kam*. By extension, they cannot accept that Jesus is the only divine being who is capable of protecting them from harm. 'Since the beginning,' I was told by one of the elders who carries out the annual *puja* honouring all Kurukh supernatural beings, 'and long before we became Christian, our ancestors have looked after us and ensured our well-being. This is why we continue to pray for protection for our farms and harvest, for the health of our cattle, our children and families.'

And herein lies the dilemma and the fundamental difference between the conceptions of the priests and the Oraons. For the priests, Jesus is unambiguously good; all other beings are forms of Satan, whose worship is unequivocally categorized as s*haitan ka kam*. In contrast, when Oraons are asked what they understand s*haitan ka kam* to be, they agree that only the act of possession, or the process by which a person gives his *viswas* and his body to a particular deity or ancestor, fall unquestionably under this category. With respect to other Kurukh practices, such as the yearly blood offerings made to the ancestors, or the consultation of a local healer and recitation of a *mantra*, there is no consensus. Only the local catechist is resolute in the view that all practices related to ancestor worship are irrefutably *shaitan ka kam*.

This lack of consensus reflects the tensions between the dualistic rhetoric of good and evil that the Oraons are taught by the Church, and the varying gradations of good and evil that underpin their experiences. As we shall see in the next chapter, healers, with their feet firmly planted within both Church and traditional practice, are particularly illustrative of this tension. The priests are determined to instil in the Oraons the notion that Jesus is the only God and that all other supernatural beings with which the Oraons have traditionally engaged are guises of Satan and therefore unambiguously evil (cf. Caplan 1987).

It is perhaps because of the regular chastisement that they get from the priests about their 'half-way' beliefs that the Oraons classify themselves as 'half half people' (*adha adha log*): those who waver between being *asli* or *nakli isai* (genuine and counterfeit Christians). *Asli*-ness is being a 'true' Christian: going to Church, holding prayer meetings and having '*viswas*' in the heart; *nakli*-ness is being a bad Christian: drinking, avoiding church and indulging in 'Satan's work' (*shaitan ka kam*). For the priests, this includes calling on healers instead of going to the dispensary, and hosting traditional rituals at times of birth, marriage and death instead of following prescribed Christian norms. Only those who are considered to be the most pious (the local catechist) and the most depraved (those who practice witchcraft) are consistently '*asli*' or '*nakli*'. For reasons described above, ordinary Oraons waver between the opposing pulls of the Church and their traditional beings, acting variously *asli* and *nakli* and calling themselves and their beliefs 'half-half'.

In short, Oraons 'inhabit a dual moral world' (Mosse 1994c: 324) wherein they must constantly reconcile the demands of their Christian faith with those of their Kurukh obligations. While Jesus' power is believed to be supreme (proven by the gift of a child), it is also elusive and undependable, and sometimes people are forced to return to their deities and ancestor spirits. To rely on the latter, the Oraons must maintain some sort of ritual relationship with them, for otherwise even these beings will get angry and withdraw. My friend Vero Tengio put it to me in this way. 'Whom shall we respect? Whichever deity's name we take, he will be pleased; and whichever name we do not take, he will get angry. If we give blood to one of our Kurukh deities, then 'Jesu' will get angry; if we do not give blood, then our ancestor spirits will get angry'. Moreover, although Jesus' power to enact good is superior, it is believed that the power of the ancestors and deities to enact harm can be even greater. Oraons have been taught that Jesus is a forgiving god. 'But if we do not worship our ancestors', I was told, 'then it is dangerous.'

Church Strategies: Becoming 'Proper' Christians

While the diabolization of local beliefs and practices has helped in propagating a notion of opposition between Christian and Kurukh beings, the increasing frustration over the Oraons' continuing engagement with the latter has recently led local priests to employ more aggressive strategies. Effected in mid-1998 and thought up specifically for the Oraon Christian congregation in this particular area, these strategies are aimed at directly opposing instead of encompassing or reinterpreting local practices. They revolve around a set of regulations that combine a sort of 'material diabolization', where a system of ostracism and fines is instituted against those found guilty of participating in 'un-Christian' activities, with a mechanism of excommunication or 'outcasting', where participants are excluded from the sacrament and their children are expelled from school until such fines are paid and confession is extracted. Such regulations, which go against the inculturation tactics traditionally employed by the Church, are comparable to those instituted in other parts of Chhattisgarh by nineteenth century Christian missionaries, whose 'civilizing mission' was accompanied by a drive to control, improve and discipline the members of the congregation (cf. Dube 1998: 75).

The primary practices for which Oraons are punished locally revolve, unsurprisingly, around the engagement in what the priests have classified as *shaitan ka kam*. This includes the refusal to call a nurse or avail of Church-approved treatment offered by the dispensary for illness. When the priests get to know that an Oraon has called a local healer, the patient's family is fined Rs 50 (equivalent to nearly two days' wages). Likewise, if it is discovered that others in the village were in attendance or somehow had knowledge of the ritual, then they are fined the same.

Another activity for which fines are meted out is the hosting of and attendance at traditional, non-Church approved marriage rites. These include the engagement ceremonies (*lota pani*), where the bride-to-be gives her final, public consent to the groom by symbolically exchanging a brass vessel of water, and the 'big feast' (*koha pani*), an event sponsored by the groom's family where the wedding date is fixed and brideprice negotiated.[19] The feasting and drinking involved in these events is accompanied by a traditional ritual element, wherein Oraon elders invoke the deities and ancestor spirits to bless the couple and ensure their future happiness. The rule instituted by the local priests holds that those families who host traditional marriage rites like the *lota pani* or *koha pani* ceremonies are to be fined Rs 500 each, while the couple will be fined Rs 250. Those who attend the traditional marriage rites held in the village are also to be fined Rs 100 (a charge that is equivalent to over three days' wages).

Nowadays, prospective brides and grooms are made to attend a five-day 'marriage preparation course' conducted by the local priests and sisters before they are allowed to be married in the church. They are charged a fee of between Rs 50–100 to attend the course,

[19]See Kujur (1989: 196–206) and Roy (1985 [1928]: 136–71) for detailed descriptions on traditional Oraon marriage rituals.

where they are taught the importance of marriage and fidelity and given advice on maintaining harmony in the home. Some Oraons choose to postpone this course, along with the traditional Catholic service, until such time that they can afford the expense and time—usually several years after the marriage, and often after the birth of one or two children.

Alongside the rules mentioned above, it was announced that those who had not been married in the church and who did not make the proper arrangements to do so within six months would be refused the sacrament. Such arrangement included the completion of the five-day marriage preparation course. If couples happened to have children, then the children would not be allowed to attend the mission boarding school until such time as their parents completed the course and consecrated their marriage in the church.

In the immediate months following the announcement of these new rules, several individuals were charged with violating them and served with the requisite fines. The rule with respect to the church marriage affected nine Oraon couples, six of whom had school-going children. All but two of these couples subsequently made arrangements to attend the marriage course and consecrate their marriage in the Church within six months' time. They agreed that it was a 'good idea' to get married in the church, but admitted that they did so at this particular time on behalf of their children's schooling. The remaining two argued that they could not afford the time and money for the course, and refused. They were subsequently forced to withdraw their children from the mission school. One of them did not seem particularly troubled by this, and was instead relieved that he did not have to pay the school fees of Rs 800. The other was angry and complained about how the priests were jeopardizing his daughter's education. He did not understand why the priests had to punish his child, and boycotted Sunday mass in protest. Most of the Oraons agreed that the priests were being unfair. Such complaints reached the ears of the priests, who refused to lessen the harsh measures, saying that 'this is the only way that the Oraons will learn'.

Other acts were regularly added to the list of prohibited acts for which similar punishments were meted out. These included the Kurukh customs that were carried out at the funeral, which traditionally involved the invocation of ancestors through *puja*. Such customs included the placement of items belonging to the deceased alongside her body in the coffin. Amongst these items were the deceased's plate and cup, her clothing and slippers, and a few rupees to ensure that she would be able to purchase what she needed in the afterlife. Other rituals that fell under this new classification included the spreading of seed-rice (*dhan*) along the path behind the coffin as it is carried from the house to the grave. This is believed necessary to provide the spirit with sufficient food for its journey to the afterlife, as well as to provide seed to plant in the after-world.

The prohibition against these practices came about after the Mother Superior based at Manpur witnessed one particular funeral in Mohanpur. Her presence was unusual, for she rarely visited the surrounding villages and had very little interaction with members of the community outside of the confines of the Church compound and dispensary, where she acted as 'head nurse'. She was surprised when she saw the traditional Kurukh practices, and commented to the priest on how little the Oraons seemed to have understood or taken the 'message of Jesus' into their hearts. She also took note of the 'waste' of the seed-rice being spread on the ground behind the coffin (which amounted to about 10 kg, an equivalent of two days of food for the deceased person's family), pointing out that this could have been donated at the Sunday service. It was at the following Sunday mass that the rule prohibiting the engagement in such rites was added to the list of prohibitions.

Excessive drinking has also been classified as 'un-Christian', although the priests recognize that this is an 'engrained' *adivasi* practice and therefore difficult to control (see Hardiman 1985; see also Chapter Seven). The priests' only recourse here was to ban anyone whom they suspected of drinking, from attending mass or prayer meetings, and to impose a fine of Rs 50 on those who audaciously attended mass while drunk.

Since the institution of these rules, Oraons have attempted to keep such practices away from the purview of the priests. However, the latter usually learn of such activities, either when a family member or neighbour informs on the guilty parties, or through the casual talk of children at the mission school. Once such an offence has been discovered, the guilty parties are summoned by the priests, who will then announce the offender's name and offence at the following Sunday mass. This 'naming and shaming' practice also serves to warn others of the spiritual and material consequences of such an offence.

As harsh as some of the consequences seem to their intended recipients, these rules and related 'civilizing' efforts do appear to have had an effect on the Oraon's piety. Proof, according to the priests, is in the growing church attendance and the increasing numbers of

Oraons who are opting for church weddings. Even the man who had boycotted Sunday mass was making plans to attend the five-day marriage preparation course when I completed my fieldwork.

Both the Oraons and the priests acknowledge that the formers' improving piety is not only due to the measures instituted by the priests against errant members, but to the recent death of the two most influential healers and primary propagators of *shaitan ka kam*. As noted earlier, when these men were alive, Oraons were more likely to consult them for ritual and medical advice than to attend mass and seek the services of the nurse at the Catholic dispensary. The deaths of these elders thus, marked a shift in spiritual and ritual allegiance, which has been further encouraged through the diabolization of traditional Kurukh beings, along with the institution of the kind of measures mentioned above and the biomedical campaigns described in the following chapter.

The Oraon people admit that these measures are helping them to become better Christians. They compare themselves with their extended kin in Pathalgaon, the town in Chhattisgarh from where many of them emigrated. There are 'thousands' (*hazar*) of guises of Satan in that area, I was often told by my Oraon informants. This is because the Oraons in that area have not abandoned their traditional beliefs, and Church influence is much weaker. There is also more drunkenness, violence and other kinds of behaviour that signifies the absence of Jesus amongst Oraons in Pathalgaon. When such behaviour occurs locally, everyone involved agrees that this is because the community has 'lost its faith'. Indeed, a drunken brawl will invariably result in a sudden increase in attendance at the following Sunday mass, in order 'to call Jesus back into the village'.

One ostensible outcome of the Oraons' growing piety is their relatively superior material prosperity. As mentioned above, the Oraon community as a whole, is considered to be wealthy by local standards. In Chapters Six and Seven, I show that this wealth, which is represented by their large houses and the relatively larger number of consumer and prestige goods, is due partly, to their participation in wage labour, and partly to the fact that they do not own land in which to re-invest their income. While the Oraons do not refute the source of this wealth, they also believe that Jesus is rewarding them for abandoning their engagement in *shaitan ka kam* and becoming better Christians.

Diminishing participation in *shaitan ka kam* and other ritual and social obligations of the sort mentioned above has, to be sure, contributed to the Oraons' relative prosperity in more practical ways.

Such obligations, which included regular propitiation of Kurukh deities with blood offerings and the maintenance of sacred sites, are not unlike those mentioned in the previous chapter in which members of the Hindu community continue to engage. These are traditionally very costly and, in the past, it was not unusual for Oraon households to incur enormous debt whilst trying to meet them. The fact that the Oraons are abandoning these practices means that their monetary outlay for such obligations is less. As we shall see in later chapters, this has not only contributed to the Oraons' economic status and relative material prosperity; it has also helped them to become moneylenders to the more impoverished Hindus, who are often forced to mortgage their land in order to fulfil the social obligations related to their rituals.

The Church and the RSS

The purpose of this chapter has been to provide an ethnographic examination of the relationship that the Oraon Christians have with the local Church, and to consider the contributions that the latter have made to the transformation of the former into the local 'threatening others'. It was suggested earlier in the chapter that the Oraons' 'Christian-ness' has not, until recently, been the primary category around which social relations with the local Hindu community have revolved. As a community whose origins, language and primary source of income are located outside of the village, the Oraons' low-caste, 'outsider' status has taken precedence over their religious identity and has underpinned the way that the Oraon Christians have interacted with local Hindus. It has primarily been through measures like inculturation, the diabolization of traditional deities and beliefs and, more recently, the outcasting of errant members, that the Church has contributed to the 'betterment' of the Oraons', thereby enhancing their 'Christian-ness' and 'civilizing' them in the process.

By drawing attention to their Christian status and distinguishing them more visibly from their Hindu neighbours, such measures have served to amplify the cultural distance between the two communities. Once again, however, it is the role that these have played in the Oraons' improved material status that has had the greatest impact on their relationship with the Hindu community. In particular, it is the contribution that such measures have made to the Oraons' ability to purchase non-essential goods and to act as creditors to members of the local Hindu community that has facilitated the tensions between the Christian and Hindu communities.

While the latter issue will be fully addressed in Chapters Six and Seven, it is important at this stage to reiterate that the measures employed by the Church to improve and 'civilize' local Christian *adivasis* are similar to those strategies being used by the RSS. Both organizations are broadly concerned with removal of '*jangli*' practices and the cultivation of appropriate religious practices and beliefs; both draw on processes of inculturation to inculcate such practices; and, as we shall see more fully in the next two chapters, both are actively engaged in the social upliftment of *adivasi* communities. With respect to the RSS, such similarities are underpinned by the broader mimetic relationship that Hindu nationalist organizations have had with the Church. As mentioned earlier, this relationship dates back to at least the nineteenth century, when Hindu reform movements sought to model and 'redefine' Hinduism after the Christian religion (cf. Thapar 1985).

It is because these similarities are part of a longer and more complex history that both the presence of the RSS and its impact in this area are a function of its relation of opposition to the Church. According to Panikkar (1999: xviii-xix), RSS strategies in *adivasi* communities like Mohanpur are possible only if the Church and its 'good works' are discredited and replaced by those of the RSS and its affiliated organizations. A total replacement of Church-related activities—namely those that revolve around education and health care—is unlikely to happen in the foreseeable future, given the Church's respected history and efforts in this area.

Successful inroads can be achieved, however, through the introduction of suitable alternatives to local people, and it is to this end that RSS activists have embarked on their own 'civilizing mission'. From around 1995 onward, concern for the physical and social welfare has been the ostensible motivation behind the increasing attention and the 'upliftment' strategies being employed by the RSS in Mohanpur. Two strategies in particular have been met with widespread local support: improved access to biomedical treatment options and the enforcement of basic monetary entitlements. My concern in the next two chapters is to examine how the employment of these strategies, which are modelled after successful Church initiatives, has not only legitimized the presence and wider agenda of the RSS, but has gone some way in counteracting the influence of the Church. As we shall see later in the book, the specific focus of groups like the RSS on such strategies is viewed as necessary to make the nationalist discourse locally meaningful and available to *adivasis*.

CHAPTER FOUR

Health, Biomedicine and the RSS

About two months into my fieldwork, I met Durga, a frail-looking Hindu woman who walked with a strong limp due to a dirty, infected lesion on her ankle. This lesion was the latest in a six-week spell of bad health, which had begun with the onset of minor aches and culminated most recently in a ten-day period of high fever and delirium. I naively suggested to her father-in-law, the village headman, that perhaps she should see a doctor about the lesion. He promptly told me that the infection was not a case of *sadharan bimari* (simple illness), treatable by doctors and biomedicine; her illness was *bhuti bimari* (supernatural illness; literally 'ghost's illness'), caused by her husband's (the headman's eldest son) neglect in propitiating a powerful local deity during a recent family *puja*. In revenge, this deity had become angry and threatened to take Durga's life. Only the divination efforts of local healers and the promise of an offering of several goats and fowls saved her from certain death.

This chance meeting with the headman while his daughter-in-law was ill, provided me with my first glimpse of local conceptions of illness and healing. Illness[1] (*bimari*), I found, is inextricably linked to beliefs about cosmology and conceived by local people to be the product of divine disapproval of human misconduct. As illustrated

---

[1] I use the term 'illness' instead of disease to refer to both the patient's subjective experience of being unwell and the patient's objective condition. It is important to note, however, that the terms 'illness' and 'disease' remain contested categories within the medical anthropology literature (see Kleinman 1988; Reznek 1987).

in the headman's response to my suggestion, members of the local Hindu community in particular remain firmly committed to the idea of supernatural illness and treatment.

In the discussion that follows, detailed ethnographic attention is paid to the beliefs, practices that revolve around local conceptions of illness and causality that underpin local treatment alternatives. This discussion is necessary in order to better understand the strategies that the Church and the RSS are employing to discourage local people's commitment to 'backward' '*jangli*' ideas about supernatural illness and healing. While the increasing legitimacy of biomedical treatment in this area can largely be attributed to the influence of the Church, the corresponding decline of supernatural modes of healing has not occurred as it has elsewhere in India (cf. Lambert 1992: 1070).[2] Instead, supernatural treatment and other 'backward' methods continue to be a legitimate and respected avenue for healing to which both Christians and Hindus regularly turn. Two prevailing norms that represent what the Church and the RSS have categorized as being particularly '*jangli*' concern, the practice of swiftly discarding biomedicine in favour of supernatural techniques, and the belief that biomedical and supernatural treatment should never be mixed.

It is ostensibly in response to the persistence of these 'backward' practices that the Church and the RSS are actively engaged in introducing and advocating biomedicine to local people. Like the efforts described in the previous chapters that are underpinned by the inculcation of 'proper' forms of worship, these strategies are at the centre of the broader 'civilizing mission' (Skaria 1999) in which both the Church and the RSS are involved locally. In this chapter, I am most interested in the strategy recently employed by the local RSS activists: the sponsorship and installation of a biomedical 'doctor' in the village. Purportedly aimed at curtailing local people's commitment to 'supernatural medicine', I argue that this tactic serves as another means by which the organization is attempting to emulate the success and counteract the local dominance of the Church. The broader objective is to gain local legitimacy and attract support from the village community as a whole.

[2]In this book, the term 'biomedicine' refers to 'allopathic' or 'western medicine'. Locally, the terms '*sadharan*' (simple), '*goli, sui-pani*' (pills, injections), '*angrezi davai*' (English medicine) or '*sikshit davai*' (educated medicine) are sometimes used to refer to the same medicine. See Lambert (1988; 1997b: 193) for further discussion on this terminology; see also Carstairs (1928: 141).

Local Conceptions of Illness Causality

The issue of causal reasoning about illness has attracted continuing anthropological interest since the time of Tylor (1974[1879]), although James Frazer (2002 [1922]) was perhaps the first anthropologist specifically to make note of 'the manner by which man attributes pains and mishaps to the spite or anger of the spirits' (p. 547) in his writings on primitive magic. Lay theories of illness causality found in early anthropological studies were rarely set apart from larger categories of misfortune. Evans-Pritchard (1937) was one of the first ethnographers to focus specifically on a set of causal explanations for general misfortunes, under which illness and other calamities were categorized (cf. Gillies 1976). Early studies of illness were also integrated within studies of religion, magical or ritual practices (Wyman and Kluckhon 1938) or symbolic systems (e.g. Turner 1968; see Sindzingre 1995: 73).

Numerous ethnographies since have shifted from an examination of illness-as-misfortune to illness as a specific social category and object of analysis (cf. Lewis 1975; for specific examples within India, see Carstairs 1955; Fuchs 1964; Hasan 1967 and Marriott 1955). Such studies have also been concerned with proposing multiple analytic categories that serve to differentiate laypersons' theories of illness causality.[3] A common feature of these accounts is the distant or exogenous nature of causality, where the event that triggers off the illness is the result of factors external to the victim.[4] Such factors can

[3]Foster (1976), for example, has differentiated between personalistic systems, where illness is attributed to the active intervention of an agent (such as a supernatural being) and naturalistic systems, where illness is explained in terms of particular events or natural states that preceded the illness (cf. Wilkinson 1988: 47). Goody (1962), and later Lewis (1975), recognized three levels of illness causation: the agent, the methods behind the illness, and the reasons. Here, the individual, natural, social and supernatural causes are not mutually exclusive but are viewed to be linked together in each particular case (cf. Helman 2000). See also Dube (1955).

[4]This is similar to Young's (1982) classification of belief systems about illness causality as 'externalizing', which concentrates mainly on the aetiology of the illness that is believed to arise outside the sick person's body, as compared to 'internalizing', which concentrates less on aetiological explanations and more on events that occur inside the individual's body. More recent work (e.g. Schweder et al. 1997) has taken these distinctions further by framing them in terms of three 'causal ontologies': interpersonal (where blame for suffering is externalized: others are held responsible), moral (where suffering is a consequence of personal transgressions, misdemeanours

be either human or non-human, subjectivised or endowed with intentionality (cf. Sindzingre 1995: 74).

While this short overview of the anthropological literature on illness causality is by no means exhaustive, it is evident that the supernatural continues to be everywhere immanent as an explanation of illness causality (cf. Murdock 1980). In the ethnography that follows, we shall see how ideas of supernatural causality predominate in Mohanpur.

As illustrated in Durga's case, local ideas about illness causality are broadly divided into two categories: 'simple'(*sadharan bimari*), caused by natural factors and cured by tablets/injection (*goli / sui pani*) or by herbal medicines from the jungle (*jaributi*); and 'supernatural' (*bhuti bimari*), caused by an angry ancestor spirit or deity, and cured through divination and ritual offerings.[5] All types of illnesses can be classified as either 'simple' or 'supernatural'. Simple illnesses are normally attributed to causes that are related to the season or to specific, identifiable circumstances. For example, a headache is often said to be due to exhaustion and too much 'hard work' during the summer; stomach ache or diarrhoea is frequently blamed on 'bad' water or the over-consumption of seasonal food items such as mangos or wild mushrooms; and fever is commonly attributed to the onset of cold weather. Similar to Lambert's (1997b: 195) observations on illness classification in rural Rajasthan, the classification of an illness locally is contingent upon the efficacy of the cure: if an illness is quickly cured through biomedical techniques, then it is said to be 'simple'; if not, then it is immediately suspected to be supernatural. There is no conception of an 'incurable' or 'terminal' illness: it is assumed at the onset of illness that the patient will recover, if not through 'simple' then through 'supernatural' means. An illness that results in an untimely death will invariably be attributed by villagers to supernatural causes.

When someone falls ill, the general pattern is to first try biomedical treatment, which usually consists of pills or an injection. As we shall see below, this pattern is illustrative of the increasing legitimacy that biomedicine has gained over the past decade, largely due to the presence of the Church dispensary in the neighbouring village. If the patient makes a swift and straightforward recovery, then the illness

---

and personal debts) and biomedical (where suffering is a by-product of events and circumstances that take place outside the realms of human action).

[5]In this chapter, I am specifically referring to physical illness, or *saril bimari*. What is locally regarded as 'mad' (*pagli*) behaviour, and what western society might categorize as 'mental' or 'psychological' illness is always classified as 'supernatural' illness.

is classified as 'simple'. The particulars of 'simple' illness vary only in terms of what the patient or the health practitioner diagnose to be the specific cause: contaminated water, exhaustion, mosquitoes. Typically, there is no further discussion of the specificities of the illness.

If the treatment fails and the illness continues beyond what is considered to be an appropriate period of time (usually between one and three days), then it is suspected to be supernatural and a healer will be summoned. It is interesting to note that, in this particular area, the failure of biomedical treatment is not attributed, in the manner described by Nichter (1996a), to the perception of power behind the medicine or strength of the dose. Instead, it is attributed to the nature and category of the illness itself: 'simple' illnesses will, by definition, be cured rapidly and through 'simple' (biomedical) means; 'supernatural' illnesses will not.

It is very rare that an illness will be re-classified as 'simple' or natural once it has been diagnosed as supernatural. It is also held that no amount of tablets or injections will cure a supernatural illness, and that no degree of mixing biomedical and supernatural treatments is permitted. Furthermore, it is believed that consulting a medical expert in such cases will cause additional anger to the affronted deity or spirit, endangering the well being of the family or community as a whole, and resulting in the death of the patient.[6]

Once an illness is classified as supernatural, there can be no progression in terms of the patient's recovery until the cause is determined. Divining a cause can sometimes be very complicated, due to the 'multiple levels of causation' (Foster 1976: 780), which makes it necessary to identify both a causal agent, to whom ritual amends must be made, and a reason, to avoid repeating the transgression in future (cf. Lewis 1975: 65). Supernatural illnesses are usually related to a variety of transgressions of the sort described in Chapter Two, such as breaking ritual taboos, neglecting propitiatory obligations, and trespassing on sacred ground.[7] Like elsewhere in central India (cf. Padel 1995: 122), supernatural beings are said to react to such

[6]While Marriott (1955: 239–68) made similar observations in a north Indian village, where the causal agent is likely to become more angry if direct medication is applied to his abode in the body, this rule appears to be more flexible elsewhere in north India (see also Lambert 1997b: 194–7).

[7]This is not unlike similar conceptions found throughout other parts of India. See Khare (1963), Lambert (1997a), Sargent and Johnson (1996) and Worsley (1982), for further discussion on the connection between human conduct and supernatural punishment; cf. Evans Pritchard (1937: 74).

transgressions by 'catching' (*pakarna*) or 'eating' people's souls. Regarded as a kind of possession, supernatural illness can also be attributed to witchcraft or to random encounters with ghosts, in the form of a sudden and accidental meeting with a spirit along a forest path. At times, the cause of an illness will be attributed simultaneously to numerous agents—ghosts, angry deities, and witchcraft—all to whom the patient and her family will have to make ritual amends.

When the identity of the deity has been determined, a minor *puja* is performed where the deity is promised a blood offering upon the patient's recovery (see Lambert 1997a for comparison). The ritual at which the deity's demands are met serves as a sort of 'atonement' for angering the deity. This ritual usually takes place around three months after the patient's recovery. The purpose of this delay is to 'test' the diagnosis: if no additional suffering befalls the patient, then the affronted deity and its demands are said to have been correctly identified and satisfactorily placated; if the patient remains unwell, then it is thought that other supernatural beings are involved, and another round of healing rituals is undertaken. The demands of all causal agents identified by various healers must be met upon the patient's recovery, irrespective of whether one healer's methods failed to evoke a cure.

Those who participate in this final ritual include the healers who conducted the rituals and all male elders who were present at the time. The blood offering (usually a fowl or a goat) is made to the deity as a mark of appreciation for 'removing of the cause of misfortune' (Helman 2000: 238). It is then cooked and consumed by all but the patient, who is prohibited from partaking of the cooked offering. It is believed that if the patient consumes the offering, which has been given to the deity in exchange for good health, then he is effectively annulling this exchange. The result is a return of the illness.[8]

Like those outlined in the previous two chapters, such beliefs and practices are representative of the kind of 'backward' *adivasi* or '*jangli*' traditions criticized by the Church and the RSS. As we shall see later in this chapter, increasingly systematic effort is being made by both

[8]This act of restricting the consumption of the sacrifice to the elders arguably has a pragmatic element, for it is an opportunity for the elders to consume meat, a rare and expensive food item. Indeed, it is sometimes said by more cynical locals that this ritual (and very tasty) 'return of services' is part of the incentive for more devious healers to regularly divine blood offerings.

the Church and the RSS to discourage local people's engagement in such practices. For now, I turn to an examination of the healing and treatment options that are most preferred locally.

Local Treatment Alternatives

Whether biomedical practitioner or local healer, the act of consulting an expert for treatment indicates that the patient and her family want two things: that the affliction and causal agent should be named and made familiar, and that the prediction should be made that 'she will recover' (Worsley 1982: 317).[9] When I first began my fieldwork, villagers had two biomedical treatment options: the Catholic-run medical clinic and dispensary, located in the neighbouring village of Manpur; or the itinerant government healthcare worker. I knew of very few people who actually consulted the latter, due to the infrequency and unpredictability of his visits to the village. Instead most villagers went to the dispensary. The latter was located one-hour's walking distance (6 km) from the village, and patients had to wait an additional hour before being seen by one of the nurses. Such visits often took up the better part of a day, and few people could afford this kind of time away from routine agricultural and household labour.

The primary illnesses for which local people travel to the dispensary include cough, diarrhoea, malaria, headache, fever and general weakness. Ordinarily, the patient is given no more than a three-day course of pills, which are individually wrapped in small paper sachets and dispensed along with careful instructions about how to take them. The patient is also told to return after the course is completed for a check-up. For more serious illnesses like malaria, the patient is given an injection along with the tablets and told to return the next day for a follow-up examination and a second injection. In extreme cases, the patient might be intravenously given bottles of glucose water, and possibly kept at the dispensary overnight for observation. Emergency cases are rushed to the city by jeep.

Whereas the primary biomedical alternative was the dispensary, the supernatural treatment choices included a range of healers, known

---

[9]Similarly, Trawick (1992) holds that one of the principal functions of the healer is to substitute meaning for the apparent meaninglessness of sickness and death, and so to lend courage to the sick and dying. See also Carstairs (1955) and Henry (1977: 309).

locally, as *gunias*. Sometimes referred to as 'shaman' or 'exorcist' in the wider literature on central India (cf. Vitebsky 1993; Hardiman n.d.; Padel 1995), a *gunia* is a ritual specialist who has been specially trained to divine illness and communicate with local deities through trance or possession. At the time of my fieldwork there were eight *gunias* (five Hindus and three Christians) who lived in the village. All of them were male (although it is not uncommon for women to become a *gunia*); and all had received their knowledge from a combination of the long process of apprenticeship to another *gunia* and their secret 'guardian' deity (*angrakshak*), who regularly instructs them through the medium of possession or dreams (cf. Sargent and Johnson 1996: 116).

The practices in which the Oraon Christians and the Hindus engage with respect to supernatural illness and healing are very similar, and it is for this reason that I do not distinguish between them in this chapter. All local *gunias*, for instance, are skilled at divining illnesses through a variety of techniques. These include *mantras*, or sacred prayers that are targeted to specific deities or ailments; *jhar-phukna*, a well-documented ritual action where neem leaves are used in an attempt to 'sweep and blow' the disease downward and out of the patient's body (see for example Lambert 1997a, Allen 1976, Hitchcock and Jones 1976 and Hasan 1967); *patta dekhno*, where the cause of illness is divined through looking into the depths of a *sal* leaf; *dhan ginte*, where scattered grains of seed rice are counted and 'read'; and trance or possession. *Gunias* also draw on a range of knowledge about local medicinal herbs and plants, which they routinely prescribe to the patient as part of the healing process.

Compared to elsewhere in India (cf. Nichter 1996b), cost does not figure in the decision to call one particular *gunia* over another, since direct remuneration beyond a meal or a bottle of liquor is not expected. Routine items used in healing rituals and for special offerings demanded by a vengeful deity can be costly for the patient's family. However, such costs are dissociated from the *gunia's* payment. It is for this reason that healing is not the primary occupation of any local *gunias*. Instead, and in common with other villagers, all *gunias* support their households through a combination of rice cultivation and the collection and sale of non-timber forest products.

It is important to note that while *gunias* can be renowned for a particular skill in divination, they will neither be credited with a patient's recovery nor blamed for a failed divination that may, in the worst-case scenario, result in a patient's death. The *gunia* is regarded only as a mediator who identifies and communicates the wishes and demands of the supernatural agent, which itself is ultimately recognized as the power behind the patient's recovery or death.

Although *gunias* are not credited with the patient's recovery, the decision to consult one particular healer over another is based in part, on his reputed powers of healing. Certain *gunias*, for example, will be consulted because of their knowledge of a particular *mantra* or for their abilities to cure a particular ailment. Others are preferred because of the mutual familiarity established between them and their patients. Indeed, it has been observed by many writers that there is a necessity for healers to be familiar with the patient's 'social field' and the conflicts that surround her (Turner 1964: 243). *Gunias* are able to gain this sort of knowledge both by living within the same social space as the patient and by questioning the family before the start of the healing sequence about the patient's (and other family members') recent movements and interactions. Referring to the kind of knowledge that is gleaned in this manner, Helman (1994) observes that 'there is likely to be a component of shrewd observations and experience on the part of the healer as to why and how people get ill' (1994: 230). This kind of experience undoubtedly contributes to the efficacy of the healing experience.

It could be argued, of course, that a basic familiarity with the patient's 'social field' is equally important to biomedical practitioners. In an attempt to identify the exact nature and cause of the illness, nurses at the dispensary will regularly query the patient about his illness, his recent food intake, his travels, and the state of his family's health. However, the important difference between a nurse and a *gunia* is the fact that, by virtue of being resident in the village, the latter invariably plays a critical and often very personal role in the patient's life. He is not only a healer who is charged with the care of a patient; he also occupies the role of neighbour, uncle, brother, drinking partner or respected elder—all of which are underpinned by complex social obligations. The nurses, in contrast, remain distant and unfamiliar with the activities and social relations that help the *gunia* in his diagnosis. As I suggest below, the kind of proximity and familiarity that local people share with *gunias* plays an important part in the continued prominence and preference for supernatural over biomedical treatment. As we shall also see later on, it is precisely these issues that help to explain local people's response to the installation of a biomedical 'doctor' by the RSS.

Because of their skill and reputation for engaging with the supernatural and treating various afflictions, *gunias* have traditionally enjoyed a strong reputation amongst Hindus and Christians alike. In addition to healing the supernaturally caused afflictions of individuals, *gunias* also manage the health and sickness of the village as a whole. Here, they serve as 'mediators' between humans and the divine at all seasonal rituals and annual festivals in which communication with local deities and ancestor spirits through possession is required.

The Church and *Bhuti Bimari*

As we saw in the previous chapter, there is a real tension between the dualistic rhetoric of good and evil that Oraons learn from the Church, and the varying gradations of good and evil that underpin their traditional practices and beliefs. It is in the realm of illness and healing that this tension is most felt by ordinary people. It is also this realm that provides the greatest obstacle to the Church's attempts to inculcate 'proper' Christian practice.

It is traditionally believed by all local people—Christians and Hindus alike—that illness and misfortune stem from committing some kind of ritual transgression, which can only be rectified through the intervention of healers, through *puja*, and through the promise of ritual offerings. What the Oraons seem to be learning from Christian tradition, in contrast, is that illness and misfortune stem from the withdrawal of Jesus' presence, due to a general weakness of faith and continued indulgence in *shaitan ka kam*. Illness and healing are also inextricably linked to *viswas* (faith, belief). Oraons are taught that illness represents a sort of *pariksha* (test) through which Jesus determines an individual's level of faith. If the patient opts for and continues with biomedical treatment, then she is said to have *viswas* in Jesus. If she consults a healer, then it is generally assumed that her *viswas* has waned and Jesus has abandoned her. It is believed by most Oraons that if the patient's *viswas* is strong enough and comes 'from the heart', then Jesus will evoke a cure.

The manner in which faith and healing are equated by Oraons is connected to early missionization strategies in India. According to Hardiman (n.d.), the 'medical missionaries' who proselytized amongst *adivasis* of Western India from the latter part of the nineteenth century onward believed that healing was brought about partly through medical skill and partly through prayer. It was also believed that western medicine was one way of expressing God's power (cf. Moorshead 1913: 15).[10] Indeed, many missionaries believed that in certain cases, patients could be cured by faith in Christ alone.

The propagation of the view that medicine could be used 'not only to care and cure but also to Christianize' (Fitzgerald 2001: 89) was not unique to Christian missionaries who worked amongst *adivasi* communities. In his research on the role of missionaries in the mid-nineteenth century creation of a South Indian princely state (in what is modern day Kerala), for example, Kawashima (1998: 138) quotes a nineteenth century missionary report on how medical work was believed to 'enable the Mission to touch the hearts of classes who otherwise are likely to remain shut up in their Heathenism ...'. To this end, high caste patients who visited hospitals and dispensaries were regularly 'taught Christianity' in the belief that this would aid '... the struggle against demonism and superstition' (ibid. 138–9; cf. Cavalier 1899; Dennis 1899).[11] The idea that people are cured as much through the power of faith in Jesus as through the power of biomedicine and nurses' skill continues to underpin contemporary Christian proselytization practices.

While local Oraons seem to subscribe to this ideology, they also believe that strong faith is sometimes not sufficient. Take the example of my friend and research assistant, Sumitra. Considered to be an *asli* Christian by local Oraons, Sumitra went to mass faithfully every week and generally had no tolerance for anything related to s*haitan ka kam*. Some years ago, Sumitra's father had purchased a piece of land from some Hindu neighbours. At that time he was warned that, as the new owner of the land, he must continue the seven-yearly goat

[10]The skills of medical doctors in the first half of the nineteenth century were seldom sought by either Catholic or Protestant missions. This is attributed by Williams (1982: 271–2) partly to the early conviction that medical work was likely to distract from the true missionary object of conversion to Christ, and partly to the fact that the medical profession had not, until the mid-nineteenth century, attained a professional and respectable reputation (cf. Fitzgerald 2001).

[11]For comparative examples, see Cavalier (1899) for a discussion on medical missionary work across northern India. See also Moorshead (1913) for a general discussion of the appeal of medical missions in Africa and China, as well as in India; see Ranger (1982) for a discussion of the history of Anglicanism in relation to healing in Africa; and Dennis (1899) for details on medical missionary work in Japan, Western Asia and China.

sacrifice to the deity who resided in the field or face divine retribution. In spite of this warning, he neglected to give the offering because, he explains, 'we are Christian and do not believe in *shaitan*'.

When Sumitra first became ill halfway through my fieldwork, she dutifully went off to the dispensary where she was prescribed a course of tablets and given an injection for malaria. She returned for two additional injections, but her condition deteriorated. In desperation, her father called a local Hindu healer, who determined that Sumitra had in fact been 'caught' (possessed) by the field deity, which had been angered by the family's refusal to make the obligatory sacrifice. Upon learning this, Sumitra's father vowed to do the *puja*, whereupon she slowly recovered.

Before this incident, Sumitra had been fond of telling me, rather smugly, how '*katta* people believe in the devil and Kurukh people believe in 'Jesu'. These sorts of comments usually came after she had witnessed some kind of *shaitan ka puja* while passing through the Hindu *basti*. After her recovery, Sumitra admitted that she now had a little *viswas* in *shaitan ka kam*, and her father agreed that 'we now have to respect this field deity'.

The actions and words of Sumitra and her father serve to illuminate the tensions between the Oraons and the Church. According to the priests, recourse to supernatural treatment at the time of illness is an example of weak faith; as maintained by the Oraons, it is an example of Jesus' withdrawal of protection at the most critical time of need. In Sumitra's case, Jesus 'turned away' in spite of her strong *viswas*, which was demonstrated by her piety and her choice of biomedical treatment. There appears to be no guarantee, in other words, that Jesus will protect the Oraons in their time of need. It is when Jesus inexplicably turns his back in this manner, irrespective of the Oraons' *viswas*, that the latter 'backslide' (Meyer 1996: 217) into their traditional Kurukh practices.

Gunias are particularly illustrative of the tension that the Oraons feel between their commitment to Jesus and their traditional deities. While not as prominent as the two deceased *gunias* mentioned in the previous chapter, the three Oraon men who currently engage in supernatural healing alongside the five Hindu *gunias* represent a direct opposition to both the authority of the local priests and to the biomedicine propagated by the Church. The priests see these men as propagators of the devil who both act as direct mediators between ordinary people and Satan, and who help to lure members of the local congregation back into their heathen ways. They are often the subject of Sunday sermons, where the lay congregation is discouraged from consulting them and indulging in what the priests have categorized as *andhviswas*, or superstitious activities. They are also regularly summoned by the priests to confess their 'sins'.

Most Oraons, however, see *gunias* as individuals whose valuable knowledge and relationship with various supernatural beings have saved many. *Gunias* themselves, moreover, do not view their practices as conflicting with Christian beliefs; nor do they regard themselves as having 'given' their *viswas* to Satan. Let us return to Manglu, whom we met in the previous chapter. A renowned healer whose skills extend to snake charming and snakebite cures, Manglu is quite proud of his knowledge and ability to cure people. His methods include a variety of secret *mantras* that invoke Shankar, known locally as the 'snake god'. These are combined with herbal medicines that are taken orally. Manglu sees no contradiction in what he is doing (saving people from certain death) and in what Jesus demands (*viswas*), and wonders why the priests are constantly after him to confess his participation in what they deem to be 'Satan's work'.

Another example concerns a healer called Gervani *gunia*, one of the few Oraons who faithfully attends mass every Sunday. Gervani *gunia* is generally considered by most Oraons to be an *asli* (genuine) Christian, and I was very surprised to discover, several months into my fieldwork, that he was also a practising healer. Gervani *gunia* uses the *patta dekhno* method, in which he 'sees' the cause of illness in the depths of a leaf. While such practices are held by the priests to be indisputably the work of Satan, Gervani *gunia* remains steadfast in his conviction that he is doing nothing in which Jesus would be disappointed. He contrasts the *patta dekhno* technique with the *supa* method employed by other local *gunias*, where uncooked rice is stirred rhythmically in a winnowing basket while the healer induces his own possession and 'gives his body' to the possessing deity. In Gervani's words, '*supa kam* (the *supa* method) is real *shaitan ka kam*. I never give my *viswas* to Satan; I never use the *supa*. I only have visions in the leaf. This is why my heart is clean.'

As we saw in the previous chapter, there is no strong consensus about what precisely constitutes *shaitan ka kam*. For healers as well as for ordinary Oraon Christians, this issue seems to be related to possession, or the process by which a person gives his body, along with his *viswas*, to a particular deity or ancestor spirit. Neither Manglu nor Gervani see their respective healing techniques as acts wherein deities (or *shaitan*) are summoned. By extension, they see no contradiction between what they are doing—healing people through *mantras* and divination—and maintaining *viswas* in Jesus. Local Church authorities, however, view these as superstitious practices that unequivocally represent the work of Satan. It is for the purpose of discouraging engagement in such practices that the priests have instituted strict measures like imposing costly fines and outcasting errant members.

Efficacy and Power of Supernatural and Biomedicine

It is in the context of their work at the dispensary that the Sisters and priests regularly see what they maintain are the consequences of supernatural healing. Their strong opposition to such practices is not reserved for their Oraon Christian flock alone; they often express dismay and concern for the local Hindus, who make up the majority of their patient list at the dispensary. Local *adivasis'* engagement in *shaitan ka kam*, I was told by one of the sisters who works in the dispensary, creates 'unnecessary suffering', particularly amongst Hindus, who will often refuse biomedical treatment until it is too late.

As mentioned above, supernatural healing is particularly representative of the kind of '*jangli*' practices that both the Church and the RSS oppose. As *gunias* are the kind of people most steeped in such practices, moreover, they are the individuals who are considered to be the strongest opponents of the efforts promoted by Church officials and the RSS. To be sure, *gunias* have always been the primary mediators between humans and the divine. This kind of responsibility has contributed to the authority and respect that they have traditionally enjoyed locally. Indeed, most *gunias* saw the arrival of biomedicine in the 1970s (in the form of the Church dispensary) as a threat to this authority. As a consequence, *gunias* provided the strongest resistance to the introduction of biomedicine. They did so by actively discouraging local people from visiting the dispensary and warning that such actions would result in the increased wrath of local deities and ancestor spirits. According to both local people and the nurses, it was the latter that contributed most markedly to the relatively low numbers of (especially Hindu) patients during the early years of the dispensary's existence.

Such resistance has weakened since then, and biomedicine is no longer viewed as threatening the *gunias*. One reason for this is related to its obvious efficacy. It is undeniable to local people that biomedicine successfully treats certain kinds of ailments, such as fever, rash, and stomach problems, and nowadays, even *gunias* send their families to the dispensary or summon a health worker at the first sign of illness. While biomedicine is effective for some illnesses, however, it is not effective for all, and both *gunias* and local people realize that there will always be an imperative necessity for supernatural healing. Indeed, it is perhaps for this reason that the local distinction between simple and supernatural illness endures. Another reason is connected to the *gunias'* wider position in the village, which goes beyond their role of healer. As the primary mediator between humans and the divine, *gunias* play an integral part in life-cycle rituals and annual festivals. A nominal threat to their role as healers by the increasing legitimacy of biomedicine in no way jeopardizes their larger position as ritual leaders.

The refusal of local *adivasis* to completely turn away from superstitious practices is one issue about which the RSS holds similar views to the Church. According to the local RSS *pracharak*, Raj, the greatest hindrance to the RSS's 'civilizing' efforts amongst *adivasis* is *andhviswas*: the superstition that underpins supernatural illness and healing and that leads local people to discard biomedicine in favour of supernatural therapies. As outlined earlier, *andhviswas* is characterized by the practices and beliefs that underpin traditional *adivasi* cosmology and worship, including the propitiation of ancestor spirits and local deities with alcohol and blood offerings, and the mediation between such beings and local people through the vehicle of possession. It is the eradication of *andhviswas*, which is opposed to both 'proper' Hindu and Christian practices, that underpins and, in the view of their proponents, justifies the Church and the RSS's respective 'civilizing missions'.

Abandoning and Blending Medicine

One of the issues about which both the Church and the RSS are particularly frustrated is the practice of prematurely abandoning biomedical treatment in favour of supernatural methods. As mentioned above, the efficacy of biomedicine is demonstrated by the patient's rapid recovery, although the degree to which this is measured differs for the Christian and Hindu communities. As demonstrated with Sumitra's case, Oraon Christians are more likely to return to the dispensary several times over several days or weeks for biomedical intervention before resorting to supernatural treatment. In contrast, the majority of the Hindus will typically make an assessment soon after the first pills are taken: if the patient does not recover shortly after the initial injection or dose of pills, then a *gunia* will be summoned.

To illustrate, when my friend Bijay, a young Ratiya Kanwar man, became ill, he immediately went off to the dispensary. There, he was diagnosed with 'ordinary fever', given an injection and a three-day course of tablets, and instructed by the nurses to return for a check-up. When his fever continued after the first day's dosage, he was convinced that his illness was *bhut ka*. He promptly called a local healer called Deheria *gunia*, who checked Bijay's wrist in order to ascertain that the illness was in fact 'supernatural'. This is a routine practice for healers in this area and elsewhere in India (see Carstairs 1955 and Lambert 1996). Occasionally, healers might discover that the illness is 'simple' after all, and they advise the patient to return to the doctor or continue the initial course of prescribed medicines. In Bijay's case, the rapid 'blinking' of his pulse indicated that he had indeed been 'caught' (*pakarna*) by an unknown spirit.

Returning the following evening, Deheria *gunia* moved on to what Helman (2000: 238) calls the diagnostic or 'divination' phase of the ritual. Here, he used the *dhan ginte* (seed-rice counting) method described above to determine that the illness was due to the random encounter that Bijay had with a nameless *bhut*. The exact identity of the *bhut* and the specific details of the offence remained vague, but these were not important: a causal agent and transgression had been found. After establishing the *bhut*'s demands, a minor *puja* was performed wherein Deheria *gunia* promised that an offering of two hens and a coconut would be made as soon as Bijay recovered.

One explanation for the local pattern of quickly discarding biomedical treatment after the initial dose is the assumption that if the illness is 'simple' then the patient should make a recovery soon after taking biomedicine. This assumption, based on people's experience, is buttressed by the fact that people *do* regularly recover after a particular dose of biomedical treatment. By this logic, if a patient *does not* recover after taking the same kind of medicine, then the illness must be supernatural.

Another explanation is related to the presumed efficacy of the medicine. In supernatural cases, if the cause of illness has been identified and the promise of a blood offering extracted—stages in the course of treatment that could together be encompassed within a sort of 'dose' of supernatural medicine—then the patient should expect to recover. In the event that a particular divination and promise of offerings have failed to initiate the expected recovery, subsequent divinations will never reveal the identical causal agent; a second or follow-up 'dose' of the same 'ritual' medicine, in other words, will never be prescribed. Indeed, this would be viewed as ineffectual and pointless, and additional divination rituals will invariably reveal a different causal agent.

I suggest that there is a parallel expectation with respect to the presumed power of biomedicine and the view that a second dose of the same medicine will not be effective. When I asked people why they did not complete their prescribed course, I was invariably told that 'the medicine did not work', proof of which was in the fact that the patient did not recover after the initial dose. Following the above pattern, where the same agent is never identified more than once as the cause of illness, it is believed that a second dose of the same biomedicine will be ineffective, particularly if the first dose has failed to produce the desired result. It is this kind of belief that is considered to be particularly 'backward' by both the Church and the RSS.

In addition to the regular practice of abandoning biomedical treatment in favour of supernatural therapies, a second issue that concerns both the Church and RSS is the persisting belief that the blending of biomedical and supernatural techniques is very dangerous. It is useful to illustrate this with an extended ethnographic example that involves Kirtan, a lively four-year-old Ratiya Kanwar boy who had been down with fever for nearly two weeks. Following the usual pattern, no further attempt to seek biomedical treatment had been made after Kirtan was initially prescribed pills for 'fever' by the itinerant health worker. When his condition did not improve, his parents consulted a local *gunia*, Mahu, who attributed Kirtan's illness to his father's failure to propitiate the village deity, Mahadev, at a family *puja*. A minor offering was made, along with the promise to sacrifice a goat to the deity as soon as Kirtan became well.

Instead of recovering, Kirtan's condition continued to deteriorate. I was particularly fond of Kirtan and, at my suggestion, his parents agreed to take him to the dispensary to be examined by a nurse. This was dangerous, for Kirtan's illness had already been classified as 'supernatural'; as such, disrespecting the deity's demands would risk additional wrath. Kirtan's parents agreed only if Mahu accompanied them to the dispensary. Seeing his condition, the nurse suspected malaria and advised Kirtan's parents to keep him at the clinic overnight for further observation. His parents insisted on taking him home. After giving Kirtan an injection to reduce his fever, the nurse instructed his parents to give him three doses of a 'strength-giving' tonic and two chloroquine tablets later that evening, and to return first thing the following morning for another injection.

Kirtan's condition seemed to improve after he reached home, and his parents wondered aloud if perhaps his illness was 'simple' after all. Several hours later, however, his fever returned: a sure sign that his illness was in fact 'supernatural'. The journey to the dispensary had been a grave mistake; the deity was clearly angry. As his fever raged into the evening, I suggested that Kirtan should be taken straight back to the dispensary for urgent treatment. But his parents adamantly refused and insisted that their decision to take my advice in the first place was the reason that Kirtan was in his current state. Later in the night, his fever finally broke and his body became cool: a sign to Kirtan's family that death was imminent.[12] As Kirtan displayed a weakening pulse and shallow breathing, his mother and grandmother began the customary death wail.

By now, there was a large cluster of people gathered outside his home, waiting for news of Kirtan's death. I had returned home for a quick meal and discussed the case with some of my Oraon neighbours. Their views were predictable: 'It is very difficult to make *katta* people understand', I was told by my 'brother', Bahadur. 'They have no faith in Jesus and no respect for pills and injections, only for *bhut.*' Another man agreed that this was why Hindus often die of illnesses like malaria. Oraon people, it seems are protected 'because they pray to 'Jesu' and go to the dispensary'.

The Oraons' belief in the relative superiority of biomedicine appears to be based as much on their conviction of Jesus' superior power over that of local deities (or *shaitan*) as it is on their relative confidence in biomedical therapies. One day, I queried a local Hindu elder about what he thought of the Oraons' well-known views of superiority with

---

[12]Local people believe that a cold body is a strong indication that death is near, and female relatives will frantically try to ward off the inevitable by warming the patient's head and feet with their hands.

respect to treatment choices. He countered that it was the Oraons themselves who did not understand. 'Their deity is different; therefore their illnesses are different. We Hindus do not believe in their 'Jesu'. We have our own deities, and we must respect them. When we do not, they punish us through illness'. Indeed, the only time that local Hindus are vocally critical about the Oraons' treatment-seeking behaviour is when the latter refuse to consult a *gunia*, even after biomedical treatment has had no effect and the illness is clearly supernatural.

The Oraons were not alone in their assessment of Kirtan's case and the decision of his parents to continue with supernatural medicine. Raj, who had conducted a training meeting in the village the day that Kirtan's condition deteriorated, used the occasion to reiterate his complaints that *adivasi* people always wait until it is nearly too late before they seek biomedicine. 'This is the problem here,' he grumbled to me, when I saw him later at Kirtan's home. 'People in this village do not know what causes illness and they do not know how to take medicine. They have *andhviswas*. It will take years before they will learn.'

It had become evident to Mahu, the healer, that there were other beings responsible for Kirtan's illness. Had Mahadev been the sole being involved, then Kirtan's condition should have improved after the first set of demands had been issued. Cases such as this that do not respond to ordinary divination methods require more extreme forms of divination, which take the form of possession. The purpose here is to allow the illness-causing agent a voice through which it can make its identity and demands directly known. It was eventually discovered that multiple beings were responsible for Kirtan's illness. These included Mahadev who, as suspected, had become further angered when Kirtan was taken to the dispensary, along with a local ghost for reasons unknown and a jungle deity on whose land Kirtan's father had trespassed months before. Once the identity of these beings had been discovered, the healers promised that the combined demands (two goats and several hens) would be met as soon as Kirtan recovered. Sometime during the night, Kirtan's condition stabilized, and he eventually made a full recovery.

Preferences for Supernatural Healing

All of the cases described above were believed by those involved to be straightforward examples of supernatural illness, where no amount of biomedical intervention would have been effective. Evidence in the cases of Bijay and Sumitra was in the fact that, the patient did not respond to biomedical treatment; proof in Kirtan's case was his worsening condition after a resort to biomedicine in the midst of supernatural treatment. It is such experiences that drive people's treatment-seeking behaviour and reinforce local dogma about abandoning biomedicine and the dangers of blending treatments.

Two other factors have contributed to people's general unwillingness to follow through with their biomedical treatment or return to the dispensary for additional medicine. The first concerns cost and mode of payment. Costs of biomedicines, whether from the itinerant health worker or the dispensary, average around Rs 15–30 for each injection and three-day course of pills. Expenses can grow if additional injections, pills or glucose drips are needed, and in rare cases, people face costs of several hundred rupees. Significantly, payment is always demanded in cash.[13]

Locally, supernatural treatment can be considerably more expensive than biomedicine.[14] As mentioned above, *gunias* do not normally charge for their services, beyond a meal and a bottle of liquor, expenses that do not usually exceed Rs 15–20. Unlike observations made by Marriott (1955: 255) and Nichter (1996b), where gifts of food to healers are sometimes expected to precede the treatment, such 'fees' in Mohanpur are not required to be paid until the patient recovers. The patient, however, is responsible for procuring the basic items (liquor, coconut, incense) used in the ritual, the cost for which amounts to a minimum of Rs 30.

While biomedicine is generally less costly than supernatural treatment, one of the reasons that local Hindus give for not indulging more regularly in biomedical treatment is that they do not have the money. 'Doctors are too expensive', is the common refrain from the majority of my Hindu informants. Upon initial consideration, this assessment seemed to me to be incorrect: how could people afford a basic, upfront cost of Rs 30 for a *bimari puja*, and not afford the same for an injection and course of pills? At closer inspection, I realized

[13]See also Marriott (1955) and Lambert (1992) for discussions on how payment and expenses influence patient decision-making on type of treatment in western Rajasthan and northern India, respectively.

[14]Compare with Lambert's (1997a) observations that it is cheaper to take a patient to consult a local healer than to seek biomedical treatment in Rajasthan.

that what I was told was accurate: local Hindus generally have little cash, which is what biomedical practitioners demand for their services. In contrast, *gunias* (or supernatural beings) demand to be paid in ritual kind: coconut, rice, or beer. These are items that all Hindu families invariably have on hand. Additionally, each family owns at least some amount of small livestock (chickens, small goats) and can acquire other items through the exchange of seed-rice. In extreme cases, such as when a costly goat is urgently required for a sacrifice, households will mortgage a parcel of land (see Chapter 6).

Unlike the immediate (cash) payment demanded by nurses and health workers, moreover, the costs for supernatural treatments are spread out over time: the final payment, which is usually a blood offering, is not generally required until two or three months after the patient's recovery. Because they invariably possess the means to make the payment, and because the payment is delayed, Hindus can thus afford the costs for supernatural treatment more easily than they can afford biomedical treatment. It is true that seed-rice could easily be exchanged for cash to pay for biomedical treatment, but this does not appear to be a well-inculcated practice for the local Hindus.

In short, the two forms of treatment (biomedicine and supernatural) require two forms of payment (cash and kind). This fact appears to have influenced the treatment choices of the local Hindus, who typically have less cash, and for whom payment in ritual kind has always been the norm. Reasons for this will be further explored in Chapters Six and Seven. This becomes even more significant when compared to the Oraons, who normally pay for all of their goods, including their medicines and treatment, with cash acquired through wage labour.

The second factor that has contributed to local people's reluctance to fully embrace biomedical treatment is the time and distance-related inconvenience of the dispensary. While it has been the most reliable source of biomedicine in the area for nearly three decades, it is located six kilometres away, a substantial distance to travel by foot or cycle with an ill person in tow. It is only open in the morning and again for a few hours in the afternoon. Patients who visit during closing hours are told to wait and, unless it is an emergency, patients are never seen by the nurses at night. As noted above, visits to the dispensary can sometimes take up the greater part of the day and are thus thought by many local people to be inconvenient in all, but the most critical cases. In short, the trouble that a visit to the dispensary entails, particularly in comparison to the convenience of availing of the services of a local healer, invariably adds to villagers' reluctance to totally abandon their traditional healing practices.

In view of this, I asked the nurses why they insisted on giving patients pills to last them only three days, instead of giving them the entire six or seven-days' worth that normally comprises a 'course' of medicine. This would, after all, spare many patients a return trip to the dispensary and perhaps persuade a few to carry on with their treatment. I was told that the restriction of dosages allowed for careful monitoring of people who 'did not understand about the importance of taking medicine'.[15] This practice, moreover, saved money. 'Medicines are expensive,' one of the nurses complained, 'and local people do not appreciate this.' Her biases were revealed when she informed me that medicines are often wasted, especially by Hindu people 'who believe in the devil' and who throw their pills away even before the three-day course is finished. As illustrated in the ethnography presented in this chapter, it is true that Hindu patients as a whole, rarely return to the dispensary for follow-up examinations or additional doses of medicine. It is equally true that a small pile of disused pills 'that did not work' could be found lying in the corner of not only every Hindu household, but in Oraon Christian households as well.

Biomedicine and the RSS 'Doctor'

That biomedicine has gradually gained legitimacy in the past decade amongst ordinary people and *gunias* alike is evidenced by the fact that it has become the preferred first-stage treatment when an individual falls ill. This acceptance has been helped not only by the efficacy of this form of treatment, but by the presence of the Church dispensary, which has been utilized on at least one occasion by virtually all *adivasi* families. In spite of the effectiveness of biomedicine, however, the legitimacy of supernatural treatment endures for reasons outlined above. This persistence is of continuing concern for the Church and, more recently, for the RSS.

---

[15] This practice is also common amongst ayurvedic practitioners in South India, where *vaidyas* monitor the number of days' worth of medicine given to patients (see Nichter 1996a: 245). This has to do with what Nichter calls the 'lay cost reckoning', where, if costs of medicines go beyond patient's expectations, then the patient will likely not return for further medicine.

Aware that the distance between the dispensary and neighbouring villages is one factor that contributes to local people's attachment to traditional therapies, and in an effort to further encourage people to avail of biomedicine, in early 1998, the Church began an outreach programme where it conducted monthly 'health workshops' with select Oraon representatives from surrounding villages about the benefits of biomedicine. Held after Sunday mass, these representatives were given short lectures about the causes of the most common local illnesses, including malaria and dysentery, and about the kind of preventive measures that could be taken. They were then instructed to take their knowledge back to their own village and hold workshops amongst the local people. They were also given samples of basic medicines (including ordinary painkillers and chloroquine tablets) to distribute to whomever was in need. Local people—particularly the Oraons—appreciated the convenience that this scheme afforded. Availing of this medicine was generally preferred as a first resort to a time-consuming visit to the Church dispensary.

A similar kind of tactic is recorded in early missionary accounts. Known as 'itineration', or the practice whereby missionaries established periodic 'camps' in nearby villages for the purpose of preaching and encouraging people to come forward for medical treatment, this is a common way in which the Church has historically been able to establish its legitimacy and win the confidence of local people in western medicine (cf. Hardiman n.d.). While this contemporary version of 'itineration' has undoubtedly encouraged greater use of biomedicine, it is uncertain whether it has succeeded in diluting the efficacy of supernatural therapies. It has, however, served as an implicit means by which the Church has further enhanced its standing and presence in the village.

Several months after the Church began its outreach programme, another biomedical option came into being. Perceiving a need for a medical alternative to the itinerant government health worker and the distant dispensary, Raj and the other RSS *pracharaks* had been discussing the possible options for some months. Shortly after the introduction of the Church-sponsored workshops, it was decided that they should proceed with their plans to install their own 'doctor'. Raj's younger brother, Panchram, was approached for the role. He was an obvious choice, with his stated interest in *vigyan* (science), his desire to make use of his Class XII education and his familial connection and sympathetic ties with the RSS. Through the sponsorship of the Korba-based RSS branch, Panchram undertook a three-month training course in primary healthcare. After he finished this course in late 1998, Raj announced in a local *panchayat* meeting that Panchram's training was complete. All villagers were encouraged to consult the new 'doctor' whenever they became ill. A red cross was painted above the front door of Panchram's family home, and Raj made a point of emphasizing that this would save villagers the long, six-kilometre walk to the Catholic-run dispensary.

Upon receiving word about the new 'doctor', the Catholic nurses and priests expressed strong reservation. Their misgivings, which were vocalized in the following Sunday mass, were directed at Panchram's lack of 'proper' training. The Oraons were cautioned against consulting this 'doctor' and encouraged to continue availing of medical treatment at the dispensary.

In spite of the Church's reservations, both Hindus and Oraons seemed genuinely enthusiastic and supportive about the fact that they had yet another local biomedical alternative. Panchram's services quickly became preferred to both the Church workshop 'representatives' who, people complained, had only basic medical supplies, and to the dispensary, which entailed a time-consuming visit away from the village. Panchram kept a basic supply of medicines in the bag that he carried everywhere, including ordinary painkillers, 'strength-giving' tonics, and antibiotics, as well as chloroquine tablets, injections and glucose bottles. Like the nurses, he referred more serious cases to the government hospital in the city.

As mentioned above, one of the primary objectives behind the RSS's sponsorship and installation of Panchram was to challenge the dominant healing traditions and beliefs that largely attribute illnesses to divine disapproval of human misconduct. It is well known that the area where this village is located has one of the highest rates of malaria-related deaths in all of Chhattisgarh. In addition to a general lack of awareness about preventive measures, this is due largely to the fact that people will either bypass biomedical treatment altogether or, in the manner described in this chapter, try and then quickly discard biomedicine in favour of supernatural treatments. Government campaigns to raise awareness about the cause and treatment of such illnesses were nonexistent during the period when this research took place.[16]

---

[16]The first of a series of health awareness campaigns started during a subsequent period of research conducted between 2002–3. However, local people find such

In response to these issues, the RSS hopes to create a viable and permanent biomedical treatment alternative to the dominant local discourse that revolves around 'supernatural' illness causality. Like the Catholic priests, who see a direct connection between waning tradition and the death of local elders and healers, Raj reckons that it will be 'at least one generation' before their fledgling efforts see any real progress. The chief impediment to the RSS's aims of inculcating biomedical habits is that the majority of the local people remain convinced about the continuing efficacy and imperative necessity for supernatural medicine. 'These *adivasi* traditions are too strong', Raj lamented to me some six months after Panchram was installed as the local doctor. 'There are many *gunias* but only one doctor. It will be a long time before things change here'. But he sees the installation of Panchram as the first step in persuading local people—particularly Hindus—to abandon their traditional healing practices and take up biomedical treatment.

In view of this objective, the installation of Panchram has seen positive results. Panchram is a constant, visible presence in the village, available for people to voluntarily call at all hours of the day or night. Like local healers who become familiar with their patients' 'social field', he has the advantage that intimate social relations and proximity affords, and he easily comes to know who is ill. Equally, he regularly enquires about the health of both Christians and Hindus, and suggests biomedical alternatives and offers services and intervention on the spot. Because of his visibility and attentiveness to local villagers, Panchram's reputation as a competent and respected health practitioner has been firmly established. The only thing that irks him is the fact that his Hindu patients insist on making payments in the form of seed rice. It is for this reason, he confided to me, that he actually prefers Oraon patients, who are willing and able to pay in cash. 'How can I accept rice as payment?' he asked me, after demanding that a patient exchange her seed rice for cash at a local shop. 'The shops in the city from where I buy my medicines do not accept anything but cash, so why should I?'

In short, before Panchram came along, the time and distance-related inconvenience of the dispensary meant that local people—especially Hindus—were less likely to seek or follow through with

---

campaigns unhelpful, largely because of the 'self-important' government doctors who arrive in their jeeps and, with the aim of educating local people, allegedly spend much of their time belittling the ignorance of the *adivasis* and their 'backward' traditions.

biomedical treatment. While people availed of the dispensary in the initial stages of an illness, they rarely returned if the illness continued, preferring instead, to seek supernatural therapies. Since he became the local 'doctor', and with his everyday intervention, Hindus have been increasingly likely to carry on with their treatment and consult Panchram for additional medicine. Panchram himself claims to have saved the lives of 'at least four people' in the twelve months that he worked as a 'doctor' before I completed my fieldwork. While certainly not verifiable, villagers insist that such claims are likely true. Local people describe in detail, certain cases where, if Panchram had not been conveniently located in the village and available to administer emergency glucose injections and antibiotics, the patient most certainly would have died.

One of these cases concerns Jaglal, a classificatory nephew of the village headman who had been gravely ill for over a month. It was towards the end of December, shortly after Panchram's medical training had been completed, and the most important annual festival, Gaura (discussed in Chapters Two and Five), was around the corner. A few days after Jaglal had come down with fever, he went to the dispensary, where he was given an injection and three-day course of tablets for suspected malaria and told to return for another injection the following day. As routinely happens after a patient receives the initial injection of chloroquine, Jaglals's fever dropped, and that evening, he declared himself to be cured: there was no need to take any more tablets or to revisit the dispensary. The following day his fever returned, and Jaglal declared the original injection a failure: the illness must be *bhut ka*. At this point, the family summoned what would be the first of a string of *gunias*, all of whom divined different supernatural causes for Jaglal's illness. Instead of showing signs of improvement, however, Jaglal's health became steadily worse.

The night before the Gaura festival was to begin, Jaglal's condition became extremely serious. To the distraught sounds of his wailing wife and mother, four *gunias* worked over Jaglal, each indulging in a different divination method in an attempt to identify the causal agent and ward off imminent death. It was particularly important that Jaglal live: being a member of the most prominent family in the village, his death would be terribly inauspicious and the Gaura ritual would have to be cancelled. Like elsewhere in Hindu India (see Parry 1994), there is a ban on rituals during the period of mourning. Locally, this period extended to when the final funeral rites were performed on the tenth day after death, long after the time declared to be most auspicious for the performance of Gaura. The cancellation of the festival would in some ways, be worse than Jaglal's death itself, for the failure to perform the important rituals would likely bring greater misfortune to the village as a whole.

In an unusual move, Panchram was summoned by the village headman to administer a glucose bottle and injection to Jaglal. Upon cursory examination, he assessed that Jaglal's condition was extremely grave and that he would likely die very soon. Aware of the local dogma surrounding the blending of medical treatments, he feared that Jaglal's probable death would be attributed to his own biomedical interference, and he refused to intervene. Only after the village headman took personal responsibility and promised that Panchram would escape any accusations of wrongdoing did he proceed to administer the first of three bottles of glucose and two injections.

Panchram is convinced that Jaglal would have died had he not been available to give him the glucose. He is also certain that if Jaglal's family had called him early on in the illness, or if he had merely carried on with the treatment that the nurse had prescribed, he would have likely recovered quickly: for (by Panchram's estimates) this was clearly a case of 'simple' illness.

In view of the ethnography presented earlier in this chapter, and as illustrated by Panchram's initial refusal to treat Jaglal for fear of being implicated in the latter's possible demise, what is unusual about this case is the fact that different kinds of medical treatments were allowed to be mixed. This would not have happened ten, maybe even five years ago, I was told by one of the local *gunias*. Even nowadays, as illustrated in the earlier example of Kirtan's illness, the ideology and accompanying practice of not mixing supernatural and simple treatments persists. It is perhaps because of the imminent Gaura celebrations and the possibility of his inauspicious death that the exception was allowed in Jaglal's case; Panchram's intervention was viewed as necessary to maximize the possibility of his recovery.

In short, the presence of a biomedical practitioner has helped to encourage local people who would otherwise not seek biomedical treatment for certain illnesses due to time and distance-related inconvenience. While Hindus, compared to Christians, still give biomedicine a relatively limited period in which to take effect before they resort to supernatural treatment, they are increasingly likely to avail of biomedical treatment for a longer period of time and for a wider range of ailments than they would have done in the past.

The RSS and Biomedicine: Challenging the Church

The foregoing discussion has been necessary to better understand the reasons why supernatural treatment and other 'backward' methods continue to be a legitimate and preferred avenue for healing to which both Christians and Hindus regularly turn. This, in turn, has facilitated a more comprehensive understanding of the strategies that the Church and the RSS are employing to discourage local people's commitment to 'backward' ideas about supernatural illness and healing. The successful 'education' of local *adivasis* about the benefits of biomedicine over traditional healing techniques is the ostensible objective behind the RSS's sponsorship of Panchram as the local 'doctor'. This objective serves as a kind of contemporary 'civilizing mission' (Skaria 1999) that has at its centre the betterment of 'backward' peoples. It is clearly characteristic of the activities that underpin the broader 'civilizing mission' in which the Church has historically been involved.

As noted earlier, medicine has been used by Christian missionaries as a proselytizing tool throughout India since at least the nineteenth century (Arnold 1993; cf. Mann 2004). With hundreds of Christian hospitals scattered around the country, the association between Christianity and biomedicine carries on to the present day. Locally, this association has been compounded by the fact that, since its arrival in the 1970s, the Church has operated the only dispensary and biomedical clinic within a 20 km radius. Moreover, the majority of the dispensary's patients have come from the Hindu communities in surrounding villages since at least, the early 1980s when records for the dispensary began to be kept. Given the demographics of this area, which sees a three-to-one Hindu-to-Christian ratio, this is not particularly surprising. However, the steadily increasing patronage of the Church's medical facilities by local Hindus has also given the Church a great deal of authority and influence over the local people and their treatment choices. This has proved to be increasingly alarming for the RSS.

The fear of conversion to Christianity is one that the RSS has harboured since its inception (cf. Dube 1998). Although it has been illegal for Christians to actively proselytize in both Madhya Pradesh and Chhattisgarh since 1991, critics of the Church argue that Christian-sponsored schools and hospitals are themselves a form of proselytization (see Shourie 1994). At the time of my fieldwork, the mission school in the neighbouring village was not of great concern for RSS proponents, perhaps because it catered mostly to Oraon Christians and did not actively seek students from the Hindu population. Instead, it is the Church dispensary and, more recently, its medical 'outreach' programme that has generated the greatest concern. As far as Raj and the other RSS *pracharaks* are concerned, the latter in particular is an example of how the Church is implicitly paving the way for future conversion of local Hindu *adivasis*. Beyond an apparent concern for the physical welfare of local *adivasis*, then, a more significant motivation behind the RSS's installation of a dedicated 'doctor', is to prevent this from happening.

According to Hansen (1999: 103–8), a similar motivation—to counter the increasing Christian influence in areas where, for decades, missionary hospitals, schools, and other social-welfare schemes are thought to have contributed to mass conversions—is behind the dedicated social work being carried out by RSS activists in other tribal areas. By sponsoring Panchram, local RSS activists have gone some way in attracting Hindu *adivasis* away from the dispensary.

In response to the RSS's growing interest in medicine and sponsorship of Panchram, Church authorities agree that it is ultimately beneficial to have additional biomedical options available to the local people. As mentioned above, however, they have actively discouraged the Oraon Christians from seeking the services of someone they consider to be an improperly trained medical worker. When I completed my fieldwork, the Catholic priests and sisters were even considering the possibility of introducing another 'rule' that prohibited Christians from consulting Panchram. So far, however, the Oraons have generally complied with the priests' requests and continue to visit the dispensary for most of their medical ailments. Nevertheless, they do find it reassuring and convenient to have a 'doctor' based in the village too, particularly at times when it is difficult to travel to the dispensary.

By the time I left the village in August 1999, Panchram's reputation as an efficient 'doctor' had travelled beyond the village, and his skills and intervention were increasingly in demand by people who lived in villages up to 15 km away. In contrast to the sisters at the dispensary, he was willing to visit patients at their homes and was regularly accompanied on these journeys, by one of the ten young men who participated in the training meetings conducted by Raj and his cohorts, and about whom we will hear more in the following chapter. During times when Panchram was absent from the village, local people who wanted to avail of biomedical treatment were once again, forced to make the 6 km trek to the Catholic dispensary. This defeated one of the objectives of Panchram's presence in the village: to provide people with a locally convenient biomedical alternative to that provided by the Church. The long-term biomedical aim of the RSS therefore, is to establish its own medical clinic in the village, with Panchram as the in-house doctor. The RSS hopes to achieve this aim in the next few years.

The installation of a medical 'doctor' may not seem like an especially obvious tactic to propagate *Hindutva*, particularly compared to the more aggressive strategies that will be discussed in Chapters Six and Seven. However, it is in many ways more successful and powerful because it is more insidious. For example, while people were aware of the role that Raj and the other RSS activists played in the sponsorship and installation of the 'doctor', they did not associate his involvement with the wider 'civilizing mission' of the RSS or the broader *Hindutva* agenda; nor did they comment on the similarities that this particular 'good work' had with the kind of social upliftment programmes in which the Church has historically engaged. They were simply grateful to Raj, who they considered a trusted 'son of the soil' intimately familiar with local needs and concerns, for presenting them with a convenient alternative to existing healthcare options.

This kind of strategy is insidious precisely because it is cloaked within the agenda of social upliftment of a 'backward' *adivasi* community. By identifying a social need and mobilizing a response to that need, Raj and the other RSS activists were successfully able to endear themselves and engender respect and trust from the community as a whole. In this way, they were able to establish a platform from which more aggressive strategies could be initiated later on, and to ensure that their appeals would be taken seriously. Along with those outlined later in this book, this is another example of the way in which 'conversion specialists' (Brass 1997: 16) like Raj tailor a particular strategy to suit the situation and context at the local level. This particular strategy was underpinned by the broader mimetic relationship that the RSS has with the Church. In the following chapter, focus is on a different way in which the social upliftment of the community has been achieved.

CHAPTER FIVE

Local Corruption and the Politics of Inclusion

I n the previous chapter we saw that one of the strategies by which the RSS has successfully endeared itself to the local community is through its sponsorship of a biomedical 'doctor'. A second strategy through which the RSS has attracted local support is by lending its legitimacy to those who wish to contest the traditional authority of corrupt local power holders. Like their engagement with local health concerns and the introduction of an additional treatment alternative, this strategy is another means by which the RSS can be seen to 'emulate' (Jaffrelot 1996) Christian missionizing tactics. The particular form of mimesis in this case concerns the intervention of an external authority (the RSS) in a matter that revolves around the challenge to traditional authority and the return of basic monetary entitlements to the local people. As we shall see in the following ethnography, it is this sort of strategy that has enabled local RSS activists to further legitimize their presence in this village.

In order to understand how this has transpired, it is useful to begin with the narration of events that took place in May 1999, when every household in Mohanpur was beginning to prepare for the annual *tendu* leaf collection. In three weeks time, the leaves would be declared ready for picking and the village would become deserted, as all but a few elderly people and small children would rush off to the jungle before dawn to collect as many leaves as possible. After six or seven hours, they would straggle home to begin the painstaking process of counting the leaves into bundles of fifty. Evening would see them hauling hundreds of these bundles to a designated field, where they would be sorted and recorded by the village *munshi*, the man in charge of the local collection process. These bundles would then be dried and carried off by lorries to government storehouses, from where they would be sold to the highest bidder and used to make *bidi*, the indigenous Indian cigarette.

The *tendu* leaf collection is a state-controlled enterprise managed by the forest department. Each village in the area has its own *munshi* appointed by the local *tendu* committee officials, a group of four men who oversee the collection process in seven surrounding villages. It is to this committee that the *munshi* must deliver the previous day's collection totals throughout the five-week season. These officials, in turn, are appointed by and accountable to their district and state-level superiors. Twice during the season and once after its conclusion, cash payment for the leaves is distributed by the state government to the local committee officials, who then deliver the money to each village *munshi*. As the government-appointed officer-in-charge, the latter is responsible for organizing the local collection, keeping detailed accounts and distributing the cash payments to all villagers.

The collection process is tedious and taxing, but with the possibility of earning five to ten times the 'average' daily wage of Rs 25–30, this is the one time of the year when villagers can look forward to a relatively sizeable cash income.[1] Consequently, spirits are typically high in the weeks leading up to the collection, as people contemplate how they might spend their windfall.

While ordinary villagers prepare for this process by making the grass ropes that will be used to bind the leaves, the *munshi* keeps busy dusting his record books and going over the previous year's receipts. He is in a most enviable position, for he is guaranteed a lucrative commission for his services while being spared the hard physical labour that goes into collecting the leaves.[2]

---

[1]This 'average' is based on the daily wage that local people typically earn when participating in government-sponsored public works or construction projects. During the initial days of the month-long *tendu* season, when leaves are plentiful, families are capable of picking between 400–800 bundles in a day (around 20,000–40,000 leaves). At Rs 40 per 100 bundles, this amounts to Rs 160–320. At the time of my fieldwork, Rs 40 could purchase around 4 to 5 kg of rice, which could feed a family of four for two days.

[2]In the previous year, the *munshi* had received Rs 1,400 for every 100,000 bundles that his village had collected. His total commission was over Rs 11,200, an incredibly large sum by local standards.

As I watched the preparations getting underway this particular spring, I noticed that the process appeared to be identical to what I had witnessed the previous year—the only difference being the regular visits by Raj and other members of the RSS. Over the previous year, the frequency of these visits had increased from once every two months to once weekly. As mentioned in Chapter Two, these visits often coincided with major Hindu festivals such as Mahashivratri. On such occasions, demonstrations about how to conduct festival rites in 'proper' mainstream Hindu fashion would be followed by 'training meetings' in which a group of local young men were taught the *Hindutva* ideology (cf. Basu et al. 1993; Nandy et al. 1995). More recently, these visits included brief meetings with the local 'doctor', Panchram, who would provide Raj with an update about his growing number of patients. Occasionally, Panchram would also produce a list of medical supplies required to replenish his stock, which he would then request Raj or one of the other RSS cadres to procure from the city.

It was on one of these visits, a week or so before the *tendu* season was scheduled to begin, that something extraordinary happened. Without warning, the *munshi* was approached by the local *tendu* committee officials who demanded his record books and informed him that his services were no longer required: there had been a complaint, they informed him, and he was being replaced. As word of the *munshi's* dismissal spread, people across the village quietly celebrated. For they were seeing the end of what effectively amounted to ten years of theft, a period during which they had regularly witnessed their yearly cash bonuses pocketed (for 'services rendered') by this man. Individually, these bonuses were relatively small sums that ranged between Rs 50–250 per family; in total, they amounted to thousands of rupees per year. Although his practice of pilfering was common knowledge throughout the village, in the ten years that this man had been the *munshi*, nobody had dared make an official complaint.

This was indeed a remarkable event, and I was as surprised as anyone that this man had been deposed: for the *munshi* also happened to be the headman (the Patel), the most powerful and feared individual in the village who was, in a sense, above the law. For years, villagers had been discontented with the Patel's behaviour. But he was allowed to continue with his actions in part, because of the legitimacy he received from the most powerful local deity, and in part, because of his connections to influential individuals outside the village. While the *tendu* committee officials in whose region the village was located had been aware of the Patel's conduct, they could do nothing about the situation until someone from the village lodged an official complaint. On their part, the villagers had not dared to complain because of the possible repercussions they would face. In any case, it was believed that there would have been no point: the receipt books were in the Patel's control, and the alterations that he allegedly made to cover his deeds would serve to erase any written proof of the stolen bonuses.

So why and how had control over the most lucrative local venture suddenly been stripped from the most powerful and feared man in the village? And what does his dismissal have to do with the RSS and their efforts to gain local legitimacy? To many villagers, the Patel's dismissal as the *munshi* appeared to be a straightforward sign that the lower-level state personnel—the *tendu* committee officials—had finally found some sort of legal basis on which to act. But to the respected local elders and young men 'in the know', it was a sign that the Patel had lost his traditional authority, which was legitimized by and dependent upon his connection with the most powerful deity in the area.

Through an examination of the construction and reproduction of traditional authority, this chapter focuses on the role that the RSS plays in its transformation. Unlike neighbouring villages where it has been diluted by local systems of self governance in the form of the *gram sabha* (see Chapter Two), traditional authority in Mohanpur continues to be legitimized in 'pre-modern' terms (Chatterjee 1997: 295; see also Fuller and Harriss 2001: 24), remaining rooted in a single individual and bound to notions of divine legitimacy. Here, the Patel's authority is both dependent upon divine approval and contingent upon the view of others that he is acting within the cosmological and political limits of power. As we shall see in the ethnography described below, a challenge to the Patel's authority takes place through a sort of 'customary rebellion' (Gluckman 1955, 1963), which both upholds the existing traditional order that revolves around kingship and draws its legitimacy from and seeks change through an appeal to custom. In Mohanpur, as in the African context examined by Gluckman, disputes are about distributions of power, not about the structure of the system itself; as such, the sanctity of kingship withstands the defects of the individual king (see Sundar 1997: 85).

According to Guha (1989: 90), who invokes the notion of 'customary rebellion' in his examination of traditionally sanctioned forms of resistance against unjust kings in northern India, the origins of such rebellions stem from a perceived breach of covenant between ruler and ruled.[3] A similar analysis can be applied to the situation in Mohanpur, where the breach in question revolves around the Patel's violation of the cosmological and political limits of power. As we shall see, the ensuing 'rebellion' that brought about a change to the distribution of power in Mohanpur ultimately necessitated the involvement of an external source of authority, which presented itself in the form of the RSS. By analysing the situation that led to this rebellion and the reasons behind the RSS proponents' involvement, this chapter not only contributes to the wider ethnographic literature on the construction and transformation of traditional authority, but also identifies a further strategy by which the RSS has succeeded in making inroads into this *adivasi* community.[4]

It is significant to note that the continued legitimacy of traditional authority in Mohanpur has also required the support of state structures and personnel, and a second objective of this chapter is to illuminate the processes by which the state is experienced by local people. Recent anthropological literature has commented on the relative lack of attention to the state in ethnographic work (Brass 1997; Fuller and Bénéï 2001; Gupta 1995). While this chapter does not purport to be an ethnographic analysis of the state, it does offer a glimpse of the relationship that the villagers have with lower-level state officials. Commonly, for example, local people have little regular interaction with state personnel, including land officials, the police and elected representatives, which has not been previously mediated by or filtered

[3]Other scholars who have recently utilized the notion of 'customary rebellion' in the Indian context include Sundar (1997), who examines the 1876 Bastar rebellion and argues that it was intended to emphasize the divine function of kingship and demand that the raja fulfil his role (1997: 86).

[4]The transformation of traditional authority has been one of the central issues animating the sociology of India for decades, and encompasses numerous features. These include the transformation brought to traditional forms of social and political organization (including kingship) by electoral politics (Bailey 1963); the changes brought to traditional village structures through market forces and the creation of new power bases (Béteille 1965; Robinson 1988); and the decline of traditional rights and obligations of patronage by increasing government intervention (Breman 1974). While these scholars all focus on changes that brought about a transformation of traditional authority, others look at how 'true' traditions were used to promote social reforms. For example, in Uberoi's (1996) edited collection on social reform, sexuality and the state, many authors talk about how traditional symbols of 'motherhood' were adopted, valorised and likened to ideals of nationhood. For other examples where traditional 'motherhood' and women's symbols were used as reformist ideas, see Forbes (1981), Kumar (1993), and Sangari and Vaid (1989).

through the authority of the Patel. In view of this, and as the ethnography will illustrate, far from being a 'neutral arbiter of public interest' (Fuller and Harriss 2001: 3), the state itself has served as an effective tool to buttress the traditional authority of the Patel. Notwithstanding this scenario, the chapter also examines the way in which one group of state personnel, the members of the *tendu* committee, through the strategic intervention of local RSS activists, participated in challenging the Patel's traditional base of authority.

Finally, this chapter considers how the objectives behind the RSS' intervention in this particular issue are impelled by what van der Veer has termed the 'politics of inclusion' (1994: 135). Used loosely, this term refers to the kind of social upliftment strategies that are employed to draw disenfranchized groups like the *adivasis* and untouchables away from 'foreign religions' like Christianity and back into the Hindu fold. As van der Veer points out, the rhetoric behind this initiative is informed by Gandhian concepts of social reform and underpinned by the Sangh Parivar's broader initiative of nation building (ibid.).

The objectives in which the RSS is currently engaged are not only impelled by the 'politics of inclusion'; they can also be seen to emulate the more successful strategies employed by the Church (Jaffrelot 1996). This form of mimesis is locally represented by the discouragement of traditional healing practices, along with the promotion of biomedicine and other strategies outlined in previous chapters. With explicit emphasis on the overall 'improvement' of vulnerable, 'backward' tribal communities, such strategies underpin the broader 'civilizing mission' in which both the Church and the RSS are engaged.

The particular strategy outlined in the present chapter, which concerns the intervention of an external authority in local tensions, also has parallels with Christian missionisation practices. Where nineteenth century Church missionaries familiarized themselves with agrarian laws and intervened on behalf of *adivasis*' in land rights issues (see de Sa 1975; Tete 1990), we shall see how present-day RSS activists have acquainted themselves with beliefs surrounding traditional authority, in order to secure the return of basic monetary entitlements to local people.[5] It is in the process of involving itself in the contemporary affairs of the local *adivasis* that the RSS has achieved

[5]That a condition of baptism was later tied to receipt of Christian aid in the nineteenth century suggests, of course, that the underlying objective behind missionary involvement was conversion.

a similar objective as the Church missionaries: namely, enhanced legitimacy within the local community.

The Ratiya Kanwars and Divine Authority

As discussed in Chapter Two, the dominance of the Ratiya Kanwars is replicated in most neighbouring villages and can largely be attributed to the Gandhel clan, who enjoy 'first-settler' status and preponderant control over land. In a case where 'the dominant caste reproduces the royal function' (Dumont 1980[1966]: 160–2; cf. Fuller 2004: 139), the Ratiya Kanwars can be seen as a sort of local 'royalty' of which the powerful Gandhel clan is the most important, and from which hails the 'king' (the village headman) and the 'priest' (the village Baiga). Such dominance is also reinforced by some of its younger members, namely the group of ten young men mentioned in previous chapters who have been strongly influenced by Raj and the other RSS cadres who frequent the village. It is members of this group that play an important role in facilitating the RSS's involvement in the events outlined in this chapter.

The origins of the continuing domination of the Ratiya Kanwar caste and, by extension, the Patel's authority revolve around a particular narrative that dates back to the arrival of the first Gandhel ancestor and that continues to constitute local relations of political and ritual dominance. The story goes that shortly after the first two Ratiya Kanwar families arrived in this area and began working the land at the base of a small mountain, a senior male family member suddenly died. The nervous survivors decided to request special protection from their ancestor deities in the form of a blood sacrifice. As the sacred drum (*nissan*)[6] announced the start of the *puja*, a powerful local deity suddenly descended upon and possessed Moharsai, the senior-most family member and the primary ancestor through whom all local Ratiya

[6]The drumming of the *nissan* is an integral part of every major public *puja* and life cycle event, which is known to be cancelled or postponed if the *nissan* or its drummer is not present. It is meant to house, or indeed to be, a deity, and it is venerated at every sacred event. There are four *nissans* in the village, all owned by members of the Gandhel clan (although played by members of the Chauhan caste). It is not normally handled outside ritual contexts, for it is said that the sound of the drums is an invitation to the local deities to join the rituals. Careless handling of this instrument would incur the wrath of the deities.

Kanwars trace their lineage. Through the mediation of Moharsai's brother, whose descendants have since served in the role of the village priest (the Baiga), this deity immediately announced that he was the big god (*bara dev*), Kaleshar: the god of all deities (*dev ka mukhia*), whose power exceeded that of even the most powerful village deity, Thakurdev.[7] He revealed that he was angry because the Ratiya Kanwars had trespassed on his grounds and cultivated within his territory without requesting permission. In return for this transgression, he had taken the life of their male relative.

Now that he had got his revenge, he had come to inform the surviving Ratiya Kanwars that he and his entourage of junior deities and demons who assisted him in ruling over the area, needed them for their own survival. It had been some time since any humans had inhabited the area, and it was from humans that their sustenance came in the form of ritual offerings.[8] Kaleshar offered protection to the community if the Ratiya Kanwars agreed to remain in the area.

[7]According to Andre Béteille (personal correspondence, March 1999), Kaleshar is another name for Shiva, or a reincarnation/godling of Shiva. However, when I enquired as to whether this was the case locally, I was given a resounding 'no' from both the Patel and Baiga, and reminded that Shiva resides in the village in another form, Mahadev. This connection between Kaleshar and Shiva becomes even more interesting when we consider that the primary festival in the village that celebrates the marriage between Shiva (Mahadev) and Parvati (Gauri Rani) is also the occasion at which Kaleshar not only appears as the most honoured guest, but also where his power and involvement in village affairs is most publicly reaffirmed. Local people's insistance that Kaleshar is distinct from Shiva could be interpreted as an instance of Hindu appropriation of tribal deities, which are then re-appropriated by *adivasi* people and transformed into separate and distinct forms. See Eschmann's (1978a: 94–5 and 1978b: 101–3) discussions on the possibility of the association of different kinds of tribal deities with Shiva, or with aspects of Shiva. Eschmann (1978a, 1978b, 1978c) and Tripathi (1978) also discuss the transformation of tribal deities into forms appropriate for 'high' or mainstream Hindu worship. A good example is the relationship between tribal origins and influence on the Hinduized Jagannatha cult, analysed in the impressive volume by Eschmann, Kulke and Tripathi (1978).

[8]The issue of divine needs in the form of ritual offerings varies in theory and practice. Eck (1985: 37), for example, asserts that such offerings are not a god's necessity, but shaped by human ideas of honouring guests. Fuller (2004: 69–72) concurs, but states that the issue is more complicated. At one level is the view that while deities do not actually need offerings and services, they must be worshipped *as if* they do. At another level is the position that deities not only need the offerings rendered to them in the form of *puja*, but that they actually suffer if such offerings are not provided. According to my informants, Kaleshar is clearly a case of the latter: he needs propitiation in the form of blood offerings.

In return, he requested that they shift away from this particular place near the mountain, and that they sacrifice a buffalo in his name every twenty years.

I had heard of this important and most powerful of deities quite early on in my fieldwork, but only in terms of his pseudonyms, *Baradev* (the big god) and *Gardev* (the name of the mountaintop and Kaleshar's *devras*, or sacred grove, where the buffalo sacrifice takes place). When I tried to verify his identity, I was told that it was dangerous to mention him by his real name outside of ritual contexts, for idle talk is disrespectful and could easily be picked up and carried by the winds to his *devras*, causing tremendous anger.

The mountain range that surrounds Kaleshar's *devras*, is reportedly rich with a variety of forest produce and game, and is off limits to people except during ritual occasions. Although this applies specifically to the area around Kaleshar's *devras*, the general rule of respect for the forest extends to the land surrounding the entire village, for the whole area is said to be Kaleshar's territory, carefully looked after by him and his demon sentinels. Stories of past illnesses and deaths attributed to, knowingly or unknowingly, invoking the big god's wrath by ignoring these rules were frequently narrated to me by local people.

Villagers fear this deity more than any other supernatural being, although he can be a very generous god if his rules are observed and he is regularly propitiated. Indeed, his powers seem to be infinite: 'anything is possible', I was often told by my informants, if you have Kaleshar on your side. The dialectical relationship that local people have with this deity extends to non-Mohanpur residents as well, as exemplified when a candidate for the 1999 state legislature came to the village canvassing for votes. He happened to be a member of the Kanwar caste (although non-Ratiya) from a different village, and one of the local elders informed him that he would receive more votes if he pledged a goat offering to Kaleshar. He did so, and the local Ratiya Kanwars attributed his later victory to this pledge. True to his word, this candidate delivered a goat shortly after the election, which was sacrificed at a major possession ritual held at Kaleshar's *devras* on the mountain.

In addition to being the primary divine source of dominance for the Ratiya Kanwars as a whole, it is this particular deity from whom the person who approximates the figure of the king (the headman or Patel), a hereditary life post passed down through the eldest son, receives divine authority to rule over his subjects (for an extensive review of the literature on 'divine kingship', see Feely-Harnik 1985; cf. also Fuller 2004 and Guha 1989). Since the relationship between the headman and Kaleshar was cemented when the latter first introduced himself to the Ratiya Kanwars and possessed the clan leader, Moharsai, every village headman has, by virtue of occupying the post, been delegated the task of being Kaleshar's 'representative' for local villagers.

It has long been argued that public rituals are the most prevalent way in which authority is legitimated in traditional societies (see Bloch 1989; Kertzer 1988: 37; Leach 1954: 15). The authority of the person who holds the post of the Patel is most elaborately manifested during two such rituals: the annual Gaura festival, mentioned in previous chapters, which is a public celebration of the marriage between Mahadev (Shiva) and Gauri Rani (Parvati); and the twenty-year buffalo sacrifice called Mahaseva, which enacts and re-validates the historical agreement between Kaleshar and the village founding father, Moharsai. As long as the ruling headman looks after Kaleshar's upkeep in ordinary and twenty-year *pujas* and ensures that his *devras* is respected, the ruling deity will continue to give legitimacy to the Patel and protection to his village.[9] It is at these two rituals that the acting Patel is transformed, through possession, into his supernatural counterpart, Kaleshar; and it is here, when Kaleshar begins to speak through him, issuing warnings, making demands, or simply reaffirming past promises, that the Patel's authority and position in the eyes of the public as ruler of the village appears to be completely validated.[10]

While the twenty-year *Mahaseva* celebration is said to be the most ritually important occasion for the village, attendance is restricted

[9] As is often the case where ritual convention is concerned, there is a difference here between orthodoxy and orthopraxy. The actual performance of these rituals is usually more sporadic, spanning between 15 and 30 years for the Mahaseva celebrations, and occasionally skipping one to three years for the Gaura festival. Reasons for this are invariably practical, and relate to the villagers' inability to collectively sponsor the costly rituals. For more discussion on the (ir)regular propitiation of deities, see Fuller 1992.

[10] Vestiges of the relationship between state or court deities and kings, which were seen in pre-independence Indian kingdoms, and where the king shares in the deity's divinity, are exemplified in contemporary India by the Navaratri and Dassara festivals. Here, the rituals (which, in the case of the Navaratri festival, traditionally include buffalo sacrifice) are built around the joint sovereignty of the goddess and the 'royal' village headman and are constitutive of the universal socio-cosmic order. Cf. Dumont (1980 [1966]: 160–3).

to men, and held in Kaleshar's protected space on the mountain. As such, it is on the occasion of Gaura that the Patel's power is the most publicly reaffirmed, for the site of Gaura has always been the ruling Gandhel family compound, where the re-enactment of the marriage. rituals of Mahadev and Gauri Rani are witnessed by the entire village. Throughout the four-hour rituals, up to 25 mostly male villagers circle the site of the divine wedding ceremony, having become possessed by a range of visiting deities who have been invited to attend the celebrations.

The most visible and potent sign of divine presence is when a deity descends on a human agent in the form of possession (*jhupna*). The sort of potency that is exhibited when a *gunia* induces the kind of possession described in the previous chapter is magnified when the possession takes place in the context of a formally staged public performance like Gaura. It is traditionally the Baiga who has the authority to carry out the ritual responsibilities for this event, in terms of both officiating at the marriage between Mahadev and Parvati, and greeting and questioning each of the divine guests as they descend on their human agents in the form of possession. It is also said that only the Baiga has the authority to mediate between Kaleshar and the public. This authority was established when Kaleshar first made contact with the original Ratiya Kanwar settlers. This is an important issue to which I return below.

The process by which possession takes place during Gaura is in some ways, merely an elaborated version of that described earlier. Instead of the rice-filled *supa*, however, the individual enters his or her possessed state to the accompaniment of the rhythm of numerous *nissan* drums. The shaking of the individual's body and the utterance of '*soo-oo-oooo*' indicate the presence of the possessing agent, which will be greeted by the Baiga with the customary '*johar, johar*'. After this greeting, the Baiga will ask its identity, request its protection for the duration of the festival, and ask if it has any message for the general community.

It is this impressive and highly charged spectacle of the sudden possession of numerous local people, which alternates between being humorous and playful, and erotic or violent, that is the main event at Gaura people have come to witness. None of the possessed agents are spared the comments of the crowd, which passes judgement on the formers' techniques and display. These range from the admirable ('see how he dances, he's really quite good'), to the scornful ('see how clumsy he is'), to the judgmental ('there he goes, stripping off his *lungi* as usual'). As seen by these comments, there are degrees of skill and expertise associated with the act of possession, particularly when dancing is involved. This suggests a sense of control while the subject is possessed, and while the 'novice possessed' will, over time, learn to conduct himself properly during his altered state, the possessed agent has little choice in the fact of being possessed itself. Possession, I was told, is the 'deity's wish', and if the deity wishes to possess an individual, then it will.

Consequently, the act of possession is taken very seriously by local people. It is considered to be very dangerous to 'fake' a possession, or fabricate divine presence or divine knowledge, for this invites the wrath of both the deity who is being impersonated, and the other deities who are insulted by the impersonation. For example, one woman who appeared to be genuinely possessed during Gaura was violently beaten by another man, whose possessing agent accused her of 'faking' her condition. All of those who become possessed, moreover, whether in the context of a public Gaura-like ritual or a private healing ritual, describe the experience as something about which they have no memory, and after which they are thoroughly exhausted.[11]

It is only when Kaleshar descends on the Patel that the crowd's reaction changes to one of respect and even fear. Even the behaviour of other deities, embodied in various possessed agents, becomes subdued as the possessed agents draw back to make room for Kaleshar. All eyes are on the Patel at this time, and the only comment that will be passed by people in the crowd is 'the big god has arrived'. Having been attending to the needs of the other deities, the Baiga directs his full attention to the Patel once Kaleshar's arrival has been announced.

The method by which the Patel becomes possessed is similar to that of the others. But his experience is unique for two reasons: he only becomes possessed at major public rituals, and traditionally it is only he who becomes possessed by Kaleshar (whereas others may become possessed in the course of minor rituals by a variety of different supernatural beings). It is at this moment, when the Patel becomes 'transformed into' his supernatural counterpart, and Kaleshar

[11]This is a common characteristic of spirit possession, about which there is a vast amount of anthropological literature. For specifically South Asian examples, see Gough (1976 [1952]), Hitchcock and Jones (1976), Srinivas (1965 [1952]), and Stirrat (1977).

The Patel (with Baiga mediating) possessed by Kaleshar at Gaura.

begins to speak through him—issuing warnings, making demands, or simply reaffirming past promises—that the Patel's local authority is decisively validated.

While all deities who attend the proceedings are welcomed with ordinary offerings of incense and alcohol, the Patel, or Kaleshar, receives *prasada* (divine grace) in the form of the blood of the sacrificed goat that has been offered to him by the Baiga. Once Kaleshar has drunk the blood, he joins the other possessed agents in their dancing frenzy. The consumption of *prasada* at any *puja* results in what Fuller (2004: 74–5) calls a 'merging of deity and worshiper' and marks what Babb (1987:69) identifies as the 'physiological engagement' between deity and devotee. Consumption of the buffalo blood at the twenty-year Mahaseva ritual is especially potent, and serves to be the most vital reaffirmation of the Patel's authority. For this is a substance of divine power that is, and can only be consumed by Kaleshar (embodied, at the moment of consumption, in the Patel).

These rituals together serve to completely reaffirm the village headman's authority and position in the eyes of the public, as ruler of the village, and it is said that if they are not performed, then the headman's power will diminish. Such rituals are also vital for the protection and well being of the village: if Kaleshar is not worshipped in the elaborate context of Mahaseva and Gaura, then terrible misfortune will befall the community. The first year I was in the village, Gaura was cancelled because the previous winter harvest was so poor that villagers were unable to meet the costs of the celebration. The subsequent failure of the following spring harvest, combined with an unusually high level of illness that struck the village during the summer, convinced many that the cancellation of Gaura was to blame.

At this stage, it is important to bear three things in mind: that possession is the most powerful means of communication between humans and the divine; that it is considered dangerous to the possessed agent himself if he fakes a possession, or fabricates divine knowledge; and that while Kaleshar may possess ordinary people in the form of illness, in public rituals such as Gaura this deity possesses *only* the Patel.

The Patel and Traditional Authority

While all headmen have been accorded an important association with this deity, the current Patel has enjoyed a more privileged relationship with Kaleshar than any headman before him. This is because he was directly chosen by Kaleshar for the post when he was first possessed by the big god at the age of twelve during a major public ritual, a mark of honour and indication that he was somehow special. This tribute was even more significant because he was not actually in line to inherit the position of village headman: his paternal uncle was the acting Patel at the time, and the position should rightfully have gone to that man's son, Babulal. Because the latter was a toddler at the time of his father's premature death, the reins passed to his older cousin, Umenthsingh, the current Patel. Two Gandhel elders who had witnessed the Patel's childhood possession told me that the moment Kaleshar descended on him they knew that one day he would become the Patel—in spite of the fact that it was not meant to happen in the hereditary scheme of things. His elevation to the office some two decades later was seen as the fulfilment of divine desire.

Because the current Patel's access to and legitimacy from Kaleshar dates back to this childhood possession, his authority is also viewed as superior to that of previous village headmen. The Patel sometimes flaunts his superiority, as when he claims that the reason he is in control of major rituals such as the annual Gaura festival is because he is the 'only one who understands everything' and therefore the only one who is capable of physically and ritually guiding the proceedings. He regularly extends this power over the village Baiga, for whom rituals and the worship of village deities were supposed to be a 'special province' (Babb 1975: 199). The Patel's regular interference (in dictating the time and sequence of a particular ritual, along with vital instructions on its performance) in what is rightfully the Baiga's domain has caused a great deal of animosity between them. The Patel also uses his connection to Kaleshar to advance his agenda and facilitate acceptance of his decisions. One such occasion occurred halfway through my fieldwork when, following the death of the village Baiga after a short illness, a new one had to be installed. Like the position of Patel, this has been a hereditary office 'since the beginning', and the deceased Baiga's replacement should have rightfully gone to his eldest son. However, at a *panchayat* meeting held just before the installation of the new Baiga, the Patel announced that he had had a dream in which Kaleshar appeared and informed him that the deceased Baiga's brother, Pitarsuar, and not his son should take over the ritual reins.

As mentioned in the previous chapter, dreams, along with possession, are considered to be one of the primary media for acquiring divine knowledge and receiving divine affirmation and instruction, and this dream should have been sufficient to legitimize the Patel's choice of Baiga.[12] However, there was a great deal of dissent over the decision, particularly from the deceased Baiga's own family. The Patel's choice, Pitarsuar, was considered by his own family to be compliant and weak in character, and therefore easily controlled by the Patel. Indeed, Pitarsuar himself confessed to me more than once his reservations about his ability to carry out his priestly duties. In contrast, the original Baiga's eldest son and rightful heir to the priestly throne had been groomed for this position since he was young. He was no ally of the Patel, having come into conflict with him in the past over a land dispute, and the Patel's decision created further animosity. The family's protest spilled over into the rest of the village, and there was talk of boycotting the Patel's choice. Dissent finally subsided when the public ritual to formally install the new Baiga was held. This was when Kaleshar made a surprise appearance and possessed the Patel, transmitting the message to the public that the Patel's choice was divinely validated.

Status and Power

As is evident, the current Patel's authority is 'locked into beliefs about [its] derivation and maintenance' (cf. Obeyesekere 1992: 161). It is as much related to divine authority, indicated by Kaleshar's public endorsement of the Patel's decisions, as it is to people's beliefs about, and acknowledgement of that authority. Before I proceed with an examination of how this authority is further augmented by secular power, it is worth discussing how the scenario I have just outlined, resembles the issue of the relationship between power and status, or kingship and priesthood. This issue was most prominently developed by Dumont (1980 [1966]), who asserted that secular power (the king) in traditional Indian society was 'encompassed by' religious or spiritual power (the priest). In this framework, power is subordinate to status, and the political domain is dependent upon the spiritual for its legitimacy. This view has been challenged by Dirks (1987)

---

[12]As we saw in Chapter Four, the power of dreams is also illustrated in the context of local healers, who receive much of their knowledge and instruction from dreams. See Babb (1975:199) for further discussion on dreams as a means of communication with the divine.

and other 'neo-Hocartians' who hold that Dumont exaggerated the extent to which the king is inferior to the priest, and that the ritual and political forms were fundamentally the same (see Dirks 1987: 4–5; Parry 1998).

The two figures that approximate the function of the king and the priest in the present ethnography, the Patel and the Baiga, have historically been monopolized by members of the same lineage within the Gandhel clan. This has created a sort of fusion of the political and religious domains. But these realms have always remained under the command of two distinct individuals who ascended to their roles by hereditary right, and who were responsible for separate but equally important political and spiritual functions: one was in charge of government and the maintenance of public order, the other mediated between the village and the cosmos.

However, what has happened in the village is that the current king (the Patel), through gradual appropriation of the Baiga's spiritual authority, has become the 'chief-priest of the [village]' (Dumont 1980 [1966]: 68; Parry 1998: 158). Under the auspices of divine legitimation, the Patel regularly interfered with the duties of the now-deceased Baiga. And against hereditary tradition, the Patel personally chose and installed the current Baiga for the purpose, according to widespread opinion, of appropriating and extending his control over the Baiga's spiritual authority. In spite of the fact that the Patel's choice was legitimized by Kaleshar, there was a sense of outrage that the rights of the traditional heir to the spiritual throne had been usurped by the Patel's intervention. 'Who knows', I was told by one informant who was against the Patel's choice of Baiga, 'perhaps the Patel will install himself as Baiga next.' Indeed, such a scenario, which did not seem implausible, would achieve what many believed, was the Patel's chief ambition: to transform himself into the area's exclusive priest-king. At present, however, the Baiga still retains the authority to officiate between Kaleshar and his human subjects, and the Patel still requires the ritual participation and mediation of the Baiga.

Perhaps the more interesting issue here with respect to status and power is that even within 'backward' areas like this, there is significant variation over space and time. While the power and status of the Ratiya Kanwar caste is generally replicated across all villages in this area, with the Patel and the Baiga typically hailing from this caste, Mohanpur is the only village with a political leader who commands such a high degree of ritual and (as we shall see in the next section) secular authority, and with a spiritual leader who commands so little. Moreover, the relationship between the 'king' and the 'priest' keeps shifting. Prior to the reign of the current Patel, the situation in Mohanpur was similar to the present situation in neighbouring villages, where the Patel and the Baiga have equally powerful and distinctive roles, and where the headman's overall authority is diffused by the presence of an active and respected *sarpanch*, who works under the auspices of the state-administered system of self-governance, the *gram sabha*.

The Patel and Secular Authority

In contrast to the situation in other villages, in Mohanpur, the Patel's power is further buttressed by his political power and juridical authority, which are both nearly absolute. As noted in Chapter Two, such authority is normally vested in the elected office of the *sarpanch*. Locally, however, the Patel boycotts *gram sabha* meetings and ignores the decisions made by the *sarpanch*. It is the Patel, for example, who officiates at local council meetings; it is to him, privately or publicly, that villagers turn for the airing and settlement of local disputes; and it is his word and decisions that are final in these disputes. The Patel, in other words, is in possession of the local 'capital of authority' (Bourdieu 1977: 40) which enables him to dictate and determine the parameters of his power.

The Patel's relative economic prosperity and visible material wealth also serve to reaffirm his political and ritual legitimacy. He owns the largest and most fertile tracts of agricultural land and claims the choicest sections of forestland. With the exception of one other Gandhel landowner, no other villager yields a surplus of agricultural or forest produce on the same scale as the Patel. Most locals, to the contrary, fall short of their basic subsistence needs and have to supplement their yields with other income-generating activities, or go into occasional debt by mortgaging their land or livestock. What's more, the Patel's landed and harvested wealth contributes to the accumulation of other assets, including a large amount of livestock and a recently acquired diesel-powered threshing machine. Likewise, his income from legitimate agricultural and forest resources has been augmented by more nefarious activities, such as the pilfering of *tendu* bonuses. Finally, he allegedly pockets the fines imposed by the village council upon individuals who indulge in various forms of social misconduct and that are intended for the village coffers.

The Patel's local authority has been further legitimized by power emanating from outside the village, namely from local-level state officials. Instead of the *sarpanch*, who is officially the main contact point for lower-level state and block office officials (see Pathak 1994: 79–85), it is the Patel with whom outside authorities like the District Collector and the police make their primary contact when they have official business in Mohanpur. For example, pension payments and school scholarships are issued by District officials to the Patel, who is known to charge the rightful recipient, an 'issuing fee' for their distribution. Subsidized rice allotted through the free school-lunch programme is also distributed to and controlled by the Patel, who keeps the inevitable surplus for himself. And the Patel has final decision-making powers over the appointment of local government-salaried positions, such as the forest guard assistant, the *anganwadi* (nursery teacher), and the schoolteacher. Currently, the former two posts are held by his son and daughter-in-law respectively, and the local schoolteacher was forced to pay a 'fee' of Rs 10,000 to the Patel for her appointment.

The Patel is also informed of people who are under suspicion for a particular crime, and if the incident is not taken care of (through payment of a bribe) through the auspices of the Patel, then the individual is summoned to the local police station twenty kilometres away. One incident during my fieldwork concerned three villagers who were accused of provoking the suicide of another local man. The Patel talked to the police on their behalf and the three were let off after paying Rs 500 each to the police and Rs 100 to the Patel.

As a Congress Party supporter, the Patel also hosts visiting state legislative candidates and is normally the main recipient of bribes from such people. He is also responsible for delivering local votes to the Congress Party candidates. Moreover, he is known to use his knowledge of local land ownership and his connections to land officials, to manipulate the outcome of local elections by threatening villagers that he will take away their land if the proper candidate does not win. Again, the fact that he does not have the legal power to do so does not matter to the local people; merely believing that he can is enough to sway their vote.

The Patel's connection to persons who hold external power, namely local-level state officials, not only impairs the access but also sometimes, controls the relationship that other members of the local community have with these authorities (Mendelsohn 1993: 832). A good illustration of this is the relationship that the Patel has with the Patwari, a local-level state official in charge of the land records of eight or nine area villages. Although he has an 'office' in a village some fifteen kilometres away, due to time and distance-related constraints, local people generally meet the Patwari when he makes one of his bi-annual visits to the village and sets up a temporary office in the home of the Patel for two or three days. This arrangement, an example of the 'blurred boundaries' between the state and society discussed by Gupta (1995), allows the Patel to have privileged access to the Patwari and to control the access that local people have to him. Ordinary people, in other words, have little opportunity to meet the Patwari in a context outside the purview of the Patel.

Moreover, while the official fees for the Patwari's services are very nominal, he commonly demands extra 'fees', or bribes, for performing any of the routine duties for which he is given a salary by the government. These include changing the name on the land title to the living descendant, or recording the division of a piece of land. Such bribes are enforced by and shared with the Patel, the only other person who is aware of the exact nature of local village landholdings; others, because they do not understand or are illiterate and unable to read the information in their titled documents, remain ignorant. For example, one local Ratiya Kanwar man named Dom believes that he legally possesses only two acres. A comparison of his title to official land records indicated that he actually 'owned' between eight and ten acres of cultivable land—a sizable amount that would have made Dom one of the wealthiest landholders in the village. The missing six to eight acres, however, were apparently 'given' to the (now-deceased) father of another Ratiya Kanwar man, Babulal (a relative of the Patel), perhaps as collateral for a mortgage, some thirty years earlier. This transaction was never recorded, and one generation later, Dom has forgotten, or was otherwise unaware that this land is legally his. Babulal's family continues to work and receive income from this land, believing it to be a piece of encroached land that rightfully belongs to them. This is not a unique case in the village. Apparently, several Ratiya Kanwar families, most of them members of the Patel's extended family, are working land that they believe belongs to them, but that is legally in the name of others (see Chapter Six for further discussion on land issues).

When I talked to people about land, I was often shown a tattered *patta* (land title document) and told by the household head that he had no idea what it said, but that he thought that he owned 'x' number of acres. I was very surprised at this. One might have expected that historical memory would have kept such situations in check, or that the literate few in the village would have come to the aid of those who could not read—particularly since land is a 'primordial' asset. But the combined power of the Patel and the Patwari, accompanied by rusty memories and the threat of disfavour in a potential land dispute, discourage any contestation of such a situation. In short, the authority that the Patel gains from access to such officials has allowed him to issue his own threats against local people. In one instance he successfully demanded that the Patwari should not update and change a particular name on a land record. This helped to reinforce the villagers' assumptions that he could (and would) use such power in the future.

The bribes and relationships in which the Patel engages are nothing unique to this area; they are part of a wider 'system of corruption' described by Gupta (1995) in which local superiors are also implicated. Lower-level officials like the Patwari are indeed only one link in a chain of corrupt practices that extends beyond the apex of state organizations and revolves, as we saw with the example of the state legislative candidate, around electoral politics (ibid.: 384).

In short, the institution of the state-administered system of government, the *gram sabha*, and the elected leader of this body, the *sarpanch*, means that this kind of dominance at the village level has waned in other surrounding villages and in other parts of India (Mendelsohn 1993: 833; cf. Pathak 1994: 79–82). In Mohanpur, however, the elected *sarpanch* remains powerless and invisible. Moreover, the *gram sabha* system seems to have had no effect on the Patel's traditional authority, which continues to be buttressed not only by his economic wealth, but also by his control over the local *panchayat*, his juridical power, and by authority figures and power emanating from the state. Indeed, ordinary people's experience of and access to the latter has been dictated by the Patel to such an extent that, in some ways, the state is subordinated to the Patel (see Mendelsohn 1993).[13]

Ritual Legitimacy and Divine Authority

It is not without good reason that both supporters and detractors refer to the Patel in private as *raja*, the king. On the one hand, local people respect him because he is the village headman, whose

[13]See Cohn (1987: 575–631) for a similar discussion of the power of the village headman.

continuing legitimacy, displayed by his ritual, political and economic dominance, is supported by the ruling deity. Whenever anyone is summoned by the Patel (myself included), they drop whatever work they are doing and rush off immediately, out of fear and deference. But they also despise him. He is known to be a corrupt, selfish man who has a 'bad character' and who misbehaves with people. Villagers' fear of the Patel's short temper and strong fist is illustrated in the many stories about how he beats people who try to cross him. Their fear also translates into a relationship of dependence: as one of the wealthiest men in the village, the Patel is in a position to threaten, help or withhold vital material resources from villagers in need.

Given such an unusual situation whereby authority was concentrated in one individual, it puzzled me for a long while why people continued to publicly support the Patel. Although his access to powerful external people could explain some of his invulnerablility, it became clear that the local context in which the Patel continues to enjoy support—even when he was indulging in bad or corrupt behaviour—is through his access to and continuing support from the most powerful cosmological authority. Very simply, people did not dare cross the Patel because of the legitimacy he received from Kaleshar, whose continued support of the headman's behaviour was evidenced by the latter's unremitting local power, his external connections and increasing wealth. Notwithstanding his far-reaching sources of external authority, it is the authority that the Patel receives from Kaleshar's divine legitimacy that remains primary here. In other words, conceptions of legitimacy do not have a separate existence isolated from other social processes: they are culturally constructed, and contextually significant (Pardo 2000: 6–7). As Kaleshar is the leader of the deities, I was told, so is the Patel the leader of the people: they are 'as one'.

The Patel occupies a post that links him with the historical reign of previous local headmen and therefore, directly to the village's founding father. As such, his position has a continuity that will extend beyond the current Patel and is vested in the position itself (cf. Bloch 1989: 66–80). In this respect, the hereditary position of the Patel is a classic example of Weber's traditional authority, where leaders are designated by traditional rules and status (1978 [1922]: 226). The rules in this particular case are in the form of a three-tiered hierarchy of authority in which the Patel is the pivotal factor: Kaleshar rules over the people, by giving authority to the Patel; and the people show respect for Kaleshar, by giving obedience to the Patel. There is no better illustration of this than the Gaura ritual, when whoever is the acting Patel takes on the role of 'Gaura ka malik', and when Kaleshar makes his customary visit, through possession, to that 'man-in-charge'.

The current Patel's authority goes beyond the continuity vested in the position itself. By virtue of having been chosen to ascend to the local throne by Kaleshar, he enjoys a degree of power that sets him apart from individuals who occupied the post before him. The Patel's traditional authority, augmented by the divinely-ordained charismatic authority bestowed upon him when he was a boy, thus appears to be doubly omnipotent: villagers are obliged to him not only because he is the person who happens to hold the office of traditional leader, but because the primary legitimizing authority personally appointed him, as a child, to that very office. It is the combination of these two forms of authority, inextricably linked to the Patel's proximity to Kaleshar, that has allowed him the unusual dominance he has enjoyed since he ascended to the position over two decades ago. And the power that derives from his position as Patel has been augmented by the secular power that emanates from outside of the village.

So, in reference to the episode recounted at the beginning of this chapter, what happened to the Patel's hold on the 'capital of authority'? How could one so powerful, whose actions were regularly vindicated by the support of his supernatural benefactor—the only other being that people feared more than the Patel himself—have suddenly been dismissed from managing the most lucrative post in the village?

What the current Patel perhaps did not consider was that his primary source of local legitimacy was not, to quote Leach (1983: 76), a 'remote god', whose authority is off-limits to all but himself, the traditional 'chief-priest' of the village. At one level, there is nothing remote at all about Kaleshar or any other local deity who regularly interferes in the lives of their human subjects through illness, dreams, and possession. The fact that members of the local ruling caste are descendants of the same founding father and original link to Kaleshar, means that they all have some hereditary connection with, and therefore access to, the latter's divine power. The Patel's assertion that he was the only one who had the authority to act on behalf of the divine indicated that he did not believe that others in his caste also had access to this same authority. And while the Patel's proximity to divine authority certainly gave him a monopoly over status and power, as we shall see below, it was precisely this same proximity that made him vulnerable to those who also claimed access to the divine.

In our three-tiered hierarchy of authority, then, the Patel in the middle could not maintain his traditional authority over the people below without the assumption of sole legitimacy from above. And while the Patel has enjoyed privileged access to this divine legitimacy, he is worthy of obedience from the people only if, as Weber (1978 1922]: 226) says, he observes the traditional limits of power, or obeys the 'customary rules' preserved by the historical tradition (Bourdieu 1977: 16). Moreover, since the Patel ascended the throne from two avenues of authority, he is obligated to remain within the boundaries of both. This means that if he either steps beyond the limits of his traditional authority, or if he fails to aid his subjects, then his divinity will be fractured (Sundar 1997: 85), his legitimacy will be withdrawn and, in the classic formulation of Gluckman (1955, 1963), customary rebellion will be allowed to take place.

Challenge to Traditional Authority

This, I contend, is precisely what happened, as signified when the Patel was dismissed from his duties as *munshi* in the manner described at the beginning of this chapter. The trouble began a year before these events, with the illness of the Patel's daughter-in-law, Durga (discussed in the previous chapter). Recall that my suggestion to the Patel that Durga should see a doctor was met with the response that her condition was not 'simple' but 'supernatural', caused by her husband's (the Patel's eldest son) neglect in propitiating a powerful local deity (who I later found out to be Kaleshar) during a minor house *puja*. Durga's life was spared only after the combined divination efforts of local healers and the promise of an offering of nine goats.

The Patel's explanation was common enough, as far as local beliefs about illness go. Indeed, the majority of supernaturally-caused illnesses are due to minor infractions such as trespassing on sacred grounds or neglecting deities during *puja*, as in Durga's case. For such transgressions, the promise of a coconut and one or two fowls or, at most, a single goat, will usually suffice to make amends to the affronted deity. But in Durga's case, Kaleshar would not relent until he had extracted a promise of an extraordinary number of blood offerings, the likes of which are normally reserved for an annual festival like Gaura wherein all families share the cost. Strange, I thought, that such a demand was made for a relatively minor infraction.

Months later, long after Durga had recovered, the 'real' version of her illness was narrated to me by a man named Prakash, the Patel's first-cousin and close ally. This is a man who is considered to be second in power and authority in the village, but whose affinity for alcohol sometimes diminishes this authority. Durga's illness was indeed caused by the vengeful Kaleshar, I was told, but not because of minor propitiatory neglect. Kaleshar was angry with the Patel himself, for his bad ways and disrespect for the villagers and the surrounding forestland: Kaleshar's land. As punishment and warning to the Patel to mend his ways, Kaleshar had made Durga, a valued daughter-in-law, gravely ill.

This version was revealed to the healers who attended to Durga during the divination ritual that saved her life. The healers, all respected elders in the village, did not tell the Patel about Kaleshar's true revelations because they feared punishment for what would certainly be interpreted as insubordination. The Patel could not possibly be told that his benefactor was angry with him; for he and Kaleshar were 'as one' (*anusar*). In any case, one healer told me, the Patel would hardly believe them, for Kaleshar does not ordinarily appear to healers in the form of possession.

According to Prakash, whom the healers did tell, Kaleshar was referring specifically to the Patel's practice of pocketing the *tendu* bonuses. The *tendu* leaf collection, along with legal ownership of agricultural and forestland, is locally understood to be an 'intermediate' zone of authority that falls rightfully within the operating sphere of government-appointed officials, such as the Patwari or the *tendu* committee (cf. Guha 1989: 91). I was told by several different individuals, including my friend Pradeep (Prakash's nephew), Sanjay (another relation of the Patel) and Naka Sahab (the local forest guard) that this zone is technically off-limits to the specific form of ritual authority held and claimed by the Patel, unless there is a genuine case of overlap, such as if someone wishes to cultivate in Kaleshar's grounds. But stealing peoples' bonuses, or threatening them with land seizures if they do not vote for the proper candidate, are clearly not within the Patel's rightful zone of authority. Moreover, such actions are considered to be morally wrong.

In short, this is precisely where the Patel overstepped his boundaries and exploited his position and the legitimizing force behind it. He should not have used his connections to Kaleshar for his own corrupt purposes; he should not even be interfering in what is rightfully the Baiga's realm, Prakash further complained, referring to the appointment of the new Baiga several months earlier. And he definitely should not use Kaleshar to extend his authority over people with respect to land and forest-related issues. When I asked if the Patel directly used Kaleshar's name in making these threats, I was told that he did not. But he did not have to use Kaleshar's name, because they are 'as one'. The authority behind his position, and the tradition behind that authority, in other words, was enough to instil fear and compliance into people.

Nothing was immediately done after the healers got the first sign that all was not right between Kaleshar and the 'king' until over a year after Durga had recovered and people were preparing for the new *tendu* season, as described in the beginning of this chapter. It was only then that Prakash, the Patel's ostensible supporter, suddenly had a dream, wherein Kaleshar appeared and told Prakash that the Patel must be removed from the position of *munshi* and replaced by someone else, otherwise something terrible would happen. As mentioned earlier, dreams are second only to possession as a powerful medium of communication between humans and the divine, and this particular dream, combined with Durga's near-death a year earlier, convinced Prakash that something had to be done.

After relating the contents of this dream to a small group of Ratiya Kanwar elders who were also very critical of the headman, it was agreed that Kaleshar's demands must be actualized and the Patel must be removed from his *munshi* responsibilities. Normally, such decisions would be made in the context of a village *panchayat* meeting. This was impossible, however, because the *panchayat* was under the control of the Patel himself. In any case, Prakash and the other elders knew that this particular dream represented the kind of traditional legitimacy and divine support required to initiate a challenge to the headman's authority. Notwithstanding this support, Prakash and the other elders also knew that such a challenge necessitated not only a traditional source of legitimacy, but the involvement of individuals whose allegiances lay outside of the village, and who would not be afraid of or subject to the repercussions that might befall someone from the village.

This external support was procured in the guise of Raj and the other three RSS *pracharaks*. As members of an influential organization, these four activists not only represented a powerful source of legitimacy emanating from outside the dominant local system; as residents outside of the village, they would be immune from the potential retribution that might arise from challenging the headman. Since they had been frequenting the village for nearly a year, Raj and the other three RSS activists were fully aware of both the Patel's corrupt practices and local people's dissatisfaction with the headman, and had themselves been lobbying the villagers to bring about his dismissal. When they became aware that assistance was required before the challenge to the headman could be effected, they immediately volunteered their services. Because they were officially living in the RSS quarters in the city, however, these men were not eligible to register the official complaint. So they enlisted the involvement of the ten young men who had been regularly attending the RSS training meetings and who were equally and openly opposed to the Patel's behaviour and corruption. As discussed earlier, all of these men were respected members of the Ratiya Kanwar caste; all were publicly opposed to the Patel; none feared his threats of land appropriation, for they had the knowledge, connections and means with which to stand up against such threats; and although they deeply respected local traditions and the power of the supernatural, they were also not particularly worried about the Patel's ability to exact revenge in the form of calling on supernatural powers, for they had the village doctor, Panchram, on their side. All could afford, in other words, to publicly and materially challenge the Patel. With assurances from Prakash that they had Kaleshar's approval, and accompanied by Raj and the other three RSS activists, these young men approached the *tendu* committee and registered a formal complaint against the Patel. After this, members of the *tendu* committee returned to the village and stripped the headman of his *munshi* duties, and forced the Patel to repay the pilfered bonuses.

This brings us back to the story of the Patel's dismissal in the spring of 1999. Everyone seemed pleased with the Patel's removal, although they would only talk of the matter in private. Fear of the Patel stretched wide, for he had only been dismissed from the position of *munshi*, not from the office of Patel itself. After his dismissal, Raj and the other RSS cadres were also consulted about who should be installed as the new *munshi*. At their advice, it was decided that one of the group of young men, a 30-year-old classificatory nephew of the Patel, should fill the post. Once installed, the new *munshi* admitted to me that he was extremely hesitant in agreeing to take on the responsibilities: the Patel was his uncle, after all, and there was still a possibility of divine retribution. He only took on the job after repeated assurances from Prakash that this was what Kaleshar wanted, and from Raj that the RSS would stand by him. In spite of this, the new *munshi* was convinced that the Patel had something to do with the fever that struck him shortly after the *tendu* season got underway, and he took special precautions and purchased a new amulet for future protection.

Many of the older boys and young men who usually acted as the *munshi*'s assistants (*chaprasi*) throughout the season also refused to help this particular year, or were prohibited from helping by their parents because of potential retribution from the Patel. And the two village criers, respected elders and healers, refused to go around the village and announce the arrival of the season, due to threats from the Patel. The latter even ordered the Baiga not to perform the traditional pre-season *puja*, a necessary ritual that ensures that the season unfolds without mishap. Instead, an impromptu *puja* was performed by Raj and other members of the group of ten young men. On the day the season began, when leaves are the most plentiful, the Patel's extended family boycotted the collection. When I went around to some of his family members and enquired why they had not joined others on what is considered to be the most fruitful day of the season, they responded glumly that they could not go against the orders of the Patel, their village and family head, for fear that he would get angry. Others in the village pointed out that the family was foolish, for they had lost a good day's earnings.

The Patel apparently never knew that the 'real' reason behind his dismissal was Kaleshar's disapproval of his behaviour; nor did he know that Prakash had orchestrated the affair. At least the Patel did not let on that he knew, for the dismissal was handled under the cloak of officialdom by the *tendu* committee members, who told him only that a complaint had been filed by local RSS supporters. When I asked the Patel why he thought he was dismissed, he responded that people in the village had become jealous, and vowed to return as *munshi* the following year.

But the Patel's knowledge of Kaleshar's alleged disapproval is not what is important here. The importance lies in what Kaleshar's appearance at Durga's healing ritual and Prakash's dream signified:

that divine legitimacy had been withdrawn from the Patel and bestowed upon Prakash who, along with the assistance of the RSS, used it to remove the Patel from his lucrative position as *munshi*.

Parallels with this situation can be drawn from Norbert Peabody's (1991) account of the movement of statues between kingdoms in seventeenth-century western India. These statues, which were controlled by Brahmans and said to embody the divine, served as a validation of authority for the deserving king. Power was guaranteed to the king who possessed the statues, and their removal signified a withdrawal of divine support and legitimacy. Prakash's access to divine authority, and his instrumental role in shifting this authority and undermining the singular power of the Patel, is analogous to the movement of statues between kingdoms, which weakened the authority of the king. This access served not merely as an index of the current distribution of power; it actually affected it.

In short, in the same way that new political systems borrow legitimacy from the old by claiming old ritual symbols and redirecting them to their own purpose (Kertzer 1988: 43–7; see also Sundar 1997: 97), once Prakash received Kaleshar's authority, he and others used it as a legitimizing tool to replace the very person whom it had traditionally supported: the Patel. Loss of authority, manifested in his right to act as *munshi*, was thus the consequence that the Patel paid for overstepping his legitimate boundaries of power.

Motives and Accountability

Before I go on to discuss the implications of the RSS's involvement in this affair, it will be helpful to address some of the critical issues of this account that remain unresolved. First, the Patel had been considered to be corrupt for years. Why, with this affair, had he only now been held accountable? The most obvious answer to this question comes from the villagers themselves. Very simply, people were too frightened to challenge the Patel because of his connection to the most powerful legitimizing authority, Kaleshar. The Patel's authority, which was derived from a dual source of traditional office and divine selection, made him invulnerable to local opposition.

Additionally, the Patel had connections to sources of power that emanated from outside of the village, such as the police, the Patwari, and the Congress Party. While this power undoubtedly contributed to the Patel's political invulnerability, it has been suggested that the Patel would not have had access to such power in the absence of support from Kaleshar. Divine legitimacy thus seemed to be pre-eminent.

It is interesting that, in line with Prakash's narrative, no action was taken—nor indeed could be taken—before permission was granted (or the order given) by Kaleshar. However, this is not unusual. Bourdieu (1977: 22), for instance, observes that in social settings in which political authority is relatively uninstitutionalized, political strategies for mobilization can be effective only if they are presented in the guise of the values and customary rules that the group recognizes. Locally, such rules revolved around the diktats of Kaleshar, which were traditionally carried out through the customary authority of the Patel. Only when this authority was transferred away from the Patel were his detractors in a position to act. In this way, Prakash and others were able to instigate a successful challenge against the Patel by upholding the existing order and respecting the customary rules that the group honours: the most important being obedience to the big god.

Similar to Guha's (1989: 98) observations, what this scenario has demonstrated is that the locally dominant tradition possesses a certain openness that allows for resistance. And while the Patel's proximity to divine authority gave him a certain monopoly over status and power, it was his abuse of this privileged proximity that made him vulnerable to those who also claimed access to the divine.

This raises the question of Prakash's motives in initiating the process that led to the Patel's removal. Because he was not a contender for power against an established authority, Prakash's personal motives must remain a matter of conjecture (cf. Gluckman 1963: 127). In terms of public discourse, Prakash became the instigating force behind the Patel's removal because it was he who had the dream wherein Kaleshar gave the order for the Patel's dismissal. Having received the first 'sign' or warning from Kaleshar one year previously in the guise of Durga's illness, Prakash and others probably felt that they had no choice but to act, for fear of divine wrath. At a political level, Prakash was afforded public legitimacy because he was the elder closest to the Patel. While he remained a public supporter of the Patel, he was also a known sympathizer of those who hated and feared him. He, like everyone else, privately disapproved of the Patel's behaviour;

and, like others, he had been robbed for ten years of his hard-earned *tendu* bonuses.

Being an ostensible supporter of the Patel, Prakash could not afford, politically or materially, to mount the challenge on his own and go to the *tendu* committee himself, even though, by virtue of the dream, he clearly possessed the necessary 'capital of authority'. For contesting the Patel was politically subversive and potentially dangerous, and while Prakash was a powerful and respected elder, he was still the Patel's social and political junior, a 'subordinate officer' (Gluckman 1955: 34) who while remaining loyal to the Patel in order to protect his own status, went about orchestrating the Patel's removal from behind the scenes.

What would happen next in a normal course of events would be for Prakash to announce the contents and instructions of his dream in the context of a local *panchayat* meeting. But the methods that would ordinarily be used to carry out Kaleshar's instructions could not go through this proper channel because the local *panchayat* was under the control of the Patel, who could impose and enforce punishment. Prakash would never have stood up to a public challenge from the Patel who, it was feared, was still capable of hijacking Prakash's dream and overturning Kaleshar's orders with a dream of his own, as had happened with the replacement of the Baiga. In short, while Kaleshar's authorization was in the first instance necessary, it was not sufficient. An alternative source of power emanating from outside the dominant local system was needed from which this divine authorization could be effected. This came in the form of the RSS, which provided Prakash with the legitimate means through which Kaleshar's order could be implemented.

One final question remains: given the accompanying legitimacy afforded by their association with and backing of the RSS, why could this group of young men have not acted on their own initiative? Why did they need Prakash's intervention? I suggest that before they could act, these young men, along with the elders, had first to be assured that they would not face divine retribution by challenging the Patel. While they were increasingly influential, these young men were also aware and afraid of Kaleshar's potential disapproval, and the latter's permission had to be guaranteed before any action could take place. This permission had a dual importance in initiating this process: not only did it ensure legitimacy of action and sanction against divine repercussion, but it also resolved any questions of Prakash's personal motivation and self-interest that may have arisen from other villagers. At a more practical level, I would suggest that this group of young men could not act earlier because the RSS connection had developed into a locally recognizable alternative source of legitimacy only during the course of the previous year, when their local visits increased from a monthly to a weekly frequency. In short, while both the elders and the young men wanted to change the situation, neither felt that they could do so single-handedly. The former needed the connections and courage of the latter; the latter needed the permission and traditional legitimacy of the former.

Traditional Authority, the State and the RSS

Against the backdrop of the ethnography described above, we have seen how traditional authority was bound to notions of divine legitimacy and buttressed by external sources of power, including those emanating from local-level state personnel. The transformation of this authority revolved around the Patel's violation of the cosmological and political limits of power, and took place through a sort of 'customary rebellion' that drew its legitimacy from both traditional and external sources.

By illuminating the way in which the Patel impaired villagers' access to lower-level state officials, this chapter has also shown how the state is experienced by ordinary members of a 'backward' *adivasi* community. To be sure, the removal of the Patel from the position of *munshi* did not translate into his dismissal from the post of village headman. However, it was an indication to local people that his all-encompassing, corrupted authority was no longer guaranteed. This meant, by extension, that local access to state officials and external avenues of power was no longer contingent on the Patel's control. The *munshi* affair thus succeeded in demonstrating how the 'everyday state' (Fuller and Bénéï 2001) is not a discrete entity acting on behalf of a single powerful individual, but is in fact available to local people as a representative tool that can be used to enforce basic citizen's rights (see Gupta 1995; Lerche 1995).

While villagers perhaps recognized that the state can be utilized in this way, they had long been resigned to the fact that corruption of the sort practised by the Patel was a reality about which they could do nothing. It was only through the instrumental involvement of the RSS activists that it was confirmed to local people that existing state personnel, represented here by the *tendu* committee, could be employed to their advantage.

One of the most important outcomes of these activists' intervention was the increased local legitimacy that the organization was able to gain. As with other strategies outlined in previous chapters, the participation of an external authority in the *munshi* affair can be compared to one of the more successful social upliftment strategies used by early Christian missionaries: namely, the legal assistance and representation offered to *adivasi*s against corrupt landlords in land rights cases. As is well known, this strategy was part of the Church's broader 'civilizing mission' and served as an important means by which missionaries were able to endear themselves to the *adivasi* communities amongst whom much of their proselytization efforts were concentrated.

By similarly lending their legitimacy and external authority to those who wished to contest the dominance of corrupt local power holders, the RSS has further revealed the mimetic relationship that it has with the Church. According to Jaffrelot (1993a: 8), the process of 'emulation' remains one of the central strategies in the propagation of Hindu nationalism. Resulting in part from the presumed threat that the Christian presence poses, the motives behind the RSS's involvement in the events outlined in this and the previous chapter were undoubtedly related to their own 'civilizing mission', which is underpinned by the wider spread of *Hindutva*. As we know, the larger 'community' of *adivasi* people has yet to be encompassed within the *Hindutva* fold. By specifically engaging in the kind of social upliftment strategies outlined above and in the previous chapter, the RSS, through what van der Veer (1994: 135) calls the 'politics of inclusion', has been able to make inroads into the local community and come closer to this goal.

All of this notwithstanding, RSS activists did perform a valuable social service on behalf of the village as a whole. By involving themselves in this affair, moreover, they received widespread support from the Hindu and the Christian communities alike. All villagers profited from the dismissal of the Patel; all, ultimately, came to know that it was at the behest of Raj and the other cohorts who were acting under the auspices of the RSS, that the dismissal came to pass; and all were grateful to these activists for their role in enforcing accountability and returning the long-overdue bonuses. Like Church missionaries before them, such intervention thereby increased the RSS's local standing and enabled it to establish a legitimate political foothold from which it could facilitate its *Hindutva* agenda.

One thing that might explain the cross-community support and appeal of the RSS in this matter is the state's own failure to fulfil its proper role and responsibilities to its poorest citizens. Local *adivasis* clearly lack the resources and connections to demand what is their due, such as convenient and affordable access to basic medical care; moreover, they feel an inability to mobilize the available state mechanisms to counter powerful, exploitative individuals and enforce what is their right. That the provision of these services necessitated the intervention of an extra-state authority like the RSS thus highlights the failings of the state to look after the basic entitlements of its populace (cf. Avritzer 2004: 58).

Similar to their engagement in illness and health practices, outlined in the previous chapter, the assistance of Raj and the other RSS activists with the dismissal of a corrupt power holder is a more benign but therefore more insidious means of propagating *Hindutva*. Local people were grateful to Raj who, acting in the role of 'conversion specialist' (Brass 1997: 16), once again demonstrated his concern for local people by familiarizing himself and intervening in a local corruption issue. It was by engaging in this kind of social upliftment activity, however, that Raj and the other RSS activists have been able to further endear themselves to the community as a whole, thus establishing a platform from which more aggressive strategies could be initiated later on.

As is clear from the successful way in which these activists has been able to engender support within this particular community, part of the RSS's broader strength lies in the fact that it performs these kinds of 'social services' even as it holds out the (unspoken) threat of aggression and violence. Before the events described above occurred, members of the *tendu* committee seemed to be held hostage to the Patel's authority, claiming that they had no power to act without local participation. Given the Patel's penchant for sharing bribes with local officials, a more plausible scenario is that members of the committee were reluctant to act because they too, were willing beneficiaries of the Patel's corrupt practices. It was only when the complaint was issued by RSS-backed individuals that the *tendu* committee officials set about removing the Patel. The disturbing implication here is that a precedent has been set whereby the transformation of traditional authority, along with the enforcement of accountability of local-level state officials, required the indirect involvement of an extra-state power that is widely associated with violence.

In short, working on behalf of the welfare of disenfranchised groups in reaction to a dysfunctional state, and engaging in the kind of civic activities that emulate historical Church practices, have provided the RSS with a vehicle through which it can gain increased legitimacy. However, such strategies have also enabled the RSS to position itself to communalize social relations and actively promote the idea of the 'threatening (Christian) other' (Jaffrelot 1996: 8). The manner in which the latter has been achieved is the subject of the following two chapters.

CHAPTER SIX

Land Relations and Local Tensions

W e have just seen how the RSS, through the provision of assistance in the form of additional biomedical treatment and the enforcement of accountability of local-level state officials, has successfully managed to endear itself to the local community. This organization is not generally lauded by its critics for its engagement in these and other kinds of social upliftment programmes. However, its involvement is appreciated by those amongst whom such activities are most commonly carried out: 'backward' *adivasis* and other disenfranchised members of the populace.

In spite of its participation in these kinds of 'social services', it is the more aggressive aspects of the Hindu nationalist movement with which the RSS is most publicly associated. Indeed, one of the more disturbing implications of the way in which this organization has managed to legitimize its presence locally is that a precedent has been set whereby the provision of basic needs requires the involvement of an extra-state power that is widely associated with aggression and violence.

It is a consideration of the more aggressive activities in which the RSS engages to which this and the following chapter is devoted. I am particularly interested in examining how the idea of the 'threatening (Christian) other' (Jaffrelot 1996: 8) is propagated locally. I am also interested in understanding the role that RSS activists play in the transformation of local tensions into wider issues of communal and nationalist interest.

The present chapter is specifically concerned with land relations and the growth in land tensions between the Ratiya Kanwar Hindus and the Oraon Christians. As noted in earlier chapters, the political and economic dominance of the Ratiya Kanwars has in part, been reinforced by the latter's possession of and claims over agricultural and forestland. Over the past two decades, however, the previously landless Oraon newcomers have steadily cleared and acquired sections of local land through encroachment and, more recently, through mortgage. Members of the Ratiya Kanwar caste in particular, have become increasingly concerned about this acquisition and, on the basis of their 'original settler' status, insist that the land rightfully belongs to them. During the course of my fieldwork, these concerns were manifested in an unusually high number of land disputes, which revolved around encroached and mortgaged landholdings. These disputes resulted in growing tensions between the 'first clearer' Oraons and the 'original settler' Hindus. The objective of this and the following chapter is to provide a detailed outline of the origin of such tensions, in order to demonstrate their appeal to local RSS activists as an effective 'conflict symbol' (Horowitz 1985: 217–18), or issue that is used to evoke deeper disputes over group entitlement and status.

The tensions that are outlined below may, upon first examination, take on the appearance of an ordinary caste conflict that revolves around 'sons of the soil' issues (Weiner 1978): a predictable response of a threatened high caste to the increasing power of an aspiring low-caste. As we shall see, however, it is through the active involvement of the RSS that such tensions have recently assumed an ethnic and communal orientation. The way in which this has happened is related to what Horowitz (1985) calls the 'politics of entitlement', or the contest for worth and place. Borrowing from Horowitz, I suggest that it is not a question of who actually came first that governs the strength of claims to local land. Rather, it is the political context of such claims and the way these have been utilized that has come to matter (ibid.: 203–4). More specifically, it is the way in which such claims have been appropriated and used by the RSS that what could have been classified as ordinary caste conflict has instead, been transformed and represented in terms of the 'master narrative' (Varshney 2002: 34) of *Hindutva*.

It is in Chapter Seven that the manner by which this has contributed to the reinforcement of communal boundaries and facilitated the emergence of communal sentiment will become fully clear. Discussions there will focus on how local tensions have been appropriated by RSS proponents and, in the process of what Tambiah (1996) has categorized as 'focalization' and 'transvaluation', attached to the wider Hindu nationalist agenda.

In the meantime, it is necessary to provide an overview of how land tensions have evolved into one of the central 'conflict symbols' that are being used by the RSS to emphasize and transmit its *Hindutva* message to local people. This is the objective of the present chapter, which begins with a brief discussion on the ritual significance of land, and on how this connects to the political dominance of the 'original settlers', the Ratiya Kanwars. The three main categories of landholdings (titled, encroached and mortgaged) and corresponding ways of acquiring land are then identified. The following two sections are concerned with household income, consumption and expenditure, which are linked to current patterns of land acquisition and distribution. Thereafter, focus is on the evolution of land disputes and the possible reasons for the increasing frequency of tensions.

Ritual Significance of Land

As mentioned in previous chapters, the importance of land and jungle to *adivasis* in this area and elsewhere in Chhattisgarh is inextricably linked to, and governed by local cosmology (Babb 1975; Baviskar 1995; Elwin 1955; Fuchs 1973). This importance is made particularly manifest with respect to those who, as the descendants of the founding lineage of the village, occupy a privileged position and are ritually responsible for much of the land designated within the village boundaries: the original settlers (*khuntkattidars*), or Ratiya Kanwars.[1]

In Chapters Two and Five, I discussed the numerous rules with respect to forest and agricultural land that were prescribed by the

---

[1] Local connotations of this term are very different from the way in which it has been employed in Jharkhand in the context of the Mundari *khuntkattidar* system. In Mohanpur, it is used to refer to the descendants of the Ratiya Kanwar 'original settlers'; in the Mundari context, it carries specific legal connotations with respect to recognizing the 'non-transferability' of land belonging to the descendants in the male line of the original founders of the village, and the rights of the village community over both agricultural and forest land. See Hoffman (1950: 2389); Kelkar and Nathan (1991: 73) and Singh (1978) for a fuller discussion.

supernatural 'owners' when the 'original settlers' arrived in this area. Such rules largely revolve around the protection of sacred space and the regular propitiation of supernatural beings. As the 'original settlers', the Ratiya Kanwar are obliged to perform certain rituals on behalf of the rest of the village and to interact with certain deities. There is a great deal of prestige attached to these obligations which, as we saw, helps to explain why this caste has been able maintain its local dominance (see Agarwal 1994: 17–18; Gell 1992: 87).

It is the 'time of arrival' issue that seems to be the most pertinent here, and that serves, as Horowitz (1985: 202–4) has observed, to invoke a sense of proprietorship and superiority. As we shall see, however, the issue of 'original settler' claims is less important than the communal end to which such claims are used.

In spite of the ritual maintenance of the land being the primary responsibility of the Ratiya Kanwars, all Hindu households are obliged to obey and propitiate the local deities. This sort of obligation has been observed in Bastar amongst the Muria Gond and is derived from what Gell calls the 'moral bond' between people and divinities (1992:112). This bond is based on reciprocity: because all people in the community supplement their livelihoods and income from the local land and jungle that belongs to the deities, they are obligated to return the favour with ritual offerings. As we saw in Chapter Four, ignoring such obligations can result in divine retribution in the form of illness and even death.

The Oraon Christians, as an 'outsider' community whose ritual allegiances lay elsewhere, are largely exempt from many of the obligations that must be carried out locally. Those few Oraon households who observe these obligations tend to do so out of fear that they will invoke the wrath of the previous (Hindu) owner's deity. Take the example of Laxmi Shankar, a Ratiya Kanwar landowner who had recently mortgaged one of his fields to Anand Tamba, an Oraon Christian. It was the anniversary of the annual field *puja*, a costly event that required the sacrifice of two large goats. As the new *khet malik* (person in charge of the field), Anand Tamba was expected to sponsor the *puja*. He initially refused, on the basis that he was Christian and 'did not believe' in such practices. Laxmi Shankar countered that the deity did not care if Anand Tamba was Christian or Hindu: since he was now the *khet malik*, he was not only obliged to participate in and contribute to the costs of the *puja*; he or his family would be harmed by the field deity if he failed to do so. Out of concern for his family's welfare, Anand Tamba agreed to cooperate.

Similar obligations can also accompany an actual purchase and transfer of ownership. As illustrated by Sumitra's illness, which was discussed in Chapter Four, disregarding such obligations can have harmful consequences. In spite of such risks, most Oraons refuse to participate in the frequent *pujas* that are held on behalf of the entire village because they have their own god and 'do not believe' in such practices. As I shall argue below, this refusal serves to reinforce the Oraon Christians' outsider status and amplify the cultural distance between them and the Hindu community. For now, we turn to the economic importance of land.

Landholdings and Tenancy Arrangements

Agricultural land is the most valuable economic good in this area, owing to the fact that seasonal rice cultivation is the primary source of income for people in this part of Chhattisgarh (cf. Babb 1975: 7). As a productive asset, arable land in particular is the 'supreme good' (Gregory 1997:111), having a permanence and importance that no other asset possesses.[2] Similar to Hill's (1986) observations about rural south India, access to such land has traditionally been the most important source of economic and political power. No family is considered to be particularly influential unless it holds—and preferably owns—a sizeable amount of arable land that reaps a substantial yield (1986: 166).

There are three categories of landholdings in this area—titled, encroached and mortgaged—and three corresponding ways whereby locals commonly acquire land: through inheritance, encroachment, or mortgage. There is a fourth way in which land can be acquired locally, and that is through purchase. Being the most ritually and economically valuable asset locally, however, land is rarely sold. Moreover, it is difficult, if not impossible, for outsiders to legally acquire land in this area. As such, I have deliberately ignored the issue of purchasing as a means of acquiring land.

[2]The economic importance of land in India has been thoroughly discussed elsewhere. See Bailey (1957); Baviskar (1995); Gell (1992) and Sundar (1997). See also Dumont (1980 [1966]).

Titled Land

While forestland, rivers and most trees are owned and utilized in common by members of the village, titled landholdings include wet and dry paddy fields (*khet* or *dhan tikra*) and dry fields (*tikra*) where pulses, oilseed and vegetables are sown. I am not concerned with the specific types of fields, however, since 'ownership' in general, is the primary focus in this chapter.

It is unsurprising that the descendants of the 'sons of the soil' (Weiner 1978) are in possession of the majority of titled landholdings (*kabja jamin*).[3] Out of the 763 titles recorded locally, the majority (94 per cent) are held by the Hindu community, of which over three-quarters belong to Ratiya Kanwar households. Significantly, only 6 per cent of these are held by Oraons (see Table 6.1 and Graph 6.1). Landholdings average 2.6 acres, although these range from a low of five *dismil* (0.05 acres) to a high of 15 acres.[4]

This distribution is largely reflective of 'original settler' dominance, which is manifested in sheer numerical strength and length of residence. The fact that Ratiya Kanwars have been in the area for around ten generations and comprise nearly half the village population helps to explain why members of this caste currently account for 75 per cent of all titled land ownership.

While I have no data on when the original titles were first issued, the records to which I did gain access date back to 1931. To the

[3]It has been pointed out numerous times that it is very difficult to get an accurate idea of the extent of land ownership and use in rural villages (see Dewey 1978; Hill 1986; Ludden 1984). Locally, land revenue records are negligently kept and are sometimes two-generations out of date and as such, don't reflect current ownership. Moreover, most local cultivators cannot report their total acreage with accuracy in part because the holdings consist of a set of separate, scattered plots. Instead, people tend to describe their acreage by the amount of seed they plant: '*barah-tami khet*' (24 kg) or '*ek-kandi*' khet (40 kg) cover areas of roughly one-half and one acre, respectively. These problems notwithstanding, I have tried to give the most accurate picture possible by cross-checking oral data (including estimates of plot size, average amounts of seed planted and yield), with official land records.

[4]I have chosen to ignore specific details about land area for the following reasons: a) the land records are out of date and do not reflect the true acreage of titled land, much of which has been expanded through encroachment, or mortgaged; b) people do not actually know their total acreage, or c) are not willing to admit their total holdings due to encroachment. However, I do not think that actual area is a particularly important detail for this chapter, which is more concerned with general patterns of ownership across the community.

Table 6.1: Titled Landholdings

	Number of households	No. hh with titles	Number of Titles	% of total titles
Oraon Christians	43	7	46	6
Hindus	121	89	717	94
Ratiya Kanwar	75	67	576	75.52
Dudh Kanwar	4	0	46	6.03
Majhuar	27	16	76	9.96
Yadav	8	3	12	1.57
Panika	3	2	6	0.79
Chauhan	2			0
Lohar	2	1	1	0.13
Total	164	96	763	

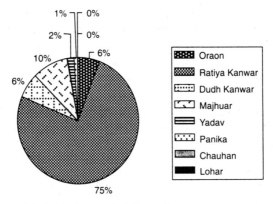

Graph 6.1: Titled Landholdings (by percentage of total)

frustration of all local people, very few new titles have been issued post-independence. This has been due to government legislation about the use of forestland, which was largely related to the emergence of timber as an important commodity (cf. Gadgil and Guha 1995: 84–8, 1992). In continuity with forest policies in colonial India, the post-independence implementation of the 1952 National Forest Policy saw individual ownership of forestland and products being further restricted whilst state control over forest protection, production and management was reinforced (Gadgil and Guha 1992:

185; cf. Sundar 1997: 197–9).[5] The view that government forest policy should be based on national needs was favoured until 1980. This was when the Forest Conservation Act (FCA) sought to limit the implicit commercial bias in this policy by prohibiting states' indiscriminate use of forestland for non-forest purposes without the approval of the central government (Pathak 1994: 57–60).[6] The central government also insisted on the protection of the forests from encroachment, and ordered that encroachers (mainly *adivasi* cultivators) be served with eviction notices. Encroachment, access to forestland by local people, and the security of land tenure, are all issues that yield strong electoral mileage at the state level, particularly during election years (Pathak 1994: 93), and following establishment of the FCA, several state governments issued notifications to regularize encroachments, which created provisions for the legal recognition of existing cultivation. Amongst these were Madhya Pradesh, which, in an ostensible effort to combine the protection of forestland with the rights of *adivasis* to sustainable livelihoods, recommended that those (largely *advasi*) forest dwellers who have been cultivating land prior to 25 October 1980 be awarded a *patta* (legal title) to their land (ibid.: 96). Those found to have been cultivating land after this date were liable for eviction.

Local *adivasis* and others who qualified for a *patta* were required to obtain official verification of their residency and length of cultivation from the village headman, the Patwari and other land officials. As we saw in Chapter Five, these officials regularly charge sizeable 'fees' or bribe money in amounts that local people cannot typically afford. This, combined with the expensive and time-consuming legal process involved in proving ownership, has further discouraged people from

[5] The history of forestland rights and legislation within India is long and complex. For a brief synopsis of land regulation from the mid-nineteenth century onward, see Kulkarni (2000). For a fuller history, see Gadgil and Guha (1995), and Guha (1989). For accounts of encroachment and contemporary forest policy issues surrounding them, see Jeffery and Sundar (1999), Sundar, Jeffery and Thin (2001), Pathak (1994) and Sarin (2005).

[6] There were ambiguities with the terms of this Act, including the meaning of 'forest land' itself, as well as what was meant by 'putting forest land to non-forest use'. Consequently, states interpreted the Act to mean only reserved forests, or land under the control of the Forest Department (see Pathak 1994: 58). After clarifications from the Central government, 'forest land' came to include not only reserved, protected and village forests, but also revenue forests, *panchayat* forests and village common forests.

applying to transfer their plots into legal holdings.[7] In 1988, a new Forest Policy was passed that stressed the welfare of forest-dwelling communities and categorically stated that the rights of *adivasis* and others living within and near forests should be fully protected (see Kulkarni 2000). This Policy should have made it easier for local people to apply for and receive the legal titles that were promised with the 1980 Forest Conservation Act. However, this Policy was never translated into law, and at the time of fieldwork, it remained essentially a broad statement of government intent specifying the legal rights owed to (largely *adivasi*) forest-dwelling communities.[8]

Given the difficulty of acquiring them, land titles are rarely sold. Instead, they are traditionally passed down from father to son after the former's demise. As discussed in the previous chapter, changing the name on the title to the living descendant of the original owner requires several thousand rupees in bribe money, which must be paid to the Patel, the Patwari and other officials in charge of recording land ownership. This is an impossible amount to afford for people in this area, which explains why the majority of legal titles are usually registered in the names of the original owners: a father, grandfather or great-grandfather of the surviving (male) household head.

Encroached Land

It is because titled land is so difficult to secure that encroachment is the most common means by which local people increase their landholdings. This type of landholding is known locally as *beja kabja jamin*, or 'land without title'. Officially illegal, it involves clearing a

---

[7]This entitlement dates back to the Rent Act of 1859 that confers 'occupancy rights' or legal title to people who have worked a plot of land for more than twelve years. See Neale (1962: 82–102), Patel (1974: 59–61) and Behuria (1997: 61–4) for details on the Rent Act of 1859 and its various reforms and amendments that confers occupancy rights on tenants.

[8]For fuller details, see Sukhendu Debbarma at www.international-alliance.org/documents/india_eng_full.doc. In 2005, the government drafted a Scheduled Tribes (Recognition of Forest Rights) Bill, which aims to provide *adivasis* with protected rights to forest land and resources, including legal titles (*patta*) to forest lands occupied before 1980, along with ownership rights to forest resources, grazing rights and habitation rights. Whilst not without limitations, if enacted, this Bill would represent an important step in securing the land rights of *adivasis*. See Gupta (2006), Kothari and Pathak (2005), Krishnaswamy (2005) and Shah (2005) for extended discussion about this new Bill.

part of the forest and building a field on what is classified as government land (*sarkari jamin*).[9]

Encroachment became a widespread practice in the early 1900s, after the forest department 'reserved' over 20 per cent of India's total land area and curtailed local use rights (cf. Baviskar 1995: 150; see Guha and Gadgil 1989: 147). As mentioned above, a system of management was introduced in the early 1950s that favoured commercial priorities and further diminished the self-provisioning capability of *adivasi* cultivators. It was at the same time that the government of India officially prohibited *adivasis* from expanding their landholdings and halted the issuance of land titles. Since such holdings were in any case generally very small, it became necessary for *adivasis* to further supplement them through encroachment.

Encroachment has long been recognized as a major cause for loss of forests in India (Kothari 2004: 78), and the extent to which forestlands have been encroached currently stands between 10–30 per cent of India's total forestland (see Kulkarni 2000). As acknowledged by scholars and activists alike, however, *adivasis* are often unfairly labelled as 'encroachers' (Kothari 2004: 78). Forests have been an intrinsic aspect of *adivasi* economy in Chhattisgarh and elsewhere in India long before such land was reserved under the various acts that have been instituted since the mid-nineteenth century (cf. Baviskar 1995: 150).

For reasons noted earlier, local people have been discouraged from taking advantage of the 1980 Forest Conservation Act. Instead, they continue to cultivate on and expand their illegal landholdings. Understandably, they are reluctant to acknowledge their exact number of encroached landholdings and related yields, for they can be fined and even ordered to abandon or destroy a field if they are found without legal title (see Baviskar 1995 for a similar discussion on the

[9]The 'government land' on which local people have encroached is officially 'forest land', or land that is controlled and protected by the Forest Department. This is in contrast to 'revenue land', which is forestland that has been surveyed and transferred to the Revenue Department. The latter is a process that regularizes cultivation and gives recognition to forest dwellers' access to such land (cf. Pathak 1994: 57–9; Debbarma n.d.). Forest department officials and conservationists, for whom protection of the forest and wildlife is of chief importance, are historically antagonistic to the use of forests by local people, and actively seeks to obstruct attempts by the state to regularize encroached holdings (Pathak 1994: 93; cf. Kothari and Pathak 2005).

difficulty of acquiring information about encroached land). However, I gradually came to know that nearly two-thirds (104 of 165) of all households in the village possess some amount of encroached land. This land included both *tikra* (dry fields) and *khet* (wet-paddy fields), the most valuable type of landholding due to its high productivity and dual-season cultivating capacity (see Table 6.2, Graph 6.2).[10]

Table 6.2: Control of Encroached Landholdings

	Number of households	*No. hh with encr. land*	*% of group with encr. holdings*
Oraon Christians	43	38	88
Hindus	121	66	54
Ratiya Kanwar	75	41	55
Dudh Kanwar	4	1	25
Majhuar	27	22	81
Yadav	8	1	12.5
Panika	3	1	33
Chauhan	2	0	0
Lohar	2	0	0
Total	164	104	

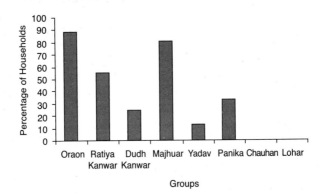

Graph 6.2: Percentage of Each Group with Encroached Land Holdings

[10]Because of the difficulty in getting exact figures in this area, I have relegated my information here to number of households that possess encroached holdings, instead of number of holdings. Although this prohibits any sort of accuracy with

As we can see, just over half (55 per cent) of all Ratiya Kanwar households possess some amount of encroached landholdings, compared to the majority (88 per cent) of the Oraon Christians and the majority (81 per cent) of the Majhuars. These proportions perhaps reflect the need for the latter two communities, compared to the Ratiya Kanwars, to increase their nonexistent or relatively small amount of titled landholdings through encroachment.[11]

The important point here is that it is this category of landholding that has come to the attention of the RSS. More significantly, it is the pattern of Oraon Christian encroachment—not that of the Majhuars or Ratiya Kanwars—that is being transformed by local RSS activists into a communal issue. Reasons for this attention are connected to the relationship that the Oraon Christians and Hindus have to land, labour and access to cash, and will be discussed later on.

For now, it is important to emphasize that the creation of a field out of forestland is a costly, time-consuming process that can take several years of continuous labour and attention. A large area of forest must be cleared of trees and other growth, then drained and levelled before it can be transformed into a productive parcel of land. In a practice that Gregory (1997: 88) calls the 'ancestral labour principle', the householder who originally cleared a piece of vacant forest land and laboured to make the area into a cultivable field had permanent user-rights to it (cf. Kelkar and Nathan 1991: 45). Conversely, without this labour, the householder could not claim rights to the land. This principle, which traditionally favoured the 'first clearer', has been traced as far back as the laws of Manu and, according to Gregory (1997: 88), evidence of its existence in some form or another can be found throughout India today.

Up until recently, this principle applied locally as well, as the 'original settler' Ratiya Kanwar who first cleared and laboured on a parcel of land was recognized as the 'owner' of that land. Later, their efforts were legally recognized with the distribution of land titles beginning in the 1920s and 1930s (Behuria 1997; cf. Neale 1962).

---

respect to actual numbers and thus creates a problem for cross-comparison, it nonetheless, provides a good indication of general distribution of encroached landholdings. There is obviously some overlap between those who possess both titled and encroached plots, the details of which are not important at this time.

[11]Given the relatively low number of other caste households and their reliance on other forms of income (e.g. goat-herding etc.), I am only interested in those groups that have the largest amount of encroached landholding.

Oraon man preparing field for rice cultivation on encroached forestland near the Petfora river.

When this was halted post-independence, those who claimed and cleared such land—irrespective of whether they happened to be an 'original settler' Ratiya Kanwar—were considered to be the de facto 'owners' of it by locally recognized rules of ownership. Indeed, it is through recognition of the ancestral labour principle that those who arrived in the area years and sometimes generations after the Ratiya Kanwars have been able to acquire (encroached) land for themselves. Recognition of this principle went so far as to allow the 'first clearer' to dispose of his land through mortgage or sale—even though there was no 'legal' right attached to it.

In recent years, recognition of this principle has diminished, with rights of the 'ancestral owner' taking precedence over rights of the 'first clearer'. In a manner that will be outlined later on, members of the Ratiya Kanwar community have begun to assert their claims over tracts of land on which they have never laboured. Such claims are being made on the basis that, as the 'sons of the soil' and rightful proprietor, this land 'belongs' to them. During the course of fieldwork, these claims evolved into a number of land disputes over encroached land on which the Oraon Christians have been cultivating for nearly three decades.

As we shall see later on, at the centre of these disputes is what Horowitz (1985: 186) calls the 'politics of entitlement', which is underpinned by the contest over time and place. The 'original settler' Ratiya Kanwars arrived first and therefore, claimed ownership of the surrounding forestland. Those who migrated later were traditionally obliged to seek permission from the Ratiya Kanwars before they were allowed to live in the village and cultivate land in the area. As the most recent immigrants, the Oraons' were forced to do the same, and it is the land that they were 'given' and first cleared when they arrived that is currently under dispute. They are beginning to feel increasingly apprehensive about their ability to hold on to this land, even though they are nominally protected by the fact they have been labouring on it since before 1980 and thus have a right to apply for legal title. However, the procedure to do so involves signatures and verification from the Patel and the Patwari. The 'fees' (bribes) for such services are even more exorbitant than those required to amend the name on the title, and neither the Oraons nor any other local group can afford to go through the process.

Such disputes could be construed as an ordinary caste conflict, where a threatened high caste community reacts to the upward mobility of an aspiring low-caste community. As we shall see below and in the following chapter, however, this issue has moved beyond the confines of an ordinary caste conflict and has been appropriated by local RSS activists and, through the process of 'transvaluation' and 'focalization' (Tambiah 1996), aggregated into the wider Hindu nationalist agenda.

Mortgaged Land

The increasing tension over encroached land is only one of the issues in which the RSS has become involved. The other issue concerns mortgaged land, particularly those arrangements made between Hindus and Oraon Christians. For reasons mentioned above, land in this area rarely comes into the market. Instead of selling, people choose to 'pledge' (Hill 1986: 157) or mortgage their titled or encroached land if they are in need of cash or other items.[12] Entering into such a transaction is preferred in this area for the simple reason

[12]This is in contrast to the observations made by F.G. Bailey (1958), where *selling* land in neighbouring Orissa, as opposed to mortgaging, was the most popular method of acquiring urgent cash.

that it allows land to remain in the household's possession and thus lacks the finality of an outright sale (ibid.; cf. Bailey 1964: 111).

There are three kinds of mortgage or 'tenancy' arrangements in this area.[13] The first is *sahaji*, a basic sharecropping arrangement where the harvest is split fifty-fifty between the landholder and the creditor/tenant, who provides the seed and labour. A second is called *regha*, where the landholder gives his land to a creditor/tenant for a single season and a fixed return, such as ten quintals (1,000 kg) of paddy (unhusked rice). If the yield from the land happens to be less than the amount agreed between landholder and creditor/tenant, then the latter must still pay the full amount to the landholder in cash or kind.[14]

The possibility of a financial loss for the creditor with these two arrangements is high, given the unpredictable nature of the monsoon in this area, along with the mediocre grade of the soil, which is mixed with sand and known as *balu mitti*, and the ever-increasing cases of blight and pests. In a *sahaji* arrangement, for example, the creditor risks losing (at the minimum) his seed input; in a *regha* arrangement, the creditor risks losing the entire fixed amount. Both of these arrangements favour the landholder, who ensures a return regardless of the value of the harvest. For this reason, most creditors refuse to enter into either of these kinds of arrangements and they are rarely mentioned as an option by those who wish to negotiate a mortgage.

With little exception, the most common type of tenancy arrangement is *gahana*, a sort of 'usufructuary mortgage' (Jain 1929: 60-1) wherein the landholder gives a parcel of land to a creditor in exchange for immediate remuneration, usually cash, sometimes paddy, rice or livestock. 'Usance' rather than interest rate is the essence of such mortgages (cf. Gregory 1997: 225).[15] Throughout the period of a

[13] I hesitate using the term 'tenancy arrangement' because there is no 'rent' as such, involved in any of the local transactions. It is for this reason that I also prefer the term 'creditor', because 'tenant' implies rent. However, as Gregory (1997: 220-1) points out, this sort of contract could be analysed as a 'tenancy' agreement from the perspective of the lender who gets land for which all 'rent' is paid in advance. The borrower is therefore, acting as a landlord and the lender as a tenant.

[14] For comparison, see Jain (1929: 60-1), who also describes an arrangement called 'rahan', found in north and central India, wherein money is obtained through mortgaging landed property or houses, and *girvin*, where money is loaned against jewellery.

[15] Hill (1986: 88) discusses the inappropriateness of the notion of 'interest' when applied to such arrangements due to the 'timelessness' of such transactions. Bailey (1964:111) pointed out long before, however, that the creditor's 'use of the land represents the interest on the sum borrowed'.

gahana arrangement, which can range anywhere from one to 10 or more years, the creditor has full rights to the land and harvest, and payment must be returned to him before the landholder resumes 'ownership' rights. The payment ranges from a few hundred to a few thousand rupees and is determined by a combination of plot size, quality of soil and urgency of cash. In contrast to *sahaji* and *regha*, this is a 'creditor's market'. Although there is some scope for negotiation between landholder and creditor, in that the former puts forward the terms for the specific tenancy arrangement, the mortgage arrangements and relationships which stem from them clearly favour the creditor, who is allowed to keep the harvest and sees a return on the capital— potentially for generations.[16]

A typical example of a mortgage transaction will occur when a Hindu landholder will suddenly arrive in the Oraon *basti*. This is an unusual event, for Hindus do not ordinarily visit Oraon Christians unless they want one of two things: to negotiate a piece of *gahana* land or to purchase liquor. The latter will be discussed in Chapter Seven. When the issue is the former, the landholder usually visits the Oraon *basti* in the early morning or around mid-day, when he will be sure to find people at home (negotiations are invariably between men). When it is discovered that he has come in search of a creditor, it is immediately assumed that something sudden or tragic has happened for which he needs urgent cash, and the first question by the Oraons will be *'ka huis'* (what happened)?

After a brief rendition of the story, which generally revolves around a relative's sudden death or a forthcoming wedding, the landholder will get down to the business of informing those present that he is interested in mortgaging a piece of land. He will invariably find an interested party who will ask for details: size and location of the plot, number of seasons and average yield, asking price and period of time for which the owner wishes to give up rights to the land. If the potential creditor is still interested then he will ask to be shown the land, which may lie several kilometres away from the village. There is generally no bargaining for the asking price (which is always, according to Oraons, within reason), for the 'seller' has a specific need, and thus a fixed price. If, finally, everything meets with the creditor's approval, then

---

[16]This is in contrast to what Bailey (1958: 59–60) described as a 'buyer's market' in 1950s Orissa, where the eagerness of the seller and the ludicrous display of indifference of the buyer characterized the situation (cf. Bailey 1964: 111).

there will be a verbal agreement between the two parties and plans will be made for the formal exchange of cash (or kind). In this respect, both parties benefit: the Oraon Christians receive land, the Hindus receive cash.

During the time that I conducted my fieldwork (1997–9), there existed a total of 41 *gahana* arrangements. All but one of these had been mortgaged by Hindus (over half by members of the Ratiya Kanwar caste alone), mostly to Oraon householders, who held the majority of mortgages (see Table 6.3, along with Graphs 6.3a and 6.3b). The significance of this is not only in the fact that Oraon Christians, compared to Hindus, do not tend to mortgage their land, but also that over 50 per cent of all Oraon households had the cash with which to invest in a *gahana* arrangement.

Locally, the average amount of land mortgaged was 0.5 acres, and the average price for such a plot was Rs 1,200. During my fieldwork, plots ranged from ten *dismil* (0.10 acre) to two acres, and prices for a single plot ranged correspondingly from Rs 200 to Rs 3,500. These are relatively small transactions, even by local standards. However, size of plot had nothing to do with productivity of the soil or the price obtained for the mortgage, and there was no systematic 'size-cash-productivity' relationship as such. Large, fertile plots could be mortgaged for a few hundred rupees, and small, less fertile plots could go for a couple of thousand rupees. Indeed, it was not unusual to hear of a mortgage of Rs 2,000 for a 0.5 acre plot, or Rs 500 for 1.5 acres. During my fieldwork, the maximum total that a (Hindu)

Table 6.3: Mortgaged Landholdings

	No. Mortgages Given	% of Total Mortgages	No. Mortgages Held	% of Total Mortgages
Oraon Christians	1	2	36	88
Hindus	40	98	5	12
Ratiya Kanwar	21	50	2	5
Dudh Kanwar	–	0	–	0
Majhuar	9	22	–	0
Yadav	8	20	–	0
Panika	–	0	3	7
Chauhan	2	2	–	0
Lohar	–	4	–	0
Total	41		41	

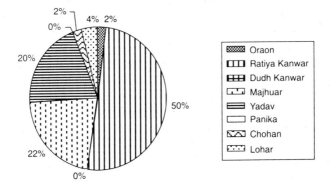

Graph 6.3a: Mortgages Given (by percentage of total)

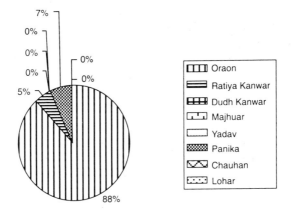

Graph 6.3b: Mortgages Held (by percentage of total)

landholder received when he mortgaged several pieces of land at once to different creditors was Rs 6,700, and the maximum total that a single (Oraon Christian) creditor was owed was Rs 3,750 (for three separate mortgages).

Instead of size or relative productivity, asking prices were directly related to financial necessity. Hindus did not mortgage their land without urgent or obligatory necessity, for land is the 'supreme good'. 'What do we have left if we give our land away?' I was often asked. Indeed, mortgaging a plot of land means not only that the landholder loses a significant amount of paddy income for several years, but also that he has to return the loan to the creditor. To put this in perspective, if we calculate the amount of seasonal yield from a half-acre plot (the kind usually mortgaged for something like Rs 1,200) to be six quintals (500 kg of paddy or 250 kg of rice, roughly Rs 2,125), then the creditor is recovering the loan value of the land in the first season alone. Moreover, such arrangements were undertaken for a particularly wide span of time. While the landholder always intended to pay off the loan within one or two seasons and thus re-acquire the rights to his yield, I am aware of only one loan that was paid off after only a single season. Instead, most were paid off after an average of four years, although the longest mortgage arrangement with which I was familiar, had entered its eleventh year.

While the landholder appears to be the long-term loser in this arrangement (making it a 'creditor friendly' market indeed), local people do not see this kind of arrangement as particularly imbalanced. For them, the transaction of land for cash is a sort of barter exchange that is determined by the interest each side has in the object of the other. In this case, the participants have decided that one object (land) is worth another (urgent cash), and the exchange is construed to be equal. As Gregory (1997: 74) has observed, when goods (including land) become commodities, the price they receive may be higher or lower than that which market valuation would predict. Locally, it is the 'urgency of cash' factor that, when figured into the actual (and apparently nominal) amount of cash given for the land, brings the amount of cash up to the level of what the land (and its returns) might actually be worth. There is, in other words, no criterion by which it can be judged that the land and the amount of cash for which it is mortgaged are equal or unequal in value (see Humphrey and Hugh-Jones 1992: 1–8).

In short, it is through mortgaging land that the urgent financial needs of landholders are met. As those with the most titled land and less cash, it is normally a member of the Hindu community who enters into such a transaction; as the community that happens to be in regular possession of cash, in turn, it is the Oraon Christians who usually act as moneylender. Most importantly, it is through serving as creditor in a mortgage arrangement, that the Oraon outsiders are able to gain access to titled land. As will be discussed later on, it is this particular arrangement, which is underpinned by the Oraon-creditor/

Hindu-tenant relationship, that has become one of the central issues around which local tensions have revolved.

Local Contingencies

All of this notwithstanding, the landholder does not enter into such an arrangement unless very hard-pressed for cash. This is an issue that has been thoroughly examined by Bailey (1958), whose reasons given for selling land in rural Orissa in the 1950s closely parallel those for mortgaging land by Hindus in Mohanpur between 1997–9. These are reflective of costly social and ritual obligations and revolve around 'contingencies' (ibid. 50) that suddenly arise. As with Bailey's observations, local contingencies revolve around birth, marriage, funeral and healing rituals, where costs that sometimes run into thousands of rupees can be met only by selling (or mortgaging) the main asset available: land. Weddings are a particularly expensive undertaking (especially for members of the Hindu community), with expenses ranging between Rs 10,000–25,000. While families are invariably helped by the donations of others, they are obliged to reciprocate these favours later on. For example, one Ratiya Kanwar mortgaged a quarter-acre plot of land for Rs 500, the amount he needed for the gift that he 'owed' another Ratiya Kanwar family whose daughter was soon to be married, and who had given his own daughter a similar gift at the time of her marriage four years previously.

Funeral expenses are also extremely costly, ranging between Rs 6,000–10,000. Likewise, I came across several cases of illness, including that of Jaglal mentioned in Chapter Four, that required lengthy and expensive healing rituals for which land had to be mortgaged. Of the 41 mortgage arrangements that existed during my fieldwork, all but one was contracted for one of the events described above, the exception being for the purchase of a pair of buffaloes.

A useful case study of how a mortgage agreement transpires is that of Laxmi Shankar, a high-caste, landowning Yadav from Mohanpur whose sister suddenly died in early October 1998. Since she was a widow and had no surviving children, the responsibility for meeting her funerary expenses came down to Laxmi Shankar and his two brothers. Laxmi Shankar owned a great deal of land (at least seven or eight acres), but he had mortgaged the entire amount during the previous three years to mostly local Oraon families in order to meet the expenses that arose from the deaths of his parents two years before, and from his regular consumption of liquor.

When Laxmi Shankar found himself suddenly in need of cash, with no land to mortgage, he went to one of his creditors, Kirtan Dada, and asked for more money against the land he had earlier mortgaged to him. Kirtan Dada, a Ratiya Kanwar who had originally paid Rs 1,100 as mortgage for this land, was not in a position to pay an additional Rs 900. So Laxmi Shankar went to another potential creditor, Anand Tamba, a Christian Oraon who had worked for many years as a wage labourer outside of the village. Anand Tamba agreed to pay the requested Rs 2,000 to Laxmi Shankar, who returned the Rs 1,100 original *gahana* money to Kirtan Dada and kept the Rs 900 balance. This sort of repossession and transfer of creditor, along with the involvement of three parties, is unusual, but the manner in which the agreement took place is typical of the way in which such transactions occur locally.

As Bailey observed in Orissa (1958: 62), it is not possible to estimate the frequency of each type of event, since the effect is cumulative. In a year, for example, one family may be obliged to spend only the minimum on mandatory obligations, whereas another household may have hosted a marriage, or suffered a death—or both—in which case it would have been forced to acquire a large amount of cash very quickly. Although there is a system of reciprocity wherein all local villagers contribute some amount of rice or paddy to assist the hosts on such occasions, their combined contributions do very little to offset more than a minor portion of the total costs. In short, the necessity for village households to reproduce themselves (Gregory 1997: 219) requires people to spend large sums of money on life cycle rituals.

As noted in Chapter Three, the expenses for such contingencies are a great deal higher for local Hindu than for the Oraon Christians. This is due largely to the present-day influence of the Church, which not only discourages Oraons from participating in ritual practices classified as *shaitan ka kam*, but also disapproves of the more costly social obligations that accompany marriages, funerals and other life-cycle rituals. The problem of finding money for these contingencies is thus more of a central preoccupation for Hindus who, for reasons discussed in previous chapters, remain both committed to and constrained by such obligations.

The necessity and relative uncertainty of such expenditure is nothing new to people in this area, thus reconfirming the observations made by Bailey four decades ago. What is interesting for our purposes is the indirect role that it plays in the context of the recent increase in local land tensions, which have revolved around both encroached and mortgaged landholdings. I return to this issue below.

To summarize the most important data thus far, 94 per cent of titled landholdings are in the possession of the Hindu community. Of these, over three-quarters are held by Ratiya Kanwars, whereas only 6 per cent are held by Oraons. Just over half of the Ratiya Kanwars (55 per cent) have some amount of encroached land, whereas nearly all of the Oraons (88 per cent) have encroached plots. Finally, the majority of the existing mortgages consisted of Hindu-owned land given to Oraon creditors. It is also important to note that the practice of lending cash is not relegated to just a few Oraon households, but is extended to over half the Oraon community.

These data are interesting because they reflect the relationship that the two communities have with land, labour and access to cash: the Oraons are cash-wealthy but land-poor; the Hindus are cash-poor but land-wealthy. The implications of this relationship will be fully drawn out in the next chapter. At this stage, the question arises as to where the Oraons get their cash, for it is this issue that, along with land, is largely at the heart of local tensions; and it is these tensions that are being appropriated by the RSS and attached to the wider Hindu nationalist agenda. Before I address this issue, it is important to provide some background data on how yield, consumption and expenditure figure into local tensions.

Yield, Consumption and Expenditure

Land is not the only source of income for landholders, and with few exceptions, no household could live on the income from their agricultural yields alone (cf. Pathak 1994: 97–103). The average yields of rice-producing households in the village is 850 kg of rice (worth Rs 7,225) for what is considered to be a 'good' or normal year.[17] In a

---

[17]Throughout the course of my fieldwork, 1 kg of rice (or half kg of paddy) could be purchased for an average of Rs 7–10. For simplicity, I have chosen to use a single

'bad' year, such as when a monsoon arrives late, average yields can be reduced by one-third to one-half of this norm.

Following the harvest, all rice-producing landholders have a surplus of paddy above immediate consumption requirements, which include daily consumption and exchange needs, along with seed-rice for planting and for paying local labourers. This is stored in the home and acts, as Gregory (1997: 131–41) observed in Bastar, as a sort of 'bank' from which ready 'cash' is drawn and used to exchange at local shops for food and non-food items alike.

It is difficult for people to measure the exact amount of paddy that they exchange on a daily basis. An average household of four usually 'withdraws' at least 2 kg (roughly 1 kg of rice, or Rs 8.50) for basic household subsistence needs, such as tea, sugar, biscuits and spices. Factoring in the basic household consumption requirements, this surplus is rapidly depleted. Most households calculate that they are forced to purchase between three to six months of rice (in a 'good' year) and between six to nine months worth of rice (in a 'bad' year) to cover their basic consumption and social obligations. Depending on size of household, annual needs range from 360–1800 kg of rice (Rs 3,060 to 15,300), with the majority falling between 720–1080 kg, or Rs 6,120–9,180.

Significantly, this practice of 'withdrawing' paddy from the 'bank' is practiced predominantly amongst members of the Hindu community. Paddy is rarely exchanged for other goods by the Oraon Christians, who believe that it is not right to exchange something as important and basic as food. Instead, Oraons use cash for all forms of exchange. Once again, these practices are related to land, labour and access to cash: members of the Hindu community, particularly the Ratiya Kanwars, own and cultivate more land than the Oraon Christians. Hence, they are in possession of the primary local currency (paddy or rice) that is used to exchange or barter for goods. Oraons, in contrast, own very little land, and hence must earn the bulk of their (cash) income from non-agricultural sources.

Apart from the major expenditures mentioned above, all households spend a great deal from their 'bank' on ordinary ritual and social obligations. These take the form of small but regular donations made at village-wide *pujas*, weddings, funerals and births;

figure of Rs 8.50 per kg. I have also used rupee as the basic unit of measurement, although locally, rice or paddy is the primary unit of measurement.

'offerings' given to travelling *sadhus* and guests; and expenditures on medicines and minor healing *pujas* and 'simple' illnesses. Given the sporadic nature of such expenditures, these are difficult for individual households to calculate. However, several local householders and shopkeepers estimated that each Hindu household spends between two and five quintals (Rs 1,700–4,000, or Rs 2,850 average) on such obligations annually.

Oraons are also faced with ordinary social obligations of this sort. However, these amount to roughly half of what Hindus spend (Rs 765–2,000 or Rs 1,400 average). As noted above, this is due largely to the fact that many of the Oraons' costlier ritual obligations have been abandoned or scaled down with the influence of the Church. This means that additional resources are available to channel into other forms of expenditure, such as non-essential material goods (a second bicycle or a television), or land. The Oraons themselves often acknowledge the connections between local Hindus' levels of expenditure on ritual obligations and associated hardship. Whenever a Hindu person comes to the *uppar para* in search of a creditor, for example, an Oraon will invariably comment about how expensive *katta* people's beliefs are.

The point that I want to draw out from this discussion is that income from land alone is not sufficient to support most local households, whether Hindu or Christian, landholding or non-landholding. Consequently, most households are forced to engage in alternative income-generating activities. It is the kind of labour in which households and communities engage that is important here, for it is this that not only sets the Oraon Christians apart from the Hindus, but that also contributes to the increasing tensions between the communities. It is in the following chapter that I will demonstrate the specific manner by which local tensions have become mapped onto wider issues of nationalist concern. For now, I turn to the kinds of income-generating activities that serve to underpin these tensions.

Alternative Sources of Income

For members of the Hindu community, and to a lesser extent the Oraons, the most common agricultural-related labour from which income is derived revolves around the seasonal agricultural needs of local landholders. All landholders must hire labour (of between five and fifty labourers) mid-way through, and again at the end of the agricultural cycle to support their weeding (*nindai*) and harvesting (*dhan katna*) requirements. This sort of labour can last between one day and two weeks and is available to labourers over a period of two to three months. It is generally paid in kind (6 kg of paddy or 3 kg of rice per day, per person) instead of cash. Actual earnings are difficult to measure since such earnings are often immediately consumed. However, these sorts of activities are such that one member of the household, working every day for the two to three month period during which such work is available, is capable of earning up to four months of their household consumption requirements.

The most important non-agricultural source of income for Hindus is the collection of 'minor forest produce', which is sold by villagers to their local shops, from where it is sold on to outside wholesalers. Locally, such produce includes *mahua* (flowers used to make liquor), *tendu* (leaves used to make cigarettes), *lak* (hardened sap used in making bangles) and *sarai* (flowers used for making oil). Most households estimate that the collection and sale of this produce can yield an average of Rs 4,100 per year (including Rs 2,100 for *tendu* leaf, Rs 1,700 for *mahua*, and Rs 300 for *sarai*; see Graph 6.4).[18]

Oraon landholders also supplement their income through the collection and sale of local forest produce. As relative newcomers to the area, however, they do not have access to the same amount or quality as the Ratiya Kanwars and other Hindus, who lay claim to

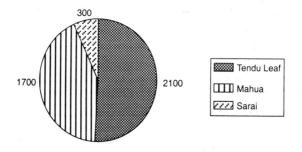

Graph 6.4: Sources of non-agricultural income
(Hindu households, annual average)

[18]I have no reliable data on income from the collection and sale of *lak*, an activity in which relatively few households engage (cf. Baviskar 1995: 141–2 for a comparative discussion on the importance of minor forest produce to *adivasi* subsistence throughout India).

the best trees or choicest plots years ago. Many Hindu households, for example, possess large, cultivated tracts of *tendu* bushes, whereas Oraons are relegated to smaller tracts scattered throughout the jungle. Although these are rarely titled holdings, ownership of such bushes and tracts is recognized as binding by the 'ancestral labour principle'. Access to better-quality forest produce like *tendu* is reflected in the comparative amounts collected by both communities, which sees the Hindu community earning an average of Rs 500 more per year than their Oraon counterparts. The latter, moreover, do not bother with collecting *mahua*, *sarai* or *lak* in any systematic fashion.

Largely for these reasons, Oraons derive much of their income from two types of wage labour (*buti kam*). The first is that which takes place outside of the village, including construction work (*mistri kam*) or other paid labour (*hajari kam*) such as cooking or public road works. Such labour is generally carried out by the male household head, who usually spends anywhere from two weeks to five months of the year away from the village. Over half of all Oraons (22 households) earn money from this sort of labour. Of this, nine households earn up to Rs 1,000 per year, five households earn between Rs 1,000–2,000, and eight households earn between Rs 2,500–5,000. In contrast, less than a quarter (24 of 121) of all Hindu households engage in this kind of labour. Of these, the vast majority earns below Rs 1,000 per year (see Table 6.4, Graph 6.5).

Table 6.4: *Hajari* and *Mistri* Income

Income Class (Rs)	No. Hindu households	% of 24 Hindu hh	% of total (122) Hindu hh	No. Oraon hh	% of 22 Oraon hh	% of total (43) Oraonhh
0–500	14	58.33	11.00	1	4.55	2
501–1000	7	29.17	6.00	8	36.36	19
1001–1500	0	0		3	13.64	7
1501–2000	2	8.33	2.00	2	9.09	4
2001–2500	0	0		0	0	
2501–3000	1	4.17	0.05	1	4.55	2
3001–3500	0	0		0	0	
3501–4000	0	0		4	18.18	9
4001–5000	0	0		3	13.64	7
Total Households	24		19	22		51
Maximum Income	3000			5000		
Minimum Income	100			500		
Average Income	727.08			2261.36		

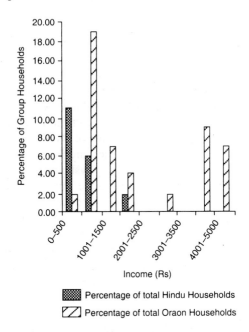

Income (Rs)

▨ Percentage of total Hindu Households
▨ Percentage of total Oraon Households

Graph 6.5: Household Incomes from *Hajari* and *Mistri*

The second most common form of wage labour is mud hauling (*matti dona*). These are generally shorter, two-week jobs where a labourer is employed to assist in the construction of a new field or a home. Such work is often carried out in a neighbouring village, allowing the labourer to return to the village at night. Nearly three-quarters of the Oraon community engages in this sort of labour, and nearly half of these earn between Rs 2,500–5,000 per year. As with *buti kam*, Hindu people rarely engage in this sort of labour. Of the 11 households that do participate in this kind of labour, only three earn a substantial income (see Table 6.5, Graph 6.6).

Part of the reason why more members of the Hindu community do not engage in this sort of wage labour is because they make a sufficient amount of supplementary income from other local sources (such as the collection and sale of minor forest products) through which, when combined with income from their land, they are able to meet their household needs. Another reason concerns habit and tradition. Hindus—especially the Ratiya Kanwars—consider themselves to be farmers who labour on the land; they are not

Table 6.5: *Matti Dona* Income

Income Class (Rs)	No. Hindu households	% of 11 Hindu hh	% of total (122) Hindu hh	No. Christian Oraon hh	% of 33 Oraon hh	% of total (43) Oraon hh
0–500	5	45.45	2.00	0	0.00	
501–1000	3	27.27	1.00	11	33.33	25
1001–1500	1	9	0.05	1	3.03	2
1501–2000	1	9	0.05	6	18.18	14
2001–2500	0	0		2	6.06	5
2501–3000	0	0		5	15.15	35
3001–3500	1	9	0.05	1	3.03	2
3501–4000	0	0		3	9.09	7
4001–5000	0	0		4	12.12	9
Total Households	11	5	9	33		77
Maximum Income	3500			5000		
Minimum Income	200			600		
Average Income	1004.55			2400		

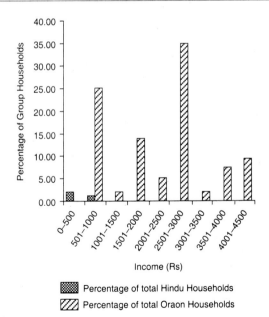

Graph 6.6: Household Incomes from *Matti Dona*

accustomed, I was told, to doing the sort of 'hard work' that Oraon people do for money.

As far as the Oraons are concerned, however, the reason that Hindus do not work so hard is due to their attitudes about caste. Bahadur, my 'brother', once complained that

> These Hindus, they think they are Brahmins. They think that they are too good for work like carrying mud; they think that we are lower caste (*chota admi*), and that this is the reason we do this sort of work. Yes, we 'lower caste' people take what work we can get, and we actively go in search of work to neighbouring villages or to the city. But we are not ashamed of this.

In addition to the labour described above, Hindus and Oraon Christians alike, augment their income through more sporadic activities that add to the overall earning power of most households. These include raising and selling pigs, goats and chickens, and selling handmade sleeping mats and brooms. Such activities can earn participating households an average of Rs 150–300 per year, although one particularly industrious Oraon household regularly earns over Rs 1,200 per year. Additionally, two Oraon households were supported by income from their teenaged daughters who worked as domestic help for a Catholic mission in the city, from where they send between Rs 3,000–4,000 per year back to their families. Finally, Oraons supplement their incomes from the production and sale of liquor, with nearly half the community (21 of 43 families) making between Rs 300–1,800 per year. It is important to note at this stage, that while the latter is not the most lucrative means of earning, it is perceived to be responsible for much of the Oraon community's social and material improvement and, as we shall see in the next chapter, has become one of the primary 'conflict symbols' (Horowitz 1985: 217) for the RSS.

Local Income and Landholdings: A Summary

There are three important points to be brought out from these data. First, and most obviously, very few local households can live off of their agricultural incomes alone, which means that nearly all—including those whose yields are sufficient to meet their needs—engage in some form of alternative income-generating activity.

Second, the sorts of activities in which the two communities predominantly engage are different. While both supplement their incomes from the collection and sale of minor forest produce, Oraons earn more from engaging in outside wage labour, whereas Hindus earn more from local agricultural labour. This is a reflection of the fact that many Hindu households have sufficient land, or claims over forestland, from which they generate a sizable proportion of their income. When this income is combined with the supplementary income activities such as *tendu* leaf and *mahua* collection, the bulk of the Hindus' subsistence needs appears to be met. Likewise, the types of earnings are different. Whereas cash is earned from the collection and sale of *tendu* leaf, most other forest produce is exchanged directly for rice, paddy or other goods. Equally, income from other agricultural forms of labour (in which mostly Hindus engage) is chiefly in the form of rice or paddy. Income from the sort of outside wage labour in which predominantly Oraons engage, on the other hand, is in the form of cash.

Which brings us to the third and most important point: the supplementary wealth of the Oraon community is largely in the form of cash and material items, whereas the wealth of the Hindus is in the form of paddy, which is derived from their own land and from the collection and sale of forest produce. What this means in terms of land relations is that when the Ratiya Kanwars' and other Hindus' need for extra cash arises, their first course of action is to mortgage a parcel of land. Because of their greater participation in wage labour, the Oraons generally have greater access to cash, a necessity for entry into the *gahana* relationship and the primary reason for the predominantly Hindu landowners to approach the Oraons for a mortgage. As Hill (1986: 83) has observed, it is inevitable that cash-impoverished households need to borrow and that cash-rich households wish to put their surplus funds to work. Mortgaging land simply enables the landholder, who is in need of money, to retain control over his land while it is temporarily cultivated by someone else (ibid. 157). Most Hindus who were part of a *gahana* arrangement during the course of fieldwork told me that they would prefer to enter into such an arrangement with their fellow caste members, and initially they tend to enquire amongst themselves. For reasons mentioned above however, Hindus are rarely in a position to enter into the agreement, prompting the landholder to enquire amongst the Oraons, where he will invariably find an interested party.

This fact is reflected in the configuration of mortgages held. The Oraons were the creditors and the Hindus were the landholders in

36 of the 41 local *gahana* arrangements that existed at the time of my fieldwork; half of these arrangements were made with Ratiya Kanwar householders. Importantly, this configuration had been the norm for as long as the Oraon Christians had resided in the area.

While this sort of indebtedness might not be unusual, it creates a power relationship between the borrower and the lender, in favour of the latter (see Gregory 1997: 218). In the case of the Oraon Christians and Hindus, the creditor-owner relationship is an ostensibly symbiotic (though creditor-friendly) relationship where all parties benefit. However, the possibility of tensions inhering between creditors (like the Oraon Christians) who belong to one ethnic group and tenants (like the Hindus) who belong to another is always very high (see Horowitz 1985: 117). The combination of this with the increasing tensions over encroached landholdings mentioned earlier, merely exacerbates the potential for local conflict, to which I now turn.

Land Tensions: 'Original Settler' versus 'First Clearer'

Land tensions in this area are nothing new and, as in the past, commonly revolve around a single plot of land claimed by two different parties. For obvious reasons, the most contentious plots in the area are encroached landholdings, and all recent disputes have revolved around such land. Disputes are normally resolved through a *panchayat* meeting mediated by the Patel, where both parties are allowed to present reasons for their rightful claims. With few exceptions, the contentious plot is divided and the two 'owners' are forced to accept equal shares.

Disputes of this sort are invariably initiated by a Ratiya Kanwar 'original settler' against an encroaching neighbour. As noted above, during the course of my fieldwork, there was an increase in the frequency of disputes between Ratiya Kanwars and Oraon Christians, all of which revolved around encroached land near a local river, the Petfora. This particular land was part of the dense jungle, lying unused by members of the Hindu community because it was home to several local deities. Members of the first three Oraon families who immigrated to Mohanpur were the first to begin cultivating in this area three decades ago, having been given permission to do so by the Ratiya Kanwar elders. This land is highly valued for its superior soil and because it allows for dual-season cultivation instead of the more common single season.

It is the descendants of these elders, most of whom are now deceased, who are today claiming to be the rightful owners of this land. They have never cultivated this land themselves, as its location was considered to be an important home of several local deities and thus, out of bounds for agricultural activities. The Oraon Christian newcomers were warned of the potential danger that would befall them if they cultivated this land. Desperately landless and armed with the protection of their own deities (including Jesus), the Oraons were less concerned with these potential ramifications (see Chapter Three), and went about transforming swathes of forestland into what are today, some of the most high-yielding fields in the area.

It was in 1995 that the descendants of the Ratiya Kanwar elders began to dispute the ownership of this land. A narration of one of these disputes that occurred two months into my fieldwork will serve to illustrate the manner in which subsequent disputes have transpired. This dispute concerned a half-acre *beja kabja* (encroached) plot that lies at the edge of the Petfora. It had been given to the father of Nicholas Tamba three decades previously by a Ratiya Kanwar family, the Porgas, whose own titled plot borders the disputed piece of land.

One morning in late 1997, as Nicholas Tamba went off as usual, to continue ploughing and preparing this plot for planting the following season's crop, he discovered eight members of the Porga family with four ploughs between them, readying the plot for their own cultivation. They refused to move from the land and insisted that they were merely reclaiming what rightfully belonged to them. They had been eying this land for the last two years or so, and had come to the decision that, since no apparent misfortune had befallen the Oraon cultivators for the past two decades, the latter must have driven the deities away from this area, rendering it safe for the original 'owners' (themselves, incidentally, encroachers) to reclaim their land.

At this, Nicholas Tamba went directly to the Patel, who called a meeting for the following day to resolve the dispute. In addition to the Patel, 16 Oraon Christian men and 35 Hindu men (both Ratiya Kanwar and non-Ratiya Kanwar) were in attendance, the former to bolster support for Nicholas Tamba, the latter to support the Porga family. Both sides claimed full rights to the land: the Porga family on the basis that the land originally belonged to them by virtue of being the *khuntkattidars* (original settlers), and Nicholas Tamba on the basis that the Porga family had given his father this land three decades ago, and because of the labour that he and his father, as the 'first clearers', had subsequently put into the land.

After an hour of argument and discussion, with supporting statements by the accompanying Oraons and Ratiya Kanwars as to the rightful ownership, the Patel divided the land exactly in half. This decision clearly favoured the Ratiya Kanwar's claim of ownership through 'original settler' status. But it also drew on the 'ancestral labour principle' and the Oraon Christians' claims of ownership due to their 'first clearer' activities and on the basis that they had put in years of labour to make this land cultivable.[19] The Oraons immediately accepted this verdict, however, and started digging the boundary lines into the disputed plot of land. But the majority of the Ratiya Kanwars protested, claiming that the Patel was favouring the Oraons unfairly. It was alleged by one Ratiya Kanwar man that the Oraons were going to continue acquiring 'Ratiya Kanwar land' in this manner, and the most senior member of the Porga family suggested that perhaps the Oraons had paid the Patel a sum of money to give a favourable verdict. The Patel, on hearing this, angrily told the group that if they (the Ratiya Kanwars) think that the Oraons were going to leave the village now, after building homes, shops and fields, then they were mistaken: the Oraons were here to stay. The Patel also warned the group that if there were any future disputes of this sort, the Ratiya Kanwars must go about their grievance in the proper fashion by taking the matter directly to the Patel and the *panchayat*, instead of suddenly assuming control over the land as the Porga family had done.

Following this dispute, and for the next several weeks, those Oraons who worked contentious plots of land near the river left their homes extremely early each morning to attend to their fields, with the expectation that their land would be targeted next. But this was the only land dispute that occurred during this particular season in late 1997. During the course of my fieldwork, however, a total of six plots near the Petfora river, all cultivated by Oraons for at least two decades, were contested by the 'original' Hindu landowners.

---

[19]Incidentally, a court of law would likely have awarded complete ownership of the field to Nicholas Tamba under the provisions of the 1980 Conservation Act. The Patel's verdict suggests an unduly strong valuation of 'original rights' over the kind of investment the first clearer put into the land. See Patel (1974) and Behuria (1997).

As illustrated with this particular ethnography, it is the assertion of the rights of the 'original settlers' that has come to define these disputes. Such an assertion effectively denies the 'first clearers' any permanent claims over the land, and is clearly in contrast to the 'ancestral labour principle' that has characterized access to local land in the past. This assertion can be compared with the traditional rules amongst the Munda and Ho, tribal groups concentrated in neighbouring Jharkhand. There, the 'first clearer' could only remain with the consent of the *khuntkattidar* or 'original settler': non-'original settlers' were liable to be ejected at any time (Kelkar and Nathan 1991: 74; Hoffman 1950). In contrast, the local Oraons' assumption that the land that was given to them three decades ago still belongs to them today, indicates that a comparable practice with respect to original settler rights has *not* existed in Mohanpur. This practice does appear to be gaining credence, however, as suggested by the assumption of members of the Ratiya Kanwar caste that they have the right to take back their land from the Oraons, in spite of the 'ancestral labour principle' and without going through proper procedure.

At the heart of this issue is the 'politics of entitlement' (Horowitz 1985: 186; 226). The resource to which the Ratiya Kanwar disputants feel entitled is, of course, land. It is by virtue of being the first arrivals, or 'original settlers', that they have not only staked such a claim; it is also for this reason that they feel justified in ignoring the 'ancestral labour principle' that favours the first clearer. Because of the strong association between Ratiya Kanwar and 'original settler' status, many Oraon Christians were surprised by the Patel's relatively favourable verdict in this (and subsequent) disputes. Oraons later speculated that this could be a kind of 'soft' bribe that was related to the fact that the Patel required their electoral support, on behalf of the Congress party, in the forthcoming *panchayat* election.

As we saw in the previous chapter, corruption, even the 'soft' sort like a favourable verdict in a land dispute, is a common practice in this area. And indeed, one of the regular 'promises' offered by local MLA candidates to secure votes in this area is a legal land title for those possessing *beja kabja* land (although these promises do not include bureaucratic assistance with the complicated legal process, and as such, usually come to nothing). From the view of the Ratiya Kanwars, forthcoming elections and the long overdue employment of the 1980 Forest Act gives the issue of the Oraons' encroachment a certain urgency. For, since the Oraons have been cultivating the land since before the 1980 cut-off date, they would be eligible for legal titles. And original settler claims would no longer be defensible.

The following two disputes occurred toward the end of the summer (*garmi* season), just before the monsoon began in late May 1998; two more occurred during the following post-monsoon harvest season in December 1998; and the last occurred in May 1999. There was another beginning to develop as I concluded my fieldwork in August 1999. All of these disputes concerned full or partial reclamation claims of dual-season *beja kabja* land near the Petfora river; all were initiated by the 'original settler', the Ratiya Kanwar Hindus, against the 'first clearer' Oraon Christians; and all were eventually resolved by the Patel, as before, in favour of both parties. Before 1997, I was told, there was at most one dispute in any given year that required the mediation of the *panchayat*; this was the first time since the Oraons arrived, that the number of disputes had been so high. It was also the first time that the disputes had been exclusively initiated against Oraon Christian landholders.

Before I explore the broader reasons for this, which relate to the increasing presence of the RSS in local affairs, it is useful to examine some demographic and ecological factors that have contributed to the increasing disputes and land tensions.

Demographic and Ecological Factors behind Land Disputes

The first factor concerns the local population, which numbered 893 persons at the time of my fieldwork. This is a figure that has more than doubled in one generation, a fact that has obviously contributed to the diminishing cultivable landholdings of most local families. The same portion of land that could sustain the basic needs of a large joint household in the past, for instance, does not begin to meet the needs of smaller households when it is divided. This gives those who depend the most on income from land (local Hindus) greater cause for concern about the source of future income for themselves and their children.

A typical example of this is the case of one middle-aged Ratiya Kanwar informant named Chamarsingh, who describes how his family used to be 'rich' two generations ago, when his grandfather had 40 titled acres to his name. After his grandfather's death, the land was divided between his five sons, each of whom received eight acres. Chamarsingh's father's portion was recently divided between Chamarsingh and his three brothers, who received two acres each.

Once Chamarsingh's three teenaged sons marry and have families of their own, each will receive an equal portion of the remaining two acres. In just two generations, then, the titled landholdings of a previously wealthy family have been subdivided to such a degree that Chamarsingh does not know how his sons are going to live when the land is divided once again. While the progressive decrease in landholdings through inheritance and divisions varies between families and is affected by accidents of birth, number of male heirs and so forth, most local families face a similar outlook.[20]

The second factor concerns the late arrival of the 1997 monsoon, an event that resulted in the paddy yields of most landholders being cut by one-third to one-half. The timing of the monsoon also reduced the harvest of the 1998 *mahua* and *tendu* crops, along with other jungle produce on which many local families depend to supplement their incomes. This event thus meant that 1998 was a very difficult year for all villagers, particularly so for members of the Hindu community who rely predominantly on the income from their crops and from jungle produce. Oraons, on the other hand, were not so badly affected because their incomes were largely supplemented by outside wage labour.

The combination of these factors—population increase and reduced harvest—may account in part, for the assertion of ancestral rights of the original settlers over the Oraon outsiders and explain the rising number of claims over land near the Petfora river. To be sure, it is when scarcity of this sort begins to be felt, as Gregory (1997: 88) has pointed out, that the 'original settlers' cling more closely to the land they think they rightfully possess (cf. Lewinsky 1913). The benefits of cultivating on the disputed land have been discussed above, and revolve around its proximity to a water source (which means dual season cultivation) and richness of soil, both of which contribute to superior yields. As a bonus, the land in question, through years of Oraon labour and attention, is ready-made into fields and therefore conveniently cultivable as well as imminently valuable.

But population increase and the division of land between sons and brothers is a gradual and foreseeable demographic fact. And a late monsoon (or blight, pests, or indeed other natural calamities that regularly contribute to reduced harvests), while unpredictable, is not a particularly unique event in this area. In short, and the presence of

---

[20]Cf. Gregory (1997: 71–117) for a comparative glimpse of the effects that rising scarcity of land through inheritance and divisions can have on subsequent generations.

these factors notwithstanding, such conditions do not always provide sufficient cause to explain rising tensions (cf. Rudolph and Rudolph 1984: 287); nor do they explain the particular reason behind the manifestations of the Ratiya Kanwars targeting encroached land held specifically by Oraons. For the latter are by no means the only community to be cultivating on land along the Petfora, or on land that 'belongs' to the 'original settler' Ratiya Kanwars. The question that interests us here, is why other Hindu groups such as the Majhuars, who also possess a sizable amount of encroached land, some of which lies along the Petfora, do not attract the same attention from the Ratiya Kanwars as the Oraon encroachers.

Caste Conflict or Communal Tension?

One possible answer to this is that these groups are part of the same community that has always been dominated by the Ratiya Kanwars: the wider Hindu community, which sees a greater degree of ritual and economic integration amongst its castes. Other members of this community have also been known to back the Ratiya Kanwars in their land claims against the Oraon Christians. It is thus conceivable that such groups feel a political and economic allegiance to each other. In contrast, the Oraons are an immigrant community that serves no particular ritual or social function for the Hindus. And although the former are obliged, to some degree, to respect the customs of the latter, as we saw in Chapter Three, they remain largely outsiders whose own god, beliefs and other ritual and social allegiances rest outside of the social and geographical boundaries of the village.

Unlike the bulk of the Hindu community, moreover, the Oraon Christians are not dependent on local sources of income. In the absence of legal landholdings, they have been forced to engage in outside wage labour, an activity that has allowed some Oraon households to become 'cash rich'. With less titled land into which to invest whatever surplus they might have, Oraons have been able to purchase more 'non-essential' items like televisions, cycles and pesticide pumps. Possession of these material goods gives them the appearance of greater income which, as we shall see in the following chapter, has bred further resentment amongst the Hindu community.

Possession of cash has also placed the Oraons in a position to purchase (the mortgages for) a primordial good (land) from Hindu landholders. While at one level the *gahana* arrangement operates at the level of basic exchange relations, where one party possesses the commodity (the land) and the other the purchasing power (the cash), at another level, this arrangement brings to light an arena in which the hierarchical and uneven relationship between a high-caste Hindu and a low-caste Oraon is subverted and renegotiated on an apparently equal basis of need.

In short, the Oraons are a low-caste group of outsiders that came to the area 'with nothing': they had no land, no homes and very few possessions. In the course of three decades, they have managed to acquire large homes, land and a variety of enviable material possessions. As my Ratiya Kanwar friend Pratap lamented to me one day, 'we Ratiya Kanwar people have been here for over 500 years. Look at us, we still have not progressed, whereas the Oraons work very hard and are becoming rich and moving ahead'. As we can see by this statement, the presence of an industrious group of newcomers like the Oraon Christians seems to be resented because their very success implies a shortcoming on the part of the 'original settlers' (see Horowitz 1985: 166–7). This kind of sentiment is echoed not only by members of the Ratiya Kanwar community, but by the wider Hindu community in general.

It is also clear that the increasing grievances that the Hindus have with the Oraons over land are underpinned by economic interests (Horowitz 1985: 102) and are inextricably related to local power relations and structures of domination. We can compare this situation with Alfred Gell's (1996) analysis of Muria consumption, where money is not just wealth, but a threat to power legitimized in a particular social organization. Newly-rich Muria found it impossible to convert their newly-acquired purchasing power into a socially coherent definition of the self, due to their sensitivity to social pressures and because it would have been seen as socially threatening and disruptive. In the current situation, and in contrast to that observed by Gell, the Oraon Christians seem to have ignored the rules of respect for their own social and economic 'powerlessness': they are not committed to the low economic position in the village that they possessed as new arrivals three decades ago. The Oraons' position, however, has begun to threaten the local entitlement that the Ratiya Kanwars feel is owed them.

As we shall see in the following chapter, the concern that the Ratiya Kanwars have for the Oraons' increasing wealth, land and overall economic advantages has created a sense of growing unease that has spilled out into the rest of the Hindu community. The Oraons were acceptable neighbours when they were poorer than their Hindu 'hosts' three decades ago. Their increasing wealth and steady acquisition of land through encroachment and mortgages not only creates resentment but also threatens the power and status of the original 'sons of the soil'. By reaffirming their rights to a given territory, the latter are attempting to deny the Oraons the rights of occupation (cf. Gregory 1997: 116). As noted above, this concern can be partly explained in terms of what Horowitz (1985: 186, 226) calls the 'politics of entitlement', where the resources—in this case, land—to which a dominant group (the 'original settlers') feels that it is rightfully entitled are being threatened by a community of industrious outsiders.

Construed in this manner, the land tensions described in this chapter could be interpreted as an ordinary caste conflict between a traditional high caste community and an aspiring low-caste community (see Bailey 1991 [1964]; Bose 1992: 375–6; Srinivas 1987). The initiators of the disputes described above happen to be the 'sons of the soil' (Weiner 1978) whose dominance and 'entitlement' to the land are being usurped by a successful outsider community. One response to this process is a rising frequency of land disputes, which are linked to two things: the claims of the 'original settlers' that encroached land rightfully belongs to them, and the growing material well being and cash wealth of the Oraon Christians, which has allowed them to acquire Hindu land through mortgages. In this respect, the increase in both frequency and manifestation of the land tensions could also be viewed as a high-caste Hindu community's attempt to 'level' (Tambiah 1996) or diminish the margin of advantage enjoyed by the upwardly mobile, low-caste Oraon community.

However, as Weiner (1978: 7) has pointed out, when the issue revolves around competition over or access to economic wealth, and when the competing groups belong to different ethno-religious communities, then ordinary conflicts can be exacerbated into a larger ethnic or communal problem. Precisely how this has happened will be fully discussed and elaborated in the next chapter, where I examine the link between the land tensions described above and the growth in local liquor tensions, and look specifically at how these tensions have been appropriated by RSS activists as part of the 'master narrative' (Varshney 2002: 34) that underpins the *Hindutva* agenda.

In the overall landholding picture, six disputes over encroached land do not seem like a particularly alarming number. However, when viewed in context of growing Ratiya Kanwar unease over Oraon Christians' encroached and mortgaged landholdings, and in context of the larger backdrop of emergent Hindu nationalism in this area and elsewhere, then the seriousness of the matter becomes clearer. Through a process that Tambiah (1996) calls 'focalization' and 'transvaluation', we shall see how local tensions, which are connected to the relationship that both communities have to land, labour and access to cash, are stripped of their particulars and attached to one of the most powerful discourses of the Hindu nationalist movement: the 'threatening Other'. It is through the strategic transformation of original settler claims into 'conflict symbols' (Horowitz 1985: 217–18) that a cultural allegiance between local Hindu *adivasis* and Hindus elsewhere in India has been successfully created. As land tensions move beyond the local, caste conflicts acquire communal elements in a process whereby religion has come to be used as a tool for economic and political gain.

CHAPTER SEVEN

Liquor Disputes and the Communalization of Local Tensions

*D*aru, or *arkhi*, is the liquor that is distilled by villagers from flowers of the *mahua* tree (*Bassia latifola*). As an important ritual, medicinal and social necessity, it occupies a central position in the daily lives of local *adivasis*. The bulk of the production and sales of the liquor is in the hands of the Oraon Christians, most of whom produce the liquor on an occasional basis, and nearly half of whom sell and make a regular profit from these sales. In turn, the bulk of the customers are Hindus, the majority of whom do not produce the liquor themselves.

The Oraons' monopoly over these sales has recently evolved into a major source of tension between the Christian and Hindu communities in Mohanpur, over perceptions of the latter that liquor profits have come to be a primary source of income for the former. As we shall see in this chapter, while the sale of liquor is a regular source of income for half the Oraon community, such income is, in fact, relatively negligible, particularly when compared to that derived from other sources of labour described in the previous chapter. But the perception remains that the income that Oraon Christians are able to generate from liquor sales has not only contributed to their material affluence, but has, more critically, enabled them to purchase mortgages for Hindu land. This is a process that is also perceived to be directly linked to the social deterioration of the Hindu community.

It is the combination of these factors that has been the driving force behind the local escalation of land and liquor-related tensions, which are nothing new in this village. What is significant is the recent involvement in these tensions by local RSS activists. The aim of this chapter is to outline the origin and evolution of these tensions, and to examine the role of the RSS in their appropriation and communalization. Specific focus is on how, through an emphasis on group entitlement (Horowitz 1985), such tensions are being used to amplify the cultural distance between Oraon Christians and Hindus. I argue, moreover, that it is through a dual process that Tambiah (1996) calls 'focalization' and 'transvaluation', whereby local tensions are appropriated and attached into wider nationalist issues, that such tensions have assumed a communal perspective.

I begin this chapter with a brief glance at the cultural importance and uses of liquor, after which I move on to consider the liquor production process. This is followed by a discussion of the expenditure and consumption practices of the Hindus (the primary customers), and the production and sales practices of the Oraon Christians (the primary producers and profit-makers). I then turn to the evolution of local tensions. Specific focus is on the meetings that take place in the context of the local women's organization (*mahila sangat*) and the village council (*panchayat*), for it is in such contexts that land and liquor tensions have been most successfully aggregated into wider communal concerns. The connections between land and liquor disputes will be fully elaborated in the final section, where the manner in which the RSS has appropriated these tensions, along with the role of the Church in this process, will become clear.

Cultural Importance of Liquor

Like *adivasis* elsewhere in India (see Hardiman 1987), local people believe that their deities and ancestor spirits are extremely fond of liquor; as such, it serves as an important ritual offering used in the propitiation of these beings.[1] Liquor also features widely within the local medicinal and healing culture. It is consumed by *gunias* to enhance the trance-like state that they enter in order to communicate with local deities. It is also mixed with herbal medicine (*jaributi*) and given to the patient as part of the healing process.

---

[1] The importance of liquor in central and north-Indian *adivasi* cultures has been thoroughly examined elsewhere (see Elwin 1950; Pertold 1931; Rao and Rao 1977; Shukla 1978).

Along with its use as a ritual libation and cure, liquor serves as a medium of exchange for the services of a healer, the loan of a pair of buffaloes, or even a piece of useful advice. It is also given as a kind of atonement for social wrongdoings, such as the failure to extend an invitation for a wedding, or on the occasion of a public insult. Additionally, liquor, along with rice beer, is a compulsory item at most local festivals and weddings. The success of such occasions is often judged by the quantity of liquor available, and several bottles of the drink will be kept aside by the hosts in the days leading up to the occasion in anticipation of the guests' needs. The host family is strongly criticised if the supply is less than adequate.

Liquor consumption also figures prominently in the practices surrounding local communal labour, known as *madad* (literally, help). The most common form of *madad* is when a large number of people are called to assist in work that needs to be completed in a single day, such as the weeding, transplanting or harvesting of a crop, or the construction of a house. Individuals are also called for *madad* to supplement the labour of the landowner with an extra pair of buffaloes and plough, usually around the time when fields are being prepared for planting. The commensality that accompanies *madad* invariably includes large quantities of liquor. A small amount is supplied before the work commences, as a sort of warm up to the physical labour which is expected from those called. This is followed by a large meal and a steady flow of liquor, which is served with great quantities at the completion of the labour to all those who participated in the *madad*.[2]

Finally, liquor is regularly consumed in the evening after a long day's labour by at least one (male) member of most households in

---

[2]The connection between labour and liquor exchange has been observed in many cultures. Karp (1987), for example, talks about the importance of liquor as an exchange for labour amongst the Eastern African Iteso. With regard to the economy behind providing 'free' food and liquor, people who sponsor *madad* admit that it would be more cost effective for them to merely pay those who come out to assist in the communal labour, which usually number around 10, a day's wage (Rs 25–30 x 10 = Rs 250–300), or the equivalent in rice or paddy. Sponsoring the obligatory meal and alcohol that accompany *madad*, which includes an average of one to two batches of *arkhi*, or 10–20 bottles at Rs 15–20 each, along with some sort of meat, can cost over Rs 1,000, up to four times that of simple payment in cash or kind. In addition to the costs of sponsoring a day of *madad*, each worker who joins in is owed a day of labour from the host in return. But while most people agree that it might be more economical to merely pay others for their labour, sponsoring a *madad* is an essential social obligation that symbolizes the individual's willingness to participate in social and economic exchanges (Karp 1987: 89).

Evening drinking after madad.

the village. Indeed, local *adivasis* often jokingly define themselves as people who 'live in the jungle, work hard and drink *arkhi*'.

The consumption that revolves around the ritual and medicinal domains described above is publicly sanctioned. It is the behaviour and practices of the 'private', individual, evening consumers that have become the subject of local tensions. This is in part due to the resulting 'madness' and violence associated with excessive drinking. More significantly, it is due to the drain on the consumers' household resources. Both of these issues will be discussed below. For now, I turn to the source of these tensions: the income derived from liquor sales.

Liquor Production and Sales

People in this area have had the knowledge to make liquor from the *mahua* flower 'since the beginning', although the drink has been made by locals themselves for the purpose of selling, only for the past 20 years or so. Prior to this, there was a government-run liquor store that operated in the village and served the consumption needs of local tribals. In response to growing concerns about widespread expenditure on liquor, these shops were closed down by the government in the early 1980s (cf. Reddy and Patnaik 1993). The task of producing and selling the drink was left to the Oraon Christians. The reason for this, according to my informants, was that Hindu people did not have the 'habit' of making a profit from the drink. Nowadays, many Hindu households produce the drink on an irregular basis. However, this is reserved for ritual or medicinal purposes, or for specific festivals. For their daily consumption, most Hindus purchase the drink from the Oraon Christians.

The tensions surrounding the production and sales of liquor cannot be understood without first discussing the economics underpinning its source and primary ingredient: *mahua*. As a general rule, *mahua* trees are considered to be the property of those on whose land they grow, or those who first claimed them from the jungle: in most cases, as outlined in the previous chapter, these are Hindus. As latecomers to the area, very few Oraons actually 'own' or are able to claim any but one or two isolated trees. As such, the collection and sale of *mahua* is an activity in which predominantly Hindus engage.

Mahua flowers are harvested between mid-March and mid-April. This is a time of year that sees mostly women and children standing guard under a *mahua* tree, watching over the sweet, yellow flowers that begin to fall from the tree at the first sign of dawn. They play games and gossip as they wait for the last of the flowers to fall, and the vaguely festive air with which they approach their duties offsets the tedium of this task. By mid-day, the space beneath the tree is covered in a solid blanket of flowers, which are then gathered into small baskets.

In a good season, a tree will yield a daily average of seven to 8 kg of *mahua* flowers, which are then spread out to dry inside a fenced-in space near each family's home. As the flowers dry and shrivel in the sun, they lose their liquid yellow sheen, along with half their mass. After two or three days, they turn a dark, reddish brown. This is an indication that they are ready to be stored in the house for use in exchange for basic goods (rice, salt, lentils). Households are able to yield an abundant crop and make a reasonable income from the collection and sale of *mahua* and over two-thirds of all Hindus earn some amount of income in this manner. Half of these earn at least Rs 1,500 per year, with a further 10 per cent earning between Rs 3,000–6,000.[3]

---

[3]In view of these figures, it is interesting to bear in mind that the Hindus are making money from the raw material of a product that they nowadays claim is undermining their community.

With few exceptions, most Hindus begin to sell their *mahua* to local shopkeepers as soon as it is harvested and dried, getting rid of most of their stock by around mid-May. This is when the price, at Rs 4.5 per kg, is at its lowest. People do not typically wait for the price to rise, which it will steadily do from late-May onward until it eventually reaches its top price of Rs 12 in December-January. May is the time of year when most households have reached the very end of their supplies of rice and the *mahua* crop thus provides them with an opportunity to replenish this and other essential goods. Shopkeepers in turn, sell most of the *mahua* for Rs 50 per kg profit to government-licensed wholesalers who are based in Korba, and who transport it out of the village for distribution in other parts of Chhattisgarh. A tenth or so of the shopkeepers' supply is reserved for local resale to Oraon Christian customers.

While *mahua* collection and sales is the domain of Hindu households, *mahua* purchases are predominantly made by Oraon Christians, who use it in the production of liquor. Having few or no trees, Oraons are forced to purchase *mahua* from local shops. If it is not available locally, if the local price is not satisfactory, or if it is not of good quality, then they will purchase it from a neighbouring village. Most Oraons who produce liquor prefer to use *mahua* flowers that have aged at least two months, as opposed to freshly harvested flowers, due to the overly pungent, sour taste of the liquor that is produced from the latter. It is for this reason, I was told, that they do not purchase *mahua*, when prices are at their lowest. When I asked why they did not purchase and then store the *mahua* in their own homes while it ages, thus taking advantage of early-season prices, I was told that it was risky to stock large quantities of *mahua* at home, as this would lend credence to what most Hindus in the village already suspected about the Oraons' profit-making intentions.

In the few months preceding the beginning of the season (December-February), *mahua* becomes scarce and expensive: the stocks of most local shops have long since depleted, and those (mostly Oraon) families who continue to purchase *mahua* for liquor production are forced to walk or cycle long distances to villages where supplies have not run out. People get to know by word of mouth, which village is selling *mahua* at the best rate, and it is not uncommon to travel 30–40 km in a day by foot or cycle to purchase 10 kg of *mahua*. In cases where lengthy journeys are involved, it is usually the (male) household head who makes the journey, taking a cycle and a wad of rupees for the purpose. The household matriarch will only make such a long journey with another woman, and only if she has a particular item like a handmade mat (worth Rs 30) to exchange. On the rare occasions when Hindus purchase *mahua*, they do so through exchanging rice or paddy.

The production of liquor begins when 10 kg of dried *mahua* flowers are placed in a large, clay vessel, along with a handful of powdered herbs that assist in the fermentation process. The *mahua* is then covered in water, sealed tightly with a piece of cloth and rope, and left alone until the '*ktik-ktik*' sound that begins to emit from the pot around the second day (as fermentation occurs and gas is released) becomes silent, usually around day four or six. This is a sign that the *mahua* is ready to be distilled into liquor. The distillation process generally takes between three and four hours, after which the saturated *mahua* in the bottom pot is discarded on the dung heap located behind the house, to be used in future as fertilizer.[4]

The production of liquor normally takes place on a hearth located in the inner room of the house, as opposed to the cooking *chulha* located in the outermost room. It is usually distilled at dawn or late in the evening, particularly during times of the heightened drink tension described below. These time and space considerations are an attempt by Oraon households to both conceal the production process from nosy outsiders (a difficult task due to the pungent smell and the smoke from the hearth fire) and to protect the production process from the eyes of a suspected *tonhi* (witch), whose gaze and presence would reportedly spoil the liquor.

It is women who are responsible for making the drink, perhaps because the distillation process revolves around what is considered to be women's labour: it is distilled within the domestic space, at the household hearth, using large amounts of water that must be carried from the village well. When the household matriarch or her eldest daughter are for some reason, unable to make the liquor after the fermentation process has been completed—due to illness, or absence from the village—a kinswoman will be asked to undertake the task, with a bottle or two given as a token of thanks in return.[5]

---

[4]This particular type of distillation has been traced back to 500 B.C. and has been recorded among tribals and rural castes throughout South Asia (cf. Allchin 1979, Pertold 1931). See Hardiman (1987: 99–128) for further details on *mahua* distillation.

[5]In many jurisdictions throughout history, both brewing and selling were monopolized by women, often with the active support of the government (see also Omori 1978: 93).

The sales and income generated by liquor are largely contingent upon the season and the availability and price of *mahua*. For example, liquor sales tend to decrease immediately after the *mahua* collection season begins in March, due to the fact that the *mahua* is new and the liquor is not tasty. Sales pick up for a month or so after the collection season finishes, due to the cheap and plentiful supply of *mahua*. Sales drop down again during the monsoon season, when wet conditions make the production process difficult, and when Hindu customers are more reluctant to make the trip to the Oraon Christian *basti*. Prices and profits will increase steadily from September onward until they reach their height at the end of February, before falling again in March when the new season begins.

In terms of the economics of production, 1 kg of *mahua* will yield approximately one litre of liquor. An average 10-kg batch of *mahua* will thus yield roughly nine to ten litres of liquor, which is stored in a ten-litre container, and measured out using a two-thirds litre bottle. One batch of *mahua* will yield roughly 14 of these bottles. At least half of this will be consumed by the members of the household and their guests; the rest is sold to local customers for Rs 15–20 per bottle.

Today, most Oraon Christian households produce the liquor on an occasional basis, and nearly half of them (21 households) sell and make a regular profit from these sales. Producers can be divided into 'low', 'medium' and 'high', depending on their rates of production and estimated income: low producers (four households) make a single batch per month, and earn around Rs 566 per year profit (an average of Rs 47 per month); medium producers (eight households) make roughly two batches monthly, and earn around Rs 965 per year (Rs 80 per month); and high producers (nine households) make between three and six batches monthly, and make a yearly profit of Rs 1,734 (Rs 144 per month) (see Table 7.1). Rates of production for the high sellers can increase to thrice weekly during festival times when it is not unusual for people to sell an entire batch in one morning, yielding Rs 150–200 (after purchasing costs). Again, I am aware of no Hindu household that produces the drink at such a frequency, and none admits to making a profit from regular *arkhi* sales.

While I am not focusing on gender or male/female divisions of labour here, it is interesting that I have come across no study that addresses the issue of or implications behind why the production of liquor is often a specifically female task, particularly in light of the fact that consumption of liquor is more frequently a male activity (see Heath 2000: 76).

Table 7.1: Oraon *Arkhi* Sales (Average Income)

Producer Status	Yearly Income Class (Rs)	Number of Households	% of (43) Oraon Households
Low	566	4	9
Medium	965	8	19
High	1734	9	21
Average	1100		

What is important to bear in mind at this stage is that the average annual income generated from liquor sales by less than half the Oraon Christian community, is Rs 1,100. This is not only substantially less than that generated by other forms of wage labour mentioned in the previous chapter (Rs 2,261 and Rs 2,400 for *hajari/mistri* and *matti dona*, respectively); as we shall see below, it also contrasts with local Hindus' perceptions that liquor production is a substantial means of income for the Oraon community. I will return to these issues later on, when I discuss some of the reasons behind such perceptions. For now, I turn to the culture of selling and drinking.

Drinking Practices: Seller and Consumer

While the production and sale of liquor has traditionally been in the hands of women, its purchase and consumption is predominantly a male activity. Apart from three exceptions, I am aware of no Hindu woman who regularly partakes of the drink. A few Oraon women drink, but they do so largely in controlled or publicly sanctioned spaces, or in the context of a *madad* or wedding celebration. In very rare cases will a woman actually initiate a purchase and consume liquor of her own accord. This is considered to be socially inappropriate, and in such cases, the woman is invariably reproached by other women in the *basti*, or beaten by her husband when he discovers her misdeed.

There are two sorts of (male) Hindu customers who purchase liquor from the Oraon Christians. The first is the customer who visits the Oraon locality any time from early morning to evening, in search of alcohol that is intended for a specific ritual offering—often related to illness—or for guests who have made a sudden appearance. This type of customer will usually be found walking swiftly, alone and with a clear objective, carrying a half-litre bottle in his hands, quite conspicuously and with nothing to hide: for he is on official, usually urgent business, publicly sanctioned by the actuality of illness or visitors.

After procuring the liquor, he might share some brief but relevant information with the seller—a daughter-in-law is ill, the *samdhi* (in-laws) have arrived—before he carries the bottle, in full public view, out of the *basti* and swiftly returns home. In a day, the Oraon *basti* will generally see at least three or four of this sort of customers, although this will increase in times of widespread illness, or during festival and marriage season, when Oraons have been known to run out of an entire batch (10–14 bottles) of still-warm alcohol the very morning it is made. During such times, Oraons are sometimes asked to reserve a bottle for a particularly trusted customer who is unable to visit the Oraon *basti* and make the purchase before the supply is likely to be exhausted.

The more common sort of customer, and the sort with whom this chapter is concerned, is the one who arrives around dusk. This is the time after a full day's work in the fields when, amidst the flurry of evening activity in the village, a man can slip out of his home, at most, telling his wife that he is going 'visiting' *(ghumne)*. This is a seemingly innocuous activity that entails an hour or so of wandering around, calling on neighbours and kin before the evening meal, to talk about a worryingly dry spell of weather or the possibility of being forced to mortgage a portion of land to meet a sudden debt. In fact, his destination is invariably the Oraon locality to purchase and consume *arkhi*.

Leaving his home, he will stroll relatively unnoticed in the growing darkness toward the outskirts of the Hindu *basti*. Unlike the daytime customer who proceeds quickly and in fully-sanctioned public view, he generally walks with a relaxed and casual gait through the shadows toward the Oraon locality: being undetected is important for the evening customer, who does not want to appear to be too anxious about his intended goal. He will often stop at a neighbour's home to collect a drinking companion, preferring to come as part of a pair. This is in part, because Oraon Christians live nearly half a kilometre away from the main part of the village, along an isolated path that becomes dangerous to travel alone after dusk, because of the deities and ghosts that are said to live in trees situated along the paths (see Chapter Two). Sometimes the men will enter the Oraon *basti* from an alternate route, a path that bypasses the main *basti* and follows the length of the village from the western outskirts. This 'secretive' and circuitous route is an attempt to mask their objective of consuming liquor, an important point to which I return below.

From the perspective of the Oraon *basti*, the Hindu 'visitors' can be seen from a distance, coming up one of the paths in the last traces of light. 'Here comes *katta*,' an Oraon child might announce. Like the customer who arrives in the morning on a publicly sanctioned mission, this customer will first go to his preferred seller. When he arrives at his destination, he will show the Oraon vendor the contents of the parcel he has brought to exchange for the liquor: sometimes a portion of freshly killed forest meat, fish or a choice vegetable, but more often resources from the household 'bank' of paddy or rice. There is rarely any haggling, for prices and amounts are relatively fixed: one glass costs Rs 4–5; one bottle costs Rs 15–20. A bottle will sometimes be produced from within the folds of his *lungi*, which the customer will take home full after he has consumed a glass or two in the company of the Oraons.

Occasionally, when the customer has been unable to procure the required exchange item, he will beg a glass of liquor from the seller, with promises of paying twice the amount next time. If the seller thinks she can trust the man, then she will proceed. On rare occasions, a customer will come bearing a brass plate or drinking vessel, or an axe or fishing basket, which he intends to 'mortgage' to the seller for a glass or two of liquor. Oraons are reluctant to accept such items because they fear, rightfully, the wrath of the customer's wife who, after noticing that the valued brass item is missing, will often come charging into the Oraon *basti*, demanding to know who has 'stolen' her property.

Households that have liquor on hand will be visited by at least one or two of this sort of customers every evening, although this number fluctuates with the season. Perhaps it is because they are an extension of the liquor production process that takes place within female domestic space, that women will invariably handle the sales. Men, on the other hand, will sit and consume with the customer, who will rarely depart immediately upon drinking. Instead, he will typically spend half an hour chatting amicably about village affairs with his hosts. This is one of the prime opportunities that Oraon Christians have to cultivate relations with their landed and more powerful neighbours.

In addition to the continuing availability of liquor, one primary reason for the regular visits by Hindu men to the Oraon locality is the relative privacy of both the locality, situated half a kilometre from the Hindu *basti*, and the Oraon Christian homes which, unlike the communal type of arrangement in which local Hindus reside, are all single-family dwellings. While the Hindu consumers' wives and fellow community members may know that they have gone to the Oraon *basti* for a drink, their temporary anonymity is guaranteed by the Oraons. In the household of their hosts, the Hindu customer will be left alone if he wishes to sit quietly in the shadows, and his demands for a drink will be indulged without overt judgment or comment by his Oraon hosts. The latter, moreover, do not publicize the fact that they have a Hindu customer in their homes, either to other Oraons (who do not care, and who themselves probably have their own customer to look after) or to other Hindus. In such surroundings, one glass often leads to two, and increasing intoxication will lead to lively conversation between customer and vendor, who might be talked into offering a third glass for free. Consequently, the Hindu customer sometimes leaves the Oraon locality in a state of drunkenness and loud revelry, as he makes his way towards his own home.

While Hindu people ostensibly spend more on liquor, Oraon Christians have the reputation for consuming more. Indeed, Oraons freely admit that they sometimes consume over half of their own liquor supplies. Moreover, there is no secret made about the Oraons' drinking, which takes place within their own *basti* and often within the domestic space itself. Everybody knows who is drinking and where and, unless it gets totally out of hand and people start to go 'mad', nobody cares. When a household's supplies are exhausted, a child is sent to a favourite producer to enquire whether liquor is available. Upon the child's return, his father will take cash—as with other items, he will never use rice or paddy to purchase liquor—and go out for a 'visit', either consuming a glass of liquor directly at the home of his kin or neighbour or, if he happens to have a visitor, returning with a bottle to be consumed at home. Often, drinks will be consumed without a demand for payment, for the host knows that his guest will reciprocate sometime in the near future.

On the rare occasions that there is no liquor available in their own *basti*, Oraon Christians prefer to go without. I am aware of no instance when an Oraon purchased liquor from a Hindu household, although they are generally aware of which families may have a supply on hand. Oraons complain that *katta arkhi* is of bad quality because it is not distilled properly. More significantly, they feel uncomfortable drinking at the homes of Hindu people, because they are treated as low-caste individuals (*chota admi*) and made to sit outside of the residence when they visit.

Liquor, then, is at once socially 'prohibited' and publicly sanctioned, depending on the context in which it is consumed. In the privacy of one's own home, or in the context of a wedding feast or a healing ritual—all of which fall within the socially approved purchasing rights of the first type of customer described above—the consumption of liquor is acceptable. Drinking acquires illicit status and begins to be socially prohibited only when its consumption ostensibly makes a significant dent in the consumer's household resources or causes public disturbance in the form of drunken behaviour and violence.

Drinking and 'Madness'

Unsurprisingly, consumption of large quantities of alcohol produces what is locally considered to be an altered state of consciousness. The euphemism for this state is *pagal* (madness), and it is invariably accompanied by socially inappropriate behaviour.[6] Drink-induced 'madness' is evidenced by at least one or more intoxicated individuals arguing over unresolved insults or offences, such as a contentious piece of land or the non-repayment of past loans or, in the case of husband and wife, the expenditure of household resources on liquor. Such arguments tend to escalate from verbal insults to physical violence, spilling out from within the confines of the house, where the parties have usually been drinking, to more public spaces like the village square. Curious neighbours will emerge from their homes to observe the spectacle, shaking their heads at the disgraceful behaviour being exhibited by their drunken neighbours or kin. At the very least, this kind of behaviour creates embarrassing and socially compromising situations with neighbours and family; at worst— particularly if social norms are violated—this behaviour risks ostracism from the entire community. Indeed, the primary reason that teetotallers give for not drinking is that, liquor changes one's behaviour and makes one lose control and 'go mad'.

[6]This euphemism is not unusual, either in this area or elsewhere in India (cf. Hardiman 1987, Rao and Rao 1977, Shukla 1978). For comparison outside of India, see Marshall's (1979) ethnography on Trukese drinking. To become drunk in Truk is to put on a culturally sanctioned mask of temporary insanity. Drunks are also referred to as 'crazy', and likened to animals.

This kind of 'madness' or loss of control is associated with the altered state that people enter in the context of possession (see Chapters Four and Five), which is often described as 'loss of mind'. Indeed, when a person becomes particularly drunk and violent, it is often said that he has become possessed by Dano, the 'drinking demon' (*pine wallah bhut*) who regularly demands liquor during ritual occasions. It is invariably husbands and sons who, after becoming drunk, tend to 'go mad' and become violent. Women, in turn, are usually on the receiving end during these incidents, either as actual victims of their husband's drink-induced violent behaviour or verbal insults or, especially in the case of Hindu women, as indirect victims of the social ostracism meted out by the Patel against the drunken man's household. The latter will normally be excluded from participation in all ritual and festival activities until such time as a substantial fine is paid to the village *panchayat*. Most women have stories about how their husbands beat them whilst drunk, or how their households were excluded from participation in an important annual festival like Gaura as punishment for their husbands' behaviour.

Because women are typically on the receiving end of this violence, it might be expected that they would be the most vocal group against drinking in the village. And indeed, like elsewhere in India, it is the women—especially those from the Hindu community—who have come out most forcefully against drinking locally.[7] As we shall see later on, however, the growing concerns of Hindu women (and the Hindu community as a whole) have less to do with the violent behaviour of their drunken husbands, and more to do with what this behaviour signifies: that valuable household resources (rice or paddy) have been squandered on liquor.

Before embarking on a 'visit' to the Oraon *basti*, the Hindu customer will quietly help himself to around 1 kg of rice from the household supply, which he will then exchange for one or two glasses of liquor. Their wives may not actually witness this action, which they classify as 'theft', but they are aware of the amount of rice that has been depleted by their husband's consumption habits because of their larger

[7]See Kapadia (1995: 208–9) who talks about the violence inflicted against women by predominantly male drinkers in rural South India (cf. Saldanha 1995). See also Reddy and Patnaik (1993: 1064), who mention that one of the impetuses behind the women's anti-liquor agitation in the early 1990s in Andhra Pradesh is the fact that invariably it is the man who squanders much of the household income on liquor, whereas it is the women of the household who have to provide for the subsistence of the children, and who end up at the receiving end of drink-induced abuse.

role and presence in the domestic space. Their concerns are magnified by the fact that it is the Oraon Christians who are benefiting from their household's dwindling supplies. In their view, the income being generated by liquor sales to people like their husbands has contributed markedly to the Oraons' material status and wealth, the latter being demonstrated by large homes and the possession of more non-essential material goods.

As we saw earlier, the total income earned from the production of liquor is just a fraction of that earned from other sources. However, it is the Hindu community's perception of these profits that matters here, and the perception remains that income from liquor sales is making a substantial contribution to the Oraon's material status. As I demonstrate below, it is this perception that has been appropriated, cultivated and used by the RSS as a 'conflict symbol' (Horowitz 1985: 217–18) to encourage anti-Christian sentiment and promote the 'threatening Christian Other' as grounds for transforming ordinary drink disputes into wider *Hindutva* concerns.

Liquor and Evolution of Local Tensions

This perception and the accompanying tensions are intrinsically related to the presence and activities of the Church. In this particular context, the relationship revolves around the local 'women's organization' (*mahila sangat*) that was established in the village a few months before I began my fieldwork in October 1997. This organization is a local branch of a larger women's organization called the *Samaj Seva Sanstha* (Community Service Organisation), a Catholic-run organization that is based in the neighbouring district of Raipur. Its broad aims revolve around the empowerment of *adivasi* women. It was set up in the early 1990s as a response to the legal prohibition of proselytization for the purpose of instituting social service and welfare projects. It is locally managed by an Oraon Christian man named Chamalsai, who liases between six local villages and the organization's Raipur headquarters. Chamalsai also conducts and records the proceedings of local meetings, and banks the small amounts of money that are collected from participants. Although a few women are aware of the organization's Catholic-connections, it is not perceived to be Christian-based or Christian-promoting by local people, and Chamalsai is accepted and respected by all local women as the leader and organizer of the group. However, Raj and the other RSS proponents are aware of the connection that this organization has to the Church, a significant fact to which I later return.

The original intention of the organization was to convene all village women for the purpose of teaching them home-based business skills, such as tailoring and chicken farming, and to create a forum for discussion of village-improvement projects. It was to be a cross-caste, cross-community organization, and the village women were meant to meet weekly to discuss various issues revolving around their role as women in the improvement of the village.

The first two meetings that I observed in early November 1997, which were attended by approximately 25 Oraon Christians and 50 Hindus, were geared towards this purpose: discussion of possible small-business projects in which groups of four and five women could get involved. The problems of drinking and drunkenness were also mentioned, but more as a general issue of concern for greater control over what was perceived as increasing drunken behaviour in the village. After these initial meetings, however, the organization's primary concerns, which were spearheaded by the numerically dominant Hindu women, came to revolve around the rate of (Oraon-produced) liquor consumption and expenditure by their husbands and sons. In response, the Oraon Christian women complained that the focus on liquor was interfering with the wider aims of the organization and that other, more important issues such as electricity and clean water were being ignored. Hindu women countered that the expenditure of household resources (namely rice and paddy, and also lentils and other goods) on alcohol were major issues that were affecting many local households, and therefore did merit regular attention. One of the more vocal Hindu women included Kudwarhin, who was the wife of Raj's brother, Santu.

Tensions between these two groups of women escalated rapidly. By early December 1997, the *mahila sangat* had evolved into an anti-drinking forum, and the main fissure over the issue—the Hindu consumer-as-victim on one side, and Oraon Christian as primary-accused on the other—began to take shape. Most meetings that were held in the month of December followed a pattern that included much loud discussion and argument revolving around the Oraons' role in producing and selling large quantities of liquor to Hindu customers, who in turn, were using household supplies of rice to purchase the drink. Hindu women's accusations were invariably met by Oraon women's denials. After such meetings, an immediate boycott from both sides would be called: Hindu men would stop going to the Oraon locality to buy liquor, and Oraons would curtail their sales to local Hindus. Meetings would adjourn with the Oraon women grumbling amongst themselves that it was not their responsibility that Hindu men could not control their drinking. The immediate ceasing of regular sales to and consumption by local Hindus would last only a few days, however, as Oraons would begin to sell quietly to trusted customers, and then more openly, to others. Within a week or so, another meeting would be called because another Hindu customer would be 'caught' drinking.

Not surprisingly, it was never the (mostly male) consumers, often respected members of the Hindu community, who were in favour of the anti-drinking direction that the meetings were taking. Indeed, those who consumed the most were generally the least concerned about control and moderation in drinking, and they often grumbled to sympathetic male kin about the increasing difficulty in being able to drink peacefully. Nevertheless, they did offer nominal support, and agreed with the general premise that it was not such a good thing that their household resources were being squandered away on liquor, not only to the detriment of their own community, but to the benefit of the Oraon Christians. It was the wives of these drinkers who were the most vociferous about calls for control.

Interestingly, the manner of being 'caught' drinking or selling was not in the actual act, but in the visible and often public effects of the sales: the drunken behaviour of the customer or his 'theft' from his own household's supplies of rice. During one of the meetings in December, for example, five Hindu women got up and narrated how they had 'caught' their husbands drinking by observing them taking rice or paddy from the home, only to return hours later, obviously from the direction of the Oraon *basti*, in an inebriated state.

Moreover, it was not just any customer to whom the Oraon Christian vendor had to be 'caught' selling: it was specifically the Hindu customer. The Oraon customer was not of concern to the Hindus. This is in part, because the Oraons' consumption and drunken behaviour takes place within the Oraon *basti* and outside of the gaze of the Hindu section. More importantly, the Oraon's consumption of the liquor, although in real terms, exceeding that of his Hindu counterpart, was of no concern to the Hindu community. The latter neither cared about the amount of resources that were being depleted from Oraon households, nor about the consequences of this on the wider Oraon Christian community. And the Oraons themselves were not particularly concerned with each other's consumption behaviour.

Because these meetings did not seem to have a lasting effect on the sale of liquor, the Hindu women became increasingly agitated. They felt that the Oraons were simply ignoring them and contributing to what they perceived to be a serious problem of local drinking; consequently, the Oraons were invariably blamed for the Hindu men's consumption. The Oraon women, for their part, became increasingly annoyed by what they construed to be a misallocation of blame. It was only they who were taken to task and held responsible for the behaviour of the Hindu consumers; the contribution of the Hindu consumer to the problem was entirely ignored, in spite of allegations by the Oraons that some of their regular Hindu customers consistently purchased liquor only after they had already consumed from their own supplies.

That the Oraon vendors have taken the brunt of the blame for the social and economic problems felt by the Hindu consumers is an important point. The attitude amongst Hindus was that consumption of liquor in itself is not bad; to be sure, it is an acceptable cultural practice when exercised within a locally appropriate manner. And indeed, at least one member of nearly every household consumes liquor on certain ritual, social or private occasions. Selling, however, is perceived as bad. It leads to domestic and social problems and worse, diminishes the household supplies of the (Hindu) customer and generates added income for the (Oraon Christian) vendor.

The friction between the two groups came to a head at the end of December 1997, when a meeting was called by Hindu women in order to discuss the fact that a great deal of *arkhi* had been produced by Oraons and sold to their husbands and sons over the previous Christmas week. The Oraon women admitted that they had been storing the drink for their own Christmas consumption, but denied actively selling to the local Hindus. Instead, they insisted that they had respected the controls that had been put into effect since early December. In response, one Hindu woman declared that her meagre harvest was already half depleted, due to her husband's evening habit of visiting the Oraon *basti*. The Oraon women accused her of lying and then walked out of the meeting, complaining that the organization was useless, and that they would not meet with the Hindu women again. In January, these meetings were temporarily halted, and alcohol sales and consumption resumed in full.

By early February, due to pressure from concerned wives and mothers, and at the suggestion of Raj, who had been kept informed of the situation by his sister-in-law, discussions about the control of liquor consumption began to enter and dominate the public, mostly male forum of the village council (*panchayat*). Locally, this forum is construed to be more important than the women's meeting. The discussion and decisions taken in this context are regarded more seriously by all villagers because it is conducted and mediated by the village headman.

It was also around this time that Raj and three other RSS activists, who had been conducting 'training meetings' with young local men on an occasional basis, regularized their presence in the village with weekly visits. By this stage, discussions had been taking place between Raj and others about how to best promote biomedical health care practices (see Chapter Four); and the four *pracharaks* were becoming increasingly familiar with the villagers' discontent with the Patel and his corrupt ways (Chapter Five). As noted earlier, these meetings specifically served as a sort of forum for propagation and discussion of *Hindutva* teachings. Importantly, they were often held on the same day as a scheduled *panchayat* meeting, which was attended by both the young men and the RSS members.

In the weekly village council meetings, which were dominated by the Ratiya Kanwar Hindus, discussions began to revolve around general calls for the Oraon Christians to control the sale of liquor to Hindu consumers. As in the women's meetings, most of the blame for production and sales was placed with the primary vendors and profit-makers. An important difference here was that, while the women were more concerned about household resources being squandered on the drink, the men were more concerned with the sort of material possessions that the Oraons were ostensibly able to accrue through liquor profits. During one particular meeting in early March, discussion centred on the new television that the Oraon shopkeeper had recently purchased—only the second in the village (the first having also been acquired a year or so earlier by another Oraon). The shopkeeper was accused by several Hindu men of making this purchase—an expense that was entirely beyond the means of ordinary villagers' income—with money he made from liquor sales. In response, the shopkeeper insisted that the purchase was made possible with the profits from his shop. This was the first time that such a connection was made between material possessions and liquor sales, and the Oraon community collectively agreed that they should totally end all sales to local Hindus.

Blame for the liquor sales also became more personal during these meetings. In a sort of 'name and shame' manner, people who had been caught drinking began to be questioned publicly by the Patel and other senior members of the *panchayat* as to where they had purchased their alcohol. Responsibility was generally placed with the Oraons, who were reprimanded by the Patel and urged to stop selling liquor to local Hindus. At this stage, the Oraon community collectively agreed that they should totally stop all sales to local Hindus. This time, the decision to boycott their local customers lasted slightly longer than a few days. But by mid-March, regular sales and consumption had resumed, and the problem of consumption was once again, raised within a village council meeting.

Bahadur, the unofficial leader for the Oraon Christian community, told me that the Oraons generally agree that 'control' of liquor sales was a good thing. And he personally tried to encourage them to honour the boycott agreements. However, he did not have any authority to enforce such pronouncements. And this, Bahadur complained, combined with the pressure by Hindu consumers who invariably came looking for a drink shortly after each boycott had been introduced, made it very difficult for the Oraons to curtail their sales for more than a few days. 'What can I do?' Bahadur lamented to me. 'If people want to sell liquor, then they are going to sell liquor.'

As far as most of the Oraon Christian vendors were concerned, the growing liquor concerns were the business of the Hindu community. 'We Kurukh people do not have a problem with *arkhi*,' I was told by one Oraon man who was the first to begin selling again after the March boycott. 'If *katta* people want to continue drinking, then why should we stop selling?' Most Oraons felt that the growing concerns about liquor sales had to do with the Hindus' jealousy over the Christians' wealth and improving material status. In support of this, Oraons cited the fact that in Kudwari, an Oraon Christian village of 25 households located a few kilometres from Mohanpur, there is scarcely any drink-related friction. And this is in spite of the fact that production and consumption of liquor in that village is allegedly greater than that in

Mohanpur. The reason for the lack of tension, I was told, is that 'there is no jealousy in that village; and there is no jealousy because there are no *katta* people living there.'

Arkhi Income and Land Acquisition

At this stage, it might be helpful to look more closely at the liquor profits that are allegedly responsible for the material wealth of the Oraon Christians. It is true that nearly half of the Oraon community engages in liquor sales, with an average household income of Rs 1,100. However, when we compare this data with the income from other sources of labour, we also find that over half the community derives a substantial income from *hajari/mistri kam* (construction labour), with household averages of Rs 2,261; and nearly three-quarters of the community supplement their incomes from *matti dona* (mud hauling), with household averages of Rs 2,400. Moreover, income from liquor sales is only two-thirds of that which Oraons earn from the *tendu* collection, which averages Rs 1,611 per household (see graph 7.1).

What these data tell us is that liquor sales contribute only 15 per cent of the Oraons' cash income. *Hajari/mistri* and *matti dona* are the leading sources of income, contributing at least 30 per cent each to the Oraons' overall wealth. Moreover, this has been the case for years: a greater portion of the Oraons' income has always been derived from wage labour activities.

If this is the case, then why is so much attention being given to liquor sales and income? I propose three possible answers to this question. First, income from liquor production is socially unacceptable,

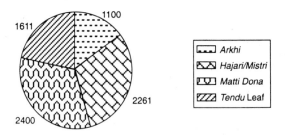

Graph 7.1: Oraon Annual Cash Income Sources (in rupees)

on account of the resource depletion and physical violence associated with its consumption. This is illustrated in the Oraon vendors' efforts to hide the fact that they produce and sell the liquor, and in the Hindu consumers' attempts to purchase and consume the liquor under the guise of evening chaos and shadows.

Second, in spite of efforts to cloak its production, income from liquor is a highly regular form of income, the generation of which occurs under the gaze of the village community. Sales of liquor are continual throughout the year; while sales dip during certain periods, such as the monsoon season, there is always liquor available from one or two Oraon households, and always a demand. Income from other sources, such as *matti dona* and *hajari/mistri*, is comparatively more sporadic. There can be months at a time, such as during the monsoon season, when there is no such work to be obtained outside of the village. The continuity of income from other sources, in other words, does not exist in the same way as income from liquor.

Related to this is the fact that income from liquor sales is highly visible: because of the labour that goes into its production and the effects of its consumption, everybody within the village knows who is making and selling liquor. In contrast, other income-generating activities in which Oraon Christians engage take place outside of the gaze of the village. While most people are aware of who has gone out of the village for work, and many get to know about the substantial amount of cash that might be brought home after a two-week or three-month period of labour outside of the village, the work itself has not been viewed by the public; on the contrary, only the continual production of liquor has been on display. This combination of regularity and visibility helps to reinforce perceptions that liquor profits constitute a substantial proportion of the Oraon community's total income.

Attention is on liquor sales and income for even more compelling reasons, however, and this is a visible squandering of Hindu households' resources and the simultaneous transfer of such resources to the Oraon Christian community. While the number of regular Hindu customers is relatively low, such customers are still visible, in that they actually travel to another part of the village. Most importantly, this is accompanied by the redistribution of supplies from Hindu to Oraon Christian households, which apparently contributes to the increasing affluence of the latter.

This is where the information from the previous chapter becomes relevant. For Hindus' concerns over the nature of the Oraons' material wealth are not only driven by the role that liquor sales play in its creation, but by the role this plays in the latter's acquisition of land. It is the relationship that the two communities have to land, labour and access to cash that is thus at the heart of these local tensions. The Hindus are the primary landowners, earning their living largely from their own land; the Oraons, in possession of little land, earn their living through engagement in outside wage labour. Having a surplus of cash (a portion of which comes from liquor profits), the Oraons have assumed the role of moneylender to Hindu landowners, acquiring Hindu land through mortgages.

While proceeds from liquor sales do contribute to the overall income levels of the Oraon community, the total profit earned from the production of liquor is just a fraction of that earned from other sources. As noted above, however, it is the perception of these profits that matters here, and the perception remains, that income from liquor sales makes a sizeable contribution to the Oraon Christian's material status.

It is important to mention here that the quarter of the Oraon households that do make a regular income from liquor sales has acquired no additional mortgages than those households whose income is derived from other sources of labour. Indeed, three of the nine households that are in the 'high producers' bracket possess no mortgaged land at all. As we shall see below, however, this makes no difference in terms of the configuration of local tensions: they are still members of the local community—the Oraon Christians—that produces liquor, the income from which contributes simultaneously to the material standing of that community and the deterioration of the Hindu community.

And this is what is at the centre of the recent tensions between the Oraon Christians and the Hindus. In the past, such tensions would have been contained locally—resolved, perhaps, in the context of the village council. During the course of my fieldwork, however, they took on a new urgency due to their appropriation and transformation by the RSS into issues of communal concern.

From Local Tensions to Communal Conflict

To see how this has happened, let us return to the women's meetings. A turning point regarding the liquor tensions, which would serve as the 'triggering event' (Tambiah 1996: 56) that shaped the future relationship between the Oraon Christians and the Hindus, came in the first week of May 1998, just before the annual *tendu* collection began (see Chapter Five). This was when an urgent meeting was called by the Hindu women, this time after the evening meal. It had been months since the Oraon women had attended one of these meetings, but because of the unusual hour, and because they were told that Chamalsai and a few other Oraon men would be present, they agreed to attend. Although this meeting was meant to be women-only, a large number of Hindu men were present, in part, because it was held in the evening at the village square, the place where young Hindu men typically engage in 'time-pass'. The subject was, as usual, liquor, with Hindu women accusing Oraon women of excessive production and sales. It soon descended into a shouting match between the Oraon Christian and Hindu women.

Just as the Oraons were preparing to leave the meeting, Raj, who happened to have conducted a training meeting earlier that day and, who, along with two other RSS activists had been observing the proceedings, got up and called for calm. As the crowd settled down, Raj posed a question to the Oraon women as to why, when the Catholic Fathers visit the village in their jeep, they go directly to the Oraon Christian locality. He did not wait for a response, but instead supplied the answer: 'because the Fathers were coming to encourage and advise the *isai log* (Christians) to make and sell liquor to the Hindu community'. The Oraon women who were present, vehemently denied these allegations, and insisted that the Fathers only came to conduct the annual Catholic mass. Raj responded that the rest of the local Hindu community believed otherwise: 'the Fathers have a secret plan, like Christians all over India, to bring the Hindu community down by encouraging Oraons to ply local Hindus with liquor'. This suggestion was met with vocal agreement from both the Hindu women and the small crowd of Hindu men who had come to investigate what the shouting was about. As Raj sat down, a few of these men joined in with accusations referring to the Christians' alleged 'secret' agenda.

After Raj's accusation, Chamalsai, the nominal leader of the meeting, took control. Attempting to redirect the meeting specifically towards local drinking concerns, he proposed a strict implementation of fines against all parties involved. To bind the agreement, it was suggested that everyone present supply a signature or thumbprint to verify his or her acquiescence to the new rule.

The meeting at this stage appeared to be getting back to order, as a sheet of paper was passed around to collect signatures and thumbprints. Suddenly, one of the young Hindu men who was involved in the jeep incident described at the beginning of the book and who happened to be present, announced that if the 'Christian sellers' did not pay up immediately when fined, they [the Hindu landowner] would take their land back from those Christians to whom they had mortgaged it, without repaying the mortgage. An Oraon woman stood up and retorted that 'you people [Hindus] had better stay off our *gahana* land [land belonging to Hindus, mortgaged to Oraons]. We paid for it, which means it is ours until you return our money. And if you so much as come walking nearby, we will beat you.'

With this, the crowd exploded. Some of the Hindu men rushed at and began beating the few Oraon Christian men who happened to be present, while others surrounded the Oraon women. Accusations against the Christians' alleged agenda of acquiring all the Hindu land through liquor sales could be heard above the din: 'you Christians are using *arkhi* money to buy our land'; 'you Christians should give us back our land and leave here'; 'you should go to Manpur [where the local Parish church is located] and live with the Fathers where you belong'; 'if you remain in Mohanpur, then you should stop selling liquor'; 'if we see you buying anything else like a television with liquor money, then we will destroy it'; 'if you remain in Mohanpur, then you should stop going to *girja* [church] and start worshipping at the village shrine'. The Hindus also insisted that they retained a right to inspect their land, even if they had temporarily given it away in a mortgage transaction. The fighting went on for 15–20 minutes, until the village headman was summoned to calm the crowd.

It is important to point out here that this was the first time that local Hindus used the category 'Christian' (*isai*) in place of 'Oraon' as a term of identification in a public context. Prior to this, Hindus would refer to Christian Oraons as 'Oraon people' when otherwise discussing the community. More critically, it was the first time that local drink disputes, and the local Christians' alleged agenda to 'bring the Hindus down', were linked to the broader *Hindutva* agenda.

What was particularly striking about this incident was the way that Raj made a direct connection between what was clearly a local issue and wider Hindu nationalist concerns, by linking local Oraon Christian's acquisition of land to allegedly similar practices elsewhere in India. It is in this way that Raj's position as 'conversion specialist'

(Brass 1997: 16), or the person who has the most instrumental role in propagating the idea that a particular community (like Christians) is the primary threat to this advancement, became manifest. The fact that rumours or allegations were used by Raj as the 'triggering event' that incited this crowd into violence is a common feature in the rise of communal conflict (cf. Tambiah 1996: 53–6). Indeed, the generation or transmission of rumours is an activity with which RSS *pracharaks* are associated more broadly, particularly during times when the level of anxiety is high (see Kanungo 2006: 246). In this particular instance, the use of rumours served as an effective strategy because it enabled a strong ethno-religious identification with wider nationalist concerns, which revolve around the idea that India is a nation that rightfully belongs to Hindus. Those living within this Hindu nation ought therefore, to be constituted along communally homogenous (Hindu) lines; those who fall outside of these boundaries are, by extension, perceived to be a threat to this homogeneity, and thus to the nation as a whole.

We can also see how livelihood and economic advantage may play a role in the creation of communal tensions, particularly if one group is relatively new to the area, and its wealth or means of acquisition has upset the existing configuration of social relations and hierarchies (cf. Horowitz 1985: 102). As discussed in the previous chapter, the concern that the Hindu community in general, and the Ratiya Kanwars in particular have for the Oraon Christians' increasing wealth, land and overall economic advantages can be explained in terms of the 'politics of entitlement' (Horowitz 1985: 186, 226). This is where a community of industrious outsiders threatens the resources to which the dominant group (the 'original settlers') feels it is rightfully entitled. As illustrated in the incident described above, this threat has been manipulated by the involvement of a group of elite outsiders (cf. Brass 1974) who are linked to a powerful organization whose instrumentalist agenda is devoted to fuelling resentment between ethnic groups and creating communal conflict.

After this incident, the Oraon Christians declared a boycott on drinking and sales, which lasted just over two weeks, at which time the 'normalcy' of drinking and selling, along with regular meetings calling for their boycott, resumed. The meetings were attended by Hindu women only, however, and the most marked change from previous meetings was the use of the term *isai* (Christian) when referring to the Oraons with respect to the latter's role in the production and sale of liquor. But the key meeting came in June, when the village headman himself announced in a *panchayat* meeting that the Hindu community had deteriorated substantially; that this was largely due to the consumption of alcohol; and that 'Christians' must no longer sell to Hindus because, as is happening throughout the rest of India, the income that is being generated from these sales is 'bringing the Hindu community down'. This was a remarkable statement made by the headman, who had until then, been a publicly neutral figure with respect to the local tensions. As the descendant of the Ratiya Kanwar headman who had permitted the first Oraon settlers to remain in the village one generation ago, this current headman's neutrality had always been a fact on which the Oraon Christian community had relied. Oraon people admitted that the implications of the headman's public acknowledgement of the connection between 'Christians' and drink tensions was potentially very serious, and there was great discussion about what could have brought about his changed position. As noted in the previous chapter, the Patel was putting himself forward as a candidate for the local *panchayat* election the following year. His use of this communal category could have conceivably been employed for the purpose of catering to the growing sentiment of the Hindus, a majority of whom had begun to use the category *isai* in a public context.

There was relative calm in the village after this latest meeting, with the most obvious manifestation of Hindu nationalism being the regularized and public use of the term 'Christian' (*isai*) by the local Hindus. But beneath this calm there was an underlying disquiet amongst the Oraons, who had been deeply disturbed by both the charges levelled by Raj and by the apparent acquiescence of the village headman with these charges. Around this time, news of the growing anti-Christian violence across India, in which RSS and other militant Hindu nationalist groups had been implicated, began to filter into the village. Oraons were concerned that, without the support of the headman, and in response to the growing influence of local RSS proponents and the wider Hindu nationalist concerns, they might be forced to leave the village and migrate from the area. These anxieties were compounded on days when Raj or one of the other RSS proponents was spotted conducting a training meeting in the main *basti*.

The arrival of the monsoons in early July temporarily halted any further 'training meetings', as the forest road became impassable. These meetings resumed in September, when the incident with the jeep described at the beginning of this book, took place. The main instigators of this incident included those young men who regularly attended the 'training meetings', one of which had taken place earlier on that particular day. In response to this incident, and to demonstrate cooperation with local concerns about liquor production, the Catholic priests immediately instituted their own system of fines against members of their parish who reportedly engaged in the production and sale of *arkhi*. They also invited some of the young men to the church to discuss the situation calmly, reiterating their own anti-drink position, and in mid-October, a sermon at Sunday mass was devoted to the virtues of sobriety. Word about the jeep incident had got around, and the Oraon Christians were given a lecture on how bad liquor was for the individual consumer and the general community. They were also reminded about how dangerous it could be in terms of their relations with the Hindu community, particularly in the context of the anti-Christian violence that was spreading across the country. Finally, and in line with the strategies to discourage traditional Kurukh practices described in Chapter Three, the priests threatened monetary sanctions against any household that produced or sold the drink.

The use of 'Christian' as an ethnic category also moved beyond the context of the local meetings and liquor disputes, a fact that underpins the degree to which local relations have become communalized. Two incidents will serve to illustrate this. In March 1999, Hindu and Christian women from all the surrounding villages were invited by the Church for a meal and festivities to celebrate International Women's Day. When the meal of rice and lentils (which was sponsored by the Church but prepared by Hindus from a neighbouring village) was served, a group of Hindu women from Mohanpur sat apart from the rest of the crowd and refused to partake, for fear that the food might contain beef which, they claimed, 'would turn us into Christians'.

Another incident occurred in April 1999, this one more serious. It will be recalled that, apart from the mission compound itself, the only other sacred space or 'social territory' (Tambiah 1996: 53) claimed by local Christians, is a small cement platform with a cross mounted on it, which is located at the top of a small hill, some two kilometres away from the mission. The hill itself is a section of uncultivated forestland on which both Hindus and Oraons regularly graze their cattle. Being non-titled land, it also traditionally 'belongs' to the 'original settlers', the Ratiya Kanwars. It is to this hill that local Oraon Christians trek for the annual 'Way of the Cross' procession.

A few days before Easter, during an RSS 'training meeting', Raj suggested to the small group of attendees that they trek to the hill, tear down the cross and construct a small Hindu shrine in its place. As a 'symbolic contestation of public space' (Hansen 1996: 190), these plans were reminiscent of the destruction of an important mosque by militant Hindu nationalists in Ayodhya, north India, in 1992, an event that led to thousands of deaths across the country. This remains a contested and politically sensitive site, currently claimed by both Muslim groups and Hindu nationalists (see Nandy et al. 1995). Local Oraons, along with the priests, got to know of these plans, and there was talk of cancelling the procession. But nothing ultimately came of these threats, and the procession went ahead as usual. However, it was the potential of the conflict which, in view of the anti-Christian violence that had spread throughout other parts of India during the previous year, gave this incident heightened importance.

In addition to these localized incidents, the RSS has also been attempting to diminish the Christian presence and influence in *adivasi* communities in this and other areas by challenging their very right to own land in such areas. The land concerned locally consists of the five acres that the Church purchased from its Hindu *adivasi* owner in 1970, and on which the Church compound currently stands. This transaction was deemed fair by all parties involved at the time. However, it became the subject of a protracted legal case that was filed in 1997 on behalf of the original owner by members of the RSS in Raipur, who argued that the Church had acquired the land forcibly and illegally. This case, along with similar ones filed elsewhere in Chhattisgarh, Gujarat and other *adivasi* areas where the Church has a strong presence, was played out in the wake of the anti-Christian sentiment that was spreading across India in the late 1990s.[8]

RSS Strategies, *Hindutva* and the 'Threatening (Christian) Other'

The events described above did not significantly transform local drinking practices; nor did they result in any further violence of the kind outlined at the beginning of this book, nor even in the unity of

[8]Local people remained largely unaware of this case, which was resolved in favour of the Church in 2001.

all local Hindus against all Oraon Christians. These events did, however, bring about the transformation of the Oraon community into the local 'threatening other' against the majority Hindu community, one of the most critical, long-term aims of the Hindu nationalist movement. By extension, this has given rise to communal distrust and communalized village-level discourse, with local *adivasis* increasingly viewing one another in terms of a more singular 'Hindu' or 'Christian' social or religious identity. These events have also had significant political impact, with the majority of local votes in Mohanpur, traditionally a stronghold for the more moderate Congress party, returned for the first time, in favour of the local Hindu nationalist BJP candidate in the state assembly elections held in late-1999.

It is the emergence of these phenomena that this and the previous chapter have sought to understand. To summarize briefly, the issue through which Hindu nationalism has been manifested in this predominantly *adivasi* village revolves around local drink tensions between the Oraon Christian vendor and the Hindu customer. These tensions first came to light in the context of the women's meetings, where Hindu women vocalized their concerns over their husbands' and sons' use of household goods for the purchase of liquor from Oraons. At the suggestion of Raj, these concerns then began to be raised in the context of the male-dominated village council. It was here that the focus of the tensions shifted to the visible wealth of the Oraon community and the latter's acquisition, apparently through profits from liquor sales, of expensive material goods. These economic concerns, in turn, came to centre on the Oraons' acquisition of (mortgages for) Hindu land. The communal tensions that evolved from these initial concerns were impelled by the involvement of RSS activists, who often conducted *Hindutva* 'training meetings' on the same day that local meetings were held, and who sometimes, attended the local meetings where disputes were aired.

Following months of growing tensions, the 'triggering event' (Tambiah 1996: 231–2) that finally signified the attachment of these concerns to wider Hindu nationalist issues was the evening meeting where the local 'Christians' were accused for the first time, of using profits from liquor to 'acquire Hindu land'. Local Hindus were also strategically warned by the RSS activist Raj, that, in tandem with patterns spearheaded by Christians throughout the rest of India, the continuation of such a practice would accelerate the deterioration of the local Hindu community. The speed with which communal categories began to be utilized locally points to the success of the introduction of Hindu nationalist sentiment—particularly the ideology of the 'threatening other'. This was related to the kind of 'conflict symbol' (Horowitz 1985)—liquor—that was utilized to transmit this sentiment.

The choice of liquor tensions by the RSS activists as the primary tool used to demonize the 'threatening other' in this *adivasi* community and thereby communalize social relations and advance their *Hindutva* agenda is interesting. On the one hand, consumption of liquor is an ingrained *adivasi* practice in this part of Chhattisgarh. By choosing liquor consumption, RSS activists thus risked alienating the very community on whom the agenda focused. Activists had to direct their attention towards what was a pre-existing local division: that between the customers (the Hindus) and the vendors (the Oraons). Such a choice also had a useful material basis manifested by the connection between expenditure on liquor and the loss of land and livelihood.

The material basis that frames these grievances makes it possible to interpret the above events as an ordinary caste conflict, whereby certain members of the high caste 'sons of the soil' (Weiner 1978) and other members of the Hindu community attempted to 'level' (Tambiah 1996) or diminish the margin of advantage enjoyed by the upwardly mobile, low-caste Oraon community. This advantage is augmented by the tremendous expenditure required of local Hindus to maintain the expensive ritual and social obligations mentioned in the previous chapter, which creates a significant strain on the average Hindu household's resources. In contrast to the Oraon Christians, whose participation in such activities has dwindled with the increasing influence of the Church, Hindus are often forced to enter into debt relationships by mortgaging their land, in order to meet such costs. The central issue here is the way that increasing tensions between the Hindus and Oraons have been framed by both the (re)allocation of scarce resources (land) that traditionally belong to and are controlled by the higher-caste Hindus, and the increasing economic wealth, helped by liquor profits, of the low-caste Oraons.[9]

Increasing Oraon wealth through liquor sales and other forms of wage labour does indeed, serve to undermine traditional structures of domination by threatening the economic and political status of

[9]See Brass (1974: 34). The scenario described here, has interesting parallels with the situation observed so long ago by Bailey (1958), with respect to the aspiring low-caste community, the Boad Distillers, whose economic success through engagement in liquor sales and land acquisition had important political repercussions for the community as a whole.

the more dominant Hindu community. In context of this, evolving Hindu/Christian communal tensions could be viewed as an amplification of pre-existing economic tensions mapped onto Hindu/Oraon caste relations. Moreover, local Hindus' enthusiastic response to the RSS activist's warning of Christian aims of acquiring Hindu land, as evinced by the formers' use of religious or communal categories, could be construed as a predictable reaction of a threatened high caste to the increasing power of an aspiring low-caste.

However, what could have been initially interpreted as the tensions distinctive of an ordinary caste conflict have rapidly become communalized by the involvement of members of the RSS, who strategically shifted attention from the (Oraon) caste to the (Christian) religious community and thus encouraged the view of them as the 'threatening other'. As Weiner (1978: 7) has pointed out, when competing groups belong to different ethnic or caste communities, and when the issue revolves around competition over or access to economic wealth, then pre-existing tensions can, and do become exacerbated into larger ethno-nationalist issues—particularly if the tensions are manipulated by a powerful group that possesses a dedicated, instrumentalist agenda (cf. Brass 1974: 45). As land tensions move beyond the local, and local incidents between individuals become contextualized or represented in terms of the 'master narrative' (Varshney 2002: 34) of *Hindutva*, what could have been interpreted as an ordinary caste conflict acquired communal elements in a process whereby religious affiliation has come to be used as a tool for economic and political gain. In short, through the strategic transformation of pre-existing land and drink claims into issues of communal concern, the RSS *pracharaks* were able to give disputes and tensions an importance beyond their particular local context.

The success of such a strategy can be attributed to the manner by which the RSS has tailored its response to the pre-existing social conditions that revolved around economic divisions and tensions over drinking (cf. Hocking 1996: 225–6). As noted earlier in the book, Mohanpur is located in a geographically remote area where, due to lack of electricity and passable roads, people have little access to the Hindu cultural mainstream. This means that the methods by which Hindu nationalism is routinely spread in urban areas, relying heavily on people's access to mass media and to popular forms of public participation, are unavailable to the local people (cf. Varadarajan 1999). The strategies of Hindu nationalist activists are thus dependent on other means of spreading *Hindutva*, such as the specific adaptation to local conditions and cleavages documented in this book. Pre-existing local tensions thus, provided local RSS activists with a convenient platform from which to strategically extend the *Hindutva* ideology.

It is perhaps no coincidence that local tensions have increased in tandem with the growing frequency of RSS 'training meetings', where RSS activists regularly disseminate information and teach young men about *Hindutva* ideology, and which are often conducted on the same day that the *panchayat* or women's meetings are held. Implicit in this analysis is the instrumental involvement of Raj and the other RSS activists who have used their positions to actively promote the idea of the 'threatening Christian other' and shape the forces through which Hindu nationalism has been delivered to the village. This is why Raj could be classified as what Brass (2003: 32–3, 1997: 16) calls a 'conversion specialist', a person whose pivotal role is to attach new meaning to local conditions or convert an ordinary local incident into communal discourse, enabling its potential escalation into communal violence.

It was not the point of this book to examine the individual agenda behind Raj and the other RSS activists' involvement in the events described above. It is important to note, however, that his role as a 'conversion specialist', in tandem with the instrumentalist involvement of groups like the RSS and the way that proponents of such groups bring their influence to bear on others' politics, is crucial for the successful production of communal sentiment in areas like the *adivasi* community where this research took place. It is, in short, through such involvement that the RSS gains influence in local affairs and initiates a connection from the ground to national-level politics.

RSS strategies to identify *adivasis* as 'true Hindus' and bring them into the Hindu mainstream can be compared to other movements, both historical and contemporary, that have revolved around questions of tribal identity or upliftment. While late-nineteenth and early-twentieth century social movements were largely aimed at changing or improving the established way of *adivasi* life by ostensibly emulating the cultural practices of higher Hindu castes,[10] the objectives of more

[10]Examples include the 1914–15 Tana Bhaghat movement, which enjoined Oraon *adivasis* to stop eating meat and drinking liquor, and to give up superstitious practices and animal sacrifices (cf. Roy 1928); the Bhumij-Kshatriya social movement, which

recent movements have also revolved around the promotion of the political and economic rights of *adivasi* people, often in reaction to powerful (usually Hindu) and sometimes exploitative outsiders (see Fuchs 1965; Singh 2002a).[11]

As discussed earlier in this book, these strategies are also parallel to what Tambiah (1996) calls 'focalization' and 'transvaluation', where local incidents were 'progressively denuded of their contextual particulars' and then 'distorted and aggregated into larger collective issues of national or ethnic interest' (ibid. 81). In tandem with these processes, RSS activists stripped drink tensions of their local particulars and attached them to one of the most powerful manifestos of the Hindu nationalist movement: the 'threatening other'. This process has occurred in the context of the allegations that the Christians' aims 'to take over Hindu land' are part of a larger national agenda, and like Hindus elsewhere in India, local Hindus must protect themselves against this process. In order for liquor disputes to become more serious communal issues, Raj and the other activists have had to direct attention towards what has become the primary local division: that between the customers (the Hindus) and the sellers (the Oraons). Focusing on the latter enabled Raj to capitalize on fears that the Hindus have of the Christians' alleged goal of 'bringing the Hindu community down'.

The process by which local tensions were attached to wider Hindu nationalist concerns can also be compared to Hansen's (1996) observations of the 'vernacularization' of *Hindutva* in rural

---

took place in Jharkhand in 1921, and which similarly, demanded that *adivasis* give up liquor, fish and meat (see Sinha 1959); and the 1922 Devi movement of South Gujarat which, along with its anti-drinking element, also invoked *adivasis* to take vows in Gandhi's name for the purpose of improving their material condition (see Hardiman 1987).

[11]One example of this is the Jharkhand movement. A region in central-eastern India dominated by *adivasis*, Jharkhand has long been occupied and controlled by higher caste Hindu outsiders who have been the primary beneficiaries of the agricultural and industrial resources of the area (Devalle 1992; Prakash, 2001; cf. Singh 2002b). Tribal demands for the region to be restored to its true 'sons of the soil' (Weiner 1978) and for Jharkhand to become a separate state were first issued in 1928. The view that such outsiders increasingly posed a threat to tribal livelihoods and ways of life contributed to the force of the movement, and Jharkhand (along with Chhattisgarh and Uttarkhand, two other regions in central and northern India that are heavily populated by tribal peoples) finally became separate states in November 2000. For comparisons with Dalit struggles, see Omvedt (2002).

Maharashtra. It was through tactics like the propagation of dominant regional idioms like the 'aggressive Hindu' that the Shiv Sena and BJP was able to 'translate' Hindu nationalist sentiment into an effective communal discourse.[12] In Mohanpur, it was through the articulation of caste disputes into wider communal issues that *Hindutva* was 'translated' into a viable local discourse. Prior to Raj's involvement in these issues, it is unlikely that ordinary local people were aware or even cared about the alleged connection between their own local tensions and those involving Christians elsewhere in India. Through the articulation of local grievances into nationalist ones, Raj was able to successfully draw attention to wider *Hindutva* concerns. In this manner, anti-Christian sentiment was not only successfully generated, but the cultural allegiance between local Hindu *adivasis* and Hindus elsewhere in India, was encouraged.

Tambiah (1996) goes on to show how the twin processes of 'focalization' and 'transvaluation' are compounded by the involvement of propagandists who appeal to larger, more enduring (and therefore less context-bound) loyalties of race, language, religion, and place of origin (ibid.: 192). Locally, such involvement also parallels parts of Brass's (1974, 1979) analysis of ethnic group politics in South Asia, particularly the attention he gives to the role played by organizations like the RSS in influencing the course of local conflict and attaching these to a nationalist agenda.

It is true that Brass has been criticised for overemphasizing the impact of the political organizations headed by elites when he writes that 'they shape group consciousness by manipulating symbols of group identity to achieve power for their group' (1974: 45; see also Jaffrelot 1996: 80; Robinson 1977). More recent writings have also expressed wider reservations with analyses of nationalism that privilege instrumental processes over others (Varshney 2002). In an article on expressions of Palestinian nationalism, for example, Jean-Klein (2001: 84) is highly critical of such analyses, in terms of how 'the masses have nationalism projected on to or prescribed for them by pervasive

---

[12]Other strategies included the systematic Hinduization of public, ritual and festival space and the provocation and exploitation of factional politics. According to Hansen (1996), not only did this successfully 'translate' *Hindutva* into a viable local discourse, but enabled the acquisition of a substantial electoral base in rural Maharashtra. See also Fuller's (2001) discussion on how the Sangh Parivar has successfully appropriated local Hindu rituals in Tamil Nadu to create a wider 'Hindu Unity'.

or persuasive (mis)representational actions of nationalist elites and leaders.' However, and as demonstrated by the ethnography above, the manifestly instrumentalist nature of RSS involvement in local affairs indicates that such analyses remain critical to the specific nature by which Hindu nationalism has been transmitted to local *adivasi* communities, and through which Hindu nationalist propagandists play an integral part in actively communalizing and therefore polarizing social relations.

CHAPTER EIGHT

Conclusion

The purpose of this book has been to bring a distinctly ethnographic approach to the wider literature on Hindu nationalism. Based on extended research that took place in Mohanpur, an *adivasi* village in rural Chhattisgarh, it is a response to the need for a systematic ethnographic analysis of the manner by which Hindu nationalism is being successfully transmitted at the ground level within specifically rural, *adivasi* areas. It comes at a time when the RSS-BJP combine, having faced recent political setbacks at the national level, is in the process of consolidating its base amongst *adivasi* communities; and when aggressive campaigns against Christian minority communities continue to be carried out by RSS activists (*pracharaks*) in states that have sizeable *adivasi* populations.

The primary objective of this account has been to identify and document the particular strategies employed by local RSS *pracharaks*, who serve as the principal proponents of Hindu nationalist ideology in Chhattisgarh, and to demonstrate how these are underpinned by the mimetic relationship that the RSS has with the Catholic Church. As noted at the beginning, the arrival and increasing presence of RSS activists in this area paralleled my own. This placed me in a unique position to observe how, in the space of two years, they managed to endear themselves to the local community. I also observed how they inculcated some of the tenets most crucial to the success of Hindu nationalism, and was able to consider the impact that this has had on the local people.

The concerns of this book have been underscored by the speed with which the Hindu nationalist movement has developed into one of the most divisive political forces within India. The long-term agenda of this movement includes the spread of *Hindutva*, or 'Hinduness', and the propagation of 'cultural unity' amongst all Hindus for the purpose of transforming India into a homogenized Hindu nation (Hansen 1999; Jaffrelot 1996). Those whose origins or allegiances lie outside the bounds of the Hindu nation have been constituted as a threat against Hindu society. It is this idea of the 'threatening other' that has evolved into one of the most powerful discourses of Hindu nationalism.

While the Muslim community has traditionally been designated as the 'threatening other' within Hindu nationalist discourse, attention of the RSS and its affiliates shifted toward Christians across India in the mid-1990s. Christians were charged with engaging in subversive activities, particularly amongst 'backward' *adivasi* communities, and were therefore, perceived as constituting a threat to the majority of the Hindus. This shift was also motivated by electoral considerations and the calculated expansion of the movement's political support beyond its urban, middle class bases. The larger 'community' of *adivasis* had yet to be encompassed within the 'Hindu fold', and as such, represented an important constituency and potentially sizeable vote bank for the main Hindu nationalist party, the BJP.

The extensive body of scholarship that has been devoted to analysing the origins and present-day trajectories of the Hindu nationalist movement has contributed enormously to our understanding of the wider historical processes and mobilizing ideologies that have led to its success. As noted at the beginning, however, the processes by which Hindu nationalist sentiment is being manifested at the ground level, particularly amongst *adivasi* communities, have remained largely undocumented and unanalysed. In light of the violence that has taken place within such areas—specifically those with a strong Christian presence—and in view of the recent political success of the BJP in states with a sizeable *adivasi* constituency, a distinctly ethnographic approach has been long overdue.

One of the central aims of this book has been to illustrate how the successful spread of Hindu nationalism within rural *adivasi* communities is related to the way in which the *Hindutva* message is tailored around the specific social relations that exist at the local level. In Mohanpur, this message was predominantly underpinned by the relationship between two *adivasi* groups: the high-caste Ratiya Kanwar 'sons of the soil', who make up the majority of the Hindu community and led the village in all ritual and political affairs; and the low-caste Oraon Christians, an upwardly mobile group of 'outsiders'. It was these particular groups that constituted the broader social cleavage between the Hindus and Christians as a whole; and it was the growing tensions between these groups around which the discourse of the 'threatening other' was cultivated by RSS *pracharaks*.

The successful transmission of Hindu nationalism can also be attributed to the way in which it was moulded around the dominant cultural beliefs and practices in which people engage. In Mohanpur, decisions with respect to issues as seemingly diverse as where people were allowed to live and cultivate their fields, the timing of their rituals and festivals, the nature of their illnesses and the particular kind of health practitioner they summoned, and even the degree of authority given to their traditional and political leaders, were all in some fundamental way, determined by the relationship that people had with their local or *'jangli'* deities and other supernatural beings. Largely constituted as 'backward' and juxtaposed against more 'proper', mainstream Hindu practices, it was these practices that influenced the way in which RSS activists engaged with people at the local level, and that determined the kinds of issues in which they became involved.

A second objective of this book has been to draw attention to the seminal role played by these activists in the spread of Hindu nationalism to this village and elsewhere. Locally, this role was occupied by Raj, a young Ratiya Kanwar man who, after failing to 'make it big' in the city, joined the RSS and committed himself to the transmission of the *Hindutva* ideology. As the primary liaison between the local branch of the RSS and the area's *adivasi* people, he served as what Brass (1997; 2003) has called a 'conversion specialist', or the principal proponent whose task it is to fuel local conflict and transform or 'convert' local grievances into violent, communal tensions. Individuals like Raj and the other *pracharaks* who frequented the village are critical in facilitating the strategies through which the propagation of *Hindutva* and the communalizing of social relations can be achieved.

In Mohanpur, there have been two principal strategies that have served as the most successful tools in the articulation of *Hindutva* as a meaningful local discourse. Both have been predicated on the 'instrumentalist' involvement of Raj and other 'conversion specialists', and both have been underpinned by the kind of mimetic relationship that the RSS has had with the Church.

The first strategy was modelled after the social upliftment activities in which Christian missionaries have historically engaged, and revolved around the RSS's ostensible concern for the physical and social welfare of *adivasi* people. It was manifested most strongly in the context of healing and biomedical intervention, activities that are traditionally associated with the Church. This association is most visible in this area in the context of the dispensary, which was constructed by the Church in the early 1970s. The reputation of the dispensary as a place where certain illnesses could be successfully treated grew alongside the efficacy of biomedicine. As the only medical facility within a 20-km radius, the dispensary was the primary point of contact between *adivasis* who lived in surrounding villages and Christianity.

It was this association, along with the support that the dispensary received from the area's *adivasi* people, which attracted the greatest concern of local RSS activists. Owing to the demographics of the area, the majority of the patients were Hindu, and RSS reservations revolved around the potential of the dispensary to serve as a vehicle for Christian missionization. While it has been illegal to proselytize in this area since 1991, the reputation that the dispensary enjoyed meant that it was in a position to exert a great deal of Christian-based influence over local *adivasis'* beliefs and practices. As such, it constituted an explicit threat to the *Hindutva* agenda.

In an effort to draw patients away from this influence, local RSS activists sponsored and installed their own biomedical 'doctor'. The younger brother of the principal 'conversion specialist', this doctor resided in the village itself and was available to local people for regular consultation and medical intervention. The time and distance-related advantages associated with the visible presence of a village-based medical practitioner translated into a small but significant reduction in the dispensary's own patient numbers. The sponsorship of this 'doctor' has been regarded by local RSS activists, as the first step towards the long-term aim of breaking the monopoly that the Church has over biomedicine in the area.

While the increasing legitimacy of biomedicine can largely be attributed to the influence of the Church, the corresponding decline in usage of 'supernatural' treatment has not occurred. Another objective behind the installation of a 'doctor' has thus been to 'educate' local *adivasis* about the benefits of biomedicine, and to further curtail their commitment to 'backward', *'jangli'* customs that revolve around supernatural healing. Such customs included the practice of rapidly discarding biomedical treatment in favour of supernatural medicine, and the refusal to blend biomedical and supernatural treatment. The RSS activists' concerns about the effects of these customs on the health of local *adivasis* are reminiscent of those of the Church. Through the employment of varyingly aggressive tactics, the latter has also been active in discouraging local Oraon Christians' participation in what it has labelled *shaitan ka kam* (the work of the devil).

The sponsorship of a biomedical 'doctor' has been one form of civic activism that has enabled local RSS activists to attract support from the community as a whole. Another social service they performed was to use their position of authority, which was derived from being members of a powerful external organization, to intervene and put a halt to the corrupt practices of a local power holder. They achieved this by familiarizing themselves with issues of local corruption and by lending their legitimacy to those who wished to contest the dominance of the village headman. As a result of their intervention, RSS activists succeeded in removing particular powers from the headman and securing the return of basic monetary entitlements to local people. Both Hindus and Christians benefited from this intervention, which can be compared with one of the more successful forms of civic activism in which early Christian missionaries engaged: namely, the process whereby the latter used their authority to intervene on behalf of *adivasis* against corrupt landlords. Such forms of activism have served as an important means by which missionaries, like contemporary RSS activists, have been able to increase their support base and enhance their local standing.

Based on the broader relationship that the RSS has with the Church, these kinds of social upliftment activities have as their primary objective, the betterment of 'backward' *adivasi* people. They are part of what could be construed as a kind of RSS-style 'civilizing mission' that is modelled after the type of civic activism in which Church missionaries have historically engaged. This 'civilizing mission' clearly represents a form of present-day proselytization, whereby RSS activists are seeking to convert so-called 'Hindu' *adivasis* from their traditional practices and beliefs and entice them further into the wider Hindu fold.

The issue of conversion to Hinduism, while seminal to the RSS's agenda amongst disparate *adivasi* communities, has been given only cursory addressal by scholars (see Thapar 1985: 17) who have been more concerned with the discourse surrounding 're-conversion' (*ghar vapsi* or *shuddhi*). This latter concern demonstrates an implicit acceptance of the recognition of *adivasis*' original identity as 'Hindu', a view that is assertively advocated by the RSS. Equally worrying, this view is supported indirectly by the state, which, by officially classifying *adivasis* as 'Hindu' in government census reports, treats Hinduism as the 'default religion' for *adivasis* (see Sundar 2006: 358). This position lends credence to the RSS view, which constantly disputes the possibility that *adivasis* are historically anything other than Hindu, and which sees 'conversion' categorically as a process of recruitment *from* Hinduism *to* Christianity or Islam (see Kanungo 2002).

The issues of conversion (away from Hinduism) and re-conversion (back to the Hindu fold) remain at the centre of the Sangh Parivar's shift toward Christians, particularly with respect to their broader agenda amongst Christian *adivasi* communities. That new and aggressive tactics are being implemented by increasingly emboldened members of the RSS against what is regularly labelled as 'anti-national' minority communities means, of course, that scholars cannot afford to shift their attention from the issue of 're-conversion'. However, it is hoped that the foregoing analysis of the kind of proselytization activities in which the RSS has engaged under the pretext of 'social upliftment' will contribute to a wider discussion on the issue of conversion *to* Hinduism.

The social services that RSS activists have performed in Mohanpur have undoubtedly had tremendous impact on the lives of local people, the most obvious of which revolves around the improvement to the latter's physical and economic welfare. Indisputably worthy, these social services have been accompanied by a more alarming outcome, and that is the enhanced legitimacy that has been afforded the RSS. Under the ostensibly constructive auspices of social upliftment, in other words, RSS activists have been able to endear themselves to the community and thereby, establish a platform from which more aggressive tactics could be initiated later on. This strategy thus constitutes one of the more insidious means through which the RSS engages with local people, for it conceals the communal agenda that underpins wider Hindu nationalist aims.

A second strategy through which *Hindutva* has been successfully propagated locally serves as an example of these more aggressive tactics, and revolves around the attachment of local disputes to wider Hindu nationalist concerns. In accordance with how RSS activists have tailored their social upliftment activities to account for the needs of local people, this particular strategy has also been underpinned by issues of local concern. The issues in this case were connected to the increasing reservations that the Ratiya Kanwars and other Hindus had about the Oraon Christians' growing economic wealth. Impoverished and landless at the time of their arrival in the area one generation ago, the latter were forced to earn their livelihoods through wage labour, which was later augmented by the sale of liquor. Such activities not only enabled many Oraon households to attain a level of material affluence that surpassed that of the Hindu 'sons of the soil', but also placed them in a position to act as moneylenders to local Hindus in exchange for the latter's land.

The Hindu community's concern about how the Oraon Christians' material wealth has contributed to their ability to acquire Hindu-owned land is related to the 'politics of entitlement' (Horowitz 1985). The local Hindus, and specifically the Ratiya Kanwars, felt that the primary resource (land) to which they were legitimately entitled as the 'original settlers' was under threat from the Oraons, a group of low-caste outsiders who had recently migrated to the area. Echoing the observations made by Weiner (1978), the resentment that the local 'sons of the soil' experienced was compounded by the fact that these particular outsiders were not only from a different ethnic community, but that, they were also economically more successful.

This resentment initially evolved into a series of caste-based disputes over access to land. In the past, such disputes would have likely remained at the level of ordinary caste conflict, wherein a high caste community attempted to 'level' (Tambiah 1996) or diminish the margin of advantage enjoyed by an upwardly mobile low caste community. Through the instrumental involvement of local RSS activists who were actively engaged in inflaming the issues surrounding the politics of entitlement, however, these grievances were removed from their local particulars and translated into broader communal concerns. It was specifically through the vehicle of the women's organization and local *panchayat* meetings that land and liquor tensions were extracted from their local context and attached to wider Hindu nationalist issues. The methods by which this transpired were similar to those that Tambiah (1996) identifies as 'focalization' and 'transvaluation', a process whereby local incidents and disputes between two individuals are progressively denuded of their local context, then distorted and attached to larger Hindu nationalist concerns. It was in the context of one particular meeting that the local RSS 'conversion specialist',

Raj, suggested that the Oraons Christians' acquisition of local Hindus' land was representative of the way in which Christians throughout India were conspiring to 'bring the Hindu community down'. This suggestion of ulterior Christian motives served as the 'triggering event' (ibid.) that facilitated the articulation of local tensions into wider nationalist issues.

Less subtle in its methods of propagating *Hindutva*, this particular strategy has been more overtly aggressive in its efforts to translate one of the most powerful discourses of the Hindu nationalist movement— the 'threatening other', or those whose origins and therefore allegiances apparently lie outside of the community of Hindus (Hansen 1999, Jaffrelot 1996)—into terms that are relevant to local people. As a result of this incident, the cleavage between local Christians and Hindus was amplified and the communal allegiance between local Hindu *adivasis* and Hindus elsewhere in India was firmly established.

While the tensions that I outlined in the foregoing account are not directly akin to the kind of violent riots to which Tambiah refers in his study of ethnonationalist conflict, the incident narrated at the beginning of this book is an illustration of the potentially violent manner to which such tensions can be manifested. There are also other similarities between the processes described in Tambiah's work and those outlined in the preceding pages, particularly with respect to the kinds of methods used by the individuals who serve as the primary instigators in converting local disputes into communal tensions. Indeed, the role of the RSS activists in this process cannot be exaggerated. The involvement of such outside 'elites' in the promotion of ethnic group loyalties to a nationalist agenda has been extensively analysed by Brass (1974, 1979). And while Brass has been criticized for overstating the impact of these elites in the production of communal sentiment, his observations are highly applicable to our understanding of the critical part that the RSS activists have played in the way that Hindu nationalism has been made available to local people.

While the emergence of Hindu nationalism in this area can be attributed to the instrumentalist strategies employed by local RSS activists, it is the presence of Christians and the Church in the first instance that has enabled this phenomenon to assume the particular trajectory that it did. The RSS and other Hindu nationalist organizations continue to see the Church as a threat to the wider *Hindutva* agenda, not only in Mohanpur, but elsewhere in India, particularly in view of the historical reputation that it has for conversions amongst India's backward classes. In response to this threat, the RSS has specifically sought to 'emulate' and 'stigmatize' (Jaffrelot 1996) those aspects of the Church that are at once useful and threatening to their broader *Hindutva* agenda. The Church's active engagement in social upliftment strategies that revolve around the social and physical welfare of the community, for example, has provided the RSS with a justification to pursue similar activities. The role that local Christians play as liquor vendors and moneylenders has also meant that ordinary, pre-existing grievances can be articulated in more threatening forms. As both the principal object of mimesis and the primary local 'threat', the very presence of Christians alongside Hindus creates the possibility of entry into the village by the RSS. In short, while the successful spread of Hindu nationalism into this area is due principally to the strategic involvement of the RSS in local affairs, the latter is also a function of its relation of opposition to the Church.

But the Church is not simply a passive participant in this process; it has also played a significant role in facilitating the communal cleavage between the two communities. Its contribution includes its attempts to transform 'backward' Oraons into proper Christians through materially and spiritually 'diabolizing' (Meyers 1999) their traditional beliefs and practices. Such strategies have played an important part in the communalization of social relations by encouraging a more distinctive, visible, Christian identity against which the identity of local Hindus can be more easily juxtaposed. More implicit, less calculating, and certainly less (potentially) violent, strategies that stress the 'Christian-ness' of the 'threatening other' have provided Hindu nationalist groups like the RSS with a convenient platform from which, through the communalization of local identities, they can emphasize the 'Hindu-ness' of Hindu *adivasis*.

As I suggested at the beginning of the book, the RSS's emphasis on the 'Hindu-ness' of local *adivasis* creates a sort of 'imagined community' (Anderson 1983), in the manner by which *adivasi* Hindus are being persuaded that they share origins, traditions and aspirations— and therefore allegiances—with the wider Hindu community. This process serves to define the *adivasis*' historical position (as 'original Hindus'), the criteria of membership in the 'imagined' ethnic group (returning to the Hindu fold), and the manner in which collective action should be carried out (through the assertion of their religious identity against the 'Christian other').

The activities in which both the Church and the RSS continue to engage to establish dominance amongst local *adivasis* amount to a kind of 'competitive proselytization' (Sundar 2006: 357). While this phenomenon is principally political in its endeavour to expand numbers whilst keeping alternative religions out, it is also part of a larger process of competitive religious assertion, where religions and religious movements within India and across the globe are becoming increasingly assertive in their efforts to mobilize and produce separate, distinctive religious identities (see Saberwal and Hassan 2006; Mahmood 2005). In Mohanpur, this kind of assertion is manifested most visibly in the further polarization of social relations and the increased solidification of ethnic and communal boundaries.

It is, to be sure, the Church and the RSS that have been the most active in producing the present situation. However, accountability must also be placed with the state, which has failed, historically, in its role and responsibility of providing for the social, physical and educational needs of some of its more disenfranchised citizens. While much of the historical success of early Christian missionaries can be attributed to the absence of state involvement in *adivasi* concerns over land, medicine and education, it is the RSS that has most recently, provided much-needed health services to local people and assisted with the return of monetary entitlements. In the process of carrying out these social services, local people have received a lesson in exercising their rights as citizens and enforcing civic accountability.

It is the state's absence and indifference, in other words, which has facilitated the need for the kinds of strategies that have been utilized as grounds for politico-religious mobilization (Sundar 2006: 383–4). Insofar as the Church and the RSS, in reaction to the absence of state involvement at the local level, continue to share a common mission under the pretext of '*adivasi* upliftment', *adivasi* communities will continue to be the object of competing political and religious assertions.

While the state must bear some responsibility for the increased solidification of communal boundaries, the primary motivation behind the RSS's interest in Mohanpur, as well as in *adivasi* communities elsewhere in India, remains the fact that the larger 'community' of tribal people has yet to be encompassed within the *Hindutva* fold. As such, *adivasi* communities as a whole remain an important obstacle to the long-term political agenda and comprehensive success of the Hindu nationalist movement.

The strategies discussed in this book have gone some way to achieving this agenda by ensuring the electoral success of the BJP in areas where *adivasis* comprise a sizeable proportion of the constituency. It is true that the BJP has seen a significant change in its fortunes between 1997 and the present. Having achieved power at the national level in 1998, it suffered a defeat to a Congress-led coalition government in the 2004 national elections. However, at the time of writing it is still in power in various state governments, particularly those with sizeable *adivasi* populations, including Madhya Pradesh, Chhattisgarh, Rajasthan and Gujarat. In such states, aggressive targeting of Christian communities, schools and Churches continues to be a regular practice amongst RSS and BJP activists. In Chhattisgarh itself, the BJP defeated the Congress party by a massive landslide, giving renewed legitimacy and license to the *Hindutva* ideology and campaigns, and raising fears amongst the more moderate Hindu and minority Christian communities about the potential for increased communalization. The local MLA is also a member of the BJP. Moreover, RSS activists are still a highly visible presence locally and across the state, and are active in various campaigns that target the 'social upliftment' of *adivasi* communities.

I began this book by highlighting the fact that the grassroots phenomena from which the Hindu nationalist movement has been constructed and around which it has revolved, have largely been ignored in favour of broader historical or political analyses that largely favours urban phenomena. The foregoing ethnography has suggested that the penetration of this movement into the everyday life of rural *adivasis*, in both its socially beneficial and more violent forms, will continue to have far-reaching implications for years to come. It is hoped that this account will assist in further understanding the role that the Church plays in this process, the strategies that the RSS activists employ to gain a broader organizational base on the ground, and the processes by which these strategies are replicated amongst *adivasi* communities elsewhere in India.

Bibliography

Agarwal, B. 1994. *A Field of One's Own: Gender and Land Rights in South Asia*. Cambridge: Cambridge University Press.

Allchin, F.R. 1979. 'India: The Ancient Home of Distillation?'. In *Man* (n.s.) 14: 55–63.

Allen, N.J. 1976. 'Approaches to Illness in the Nepalese Hills'. In Louden, J. (ed.) *Anthropology and Medicine* [A.S.A. 13]. London: Academic Press.

Almond, G.A., Sivan E. and Appleby R.S. 1995. 'Politics, Ethnicity and Fundamentalism'. In Marty, M.E. and Appleby, R. Scott (eds.) *Fundamentalisms Comprehended*. Chicago: University of Chicago Press.

Alter, J. 1994. 'Somatic Nationalism: Indian Wrestling and Militant Hinduism'. In *Modern Asian Studies* 28, No. 3: 557–88.

Anandhi, S. 1995. *Contending Identities: Dalits and Secular Politics in Madras Slums*. New Delhi: Indian Social Institute.

Anderson, B. 1983. *Imagined Communities: Reflections on the Origin and Spread of Nationalism*. London: Verso.

Andersen, W. and Damle, S. 1987. *Brotherhood in Saffron*. Boulder: Westview Press.

Arnold, D. 1993. *Colonizing the Body: State Medicine and Epidemic Disease in Nineteenth-century India*. Berkeley: University of California Press.

Avritzer, L. 2004. 'Civil Society in Latin America: Uncivil, Liberal and Participatory Models'. In Glassius, Marlies, Lewis, David and Seckinelgin, Hakan (eds.) *Exploring Civil Society: Political and Cultural Contexts*, pp. 53–60. London: Routledge.

Babb, L. 1975. *The Divine Hierarchy: Popular Hinduism in Central India*. New York: Columbia University Press.

——— 1987. *Redemptive Encounters: Three Modern Styles in the Hindu Tradition*. Delhi: Oxford University Press.

Bailey, F.G. 1958. *Caste and the Economic Frontier: A Village in Highland Orissa*. Oxford: Oxford University Press.

——— 1960a. '"Tribe" and "Caste" in India'. In *Contributions to Indian Society* IV: 7–19.

——— 1960b. *Tribe, Caste and Nation: A Study of Political Activity and Political Change in Highland Orissa*. Manchester: Manchester University Press.

——— 1963. *Politics and Social Change*. London: Oxford University Press.

——— 1964. 'Capital Saving and Credit in Highland Orissa'. In Firth, R. and Yamey, B.S. (eds.) *Capital Saving and Credit in Peasant Societies*. London: George Allen and Unwin Ltd.

——— 1981[1964] 'Spiritual Merit and Morality'. In Mayer, A.C. (ed.) *Culture and Morality: Essays in Honour of Christoph von Fürer-Haimendorf*. Delhi: Oxford University Press.

Barth, F. (ed.) 1969. *Ethnic Groups and Boundaries*. Boston: Little Brown and Co.

Bartra, R. 1994. *Wild Men in the Looking Glass: The Mythic Origins of European Otherness*. Ann Arbor: University of Michigan Press.

Basu, Tapan 1993. *Khaki Shorts and Saffron Flags*. New Delhi: Orient Longman.

Bates, C. 1995. 'Race, Caste, and Tribe in Central India: The Early Origins of Indian Anthropometry'. In Robb, P. (ed.) *The Concept of Race in South Asia*. Delhi: Oxford University Press.

Baviskar, A. 2005. 'Adivasi Encounters with Hindu Nationalism in MP'. In *Economic and Political Weekly* Vol. 40, No. 48: 5105–13.

——— 1995. *In the Belly of the River: Tribal Conflicts Over Development in the Narmada Valley*. Delhi: Oxford University Press.

Bayly, S. 1999. *Caste, Society and Politics in India From the Eighteenth to the Modern Age*. Cambridge: Cambridge University Press.

Behuria, N.C. 1997. *Land Reforms Legislation in India*. Delhi: Vikas Publishing House.

Belmont, N. 1982. 'Superstition and Popular Religion in Western Societies'. In Izard, M. and Smith, P. (eds.) *Between Belief and Transgression: Structuralist Essays in Religion, History and Myth*. Chicago: University of Chicago Press.

Ben-Ami, S. 1992. 'Basque Nationalism between Archaism and Modernity'. In Reinharz, J. and Mosse G.L. (eds.) *The Impact of Western Nationalisms*. London: Sage Publications.

Bénéï, V. 2000. 'Teaching Nationalism in Maharashtra Schools'. In Bénéï, V. and Fuller C. (eds.) *The Everyday State and Society in Modern India*, pp. 194–221. New Delhi: Social Science Press.

Bentley, G.C. 1987. 'Ethnicity and Practice'. In *Comparative Studies in Society and History*, 29.1: 24–55.

Béteille, A. 1998. 'The Idea of Indigenous People'. In *Current Anthropology* 40(3): 277–88.

_____ 1977. 'The Definition of Tribe'. In Thapar, R. (ed.) *Tribe, Caste and Religion in India*. Meerut: Macmillan Company of India Ltd.

_____ 1965. *Caste, Class and Power*. Berkeley: University of California Press.

Bhatt, C. 2001. *Hindu Nationalism: Origins, Ideologies and Modern Myths*. Oxford: Berg Publishers.

Bunsha, D. 2006. 'Festival of Fear'. In *Frontline* Vol. 23 No. 4: 39–41.

Billig, Michael 1995. *Banal Nationalism*. London: Sage Publications.

Bloch, M. 1989. *Ritual, History and Power: Selected Papers in Anthropology*. London: Athlone Press.

Bose, N.K. 1941. 'The Hindu Method of Tribal Absorption'. In *Science and Culture* Vol. 7(4): 188–94.

Bose, P.K. 1992. 'Mobility and Conflict: Social Roots of Caste Violence in Bihar'. In Gupta, D. (ed.) *Social Stratification*. Delhi: Oxford University Press.

Bourdieu, P. 1977. *Outline of a Theory of Practice*. Cambridge: Cambridge University Press.

Bowen, F.J. 1936. *Father Constant Lievens*. St. Louis: Herder Book Company.

Brass, P. 1974. *Language, Religion and Politics in North India*. Cambridge: Cambridge University Press.

_____ 1979. 'Elite Groups, Symbol Manipulation and Ethnic Identity among the Muslims of South Asia'. In Taylor, D. and Yapp M. (eds.) *Political Identity in South Asia*. London: Curzon Press.

_____ 1991. *Ethnicity and Nationalism: Theory and Comparison*. New Delhi: Sage Publications.

_____ 1997. *Theft of an Idol: Text and Context in the Representation of Collective Violence*. New Jersey: Princeton University Press.

_____ 2003. *The Production of Hindu-Muslim Violence in Contemporary India*. Oxford: OUP.

Breman, J. 1974. *Patronage and Exploitation: Changing Agrarian Relations in South Gujarat, India*. Berkeley: University of California Press.

Brubaker, Rogers and Laitlin, David D. 1998. 'Ethnic and Nationalist Violence'. In *Annual Review of Sociology* 24: 423–52.

Bryce, James 1810. *A Sketch of the State of British India, with a view of pointing out the best means of civilizing its inhabitants, and diffusing the knowledge of Christianity throughout the Eastern world, etc.* Edinburgh: G. Ramsay.

Cannell, F. 1999. *Power and Intimacy in the Christian Philippines*. Cambridge: Cambridge University Press.

Caplan, L. 1987. *Class and Culture in Urban India*. Oxford: Clarendon Press.

Carstairs, G.M. 1926. *Shepherd of Udaipur and the Land He Loved*. London: Hodder and Stroughton.

_____ 1955. 'Medicine and Faith in Rural Rajasthan'. In Paul, B.D. (ed.) *Health, Culture and Community: Case Studies of Public Reactions to Health Programs*. New York: Russell Sage Foundation.

_____ 1983. *Death of a Witch: A Village in North India 1950–81*. London: Hutchinson.

Cavalier, A.R. 1899. *In Northern India: A Story of Mission Work in Zenanas, Hospitals, Schools and Villages*. London: S.W. Partridge and Co.

Chatterjee, Partha 1993. *The Nation and Its Fragments: Colonial and Postcolonial Histories*.

_____ 1997. 'Development Planning and the Indian State'. In Chatterjee, P. (ed.) *State and Politics in India*, pp. 271–97. Delhi: Oxford University Press.

Chaudhuri, K. 2001. 'Resources Unlimited'. In *Frontline*, 7 December.

Cohen, A. (ed.) 1974. *Urban Ethnicity*. London, New York: Tavistock Publications.

Cohn, B. 1987. *An Anthropologist Among Historians and Other Essays*. London, New Delhi: Oxford University Press.

Comaroff, J. and Comaroff, J. 1986. 'Christianity and Colonialism in South Africa'. In *American Ethnologist* 13: 1–22.

_____ 1991. *Of Revelation and Revolution: Christianity, Colonialism, and Consciousness in South Africa, Volume One*. Chicago, London: University of Chicago Press.

Conklin, Alice L. 1997. *A Mission to Civilize: The Republican Idea of Empire in France and West Africa, 1895–1930*. Stanford: Stanford University Press.

Cooper, K.J. 1998. 'In India, More Attacks on Christians'. In *The Washington Post*, 17 November.

Corbridge, S. and Harriss, J. 2000. *Reinventing India: Liberalization, Hindu Nationalism and Popular Democracy*. Cambridge: CUP.

Dalton, E.T. 1872. *Descriptive Ethnology of Bengal*. Calcutta: Superintendent of Government Printing.

Danda, A.K. 1977. *Chhattisgarh: An Area Study*. Calcutta: Anthropological Survey of India, Government of India.

Das, V. 1995. 'Counter-concepts and the Creation of Cultural Identity: Hindus in the Militant Sikh Discourse'. In Dalmia, V. and Stietencron, H. von (eds.) *Representing Hinduism: The Construction of Religious Traditions and National Identity*. Delhi: Sage Publications.

Debbarma, Sukhendu (n.d.) 'An Assessment of the Implementation of the Indian Government's International Commitments on Traditional Forest-Related Knowledge from the Perspective of Indigenous Peoples'. See http://www.international-alliance.org/documents/india_eng_full.doc.

Deliege, R. 1999. *The Untouchables of India*. Oxford: Berg Publishers.

Dennis, J.S. 1899. *Christian Missions and Social Progress: A Sociological Study of Foreign Missions*. Edinburgh: Oliphant, Andersen & Ferrier.

de Sa, F. 1975. *Crisis in Chota Nagpur*. Bangalore: Redemptorist Publications.

Desai, A.R. 1975. 'Tribes in Transition'. In Thapar, R. (ed.) *Tribe, Caste and Religion in India*. Meerut: Macmillan Company of India Ltd.

Devalle, S. 1992. *Discourses of Ethnicity: Culture and Protest in Jharkhand*. New Delhi, London: Sage Publications.

de Vos, G. 1983. 'Ethnic Identity and Minority Status: Some Psycho-Cultural Considerations'. In Jacobson-Widding, A. (ed.) *Identity: Personal and Socio-Cultural*. New Jersey: Humanities Press Inc.

Dewey, C. 1978. 'Patwari and Chaukidar: Subordinate Officials and the Reliability of India's Agricultural Statistics'. In Dewey, C. and Hopkins A.G. (eds.) *The Imperial Impact: Studies in the Economic History of Africa and India*. London: Athlone Press.

Dirks, N. 1987. *The Hollow Crown: Ethnohistory of an Indian Kingdom*. Cambridge: Cambridge University Press.

Dube, S. 1992. 'Myths, Symbols and Community: Satnampanth of Chhattisgarh'. In R. Guha (ed.) *Subaltern Studies VII*. New Delhi: Oxford University Press.

_____ 1995. 'Paternalism and Freedom: The Evangelical Encounter in Colonial Chhattisgarh, Central India'. In *Modern Asian Studies* 29 (1): 171–201.

_____ 1998. *Untouchable Pasts: Religion, Identity and Power Among a Central Indian Community, 1870–1950*. New York: State University of New York Press.

Dube, S.C. 1951. *The Kamar*. Lucknow: Universal Publishers Ltd.

_____ 1955. *Indian Village*. London: Routledge and Kegan Paul Ltd.

_____ 1968. 'Caste Dominance and Factionalism'. In *Contributions to Indian Sociology*, 2:58–81.

_____ (ed.) 1977. *Tribal Heritage of India, Vol. 1*. New Delhi: Vikas Publishing House.

Dumont, L. 1961. '"Tribe" and "Caste" in India'. In *Contributions to Indian Society*: 6.

_____ 1980 [1966]. *Homo Hierarchicus: The Caste System and its Implications*. Chicago: The University of Chicago Press.

Eck, D.L. 1985. *Darsan: Seeing the Divine Image in India*. Pennsylvania: Amina Books.

Elwin, V. 1939. *The Baiga*. London: OUP.

_____ 1943. *The Aboriginals*. London: Oxford University Press.

_____ 1946. *Folk Songs of Chhattisgarh*. London: OUP.

_____ 1947. *Muria and their Ghotuls*. London: OUP.

_____ 1950. *Myths of Middle India*. Bombay: OUP.

_____ 1955. *The Religion of an Indian Tribe*. Bombay: Oxford University Press.

Epstein, A.L. 1978. *Ethos and Identity*. London: Tavistock Press.

Eriksen, T.H. 2002. *Ethnicity and Nationalism: Anthropological Perspectives*. London: Pluto Press.

Eschmann, A. 1978a. 'Hinduization of Tribal Deities in Orissa: The Sakta and Saiva Typology'. In Eschmann, A., Kulke, H. and Tripathi, G. (eds.) *The Cult of Jagannath and the Regional Tradition of Orissa*, pp. 79–97. New Delhi: Manohar.

_____ 1978b. 'The Vaisnava Typology of Hinduization and the Origin of Jagannatha'. In Eschmann, A., Kulke, H. and Tripathi, G. (eds.) *The*

Cult of Jagannath and the Regional Tradition of Orissa, pp. 99–117. New Delhi: Manohar.

——— 1978c. 'Mahima Dharma: An Autochthonous Hindu Reform Movement'. In Eschmann, A., Kulke, H. and Tripathi, G. (eds.) *The Cult of Jagannath and the Regional Tradition of Orissa*, pp. 375–410. New Delhi: Manohar.

——— Eschmann, A., Kulke, H. and Tripathi, G. (eds.) 1978. *The Cult of Jagannath and the Regional Tradition of Orissa*. New Delhi: Manohar.

Evans-Pritchard, E.E. 1976 [1937]. *Witchcraft, Oracles, and Magic Among the Azande*. Oxford: OUP.

Farmer, V.L. 1996. 'Mass Media: Images, Mobilization and Communalism'. In Ludden, David (ed.) *Contesting the Nation: Religion, Community, and the Politics of Democracy in India*, pp. 98–115. Philadelphia: Pennsylvania Press.

Feeley-Harnik, G. 1985. 'Issues in Divine Kingship'. *Annual Review of Anthropology* 14: 273–313.

Filkins, D. 1998. 'Christians Under Fire in India'. In *Los Angeles Times*, 12 November.

Fischer-Tiné, H. and Mann, M. 2004. *Colonialism as Civilizing Mission*. London: Anthem Press.

Fitzgerald, Rosemary 2001. 'Clinical Christianity: The Emergence of Medical Work as Missionary Strategy in Colonial India, 1800–1914'. In Pati, Biswamoy and Harrison, Mark (eds.) *Health, Medicine and Empire: Perspectives on Colonial India*, pp. 88–136. London: Sangam Books.

Flueckiger, J. 1996. *Gender and Genre in the Folklore of Middle India*. Ithaca: Cornell University Press.

Forbes, G. 1981. 'The Indian Women's Movement: A Struggle for Women's Rights or National Liberation?' In Minault, G. (ed.), *The Extended Family*, pp. 49-82. New Delhi: Chanakya.

Forrester, D.B. 1977. 'The Depressed Classes and Conversion to Christianity, 1860–1960'. In Oddie, G.A. (ed.) *Religion in South Asia: Religious Conversion and Revival Movements in South Asia in Medieval and Modern Times*. New Delhi: Manohar.

Forsyth, J. 1889. *The Highlands of Central India: Notes on Their Forests and Wild Tribes, Natural History and Sports*. London: Chapman and Hall.

Foster, G.M. 1976. 'Disease Etiologies in Non-western Medical Systems'. In *American Anthropologist* 78:773–82.

Frazer, J. 2002 [1922]. *The Golden Bough*. London: Macmillan and Co.

Frietag, S.B. 1989. *Collective Action and Community: Public Arenas and the Emergence of Communalism in North India*. Berkeley: University of California Press.

Fuchs, S. 1960. *The Gond and Bhumia of Eastern Mandla*. London: Asia Publishing House.

____ 1964. 'Magic Healing Techniques Among the Balahis in Central India'. In Kiev, A. (ed.) *Magic, Faith and Healing*. New York: Free Press.

____ 1973. *The Aboriginal Tribes of India*. Delhi: Macmillan Press.

Fuchs W. 1965. *Rebellious Prophets: A Study of Messianic Movements in Indian Religions*. Bombay: Asian Publishing House.

Fuller, C. 1996. *Caste Today*. Delhi: Oxford University Press.

____ 2001. 'The Vinayaka Chaturthi Festival and Hindutva in Tamil Nadu'. In *Economic and Political Weekly*, 12 May, Vol. 36, No. 19: 1607–16.

____ 2004. *The Camphor Flame: Popular Hinduism and Society in India*. Princeton: Princeton University Press.

____ n.d. 'Is Hindu Nationalism in Decline?' Unpublished paper.

Fuller, C. and Bénéï, V. (eds.) 2001. *The Everyday State in Modern India*. New Delhi: Social Science Press and London: Hurst and Company.

Fuller, C. and Harriss, J. 2001. 'For an Anthropology of the Modern Indian State'. In Fuller, C. and Bénéï, V. (eds.) *The Everyday State in Modern India*, pp. 1–30. New Delhi: Social Science Press and London: Hurst and Company.

Gadgil, M. and Guha, R. 1995. *Ecology and Equity: The Use and Abuse of Nature in Contemporary India*. London: Routledge.

____ 1992. *The Fissured Land: An Ecological History of India*. New Delhi: Oxford University Press.

Galanter, M. 1984. *Competing Equalities: Law and the Backward Classes of India*. Berkeley, London: University of California Press.

Geertz, C. 1963. *Old Societies and New States: The Quest for Modernity in Asia and Africa*. New York, London: The Free Press.

Gell, A. 1982. 'The Market Wheel: Symbolic Aspects of an Indian Tribal Market'. In *Man* (N.S.) 17: 470–91.

____ 1985. 'How to Read a Map: Remarks on the Practical Logic of Navigation'. In *Man* 20:2.

____ 1986. 'Newcomers to the World of Goods: Consumption Among the Muria Gonds'. In Appadurai, A. (ed.) *The Social Life of Things: Commodities in Cultural Perspective*. Cambridge: Cambridge University Press.

____ 1997. 'Exalting the King and Obstructing the State: A Political Interpretation of Royal Ritual in Bastar District, Central India'. In Gell, A. (E. Hirsch, [ed.]) *The Art of Anthropology*. London: Athlone.

Gell, S. 1992. *The Ghotul in Muria Society*. Reading: Harwood Academic Publishers.

Gellner, E. 1983. *Nations and Nationalism*. Oxford: Blackwell Publishing.

Ghurye, G.S. 1943. *The Aborigines—'So-Called'—and Their Future*. Poona: D.R. Gadgil Press.

____ 1959. *The Scheduled Tribes*. Bombay: Popular Book Depot.

Gillies, E. 1976. 'Causal Criteria in African Classifications of Disease'. In

Loudon, J.B. (ed.) *Social Anthropology and Medicine*. London: Academic Press.

Glazer, N. and Moynihan, D. (eds.) 1975. *Ethnicity: Theory and Experience*. Cambridge: Harvard University Press.

Glenny, M. 1999. *The Balkans 1804–1999: Nationalism, War and the Great Powers*. London: Granta.

Gluckman, M. 1955. *Custom and Conflict in Africa*. Oxford: Basil Blackwell.

——— 1963. *Order and Rebellion in Tribal Africa*. London: Cohen & West.

Gold, D. 1991. 'Organised Hinduisms: from Vedic Truth to Hindu Nation'. In Martin, M.E. and Appleby, R. Scott (eds.), *Fundamentalisms Observed*, pp. 531–93. Chicago: University of Chicago Press.

Goldenberg, S. 1999. 'Maelstrom of Militants'. In *The Guardian*, 22 January.

Golwalkar, M.S. 1966. *Bunch of Thoughts*. Bangalore: Jagarana Prakashana.

Gopal, S. (ed.) 1993. *Anatomy of a Confrontation: Ayodhya and the Rise of Communal Politics in India*. London: Zed Books.

Goody, J. 1962. *Death, Property and the Ancestors: A Study of the Mortuary Customs of the Ladagas of West Africa*. Stanford: Stanford University Press.

Gough, K. 1976 [1952]. 'Cults of the Dead among the Nayars'. In Singer, M. (ed.) *Traditional India: Structure and Change*. Austin: University of Texas Press.

Green, Maia. 1995. 'Why Christianity is the Religion of Business: Perceptions of the Church Among Pogoro Catholics in Southern Tanzania'. In *Journal of Religion in Africa* XXV, 1: 25–47.

Gregory, C.A. 1997. *Savage Money: The Anthropology and Politics of Commodity Exchange*. Amsterdam, London: Harwood Academic Publishers.

Grignard, A. 1909. 'The Oraons and Mundas from the Time of Their Settlement in India'. In *Anthropos*, Vol. IV.

Grigson, W.V. 1949. *The Maria Gonds of Bastar*. Oxford: Oxford University Press.

Guha, R. 1989. *The Unquiet Woods: Ecological Change and Peasant Resistance in the Himalaya*. Delhi: OUP.

Guha, R. and Gadgil, M. 1989. 'State Forestry and Social Conflict in British India'. In *Past and Present* 122: 141–77

Gupta, A. 1995. 'Blurred Boundaries: The Discourse of Corruption, the Culture of Politics, and the Imagined State'. In *American Ethnologist* 22(2): 375–402.

Gupta, Smita 2006. 'Limited Rights'. In *Frontline*, 8–21 April, Vol. 23 No. 7: 95–8.

Hansen, T.B. 1996. 'The Vernacularisation of *Hindutva*: The BJP and Shiv Sena in Rural Maharashtra'. In *Contributions to Indian Sociology* (n.s.) 30,2: 177–214.

——— 1999. *The Saffron Wave*. New Jersey: Princeton University Press.

Hardiman, D. (n.d.) 2005. 'Christian Therapy: Medical Missionaries and the Adivasis of Western India, 1880–1930' (unpublished) paper presented at conference on 'Reinterpreting Adivasi Movements in South Asia', University of Sussex, March.

_____ 1985. 'From Custom to Crime: The Politics of Drinking in Colonial South Gujarat'. In *Subaltern Studies IV*.

_____ 1987. *The Coming of the Devi: Adivasi Assertion in Western India*. Delhi: Oxford University Press.

Hasan, K.A. 1967. *The Cultural Frontier of Health in Village India*. Bombay: Manaktalas.

Heath, D.B. 2000. *Drinking Occasions: Comparative Perspectives on Alcohol and Culture*. Ann Arbor: Sheridan Books.

Hefner, R.W. (ed.) 1993. *Conversion to Christianity: Historical and Anthropological Perspectives on a Great Transformation*. Berkeley: University of California Press.

Helman, C.G. 2000. *Culture, Health and Illness*. London: Butterworth Heinemann.

Henry, E. 1977. 'A North Indian Healer and the Sources of his Power'. In *Social Science and Medicine* II(5): 309–17.

Hill, P. 1986. *Development Economics on Trial: The Anthropological Case for a Prosecution*. Cambridge: Cambridge University Press.

Hitchcock, J. and Jones, R. (eds.) 1976. *Spirit Possession in the Nepal Himalayas*. New Delhi: Vikas.

Hocking, R. 1996. 'The Potential for BJP Expansion: Ideology, Politics and Regional Appeal—the Lessons of Jharkhand'. In McGuire, J., Reeve, P. and Brasted H. (eds.) *Politics of Violence from Ayodhya to Behrampada*. New Delhi: Sage Publications.

Hoffman, J. 1950. *Encyclopaedia Mundarica*. Patna Government Printing.

Horowitz, Donald L. 1985. *Ethnic Groups in Conflict*. Berkeley: University of California Press.

Horton, R. 1967. 'African Traditional Thought and Western Science'. In *Africa* 37 (1 & 2): 50–7, 155–87.

Humphrey, C. and Hugh-Jones, S. 1992. *Barter, Exchange and Value: An Anthropological Approach*. Cambridge: Cambridge University Press.

Isaacs, H.R. 1975. 'Basic Group Identity: The Idols of the Tribe'. In Glazer N. and Moynihan D. (eds.) *Ethnicity: Theory and Experience*. Cambridge: Harvard University Press.

Jaffrelot, C. 1998. 'BJP and the Caste Barrier: Beyond the "Twice-Born"?'. In Hansen, T.B. and Jaffrelot, C. (eds.) *The BJP and the Compulsion of Politics*, pp. 22–71. Delhi: OUP.

_____ 1996. *The Hindu Nationalist Movement and Indian Politics: 1925 to the 1990s*. London: Hurst and Co.

_____ 1993. 'Hindu Nationalism: Strategic Syncretism in Ideology Building'. In *Economic and Political Weekly*, 20–27 March.

Jain, L.C. 1929. *Indigenous Banking in India*. London: Macmillan and Co., Ltd.

Jay, E.J. 1968. *A Tribal Village in Middle India*. Calcutta: Anthropological Survey of India.

—— 1973. 'Bridging the Gap Between Castes; Ceremonial Friendship in Chhattisgarh'. In *Contributions to Indian Sociology* 7: 144–58.

Jean-Klein, Iris 2001. 'Nationalism and Resistance: the Two Faces of Everyday Activism in Palestine During the Intifada.' In *Cultural Anthropology* 16(1): 83–126.

Jeffery, R. and Sundar, N. (eds.) 1999. *A New Moral Economy for India's Forests?*. New Delhi: Sage Publications.

Jolly, M. 1996. 'Devils, Holy Spirits, and the Swollen God: Translation, Conversion and Colonial Power in the Marist Mission, Vanuatu, 1887–1934'. In van der Veer, P. (ed.) *Conversion to Modernities: The Globalization of Christianity*. New York: Routledge.

Jordans, J.T.F. 1977. 'Reconversion to Hinduism, the Shuddhi of the Arya Samaj'. In Oddie, G.A. (ed.) *Religion in South Asia: Religious Conversion and Revival Movements in South Asia in Medieval and Modern Times*, pp. 145–69. London: Curzon Press.

Joseph, John E. 2004. *Language and Identity: National, Ethnic, Religious*. London: Palgrave.

Juergensmeyer, M. 1993. *Religious Nationalism Confronts the Secular State*. Berkeley: University of California Press.

Kakar, S. 1996. *The Colors of Violence: Cultural Identities, Religion and Conflict*. Chicago: University of Chicago Press.

Kanungo, P. 2006. 'The Navigators of Hindu Rashtra: RSS Pracharaks'. In Saberwal, S. and Hasan, M. (eds.) *Assertive Religious Identities: India and Europe*, pp. 232–54. New Delhi: Manohar.

—— 2002. *RSS's Tryst with Politics: From Hedgewar to Sudarshan*. New Delhi: Manohar Press.

Kapadia, K. 1995. *Siva and Her Sisters: Gender, Caste and Class in Rural South India*. Boulder: Westview Press.

Kapferer, B. 1988. *Legends of People, Myths of State: Violence, Intolerance and Political Culture in Sri Lanka and Australia*. Washington D.C.: Smithsonian Institution Press.

Karp, I. 1987. 'Beer Drinking and Social Experience in an African Society'. In Karp I. and Bird C. (eds.) *Explorations in African Systems of Thought*. Bloomington: Indiana University Press.

Katju, M. 2003. *Vishwa Hindu Parishad and Indian Politics*. Delhi: Orient Longman.

Kawashima, Koji 1998. *Missionaries and a Hindu State: Travancore 1858–1936*. Oxford: OUP.

Kelkar, G. and Nathan, D. 1991. *Gender and Tribe: Women, Land and Forests in Jharkhand*. Delhi: Kali for Women.

Kertzer, D.I. 1988. *Ritual, Politics and Power*. New Haven and London: Yale University Press.

Khare, R.S. 1963. 'Folk Medicine in a North Indian Village'. In *Human Organisation* 22, 1:36–40.

Khilnani, S. 1997. *The Idea of India*. London: Penguin Books.

Kleinman, A. 1988. *The Illness Narratives*. Massachusetts: Basic Books, Inc.

Kohli, Atul 1990. *Democracy and Discontent: India's Growing Crisis of Governability*. Cambridge: CUP.

Kothari, Ashish 2004. 'Rights and Wrongs'. *Frontling*, Vol. 21 No. 8: 77–79.

Kothari, Ashish and Pathak, Neema 2004. 'Rights and Wrongs'. In *Frontline*, Vol. 21, No. 8: 77–9.

_____ 2005. 'Forests and Tribal Rights'. In *Frontline*, Vol. 22, No. 11.

Krishnaswamy, Madhuri 2005. 'One Step Forward, Two Steps Back'. In *Economic and Political Weekly*, 19 November.

Kujur, A. 1989. *The Oraon Habitat: A Study in Cultural Geography*. Ranchi: Catholic Press.

Kulkani, S. 1991. 'Distortion of Census Data on Scheduled Tribes'. In *Economic and Political Weekly* Vol. 26, No. 1, 2, February.

Kulkarni, Sharad 2000. 'The Plight of the Tribal', on www.india-seminar.com/2000/

Kumar, A. 2003. *Elections in India: Nehru to Vajpayee*. New Delhi: Gyan Publishing House.

Kumar, K. 1991a. *Political Agenda of Education: A Study of Colonialist and Nationalist Ideas*. New Delhi: Sage Publications.

_____ 1991b. 'Hindu Revivalism and Education in North-Central India'. In Pannikar, K.N. *Communalism in India: History, Politics and Culture*. New Delhi: Manohar.

Kuper, A. 1988. *The Invention of Primitive Society*. London: Routledge.

Lambert, H. 1988. 'Medical Knowledge in Rural Rajasthan; Popular Constructions of Illness and Therapeutic Practice'. Unpublished Ph.D. thesis. Oxford University.

_____ 1992. 'Cultural Logic of Indian Medicine: Prognosis and Etiology in Rajasthani Popular Therapeutics'. In *Social Science and Medicine*, Vol 34, No 10: 1069–86.

_____ 1996. 'Popular Therapeutics and Medical Preferences in Rural North India'. In *The Lancet*, Vol 348, July-Dec 1996:1706–9.

_____ 1997a. 'Illness, Inauspiciousness and Modes of Healing in Rajasthan'. In *Contributions to Sociology* (n.s.) 31,2: 253–71.

_____ 1997b. 'Plural Traditions? Folk Therapeutics and "English" Medicine in Rajasthan'. In Cunningham A. and Andrews B. (eds.) *Western Medicine as Contested Knowledge*. Manchester: Manchester University Press.

Leach, E. 1954. *Political Systems of Highland Burma: A Study of Kachin Social Structure*. London: London School of Economics and Political Science.

_____ 1983. 'Melchisedech and the Emperor: Icons of Subversion and Orthodoxy' In Leach E. and Aycock D.A. (eds.) *Structuralist Interpretations of Biblical Myth*. Cambridge: Cambridge University Press.

Lerche, J. 1995. 'Is Bonded Labour a Bound Category? Reconceptualising Agrarian Conflict in India'. In *Journal of Peasant Studies* 22: 484–515.

Lewis, G. 1975. *Knowledge of Illness in a Sepik Society*. London: Athlone.

Lewinsky, J.S. 1913. *The Origin of Property and the Formation of the Village Community*. London: Constable.

Lobo, L. 2002. 'Adivasis, Hindutva and Post-Godhra Riots in Gujarat'. In *Economic and Political Weekly*, 37 (48): 4844–9.

Louis, Prakash 2000. *The Emerging Hindutva Force*. New Delhi: Indian Social Institute.

Ludden, D. 1984. *Agricultural Production and Indian History*. Delhi: Oxford University Press.

_____ (ed.) 2005. *Making India Hindu: Religion, Community and the Politics of Democracy in India*. Oxford: OUP.

Madan, T.N. 1997. *Modern Myths, Locked Minds: Secularism and Fundamentalism in India*. Delhi: Delhi University Press.

Mahmood, S. 2005. *Politics of Piety: The Islamic Revival and the Feminist Subject*. Princeton: Princeton University Press.

Mahto, S. 1971. *Hundred Years of Christian Missions in Chotanagpur since 1845*. Ranchi: Chotanagpur Publishing House.

Majumdar, D.N. 1958. *Races and Cultures of India*. Bombay: Asia Publishing House.

Mamoria, C.B. 1952. *Tribal Demography in India*. Allahabad: Kitab Mahal.

Mandelbaum, D.G. 1970. *Society in India Vol 2: Change and Continuity*. Berkeley: University of California Press.

Mann, M. 2004. 'Torchbearers Upon the Path of Progress: Britain's Ideology of a Moral and Material Progress in India'. In Fischer-Tiné, H. and Mann, M. (eds.) *Colonialism as Civilizing Mission*, pp. 1-26. London: Anthem Press.

Marriott, M. 1955. 'Western Medicine in Northern India'. In Paul B.D. (ed.) *Health, Culture and Community: Case Studies of Public Reactions to Health Programs*. New York: Russell Sage Foundation.

Mathur, K.S. 1972. 'Tribes in India: A Problem of Identification and Integration'. In Singh, K.S. (ed.) *Tribal Situation in India*. Simla: Indian Institute of Advanced Study.

Marshall, M. 1979. *Weekend Warriors: Alcohol in a Micronesian Culture*. Mountain View: Mayfield Publishing Company.

Marty, M.E. and Appleby, S.R. (eds.) 1993. 'Introduction'. In *Fundamentalisms and the State*. Chicago: University of Chicago Press.

_____ 1994. *Accounting for Fundamentalisms*. Chicago: University of Chicago Press.

_____ 1995. *Fundamentalisms Comprehended*. Chicago: University of Chicago Press.

Mattam, M.A. 1991. *Inculturation of the Liturgy in the Indian Context*. Kottayam: Oriental Institute of Religious Studies.

Mayer, A. 1960. *Caste and Kinship in Central India: A Village and its Region.* London: Routledge.

——— 1981. 'Public Service and Individual Merit in a Town of Central India'. In Mayer A.C. (ed.) *Culture and Morality: Essays in Honour of Christoph von Fürer-Haimendorf.* Delhi: Oxford University Press.

——— 1996. 'Caste in an Indian Village: Change and Continuity 1954–1992'. In Fuller C. (ed.) *Caste Today.* Delhi: Oxford University Press.

McKean, L. 1996. *Divine Enterprise: Gurus and the Hindu Nationalist Movement.* Chicago: University of Chicago Press.

Mehta, B.H. 1984. *Gonds of the Central Indian Highlands: A Study of the Dynamics of Gond Society Vol 1.* Delhi: Concept Publishing Co.

Mendelsohn, O. 1993. 'The Transformation of Authority in Rural India'. In *Modern Asian Studies* 27, 4: 805–42.

Meyer, B. 1996. 'Modernity and Enchantment: The Image of the Devil in Popular African Christianity'. In van der Veer, P. (ed.) *Conversion to Modernities: The Globalization of Christianity.* New York: Routledge.

——— 1999. *Translating the Devil: Religion and Modernity among the Ewe in Ghana.* Edinburgh: Edinburgh University Press.

Mishra, M.K. 1993a. 'Influence of the Ramayana Tradition on the Folklore of Central India'. In Singh, K.S. (ed.) *Rama-Katha in Tribal and Folk Traditions of India,* pp. 15-30. Calcutta: Seagull Books.

——— 1993b. 'A Hero of the Mahabharta in Folklore of Central India'. In Singh, K.S. (ed.) *The Mahabharta in the Tribal and Folk Traditions of India,* pp. 157–70. New Delhi: Anthropological Survey of India.

Mitra, S.C. 1935. 'Note on a Recent Instance of Human Sacrifice from the District of Sambalpur in Orissa'. In *Man in India* Vol. 15(4): 263–6.

Moerman, M. 1965. 'Ethnic Identification in a Complex Civilization: Who are the Lue?'. In *American Anthropologist* Vol. 67 No. 5: 1215–30.

Moorshead, R. Fletcher. 1913. *The Appeal of Medical Missions.* Edinburgh: Oliphant, Anderson and Ferrier.

Mosse, D. 1994a. 'Idioms of Subordination and Styles of Protest Among Christian and Hindu Harijan Castes in Tamil Nadu'. In *Contributions to Indian Sociology* (n.s.) 28, 1: 67–106.

——— 1994b. 'The Politics of Religious Synthesis'. In Stewart C. and Shaw R. (eds.) *Syncretism and Anti-syncretism.* New York and London: Routledge Press.

——— 1994c. 'Catholic Saints and the Hindu Village Pantheon in Rural Tamil Nadu, India'. In *Man* (n.s.) 29: 301–32.

Murdock, George Peter 1980. *Theories of Illness.* Pittsburgh: University of Pittsburgh Press.

Nandy, A. 1995. *Creating a Nationality: The Ramjanmabhumi Movement and Fear of the Self.* New Delhi: Oxford University Press.

Nash, M. 1989. *The Cauldron of Ethnicity in the Modern World.* Chicago: University of Chicago Press.

280   Bibliography

Neale, W.C. 1962. *Economic Change in Rural India: Land Tenure and Reform in UP 1800–1955*. New Haven: Yale University Press.

Neill, S. 1985. *A History of Christianity in India 1707–1858*. Cambridge: Cambridge University Press.

Nichter, M. (ed.) 1996a. 'Popular Perceptions of Medicine: A South Indian Case Study'. In Nichter, M. and Nichter, M. (eds.) *Anthropology and International Health: Asian Case Studies*. London: Gordon and Breach Publishers.

_____ 1996b. 'Paying for What Ails You: Sociocultural Issues Influencing the Ways and Means of Therapy Payment in South India'. In Nichter, M. and Nichter, M. (eds.) *Anthropology and International Health: Asian Case Studies*. London: Gordon and Breach Publishers.

Noorani, A.G. 2000. *The RSS and the BJP: A Division of Labour*. New Delhi: Leftword Books.

Niyogi, B.S. 1956. *Report of the Christian Missionary Activities Enquiry Committee, Madhya Pradesh, Volume I and II*. Nagpur: Government Printing.

Obeyesekere, G. 1968. 'Theodicy, Sin and Salvation in a Sociology of Buddhism'. In Leach, Edmund R. (ed.) *Dialectics in Practical Religion*. Cambridge: Cambridge University Press.

_____ 1992. 'Science, Experimentation and Clinical Practice in Ayurveda'. In Leslie, C. and Young, A. (eds.) *Paths to Asian Medical Knowledge*. Berkeley: University of California Press.

Oddie, G.A. 1975. 'Christian Conversion in the Telugu Country, 1860–1900: A Case Study of One Protestant Movement in the Godavery-Krishna Delta'. In *Indian Economic and Social History Review*, Vol. 12:61–79.

_____ 1977. *Religion in South Asia: Religious Conversion and Revival Movements in South Asia in Medieval and Modern Times*. New Delhi: Manohar.

Omori, M. 1978. 'Social and Economic Utility of Omuramba, the Chiga Sorghum Beer'. In *Senri Ethnological Studies* 1.

Omvedt, Gail 2002. 'Ambedkar and After: The Dalit Movement in India'. In Shah, Ghanshyam (ed.) *Social Movements and the State*, pp. 293–309. New Delhi: Sage Publications.

Orans, M. 1965. *The Santal: A Tribe in Search of a Great Tradition*. Detroit: Wayne State University Press.

Padel, F. 1995. *The Sacrifice of Human Being: British Rule and the Konds of Orissa*. Delhi: Oxford University Press.

Panikkar, K.N. (ed.) 1991. *Communalism in India: History Politics and Culture*. New Delhi: Manohar.

_____ (ed.) 1999. *The Concerned Indian's Guide to Communalism*. Delhi: Penguin Books.

Pardo, I. 2000. 'Introduction. Morals of Legitimacy: Interplay between

Responsibility, Authority and Trust'. In Pardo, I. (ed.) *Morals of Legitimacy: Between Agency and the System*, pp. 1–26. New York: Berghahn Books.

Parry, J. P. 1979. *Caste and Kinship in Kangra*. London: Routledge.

—— 1994. *Death in Benares*. Cambridge: Cambridge University Press.

—— 1998. 'Mauss, Dumont and the Distinction between Status and Power'. In James W. and Allen N.J. (eds.) *From Marcel Mauss: A Centenary Tribute*. New York: Berghahn Books.

—— 1999a. 'Lords of Labour: Working and Shirking in Bhilai'. In Parry J.P., Breman J. and Kapadia K. (eds.) *The Worlds of Indian Industrial Labour*, pp. 107–40. New Delhi: Sage Publications.

—— 1999b. 'Two Cheers for Reservation; The Satnamis and the Steel Plant'. In Guha R. and Parry J.P. (eds.) *Institutions and Inequalities: Essays in Honour of André Béteille*, pp. 129–69. New Delhi: Oxford University Press.

—— 2000. 'The "Crisis of Corruption" and "The Idea of India": A Worm's Eye View'. In Pardo I. (ed.) *Morals of Legitimacy: Between Agency and System*, pp. 27–55. Oxford: Berghahn Books.

—— 2001. 'Ankalu's Errant Wife: Sex, Marriage and Industry in Contemporary Chhattisgarh'. In *Modern Asian Studies* 35, 4: 783–820.

Patel, M. 1974. *Changing Land Problems of Tribal India*. Bhopal: Progress Publishers.

Pathy, J. 1976. 'Tribal Studies in India: an Appraisal'. In *The Eastern Anthropologist* Vol. 29 No. 1: 399–417.

Pathak, A. 1994. *Contested Domains: The State, Peasants and Forests in Contemporary India*. New Delhi: Sage Publications.

Pati, B. 2003. *Identity, Hegemony and Resistance: Towards a Social History of Conversions in Orissa, 1800–2000*. New Delhi: Three Essays Collective.

Peabody, N. 1991. 'In Whose Turban Does the Lord Reside?: Objectification of Charisma and the Fetishism of Objects in the Hindu Kingdom of Kota'. In *Comparative Study of Society and History* 33: 726–54.

Pertold, O. 1931. 'The Liturgical Use of Mahuda Liquor by Bhils'. In *Archiv Orientalni, Journal of the Czechoslovak Oriental Institute*, Vol III.

Pickett, J.W. 1933. *Christian Mass Movements in India: A Study With Recommendations*. Lucknow: Lucknow Publishing House.

Prakasam, G. 1998. *Social Separatism: Scheduled Castes and the Caste System*. New Delhi: Rawat Publications.

Prakash, A. 2000. *Jharkhand: Politics of Development and Identity*. Hyderabad: Orient Longman.

Prasad, A. 2003. *Against Ecological Romanticism*. New Delhi: Three Essays Collective.

Pratt, Jeff 2003. *Class, Nation and Identity: The Anthropology of Political Movements*. London: Pluto Press.

Rafael, V. 1988. *Contracting Colonialism: Translation and Christian Conversion in Tagalog Society Under Early Spanish Rule*. London: Cornell University Press.

Ranger, T. 1982. 'Medical Science and Pentecost: The Dilemma of Anglicanism in Africa'. In Sheils, W.J. (ed.) *The Church and Healing*, pp. 333–65. Oxford: Basil Blackwell.

Rao, S and Rao, C.R. 1977. 'Drinking in the Tribal World: A Cross-cultural Study in "Culture-Theme" Approach'. In *Man in India*, Vol. 57 No. 2.

Reddy, D. Narasimha and Patnaik, Arun 1993. 'Anti-Arrack Agitation of Women in Andhra Pradesh'. In *Economic and Political Weekly*, 22 May.

Reznek, Lawrie 1987. *The Nature of Disease*. London: Routledge & Kegan Paul.

Risley, H. 1908. *The People of India*. London: Thacker Spink and Co.

———— 1891. *The Tribes and Castes of Bengal*. Calcutta: Bengal Secretariat Press.

Robinson, F. 1977. 'Nation Formation: The Brass Thesis and Muslim Separatism'. In *Journal of Commonwealth and Comparative Politics* 15, 3.

———— 1988. *Local Politics: The Law of the Fishes: Development through Political Change in Medak District, Andhra Pradesh (South India)*. Delhi: Oxford University Press.

Robinson, Mark 2003. 'Civil Society and Ideological Contestation in India'. In Elliott, Carolyn M. (ed.) *Civil Society and Democracy*, pp. 377–404. Oxford: OUP.

Robinson, R. and Clark, S. (eds.) 2003. *Religious Conversion in India: Modes, Motivations, and Meanings*. New Delhi: OUP.

Roy B. 1972. 'Tribal Demography: A Preliminary Appraisal'. In Singh, K.S. (ed.) *Tribal Situation in India*. Simla: Indian Institute of Advanced Study.

Roy, Meenu 2000. *Electoral Politics in India: Election Process and Outcomes, Voting Behaviour and Current Trends*. New Delhi: Deep and Deep Publications.

Roy, S.C. 1912. *The Mundas and Their Country*. Calcutta: The City Book Society.

———— 1915. *The Oraons of Chota Nagpur, Their History, Economic Life and Social Organisation*. Calcutta: The Brahmo Mission Press.

———— 1985 [1928]. *Oraon Religion and Customs*. Delhi: Gian Publishing House.

Roy, S.C. and Roy, R.C. 1937. 'The Kharias'. Ranchi: *Man in India*.

Rudolph, L. and Rudolph, S. 1984. 'Determinants and Varieties of Agrarian Mobilization'. In Desai, M., Rudolph, Susanne Hoeber and Rudra, Ashok (eds.) *Agrarian Power and Agricultural Productivity in South Asia*. Berkeley: University of California Press.

Russell, R.V. and Hiralal, R.B. 1923 [1916]. *The Handbook on Tribes and Castes of the Central Indian Provinces of India*. London: Macmillan Publishers.

Saberwal, S. and Hassan, M. (eds.) 2006. *Assertive Religious Identities*. New Delhi: Manohar.

Sahay, K.N. 1968. 'Impact of Christianity on the Uraon of the Chainpur

Belt in Chotanagpur: An Analysis of Its Cultural Processes'. In *American Anthropologist* 70: 923–42.

_____ 1976. *Under the Shadow of the Cross: A Study of the Nature and Process of Christianization Among the Uraon of Central India.* New Delhi: Vikas Publishing House.

_____ 1992. 'A Theoretical Model for the Study of Christianization Processes among the Tribals of Chotanagpur'. In Chaudhuri, B. (ed.) *Tribal Transformations in India.* New Delhi: Inter-India Publications.

Saldanha, I.M. 1995. 'On Drinking and "Drunkenness": History of Liquor in Colonial India'. In *Economic and Political Weekly*, 16 September.

Sangari, K and Vaid, S. (eds.) 1989. *Recasting Women.* New Delhi: Kali for Women.

Sargent, C.F. and Johnson, T.M 1996. *Handbook of Medical Anthropology: Contemporary Theory and Method, Revised Edition.* London: Greenwood Press.

Sarin, M. 2005. 'Commentary on Scheduled Tribes Bill 2005'. In *Economic and Political Weekly*, 21 May, Vol. 40(21): 2131–4.

Sarkar, S. 1999. 'Hindutva and the Question of Conversions'. In Panikkar, K.N. (ed.) *The Concerned Indian's Guide to Communalism*, pp. 73–106. New Delhi: Penguin Books.

Sarkar, T. 2001. *Hindu Wife, Hindu Nation: Community, Religion and Cultural Nationalism.* New Delhi: Permanent Black.

_____ 1996. 'Educating the Children of the Hindu Rashtra: Notes on RSS Schools'. In Bidwai, Praful, Mukhia, Harbans and Vanaik, Achin (eds.) *Religion, Religiosity and Communalism*, pp. 237–47. New Delhi: Manohar.

Schweder, R.A., Much, Nancy C., Mahapatra, Manamohan and Park, Lawrence 1997. 'The "Big Three" of Morality (Autonomy, Community, Divinity) and the "Big Three" Explanations of Suffering'. In Brandt, A.M. and Rozin P. (eds.) *Morality and Health*, London: Routledge.

Sengupta, N. 1988. 'Reappraising Tribal Movements I: A Myth in the Making'. In *Economic and Political Weekly*, 7 May.

Shah, Mihir 2005. 'First You Push Them In, Then You Throw Them Out'. In *Economic and Political Weekly*, 19 November.

Sharma, J. 2003. *Hindutva: Exploring the Idea of Hindu Nationalism.* New Delhi: Penguin Books.

Sharma, V. 1978. 'Segregation and Its Consequences in India: Rural Women in Himachel Pradesh'. In Caplan, P. and Bujra, J. (eds.) *Women United, Women Divided: Cross-cultural Perspectives on Female Solidarity.* London: Tavistock.

Shourie, A. 1994. *Missionaries in India.* New Delhi: ASA Publications.

Shukla, B.R.K. 1978. 'Religious and Convivial Use of Intoxicants in a North Indian Village.' In *Eastern Anthropologist* 31:4.

Sindzingre, N. 1995. 'The Need for Meaning, the Explanation of Ill Fortune: the Senufo'. In Auge, M. and Herzlich, C. (eds.) *The Meaning of Illness:*

Anthropology, History and Sociology. Luxembourg: Harwood Academic Publishers.

Singh, A.K. and Jabbi, M.K. (eds.) 1995. *Tribals in India: Dvelopment, Deprivation, Discontent.* New Delhi: Har Anand.

Singh, K.S. 1972. *Tribal Situation in India.* Simla: Indian Institute of Advanced Study.

_____ 1978. 'The Munda Land System'. In Ponette, P. (ed.) *The Munda World,* pp. 29–35. Ranchi: Catholic Press.

_____ 1993a. *The Scheduled Castes.* Delhi: Oxford University Press.

_____ 1993b. *Rama-Katha in Tribal and Folk Traditions of India.* Calcutta: Seagull Books.

_____ 1993c. *The Mahabharta in the Tribal and Folk Traditions of India.* New Delhi: Anthropological Survey of India.

_____ 1994. *The Scheduled Tribes.* Delhi: Oxford University Press.

_____ 2002a. *Birsa Munda and his Movement, 1972–1901.* Calcutta: Seagull Books.

_____ 2002b. 'Tribal Autonomy Movements in Chhotanagpur'. In Shah, G. (ed.) *Social Movements and the State,* pp. 267–92. New Delhi: Sage Publications.

Singh, N.K. and Mahurkar, U. 1999. 'Bajrang Dal: Loonies at Large'. In *India Today,* 8 February.

Sinha, S. 1965. 'Tribe-Caste and Tribe-Peasant Continuum in Central India'. In *Man in India* Vol. 45, No. 1: 8–83.

Skaria, A. 1997. 'Shades of Wildness: Tribe, Caste and Gender in Western India'. In *Journal of Asian Studies,* Vol. 56 No. 3.

Smith, A.D. 1971. *Theories of Nationalism.* London: Duckworth.

_____ 1992. *Ethnicity and Nationalism.* Leiden, New York: E.J. Brill.

Smith, A.D. and Hutchinson, John (eds.) 1996. *Ethnicity.* Oxford: Oxford University Press.

Sontheimer, G. 1989. *Pastoral Deities in Western India.* New York: Oxford University Press.

Srinivas, M.N. 1959. 'The Dominant Caste in Pampura'. In *American Anthropologist* 61:1–16.

_____ 1965 [1952]. *Religion and Society among the Coorgs of South India.* London: JK Publishers.

_____ 1969 [1955]. 'The Social System of a Mysore Village'. In Marriott, M. (ed.) *Village India.* Chicago: University of Chicago Press.

_____ 1977. 'The Changing Position of Indian Women'. In *Man* 12: 221–38.

_____ 1987. *The Dominant Caste and Other Essays.* Delhi: Oxford University Press.

Srivastava, A.R.N. 1990. *Tribal Encounter with Industry: A Case Study of Central India.* Delhi: Reliance Publishing.

Stewart, C. and Shaw, R. (eds.) 1994. *Syncretism/Anti-syncretism: The Politics of Religious Synthesis.* London: Routledge.

Stirrat, R.L. 1977. 'Demonic Possession in Roman Catholic Sri Lanka'. In *Journal of Anthropological Research* 33.
_____ 1989. 'Money, Men and Women'. In Parry, J.P. and Bloch, M. (eds.) *Money and the Morality of Exchange*. Cambridge: Cambridge University Press.
_____ 1992. *Power and Religiosity in a Post-Colonial Setting: Sinhala Catholics in Contemporary Sri Lanka*. Cambridge: Cambridge University Press.
Sundar, N. 2006. 'Adivasi vs. Vanvasi: the Politics of Conversion in Central India, 357–90. In Saberwal, S. and Hasan, M. (eds.) *Assertive Religious Identities*. New Delhi: Manohar.
_____ 2004. 'Teaching to Hate: RSS' Pedagogical Programme'. In *Economic and Political Weekly* Vol. 39, No. 16, 17–23 April: 1605–12.
_____ 1997. *Subalterns and Sovereigns: An Anthropological History of Bastar 1854–1996*. Oxford: OUP.
_____ 1995. 'The Dreaded Danteswari: Annals of Alleged Sacrifice'. In *The Indian Economic and Social History Review* 32, 3: 345–74.
Sundar, N., Jeffery, R. and Thin, N. (eds.) 2001. *Branching Out: Joint Forest Management in India*. Oxford: OUP.
Tambiah, S. 1989. 'Ethnic Conflict in the World Today'. In *American Ethnologist* Vol. 16(2): 335–49.
_____ 1996. *Leveling Crowds: Ethno-Nationalist Conflicts and Collective Violence in South Asia*. Berkeley: University of California Press.
Tete, Peter. 1984. *A Missionary Social Worker in India: J.B. Hoffman*. Rome: Universalita Gregoriana.
Thakkar, A.V. 1941. *The Problem of Aborigines in India*. R.R. Kale Memorial Lecture, Gokhale Institute of Politics and Economics, Pune.
Thapar, R. 1985. 'Syndicated Moksha?' In *Seminar* 313: 14–22.
_____ 1991. 'Communalism and the Historical Legacy: Some Facets'. In Pannikar, K.N. (ed.) *Communalism in India: History, Politics and Culture*, pp. 17–33. New Delhi: Manohar.
Tirkey, B. 1980. *Oraon Symbols: Theologising in Oraon Context*. Delhi: Vidyajyoti.
Tonkin, E., McDonald, M. (M. Chapman [ed.]) 1989. *History and Ethnicity*. London: Routledge.
Trawick, M. 1992. *Death and Nurturance in Indian Systems of Healing*. In Leslie, C. and Young, A. (eds.) *Paths to Asian Medical Knowledge*. Berkeley: University of California Press.
Tripathi, G.C. 1978. 'Jagannatha: the Ageless Deity of the Hindus'. In Eschmann, A., Kulke, H. and Tripathi, G. (eds.) *The Cult of Jagannath and the Regional Tradition of Orissa*, pp. 477–90. New Delhi: Manohar.
Turner, V. 1964. 'An Ndembu Doctor in Practice.' In Kiev, A. (ed.) *Magic, Faith and Healing*. New York: Free Press.
_____ 1968. *The Drums of Affliction*. Oxford: Clarendon Press.
_____ 1980. 'The Social Skin'. In Cherfas, J. and Lewin, R. (eds.) *Not Work*

Alone: A Cross-culturalView of Activities Superfluous to Survival. London: Temple Smith.

Tylor, E.B. 1974 [1879]. *Primitive Culture: Researches into the Development of Mythology, Philosophy, Religion, Art and Custom.* NewYork: Gordon Press.

Uberoi, P. (ed.) 1996. *Social Reform, Sexuality and the State.* New Delhi, London: Sage Publications.

Unnithan, M. 1994. 'Girasias and the Politics of Difference in Rajasthan: "Caste", Kinship and Gender in a Marginalized Society'. In Searle-Chhatterjee, M. and Sharma, V. (eds.) *Contextualizing Caste.* Oxford: Blackwell Publishers.

Vanaik, A. 1997. *The Furies of Indian Communalism: Religion, Modernity and Secularization.* London: Verso.

van der Veer, P. 1994. *Religious Nationalism: Hindus and Muslims in India.* Berkeley: University of California Press.

von Fürer-Haimendorf, C. 1982. *Tribes of India: The Struggle for Survival.* Berkeley: University of California Press.

_____ 1944. 'Beliefs Concerning Human Sacrifice Among the Hill Reddis'. In *Man in India* XXIV (1).

Varadarajan, Siddharth 1999. 'The Ink Link: Media, Communalism and the Evasion of Politics'. In Panikkar, K.N. (ed.), *The Concerned Indian's Guide to Communalism,* pp. 160–229. New Delhi: Penguin.

Varma, Pavan K. 2005. *Being Indian: Inside the Real India.* London: William Heinemann.

Varshney, A. 2002. *Ethnic Conflict and Civic Life: Hindus and Muslims in India.* Oxford: OUP.

Vitebsky, Piers 1993. *Dialogues with the Dead: The Discussion of Mortality among the Sora of Eastern India.* Cambridge: CUP.

Weber, M. 1978 [1922]. *Economy and Society: An Outline of Interpretive Sociology.* NewYork: Bedminster.

Webster, J.B. 1976. *The Christian Community and Change in 19th Century North India.* Delhi: Macmillan Co.

Weiner, M. 1978. *Sons of the Soil: Migration and Ethnic Conflict in India.* Princeton: Princeton University Press.

Wilkinson, S.R. 1988. *The Child's World of Illness.* Cambridge: CUP.

Williams, C. Peter 1982. 'Healing and Evangelism: The Place of Medicine in LaterVictorian Protestant MissionaryThinking'. In Sheils, W.J. (ed.) *The Church and Healing.* Oxford: Basil Blackwell.

Worsley, P. 1982. 'Non-Western Medical Systems'. In *Annual Review of Anthropology* 11.

Wyman, L.C. and Kluckhohn, C. 1938. *Navaho Classification of Their Song Ceremonials.* Memoirs of the American Anthropological Association No. 50. Menasha, Wisconsin.

Young, A. 1982. 'The Anthropologies of Illness and Sickness'. In *Annual Review of Anthropology* 11: 257–85.

Government Publications
Sociological Survey 1968. *Profiles of Rural Chhattisgarh: Socio-Economic Survey of Bhilai Region.* Bombay: Popular Prakasan.

Web Site References

http://www.rss.org (as in 2002)
http://www.india-seminar.com/2000 (as in 2002)
http://www.international-alliance.org/documents/india_eng_full.doc (as in 2006)

Index